After Nicholas

Self-realization of the Japanese Orthodox Church, 1912-1956

After Nicholas

Self-realization of the Japanese Orthodox Church, 1912-1956

Ilya Kharin

To the Nagoya Orthodox parish:
my first spiritual home in Japan

Contents

Note on usages

In compiling this work, an effort has been made to standardize divergent and fluctuating customary secular and Orthodox ecclesiastical usages of English, Russian and Japanese. Transliteration of Russian, Japanese and Chinese proper names follows the modified Library of Congress, Hepburn and Pinyin systems respectively. Exceptions include customary usages ingrained in English (for example *Moscow, Tokyo, Tolstoy*), or quotes from English-language sources which use another transcription. Japanese names are introduced in the text with the last name followed by the first name, but if a Christian name is known the order is: (1) Christian name; (2) last name; (3, if known) Japanese-style first name. Russian full names appear in the order: (1) first (usually Christian) name; (2) patronymic; (3) last name. If an abbreviated appellation is used, a Russian's first name comes before the last, or else it does not appear at all.

Orthodox clergy of any nationality can be also called by their first names. The latter practice is mandatory for monastics, whose last name might only appear in parentheses. Christian names have been standardized to their Latinate English form in order to highlight the fact that, in much of traditional Christian (and contemporary Russian Orthodox) usage, names are not only personal designations, but also references to globally venerated saints, and therefore convertible into various linguistic systems. Thus, a Japanese Orthodox priest with the Christian name of *Paeru* would commonly be known as *Pavel* in Russian and *Paul* in English, his name being "translated" according to the local appellation of the prototype—the Biblical apostle.

Ecclesiastical abbreviations have been kept to a minimum; aside from Fr. ("father," a generic priestly address) and St. ("saint," as canonized by the Orthodox Church) clerical titles have been spelled out or dropped in the text. The following charts of Russian Orthodox clergy appellations, listing "black (i.e. unmarried/monastic) clergy" and "white (i.e. married/non-monastic) clergy" grades from the highest to the lowest, show that the episcopal rank is reserved for monastics, while the ranks of the priesthood and the dea-conate are duplicated in both the monastic and non-monastic tracks. Only the three ranks of episcopacy, priesthood and deaconate are invested with sacramental, and hence functional, distinction. Subdivisions into grades are honorary.

The single global Orthodox Church is subdivided into smaller self-governing "local" units with various degrees of independence—"autocephaly" (fuller independence) or "autonomy" (more conditional independence). These self-governing units are usually termed "(local) Churches" (as opposed to "churches," which are individual congregations/consecrated buildings). Alternatively, these units can be called by the title of their ruling primate-hierarch—"Patriarchate" or "Metropolia."

With respect to bibliographical references, confusion generated by identical authors being referred to by a variety of names (laic vs. monastic; last name vs. first name; in Russian, Japanese or English transcription; by a pseudonym, real name combined with a pseudonym or a full real name, etc.) has been mitigated in the footnotes by standardized English citations. The full bibliographical entry is to be found in the final bibliography, where the names of the respective authors are spelled out to the full known extent—including a full secular name, Christian name, and a secular or

Table 1: Russian Orthodox clergy appellations

Black clergy		
Rank	Grade	Comments
Episcopacy (hierarchs)	Patriarch	Primate of the Russian Church
	Metropolitan	Honorary titles
	Archbishop	
	Bishop	Basic episcopal title
Priesthood (presbyters)	Archimandrite	Senior abbot in a lofty administrative post
	Abbot	Superior of a male monastery
	Hieromonk	Monastic priest
Deaconate	Archdeacon	Honorary senior monastic deacon
	Hierodeacon	Monastic deacon
White clergy		
Priesthood (presbyters)	Protopresbyter	Exceptional rank for a handful of elders
	Protopriest	Senior priest
	Priest	
Deaconate	Archdeacon	Exceptional rank for only two-three deacons in the entire Church
	Protodeacon	Senior deacon
	Deacon	

In addition, two female grades must be named, which do not carry sacramental function, but denote a specific service in the Church.

	Abbess	Superior of a female monastery
	Deaconess	Missionary aide

ecclesiastical rank where applicable. While many articles in the Japanese Orthodox press were signed with an abbreviated version of the name, notice is given in parentheses only when a distinct pseudonym was used. Although both the Russian and the Japanese languages have undergone notable spelling and grammar reforms in the course of the period under scrutiny, bibliographical entries employ prevailing present-day sets of characters and grammatical endings.

The Russian imperial state employed the Julian calendar, which remained in use widely among Russian émigrés for decades after the 1917 Revolution, and persists as the liturgical calendar of the Russian Orthodox Church to the present. Meanwhile, the globally dominant Gregorian calendar has prevailed in the USA since the country's inception, in Japan since 1873, and in Soviet Russia since 1918. This work strove to standardize dating according to the Gregorian calendar, but in a few instances usage remained unconfirmed. For practical calculations, the Gregorian date is ahead of the corresponding Julian date by 12 days in the 19th century and by 13 days in the 20th and 21st centuries.

Acknowledgements

This work relied on research conducted in the libraries of the US Congress and the Japanese Diet; the city of Hakodate; St. Vladimir's Orthodox Seminary in Crestwood; Princeton, Stanford, Hokkaido, Kansai, Osaka, Nanzan and Nagoya Universities. Archival collections accessed for compiling this work include the State Archive of the Russian Federation in Moscow, State Archive of the Khabarovsk Krai in Khabarovsk, Archives of the Orthodox Church of America in Syosset, Archives of the Department of External Ecclesiastical Relations of the Russian Orthodox Church in Moscow, Archives of the Hoover Institute in Stanford, collections of the Osaka, Nagoya, Kobe and Handa Orthodox churches and the Matsuo Orthodox monastery.

Bishop Seraphim (Tsujie) of Sendai has been especially generous in sharing his time, insights, and a uniquely valuable collection of materials. In particular, all the otherwise unattributed illustrations in this thesis derive from Bishop Seraphim's extensive collection. Professor Macarius Hirooka Masahisa and John Basalyga have also kindly provided materials from their personal collections, shared reminiscences and perspectives on the subject. Others, notably Fr. Demetrius Grigor'ev and Lydia Kosar of Washington, DC, George Shima Toshihiko of Nagoya, Basil Matsumoto Nozomu of Kobe, choirmaster Andrew Shibayama Masao of Tokyo, Zosimas Nishizawa Kyōji and Fukui Shōji of Osaka, disclosed valuable testimonies. Many more, especially Professors Naganawa Mitsuo and Igor' Shimizu Toshiyuki; Bishop Seraphim (Sigrist); Priests George Matsushima, David Mizuguchi, John Ono, Constantine White, Nicholas Dmitriev, Dionysius Pozdniaev and Theophanes (Kim); archivists Michael Shkarovskii and Alexis Liberovsky; researchers Galina Besstremiannaia, Natalia Sukhanova, John Shōji Masatoshi, Oguri Tokio and Igaue Naho; choirmaster Mary Matsushima Junko, subdeacons Gregory Itō Yoshirō and Raul Sylva, shared their unique expertise and viewpoint on the question, stimulated and supported my inquiry.

My primary academic guides and advisors in this venture have been Professors Stephen Kotkin, Sheldon Garon and Ikuta Michiko, and I likewise enjoyed incalculable help from my entire family, especially my beloved wife Maria, as well as the broader academic and ecclesiastical communities with which this project involved me. Material backing for my work has been generously provided by Princeton University and the Japan Foundation. Finally, the conversion of the dissertation into a published monograph has become a reality thanks to the initiative and collaboration of Simon Cozens of Wide Margin Books.

Without the beneficence of these, as well as many other, institutions and people, this work would have been impossible, and I remain deeply grateful and indebted to them. While striving for truth and accuracy, I am painfully aware of the many possible errors and obvious imperfections which beset my humble effort, for which I bear responsibility and ask forgiveness.

Introduction

Japan's Meiji period (1868–1912) was a time of sweeping Westernization in many spheres of the life of the country and its people. However, embracing Christianity, a religion which the previous 13 generations of Japan's inhabitants were instructed to fear and despise, was one of the more radical acts for a Japanese even during this radical era. Accepting the form of Christianity imported from Russia, commonly seen in Japan as both the most backward and the most dangerous of all Western powers, would easily appear as the most bizarre and extreme form Christian conversion could assume. In these conditions, Archbishop St. Nicholas (Kasatkin), aided chiefly by Russian funds and Japanese converts, established a 30,000-strong community of Orthodox Christian Japanese believers by the end of his half-century-long career in Japan (1861–1912). In terms of missionary-to-convert ratio, the growth of Nicholas' Russian Orthodoxy outpaced other Christian denominations which surged into Japan at this time.

This accomplishment has attracted much inquiry into the method and context of Nicholas' mission. Most analysts have grappled with explaining the mission's success, many were fascinated with its founder's personality, some were eager to catalogue its accomplishments, and a few used it as a prism for diverse socio-cultural inquiries into the age of Japan's rapid Westernization. In addition to Japanese Orthodox in-house writers, specialists in Russo-Japanese relations, in Japanese

Christianity, and in Orthodox Christian missions could not leave the subject unaddressed.[1] Surprisingly, these inquiries left fundamental and long-term results of the mission sorely understudied. Investigators have avoided elucidating the identity of the new religious body. Albeit for different reasons, most took the "Japaneseness" and "Orthodoxy" of this "Church" for granted. Indeed, each of these three terms is so fundamental, so loaded with meanings, so extensively treated and debated elsewhere, and all the while used as a self-designation by the community in question, as to render such a discussion supremely difficult. Yet, only by addressing these basic parameters can one discern the internal dynamics of this community.

In other words, before one might properly evaluate why their experience diverged so much from that of Western Christian missionary bodies in Japan, how the Japanese Orthodox Church bridged different cultures and communities, and what set them apart from their coreligionists belonging to traditionally Orthodox populations, one needs to answer the surprisingly little-asked question: What, in essence, was

---

[1] Major treatments of Nicholas' mission usually center upon his person. The leading works in this biography-as-institutional-history pattern are Consistory (1936), Ushimaru (1969), Nakamura (1996), Takahashi (2000) and Sablina (2006). The landmark contemporary history of on-the-ground progress of the mission has been produced by Ishikawa (1901)—the principal source for the pertinent part of Cary (1909). The best comprehensive coverage of the Meiji-period Orthodox Mission as a cultural importer from Russia to Japan is Potapov (2004). Many valuable works have been recently produced by a Japanese Russianist, Naganawa Mitsuo, among which Naganawa (1989, 2007) are most notable.

Another prominent specialist, Nakamura Kennosuke, has teamed up with his wife to produce a pioneering study of Japanese Orthodox women-leaders in Nakamura & Nakamura (2003). Amid a large body of biographical studies on Meiji-period Orthodox Christians, the literature on Irene Yamashita Rin—the first Japanese woman in the modern era to study art abroad—stands out in volume and quality, with the latest recapitulation in Ōshita (2004). Micro-studies of individual local Japanese Orthodox communities like Utsumi (1979) and Higuchi (1996) also dwell predominantly on the period of Nicholas' mission.

this Japanese Orthodox Church which Nicholas left to his successors?

To address this question, this book focuses on the period between 1912 and 1956—a period of relative independence, isolation and introversion of the Japanese Orthodox Church. The starting point for the inquiry is the death of the Church's irreplaceable founder, Archbishop Nicholas, which signaled a fundamental reconfiguration of the community. The endpoint coincides with reimposition of extra-Japanese controls and reactivation of exchanges with the "far abroad." The story of Japanese Orthodoxy between those dates passed in the shadow of war and deprivation, on the smoldering fault-line between Russia and Japan. In its survival, shriveling, and self-searching, this Japanese community became the first large East Asian body of Orthodox Christians who were free of compelling external controls in defining the shape and course of their collectivity. It is with this Japanese Orthodox ecclesiastical "self," as corporately enacted, discovered, and thus realized, that this book is primarily concerned.

Historical perspectives

Of the major historiographical and conceptual fields in which the Japanese Orthodox experience has been—thus far rather tenuously—situated, the literature on the Russo-Japanese relationship is perhaps most widely known. The common conception of this relationship, reproduced countless times in the dominant historiography, centers upon the seemingly irreconcilable tension over the boundaries since the latter 18th century down to the present standoff over the Southern Kuriles/Northern Territories. Even such sapient treatments as Hasegawa's opine that "it may be justified to view Russo-Japanese relations as a history of uninterrupted conflict."[2] However, this popular view, built

[2]Hasegawa (1988), vol. 1, 13.

upon the exotization of commonplace borderland irredentism and the obfuscation of the sometimes dramatic fluctuations in bilateral policies and perceptions, masks an increasingly rich and well-founded store of counter-narratives.

A study of Russo-Japanese diplomatic relations, influentially undertaken by Lensen and Berton,[3] punctures the simplistic "archrivalry" model by illustrating the very significant shifts in this realpolitik relationship. It was contact, not conflict, which was inevitable—in other words: "the Japanese and the Russians could be friends or enemies; they could not be strangers."[4] But what about alter-egos, cohabitants, spouses—both figurative and quite literal? It was up to John Stephan to mark a major departure into the realm of borderland, émigré and cognitive histories, where mutual Russo-Japanese impregnation, hybridity and merger could be discerned—the "Northeast Asian Ecumene," where "distinctions between domestic and foreign policy break down."[5] Since the 1990's borderland studies have been complemented with an increasingly probing wave of inquiries into Japanese and Russian perceptions of each other. A major attempt at synthesizing this identity-history is the recent effort by Bukh, who suggested seeing Russia as Japan's centrally significant alter-ego. Developing Edward Said's influential typology beyond Stephan Tanaka's treatment of China as Japan's alienated "Oriental" other,[6] Bukh provocatively argues that it was the construction of the Russian "other" as the barbaric "Orient of the West," which allowed Japan to counterpoise itself as civilized in both the "Western" and "Asian" discursive regimes.[7] Yet, in doing so Bukh admits to leaving out the

---

[3] Among their many works Lensen (1959, 1962, 1970) and Berton (1956) bear special significance for the discussion.

[4] Lensen (1962), 347.

[5] His pathbreaking works on the Kurile Islands, on the Russian fascists in Manchuria and the US, and on the Russian Far East are respectively Stephan (1974, 1978, 1994). The quote is from the latter, pp. 1-2.

[6] See Said (1978), Tanaka (1993).

[7] Bukh (2010), see especially 125-133.

less influential alternative Japanese vision of Russia—that of a benign parallel, Japan's natural "companion on the road to modernity where both nations should share their experience and learn from each other"—a vision he identifies with the postwar Japanese academic left in general, and with the prewar Japanese Orthodox Christian publicist, Daniel Konishi Masutarō, in particular.[8]

This invocation begins to make clear the distinctive location of the Japanese Orthodox Church in the fabric of Russo-Japanese relations. It has been often noted that, especially in the pre-1917 period, "perhaps the most notable role in the propagation of the Russian language, Russian concepts, and beliefs in... Japan was played by the Russian Orthodox Church."[9] By illuminating the experience and evolving self-consciousness of this group, the present work aims to shed light onto a community which played a unique role of a non-state corporate agent that was inextricably Russo-Japanese—a would-be locus of national-level synthesis rather than an evanescent borderland community. Despite the prevailing adversarial climate of political relations and the precipitous loss of what had been extensive support from pre-revolutionary Russia, this overwhelmingly native community stayed afloat throughout the first half of the 20th century without shedding its inconvenient double identity. What kind of Russo-Japanese microcosm did this group embody and why did it not break up under the strains of conflicts and "othering" identity polarization? These questions appear salient to the entire body of Russo-Japanese relations literature which does not provide a satisfactory response.

At this point one might reasonably turn to the next best developed historiographical field of Japanese Orthodoxy— the study of Christianity in Japan. Its popular presentation revolves around two barely connected eras, separated by a

[8]Bukh (2010), 23, 126-128.
[9]Lensen (1959), 399.

period of forcible suppression of Japanese Christianity—the Roman Catholic "Christian century" starting in 1549, and the Protestant "modernity" since the late 1850's. Although the latter period saw the re-legalization of Roman Catholicism and the introduction of Orthodoxy, it is primarily Anglo-American Protestantism which has come to dominate the discourse of generic "Christianity" in modern Japan. Furthermore, since the formative era of growth and institutionalization of presently operative Japanese Christian groups occurred during Japan's Meiji period (1868–1912) of rapid Westernization, it is specifically "Meiji Christianity" which magnetizes the scholars' attention.

One can gauge the extent to which the resulting interpretive models remain skewed in favor of American Protestantism by the work of the leading scholar on the sociology of "Meiji Christianity," Morioka Kiyomi. His meticulously researched studies take stock of a broad array of contextual and internal institutional factors to discern the patterns of church growth, inscription and transformation in local society, and institutional evolution—but the circle of his subjects is limited to establishment Protestants. His typology of early convert-leaders—samurai youth who lost their material, social and spiritual supports in the course of the Meiji Restoration and sought the supposed civilizational benefits of the "Christian package" at least as much as they did the spiritual message of salvation—fits the Orthodox case adequately enough, revealing the shared roots of the modern Japanese Christian movement.[10]

However, when it comes to institutional organization, Morioka manages to construct a dichotomy between "Christian" and generic "Japanese" religious bodies according to which Japanese Orthodox are almost wholly excluded from the former category. In his conception, "Christians" formed brotherhoods of individuals with a leveling tendency, their

[10]For Morioka's terse summary of this well-known pattern see Morioka (2005), 65-67.

individual congregations were held together in nation-level bodies by means of contracts; they lacked symbolically and bureaucratically central institutional headquarters, and operated on an assembly-centered basis. "Japanese" religious bodies, on the other hand, are represented as associations of households or persons attached in a hierarchical relationship to a charismatic "parent" (*oya*) as spiritual "children" (*ko*), held together by "automatic incorporation" via allegiance to religious leaders and to symbolically and organizationally central religious headquarters, functioning by means of bureaucratic establishments.[11] With the unambiguous administrative and charismatic centrality of St. Nicholas and the Tokyo Resurrection cathedral compound, organized on the basis of households, stratified through a hierarchy of ordained clergy, and devoid of detailed institutional regulations, the Meiji-period Japanese Orthodox Church possessed far more marks of generic "Japaneseness" than of "Christianity," if Morioka's typology is employed. Clearly, this most influential reading of "Meiji Christianity" remains a misnomer for Meiji mainline Protestantism.

A long-standing interest in overcoming the Christian vs. Japanese dichotomy created a diverse literature on the theological and ritual indigenization inside mainline Christian groups, on the relationship of Christianity and Japanese culture and on Japanese Christian leaders. It was up to Mark Mullins to decisively reorient the field by expanding the array of actors in an uncharted direction. His *Christianity Made In Japan* situated a large body of Japanese indigenous breakaway Christian movements as a central locus of a rather radical and diverse indigenization which had occurred on the fault-line of mainline Protestantism and Japan's syncretic "new religions." Most of them long shunned by the Protestant establishment as illegitimate offspring, these groups grew up as a consequence of the institutional and creedal diversity of Protestant denominations, which suggested a possibility of

[11]Morioka (2005), 442-446.

a distinct "Japanese" Christianity to go along with its many jostling "American," "English" and "German" guises. In light of this work it is evident that, while Japanese Orthodoxy did exhibit much more ritual "spirit world" interaction than Protestants and did center overwhelmingly on the figure of its charismatic founder, it was hardly a "Christianity made in Japan"—if only because it failed to break with the institutional and theological tenets binding it into a single whole with a global communion. Too "native" to belong with archetypal mainline Protestantism, it is too "foreign" to squeeze inside the rubric of Japanese Christian new religions.

Native or foreign, all of Japan's religious bodies were subject to a shared regulatory regime of modern Japan. This regime has commonly been read, following the lead of Communist theoreticians, as an "emperor-system"—an oppressive ideology of mandatory state-worship forcibly foisted upon the public and strictly maintained by the Japanese state since the close of the 19th century until 1945. However coveted, a consistent resistance narrative remained difficult to script in the context of widespread conformism of modern Japanese religions. As a result, the reflection of the "emperor-system" thesis in the historiography of Christianity usually assumes the guises of victimization or failure narratives, reflective of the overall historiography of pre-surrender Japan. On the one hand one reads much about official pressure for Christians to accept the rites and pseudo-doctrinal formulae of state Shintoism, the official de-legalization and suppression of some Christian groups since the later 1930's, the superabundant policing and eventual hounding of most foreign missionaries. On the other hand are the self-searching accounts about the Christian inability to reform the "feudal" elements of Japanese society into "modern" ones, the lamentations about Christian "surrender" to the imperial and imperialist discourse and practice. The failed victim paradigm is characteristically integrated by

Morioka as the counterpart to the indigenization problematic. He writes:

> [Japanese Christian] stabilization at the denomi-
> national level may have been limited to deforma-
> tion (tension) in intra-denominational modifica-
> tions, but as far as contact with state power—and
> with the national identity swayed by that state
> power—it appears to have frequently descended
> into a denaturing (lapse).[12]

Behind this summation stands the presumed normativity of anti-imperialist (and anti-imperial) democratism, which makes the widespread Japanese Christian accommodation and incorporation of imperial ideology and colonial projects into aberrations bordering on moral and doctrinal heresy. Even more fundamentally, the ideologized rigidity of the "emperor-system" construct unduly trivializes the very real shifts in the state-religion relationships during the pre-1945 period.

While marginalized in the historiography of Japanese "civil society" or "public" in general, religion finds its niche in the more nuanced studies emphasizing the constructive, even synergistic, state-society give-and-take in imperial Japan—whether those, like Carol Gluck's, which aver the centrality of Meiji-period ideological construction,[13] or the more practical-minded perspectives like Sheldon Garon's, which trace the long haul of modern social management efforts.[14] The latter has influentially argued that "elite bureaucrats, established religious leaders, and intellectuals had more in common than is usually recognized."[15] The resulting broad national "orthodoxy"—both rationalistic and moralistic—had room for both a mandatory but ambiguous "state Shintoism"

[12] Morioka (2005), 451.
[13] Gluck (1985), 132-143.
[14] Garon (1997), 60-87, 206-215.
[15] Garon (1997), 86.

as well as for a practical normalization and expansion of diverse established religions. This was the condition for the cooperation between the state and established religions in what both parties frequently perceived as mutually beneficial projects, especially in the 1910's and 1920's. In the case of Japanese Orthodoxy, in addition to providing a unique venue for Russo-Japanese political, this Christian group was a bearer of a tradition of emperor-reverence and state-alignment distinctly apposite in the Japanese context.

It is thus as a juncture of "foreign" and "native" typologies, and a case particularly well-tailored to the cooperative state-society model, that the Japanese Orthodox Church acquires salience to the discourse on Christianity in Japan. Yet, lacking in foreign support which characterized mainline Western Christian bodies, low on magnetizing syncretism of native ritual and belief which buoyed Japanese Christian new religions, and devoid of domestic extra-liturgical activities which might align with state projects, how—and toward what purposes—did the interwar Japanese Orthodoxy manage its operations? As has been noted about the Japanese Orthodox Church by one Protestant observer of Japanese Christianity in the 1950's, "with no affiliated institutions, no assistance from outside its membership and almost no ecumenical contacts it is a miracle for it to have survived at all."[16] The Japanese Christian context, like the Russo-Japanese one, does not offer a satisfactory roadmap for the experience of Japanese Orthodoxy.

While noting that the Japanese Orthodox experience is both too "native" and too "foreign" for prevalent typologies of Japanese Christianity, one might just as well remark that it is too "global" to be treated solely within a national or regional framework. The splintered historiography on the modern Orthodox Church, largely absorbed with the traditional habitat of Orthodox Christians riddled by "the equation of

[16]Iglehart (1959), 336.

religious unity with political unity and later with national identity,"[17] has limited explanatory power in the Japanese context. The specific historiography of the Russian Church—the Mother-Church of the Japanese—usually subsumes the Japanese experience under the headings of pre-revolutionary "mission" and of post-revolutionary "ecclesiastical diaspora," being unprepared to systemically address the unique case of a mission-turned-local Church.[18] Unlike almost all other local Orthodox Churches, the Japanese community emerged on a ground shorn of age-old Orthodox roots, without the benefits and banes of "historical" intimate relationships with the local state and society. Often suspended in an administrative limbo, the Japanese Church in the first half of the 20th century, while thoroughly native and local, operated in a global setting which activated or adumbrated transformative high-level relationships with ecclesiastical centers as far apart as the Russian St. Petersburg and Moscow, Serbian Sremski Karlovci, German Munich, Chinese Harbin, US New York, Turkish Istanbul and Greek Athens. Needless to say, if the supra-nationalist and supra-autocephalous dimensions of Orthodoxy were in fact as invisible as the particularist model would have it, the Japanese Orthodox case would simply not exist.

As a legacy of a pre-revolutionary Russian mission, the Japanese Orthodox Church can more fruitfully be situated in a distinctive sub-field of Russian Orthodox studies—the historiography of missions. Frequently subsumed by earlier scholars in the narrative of imperial expansion, Russian Orthodox missionary activity has recently begun to garner broader and more sober attention, yielding such landmark syntheses as the work of Andrei Znamenski on the inter-action of native shamanistic societies of Russia's eastern periphery with Orthodox Christianity. Znamenski shows that "mission" involved—whether willingly or not—the whole

[17]Ramet (1988a), 6.
[18]As in Tsypin (2006), 312-314, 779-781.

xxi

Russian society of Christians who in some fashion faced the indigenous peoples. The oft-touted invasive "Russification," according to Znamenski, was a non-issue, since neither the Russian Orthodox tradition of "using indigenous languages and native clergy to convey the Christian message," nor the feeble reach of the Russian state and Church on the imperial periphery, provided the necessary overwhelming context.[19] It was up to the indigenes to arbiter whether and how they would approach the religious dialogue, a choice that often appears to have involved native societies at a group level, with participants eager and able "to maintain personal and communal integrity."[20] A positive choice for open dialogue—which would invariably yield syncretic Orthodox-shamanistic combinations—might be made only if the indigenous group were convinced by "spiritual power considerations and a search for meaningful explanation of reality."[21]   A key syncretism one would expect to find in the elaboration of Japanese Orthodoxy is a "syncretism" between mandated ecclesiology and what Gluck has aptly called "Japan's modern myths"—evolving political ideologies. In tracing the history of Japanese Orthodoxy as a polity, the present work will show the corporate practice and limits of such a "syncretism."

However, the fundamental question of the present study involves a deeper issue beneath the layer of missionary historiography—the transformation of a "Mission" into a "Church," a practical elaboration of corporate selfhood at the balance point between prescription and predilection. There is comparatively little theorizing in the way of Orthodox missiology, and a rare exception—a study by James Stamoolis—helps show why. After an overview of the history (which gives the Japanese experience pride of place), aims, methods and motives of Orthodox missionary activity, Stamoolis attempts to define "mission" and ends up by dissolving it in the notion

---

[19]Znamenski (1999), 256.
[20]Znamenski (1999), 262.
[21]Znamenski (1999), 262.

of the "Church." Just as the Orthodox Church failed to gener-
ate a stable institutional pattern for missions, its thinkers are
unprepared to delineate mission as anything other than the
action and the essence of the Church. As Stamoolis affirms,
"any exploration of Orthodox missionary thinking inevitably
must arrive at a consideration of Orthodox ecclesiology."[22] In
discussing the latter, in turn, he emphasizes its "corporate
character," which requires that "as in worship, so also in
mission, all participate... even if not all perform the same
task of service."[23] Mission is ultimately presented as "the
advance of the Christian's spiritual perfection,"[24] an endeavor
for the Church as a whole, for the congregation, and for each
individual in particular. One needs not follow Stamoolis from
analysis to prescription in order to appreciate his increasingly
broadly-accepted insight that conversion is not only a singular
moment, and mission is not solely an extraverted task. Rather,
the mission of the Orthodox Church might be defined as
becoming in practice closer to what it holds up as its own
ideal. This often contested and rarely conscious process of self-
realization appears to be the central internal meaning-making
dynamic in the experience of the Japanese Orthodox Church,
which thus provides one of the best-documented and recent
instances of Orthodox ecclesiastical genesis.

While mindful of the above three principal contextual
fields—Russo-Japanese, Japanese Christian and global
Orthodox—this work has been structured with a view
to facilitating the entry into the fundamental level of
discussion—the process of the practical elaboration of
corporate identity. Part I tackles the principal contexts
necessary for engaging the topic. Chapter 1 attempts to
provide an interpretive sketch of the histories of Christianity
in Japan, of Russo-Japanese relations and of Orthodox
Christian global expansion to illustrate both the significance

---

[22] Stamoolis (1986), 103.
[23] Stamoolis (1986), 117.
[24] Stamoolis (1986), 123-124.

and the deviance of the Japanese Orthodox experience. Chapter 2 charts a skeletal outline of the first century of Orthodoxy in Japan from 1850's to 1950's, conceived as a guide to principal events, institutional statistics and surface dynamics. Chapter 3 delves into the discourse of the Japanese Orthodox themselves in order to apprehend their formulae of self-definition—the analytical key to the fundamental processes of self-realization. At this point the tension between explicit identity-statements and the practical elaboration of that identity emerges as the drama of the Japanese Orthodox experience. Two core self-definitions stand out as particularly problematic in practice. The first is the Church's claim to be "apostolic"—usually interpreted as having to do with the centrality of the community's ruling bishop. Correspondingly, Part II is devoted to tracing the evolving role of bishops in the life of the Japanese Church. Another fraught claim of the Church is "catholicity"—a quality denoting universal reach. The attendant dilemma of defining the boundary of the corporate self and of conducting corresponding external relations is investigated in Part III. Each of the three parts concludes with an attempt at a partial answer to the question about the evolving Japanese Orthodox identity. The work then concludes with a brief summation and perspective on further research.

Bibliographical basis

The remainder of the introduction is focused on the narrow historiographical and bibliographical basis for the study of the Japanese Orthodox Church between 1912 and 1956. In comparison to the literature available on the "Nicholaevan period" of Orthodox mission in Japan, post-1912 history of the Japanese Orthodox Church remains poorly charted terrain, a postscript to former prominence. The precipitous loss of the charismatic founder, of Russian support, and of the missionary apparatus in the course of the 1910's edged the Japanese Orthodox Church into oblivion. Outsiders usually lost interest in what appeared to have become a stunted and introverted community, while most insiders found themselves too uncertain and isolated to reach a broad audience. It took a major shift in the global religious and political context to stimulate interest in the recent history of the Japanese Orthodox Church. Specifically, the dissolution of the USSR in 1991, which sealed the collapse of the communist experiment in atheistic modernity, facilitated a revival of the Orthodox Church in its Eastern European heartland and the consequent efflorescence of Orthodox studies.

Continual retellings of corporate history form an integral part of the life of the Japanese Orthodox community. However, foundational work of narrating and appraising its experience after St. Nicholas has been carried out by its premier historian, Protopriest Proclus Ushimaru Yasuo. His output, especially the two monographs on the subject, first published in 1978 and 1985 respectively, traced many of the basic dilemmas which confronted the Japanese Orthodox community. Although marked by occasionally significant gaps in the record and overreliance on the victimization narrative, wherein supposed inevitabilities obscure choices, Fr. Ushimaru's treatments remain basic references.[25] They reflect a large, but much less accessible, volume of locally published commemorative church histories produced by Japanese Orthodox communities across the country down to the present. These meticulous chronicles of communal and

---

[25]The two chief works are Ushimaru (1978b, 1985). His prominent contribution to this subject can be seen in the authoritative Japan Christian dictionary (1988), wherein he authored most of the material dealing with the Orthodox Church. Fr. Proclus also penned numerous articles and a few booklets on the history of Orthodox parishes in Western Japan, the most significant being Ushimaru (1978a, 1979). His articles are especially numerous in the Orthodox magazines which he edited in the 1970's and 1980's—*Dawn* (*Akebono*) and *Naniwa Orthodoxy* (*Naniwa Seikyō*).

personal lives occasionally offer data which supplement and even reorient parts of Ushimaru's narrative—most notable in this respect are the histories of Orthodox communities in Sapporo, Kushiro, Tokyo, Sendai and Nagoya.[26] Yet, in the majority of these works, the death of Archbishop Nicholas, the Russian Revolution, the Great Kantō Earthquake, World War II, and the Cold War form a catastrophic master-narrative so encompassing as to subsume potential questions about Japanese Orthodox self-definition. Much of this literature thus dovetails with Japan's prevailing national victimization narrative, exacerbated in the case of the Orthodox by the additional shocks of Russia's tumultuous 20th century experience.

As the decay and collapse of the USSR gave a new impetus to the study of the Orthodox Church, Japanese scholars with a greater degree of independence from the above collective narrative have begun to open new horizons by focusing on individual members of the Japanese Orthodox community. Pioneering works of this kind by Professor Naganawa Mitsuo in 1989 and Kaneishi Naka in 1993—the first armed with the professional training as a Russianist, the second endowed with the unique access and sensitivity of a family member—represent contextualized biographies of two prominent Japanese clerics, Nicholas' disciples who lived until the 1940's.[27] As the Japanese Orthodox Church continued to hold Naganawa's attention between 1995 and 2007, he went on to explore the life of Nicholas' successor at the helm of the Church, Metropolitan Sergius (Tikhomirov), who appears simultaneously as a central actor and a foil of a Russo-Japanese Orthodox story in Naganawa's dramatized presentation.[28] His work generated a response from within the Orthodox

---

[26]Sapporo church (1987); Kushiro church (1992); Tokyo cathedral (1998); Sendai church (2004); Itō (2010).

[27]Naganawa (1989); Kaneishi (1993).

[28]Naganawa (1995, 2001, 2003, 2005). In Naganawa (2007) see especially 320-385.

community, in the writings by Gregory Itō Yoshio,[29] and especially by Bishop Seraphim (Tsujie), the Orthodox bishop of Sendai. The latter published what is at present the most documented and thought-provoking study of the person and office of the bishop in the Japanese Orthodox Church from early 20th century to the American occupation.[30] In this strain of person-centered writings the Japanese Orthodox community figures as a microcosm with distinctive agendas and dynamics, powerfully impacted, but hardly dictated by global catastrophes.

The above evolution of the Japanese bibliography was in part fuelled by the emergence of a parallel discourse on Japanese Orthodox history in Russian scholarship. Russian inquirers brought a different set of preoccupations by placing the Japanese Orthodox Church firmly into the framework of the 20th century Russian Orthodox experience, with its unprecedented persecutions, global dispersion, politicized schisms. Scattered Russian summaries of the history of the Japanese Orthodox Church in the 20th century were initially informed by the material published over the decades by the Russian Church's official *Journal of the Moscow Patriarchy*,[31] while Eleonora Sablina's voluminous work drew on Japanese sources to introduce the Russian reader to the 20th century history of the Tokyo Orthodox community.[32] Since the early 2000's post-Nicholaevan history of the Japanese Orthodox Church found its thorough researcher in the person of Natalia Sukhanova, whose scholarly work for the first time brought together the bulk of key Japanese Orthodox primary documents, newly available Russian archival documents, and a few pivotal materials from US holdings. Her work set a new benchmark not only by synthesizing the amassed

[29]Itō (2008a, 2008b).
[30]Seraphim (2007a, 2007c, 2007-2008). The work of special significance is Seraphim (2008-2010).
[31]Notable articles include Vedernikov (1951), Yoshimura (1968), Tyshchuk (1970).
[32]Sablina (2006).

data, but by offering a powerful pragmatic analysis of the interplay among such factors as the Japanese ecclesiastical independence movement, the struggle of rival groupings for the title of the globally legitimate Russian Orthodox Church, the manipulations of the superpowers in the religious sphere, and the attendant fiscal realities.[33]

Although between 1947 and 1970 most of the Japanese Orthodox Church was subordinated to a US-based body, the Russian Orthodox "American Metropolia," Western scholarship has hardly formed a bibliography on the subject. The best readily available text remains Drummond's five-page summary from 1971, while the most recent encyclopedic *Handbook of Christianity in Japan* writes off post-Nicholaevan history of the Japanese Orthodox Church in a few lines.[34] A useful 2003 collection of writings on St. Nicholas and the Japanese Orthodox mission introduced the English-language reader to the work of Japanese and Russian researchers, tangentially illuminating some of the community's post-Nicholaevan history.[35] Also, a valuable, although minuscule, entry on the Japanese Orthodox Church is found in Woodard's magisterial work on Japanese religions during the US occupation.[36] However, since George Lensen's post-WWII foray,[37] there have been no independent investigations by Western scholars into the post-Nicholaevan Japanese Orthodox community. By far the most interesting and informed work in English has been produced by Orthodox seminarians, especially John Shōji Masatoshi, whose brief but insightful thesis not only introduced previously untapped documents from US archives, but discerned the drama of 20th

[33] She introduced her work in a number of articles, integrated into a dissertation format in Sukhanova (2008).

[34] Drummond (1971), 355-359; Ion (2003), 71.

[35] Remortel & Chang (2003).

[36] Woodard (1972), 214-215.

[37] Lensen (1952). See also Lensen (1973), 104-110.

century Japanese Orthodox Church's history in the believers'
ignorance of their community's prescriptive self-definition.[38]

Part of the distinctive challenge and interest of post-
Nicholaevan Japanese Orthodox history is the breadth and
obscurity of its source-base. In-house materials heavily pre-
dominate, many of them unavailable in any secular archival
collections. This field requires significant socialization into
the Orthodox Christian—Japanese, Russian and American—
milieu in order to access pertinent materials from various
ecclesiastical and private holdings on three continents.

However, first a few words must be said of the primary
documents emanating from outside the Orthodox Church.
Sources produced by secular governments are by far the
most important. Despite the mass destruction of Japanese
government documents at the close of World War II, archives
still hold some pertinent fragments of the record. Accessed
Japanese documents deal with the state-sponsored dispatch
of the Japanese Orthodox delegation into the Russian Far
East during the Russian Civil War; the routine policing of
religion in the Japanese Empire; the oversight of Japan's
resident Russian Orthodox émigrés in the interwar era; the
government's efforts to contain and quell the disorder in the
Japanese Orthodox Church in 1940-1941; the official position
on the relationship of the state and Orthodox Christianity
in Manchukuo.[39]   On the Soviet side are the propagandist
anti-Orthodox and anti-Japanese polemics[40] as well as the

---

[38] Shōji (2007).

[39] Most of the materials have been drawn from the selection of Japanese
Foreign Ministry materials made available by Japan Center for Asian Historical
Records. Those with special pertinence include Siberian dispatch (1918);
Maruyama (1930); Oka (1931); Thought Section (1945). Salient excerpts
from the 1940-1941 *Special Higher (Police) Monthly* (*Tokkō geppō*), issued by the
Peace Preservation Division of the Policing Department of the Internal Affairs
Ministry, are collected in Dōshisha (1981), vol. 1, 298, 302-303, 323; vol. 2, 72-
76, 107. Materials on the Manchurian state-religion relations derive from the
State Archive of the Khabarovsk Krai, notably Kyō-wa-kai (1942) and Maeda
(n/d).

[40] Kandidov (1932, 1937).

documentation on the attempt to attract and employ the Japanese Orthodox Church in the global post-war religio-political gamble of the late Stalinist state.[41] Japanese ecumenical circles appear to have been the salient non-state locus of information-gathering about the Japanese Orthodox Church. The materials from this quarter provide a perspective on the external perception and self-presentation of the Orthodox community, including bare-bones annual assessments of the community's size and status,[42] as well as a lone publication in a set of manuals on comparative religion.[43] Of the contributions from secular media the most significant is the sensationalized reportage of Japanese Orthodox Church's principal crises and triumphs, publicized in Japan's papers—especially the *Asahi Shimbun*—and the Russian émigré press worldwide.

Turning to the pool of in-house resources, one must single out as most significant the minutes of the Councils of the Japanese Orthodox Church. These events as a rule happened annually, with a pause between 1942 and 1945, and with additional extraordinary (provisional) Councils held in 1923, 1941, 1946 and 1947. The pressing issues of the Church were vigorously debated and ruled upon at these well-attended community-wide gatherings. Almost always published within a few months after each Council, the brochures recount the proceedings in detail, including the listing of communities and church-servitors, the financial and membership statistics, and the transcribed texts of debates and reports. At times these transcripts are rather summaries, than literal records, and in one case—the hotly contested Council of 1940—there are even notably divergent versions of the transcript, published by rival factions. However, an overview of the minutes through the decades reveals identifiable points of

---

[41]The materials of the State Archive of the Russian Federation in ГАРФ, ф. 6991, оп. 1, д. 23; д. 588.

[42]Presented in *The Japan Mission Year Book* and its successor, *The Japan Christian Year Book*. Notably, the statistics are at times wishful or else recycled data from more or less dated Orthodox sources.

[43]Mii (1934).

view, specific turns of phrase and even sharp expressions associated with key individual participants. These annual brochures were made public, but their print-runs appear to have been relatively limited. The broader reportage about the Councils, presented in the official periodical organ of the Church, usually reproduced the minutes in a somewhat abbreviated format.[44]

In-house periodicals represent a vast stratum of primary materials. By far the most significant is the *Orthodox Messenger* (*Seikyō Jihō*), the official organ of the Japanese Orthodox Church from 1912 until the present. It has been issued in various formats—from a illustrated thick biweekly magazine of over 60 pages before the Russian Revolution to a pair of irregularly provided screen-printed sheets in mid-1940's—but endured as the chief, at times sole, Japanese Orthodox media outlet, with theological, moralistic, historical, biographical and analytical pieces, as well as ample reportage on current events. Other Japanese Orthodox periodicals had briefer and punctuated life-spans. Pre-revolutionary centrally-issued publications, discontinued in 1910's, included the broadly targeted *Orthodox Discourses* (*Seikyō Yōwa*) and the philosophical-theological *Trends of Orthodox Thought* (*Seikyō Shichō*). Interwar attempts by the Tokyo headquarters of the Church to broaden the media field included the literary-leaning journal *Dawn* (*Akebono*), published by Metropolitan Sergius of Japan in 1925-1928, and *Japanese Orthodoxy* (*Nihon Seikyō*), a magazine issued from 1931 for a brief time by the nativist "League of Japanese Christian Orthodox faithful." Of the local ventures,

---

[44]The publication data for the Council minutes vary slightly through the years, as detailed in the bibliography. The factional publications dealing with the Council of 1940 and the subsequent gatherings of early 1941 are Council (1941), presenting the Iwasawan version, and the anti-Iwasawan Council Provisional (1941b). The latter, however, is severely abbreviated and censored in comparison to the handwritten draft of the same, found in the Osaka Orthodox church's collection and designated below as Council Provisional (1941a). A note must be made of the minutes of the Protopriests' Conference (1943)—a gathering of senior clergy, conducted in 1943, at a time when the state forbade the gathering of a bona-fide Council.

undertaken by significant parishes across Japan, only *Yeast* (*Pandane*), published by the Nagoya Orthodox youth society between 1921 and 1935, achieved the breadth and significance comparable with Tokyo publications.[45]

Valuable data are also found in Russian Orthodox press, both from Russia and from the diaspora. Before the Russian Revolution the Russian Church's *Christian Reading* (*Khristian-skoe chtenie*), *Church Messenger* (*Tserkovnyi vestnik*) and *Orthodox Evangelist* (*Pravoslavnyi blagovestnik*) carried reports from the Japanese mission. Between 1920's and 1940's the press of the Harbin Orthodox diocese in Manchuria, especially the journal *Heavenly Bread* (*Khleb nebesnyi*), offered useful reportage. In the wake of World War II news and articles about the Japanese Orthodox Church become a fixture of *The Russian American Orthodox Messenger* (duplicated in Russian as *Russko-Amerikanskii pravoslavnyi vestnik*) and *The Russian Orthodox Journal*—principal periodicals of the Russian Orthodox Greek-Catholic North American Metropolia which assumed leadership over the Japanese Church.

An important testimony and reflection of the community's existence were its occasional publications, issued almost exclusively from Tokyo or Nagoya. The majority of these were authored by Japanese Church's clerics and laity, but some translations from Russian were republished or carried out anew. These booklets and monographs bore dogmatic, moralistic, historical, hagiographic and propagandistic character, focusing on the teaching and history of the Orthodox

[45]Other briefly-published local periodicals have included *Orthodoxy of the North Seas* (*Hokkai no Seikyō*), Sapporo, briefly from 1919; *Orthodox* (*Ōsodokkusu*), Kyoto, in 1950; *Orthodox Naniwa* (*Naniwa Seikyō*), Osaka, 1925-1940, restarted in 1955. Sergius' *Akebono* was preceded by the homonymous occasional Tokyo youth group publication, issued since 1921. Evanescent one-man provincial missionary publications, initiated in 1920's, included *Awakening* (*Kakusei*) from Handa; *Mustard Seed* (*Karashidane*) from Kyoto and *Jar of Oil* (*Abura no tsubo*) from Yokohama. In 1913 there was also a one-man attempt at a dissident periodical, *New Orthodoxy* (*Shin Seikyō*).

Church.[46] Also reissued were the liturgical and Scriptural books necessary for the minimal routine of Church life. The few Russian-language manuals, also published by the Japanese Church, revealed the enduring significance of attenuated international ties. Finally, a group of publications, both centrally authorized and dissident, dealt with the current celebrations or crises of the Japanese Orthodox Church.[47] These publication types reflect integral aspects of the community's activity—its continual self-propagation, daily prayer-life, supranational involvement, and responses to outstanding events.

Private writings by central figures of the Japanese Orthodox Church history afford unique insights into their personal and institutional lives. While only one notable diary has come to light—that of the head of the Russian-American Metropolia, Metropolitan Leontius (Turkevich)—two correspondence clusters illuminate the history of the Church's central governance. The first one is centered on the ruling Orthodox hierarch of Tokyo, Sergius (Tikhomirov)—these are his missives to Russian hierarchs throughout the world, his letters to Russian and Japanese laymen in Asia, and correspondence about him in Russian émigré circles.[48] A

[46]Among the original writings are Shibayama (1928); Mii ([1928] 1935); Yoshimura (1929); Takeoka (1932); Sergius ([1941] 1971); Iwama (1937); Hibi (1948); Iwama (1955). Translated publications include Morita (1931); Basil (1952); John (1953a, 1953b).

[47]Sergius (1913, 1914, 1924, 1930); Consistory (1920a, 1920b, 1933, 1936, 1942); Theodosius ([1926] 1999); Mochizuki (1930, 1951); Nicholas ([1934] 1976, 1944a); Iwasawa (1941); Kamada (1941); Kitamura (1941); Satō (1946).

[48]Select letters include Sergius (1931a, 1931b, 1935b, 1939, 1944, 2000, 2007); Benjamin (2000); Bulgakov (1920). These and other private letters by and about Sergius, are scattered in various holdings, with only a handful published. A great deal of Sergius' correspondence with the disgruntled Russian priests in Japan, Frs. Bulgakov and Seryshev, is contained in Seryshev's files, as well as in a few other collections at the Hoover Institution Archives. In addition, the most important holdings are those of Bishop Seraphim (Tsujie) of Sendai, of the Russian Orthodox Church's Department of External Ecclesiastical Relations, and of the Archive of the Orthodox Church in America.

much smaller body of writings belongs to the US occupation officer, Colonel Boris Pash, whose correspondence with the leaders of the Russian-American Metropolia shows his centrality to the post-war reconfiguration of the Japanese Church's governance.[49] While a few of these letters have been published in narrowly circulated ecclesiastical press, most are to be found only in archival collections in Russia, the US and Japan.

Some individual parishes across Japan preserve clusters of local sources in the form of metrical and accounting books, occasionally recorded minutes of various parish meetings, unpublished recollections and photographs of believers. Although the fires of World War II and the lack of proper maintenance have wiped out many records, church-collections and publications are continually supplemented by parishioners' contributions. Such materials form the valuable core of local ecclesiastical histories, which have been published by Japanese Orthodox parishes for over a century on occasions of their temple-consecrations and anniversaries. These works range from pocket-sized popular booklets to some three-hundred-page meticulously researched tomes. While only some of these works, as mentioned above, belong to the general bibliography of the Japanese Orthodox Church, most represent or contain at least some primary sources.[50]

Aside from such community-sanctioned publications, a diffuse body of independently issued memoirs is growing continuously. This layer reflects a wide variety of view-points,

---

[49]See some of Pash's letters in Shōji (2007), 62-69; a few others are located in the Japanese folders of the Archive of the Orthodox Church in America.

[50]In addition to the more prominent works, listed in the bibliographic section above, such publications include Anthony et al. (1927); Kannari church (1934); Izawa (1955); Iwama (1959); Mizuno (1972); Nakahara (1975); Tōhei (1976); Yoshikawa (1977); Kyoto church (1978); Ushimaru (1978a); Toyohashi church (1979); Tokushima church (1980); Kobe church (1983); Aizawa & Kumagai (1983); Ashikaga church (1983); Ise (1984); Kikuchi (1986); Kuriyagawa (1994); Baba (1996); Nobata (1997); Tomakomai church (1998); Odawara church (2002); Shirakawa church (2006).

driving narratives and preoccupations, which defy monolithic categorizations. Particularly valuable perspectives and facts emerge from the memoirs of Frs. Symeon Mii Michirō, Alexis Mitani Takeo, Basil Takeoka Takeo, Innocent Seryshev and Barnabas Osozawa Eiji, choirmaster Titus Katō Najirō, Eugenia Kaminaga Mitsue, Col. Boris Pash, Alexander Manabe Rijū and George Chertkov.[51] Those who have kindly shared their recollections have been thanked above in the acknowledgements.

---

[51]Mii (1982); Mitani (1960); Takeoka (1989); Seryshev (1952-1968); Osozawa (1976); Katō (1985); Kaminaga (2000); Pash (1958); Manabe (1996); Chertkov (1977).

Part I

The Japanese Orthodox experience: contexts, contents and claims

Born in Japan to Russian émigré parents, Lydia Pokrov-skaia grew up in and around the Tokyo Orthodox cathedral compound, where her father served as a choirmaster, and where she lived next door to Japanese churchmen and their Russian bishop. In her childhood games with Japanese peers she had no occasion to confront her exotic identity until the wave of wartime ultranationalism in the 1930's reached the world of children. Then her playmates suddenly turned her away—for being White, Russian, and therefore "alien." Distraught and astonished, she ran to her father in tears with a question: "Am I Russian or am I Japanese?" The response was: "You are Orthodox." Taking this instruction to heart, Lydia went on to marry an American occupation officer and remain a devout parishioner of the Orthodox cathedral—in Washington, D.C.[52]

This life-story not only has much to do with how the author came in contact with the Japanese Orthodox Church, but is a fitting epigraph to the history of this religious community in the first half of the 20th century. Orthodox Christianity, incarnated by this group, was something fundamentally Russian that was expelled from Russia; something that became native to Japan and was considered alien by most Japanese; something that unexpectedly linked Japan with America

[52] Author's interview with Lydia Kosar (nee Pokrovskaia), Washington, D.C., July 2003.

chiefly by means of Russians and the US military. Most importantly, it was something which provided an implicit and incarnate mode of corporate being meaningfully discovered and actuated by Japanese adherents in the process of an acute wartime identity crisis. The Japanese Orthodox Church's genesis and development appear aberrant within those principal conceptual categories—of Christianity in Japan; of Russo-Japanese relations; of Orthodoxy's globalization—which were obliged to encompass, but ill-equipped to interpret the course of this community. This marginalization was neither artificial, nor unwarranted, since the prevalent logic of the archetypes and plots inside each historiography suggested that a body like the Japanese Orthodox Church was not "supposed to" emerge and function. The aim of the first chapter is to provide a brief interpretive sketch of the three broad fields into which the Japanese Orthodox Church has been incongruously inscribed. While necessarily very generalized, these profiles aim to highlight endemic narrative ruptures for which the Japanese Orthodox experience serves as a vital missing link.

An overview of a century of Orthodox Christian mission in Japan—from the end of the Tokugawa period to end of the American occupation—shows that many of the principal processes and events, taken up by the above three major contextual fields, were manifestly at work among the Japanese Orthodox, often with sweeping strength. Even the towering figure of St. Nicholas, whose outstanding zeal and charisma at times appeared to be "making history," might well be inscribed into the systemic rise of vigorous reformer-contemporaries—the Russian "men of the 60's" and Japanese "men of Meiji." With Nicholas' demise and the Russian Revolution, the sway of the "trends of the times" upon the course and condition of the Japanese Orthodox Church increased exponentially. Yet, inherent incongruities and internal forces thwarted this community's comprehensive inscription into dominant contexts. The second chapter presents a skeletal plotline of the Japanese Orthodox Church's history down to the mid-1950's, with emphasis on dates, statistics, infrastructure and sociology—meant as a reference guide for the rest of the work as well as a springboard for deeper inquiry.

The third chapter aims to apprehend the basic premise for such an inquiry—the evolving public self-definition of the Japanese Orthodox Church during the first period of its relative independence. The chief authoritative catechism, formal corporate constitution, theological manuals and apologetics, reformist wartime manifestoes, and a historical self-presentation by leading figures of the Japanese Church are introduced here in their particular context, as snapshots of key figures and junctures. Distinctive in-house identity discourse appears not only as a manifestation of autonomous agency and corporate self-consciousness, which are of central interest for this study, but also as a necessary analytical tool for an interpretive reading of the processes inside the community.

The significance of explicit identity-statements is not only—and not primarily—descriptive, as it is prescriptive, enmeshed in the power-structures of legitimization and normativization through adherence to the "right teaching." Formal definitions of the Church are of vital importance because they dictate not only the mandatory beliefs about the Church's nature, but also imply corresponding core institutional arrangements, in effect postulating not only a theological, but an administrative "Orthodoxy." Although it might appear impossible to ascertain metaphysical beliefs, the evolution of the Japanese Church's administrative and institutional arrangements is well within reach of research, allowing one to discern the relationship between organizational incarnation and professed faith. Thus, a survey of a Japanese Orthodox ecclesiology offers both a definitional and an evaluative criterion for an analysis and appraisal of the process of collective self-realization.

Chapter 1

The missing link in ruptured contexts

Native-foreign nexus of Japanese Christianity

The 1549 arrival of the Roman Catholic apostle, Francis Xavier, ushered into Japan's "Christian century"—a period of dramatic growth and even more dramatic suppression of Iberian mercantile, religious, cultural and political presence in Japan. Methodical, inculturated and elite-targeted mission by Portuguese Jesuits yielded a rich harvest especially in Southwestern Japan, with some 300,000 baptized—mostly by fiat of converted lords—by the close of the 16th century. Yet, this success rested on the precarious balance of political disunity of Japan, propitious trade with Portugal, personal diplomacy of the Jesuits and practical adaptation to Japanese mass religiosity—a balance upset by the arrival of Anglo-Dutch Protestant competitors, the intrusion of the far less tactful Spanish Franciscans, and the success of Japan's political unifiers. The specter of eradication hung over the Roman Catholics since the unenforced expulsion edict of 1587, and in 1612 Japan's ascendant dynastic founder, shogun Tokugawa Ieyasu, launched a brutal campaign of Christian extermination and reconversion. By the middle of the century surviving Roman Catholics were reduced to "hidden Christians," preserving the rudiments of their faith behind a façade of official Buddhism.[1]

The anti-Christian campaign itself became the mission's main legacy to Japan, emerging as a vital force for unification. Anti-Christianity defined the syncretic and multireligious Japan in terms of its civilizational "other" and constructed Japan's first realm-wide thought-police network—which included an obligation for every Japanese to regularly trample on Christian sacred images and maintain registration with a Buddhist "parish" (the latter being a key organizational Christian borrowing). In the 17th century Christianity's radical monotheism, criticized for undermining the lord-subject relationship, helped consolidate a Confucian-dominated orthodoxy.

More important still, by the 19th century the threatening notion of Western monotheistic mass-mobilization drove Japan's leading scholars, notably Aizawa Seishisai, to jettison the earlier model of Confucian hierarchy and infuse the Japanese emperor with the qualities read into the Christian God—those of a direct personal lord and father over each individual subject. When the Japanese "emperor system" was being elaborated in the course of a precipitous defensive Westernization in the latter 19th century, this seminal adaptation from Christianity ensured that the end result would feature

---

[1]The cosmopolitanism and tumultuous drama of the "Christian century" have generated a vast literature, but the summary works specifically on the early Japanese Roman Catholicism itself are not as numerous. The major monograph by Boxer (1951) remains a basic reference; Higashibaba (2001) portrays the adopted popular Japanese Christian religiosity of the period; Elison (1973) treats theological conflict and the emerging Japanese image of the "evil cult".

not only Western technologies of "modern monarchy," but the genetic linkage to the Christianized Roman imperial model, in which the emperor was an "image" of God just as the empire was an "image" of the universe. Profusely coated with the rhetoric of resuscitated native antiquity, the turn toward an emperor-centered "national polity" in the Meiji period represented Japan's most consequential assimilation of a Christian religio-political concept.[2] The resulting regime became the overwhelming context for the modern history of Christianity in Japan until 1945.[3]

The fundamental transformation of the Japanese polity towards emperor-centrism was accompanied by the long-expected and comparatively mild Christian penetration. In 1859 foreign missionaries appeared in the open treaty ports, while in 1865 over 4,000 "hidden Christians" astonished public opinion by reemerging into effective contact with the Roman Catholic hierarchy. Yet it took the Western powers well over a decade after Japan's "opening" to communicate a concerted demand for the Japanese state to stop persecuting Christians. In response, the new Meiji regime suspended the anti-Christian edicts in 1873, and formally granted conditional religious freedom with the Meiji Constitution of 1889. By the latter date three missionary tracks emerged—an abundance of mostly Anglo-American Protestant missionaries aimed at an elite activist ex-samurai urbanite following; a smaller number of mostly French Roman Catholic missionaries and monastics concentrated on a less publicized build-up of core

---

[2] The pioneering work in elucidating the constructive significance of Japan's Tokugawa-Meiji anti-Christianity is Paramore (2009). Fujitani (1996) influentially described the practical process of the Meiji-period rearticulation of the Japanese emperor.

[3] Comprehensive perspectives on Christianity in Japan are provided most notably by a thorough handbook edited by Mullins (2003) and by the extensive *Japan Christian Dictionary* (1988). Significant monographs on Japanese Christianity in general include Ebisawa & Ōuchi (1971) in Japanese and Drummond (1971) in English, while an inquiry into the dynamic of transmission and appropriation of Christianity in Japan is presented in Breen & Williams (1996).

communities and on expanding their "hidden Christian" inheritance; a minute Russian Orthodox missionary presence could do little but rely on native catechists, who actuated Japan's most locally-attuned mission of the day.[4]   The 1870's and 1880's saw Japan's flood-tide period of Western borrowing—"West-worship"—which, however, netted only some 30,000 believers into Protestantism, the most visible brand of Christianity of the new era.

Protestant missionaries exerted themselves in the educational, medical and social fields, gaining national prominence as school-founders and rights activists, but their tendency to speculate on the comprehensive package of Western modernity under the rubric of "Christ against (Japanese) culture" backfired in the hands of the educated Japanese elite, which quickly asserted its ability to effect a non-Christian Westernization.[5]   Contemporary Western philosophical discourse was grafted onto Japan's enduring anti-Christianity by highly-placed commentators of Japan's new "creeds"— the 1889 Meiji Constitution and the 1890 Imperial Rescript on Education.   With the advent of large-scale imperialism and industrialization at the close of the century, the growing strength and integration of the Japanese metropole sparked the consolidation of a popular nationalism, which encoded the need for "alien" Christians to perpetually prove their "Japaneseness." By this time some basic aspects of Christian innovation—notably the calendar and the nuclear family roles—had gained wide acceptance. Christianity was tacitly in-

[4]The proportion of foreign missionaries in 1877, when Protestants numbered 99 missionaries, Roman Catholics—45, and Orthodox—4, represented the high point of foreign Orthodox presence. Nakamura (2007), 27.

[5]The period of initial receptivity to Christianity has attracted particular attention in the context of modernization/Westernization of Japan, giving rise to the historiographical construct of "Meiji Christianity." A valuable basic source is still Cary (1909); for a study on the pattern and significance of ex-samurai Christian conversion see Scheiner (1970); for a social history linking Christianization and modernization see Morioka (1976); for the distinctive Roman Catholic experience of Meiji see Takagi (1978-1980). Systemic study of missionaries began more recently, most importantly by Ion (1990, 1993).

scribed into the wide parameters of Japan's social "orthodoxy" through participating, en par with Shintoists and Buddhists, in officially-sponsored conferences to mobilize religions for state-mandated "moral suasion" campaigns. However, this precarious "establishment" cost Christians a loss of leadership in social activism, while continued dependence on foreign staff, supplies and prestige marginalized them in the newly "nationalized" Japan. Radical champions of social betterment increasingly turned to direct political action and away from Christianity, while the Christian mainstream was drawn into the construction of the Japanese mixed-nation imperialism.[6]

Central protagonists of Japan's modern religious history were native "new religions"—syncretic or synthetic popular movements centered on charismatic founders. They began to spring up amid the ferment of the late Tokugawa period and continued to multiply apace with the advance of urbanization and attendant social dislocation, reaching a pre-war peak during the Great Depression. A digest of folk religiosity, organized lay Buddhism, and Confucian moral self-cultivation, this diverse phenomenon began to embrace and remake Christian elements in the 20th century. Aside from the outstanding preacher Kagawa Toyohiko and his pan-Protestant "Kingdom of God" campaign in 1929-1934, few Japanese Christian leaders engaged the common laborers, among whom "new religions" flourished. Yet, the process of radical indigenization had already occurred in the "hidden Christian" tradition, which, upon emergence into legality, split into self-recognized Roman Catholics and those who remained attached exclusively to distinctive ancestral ways.[7]

[6] On the notable Christian input into the emergence of the Japanese mixed-nation concept see Oguma (2002), 31-52. For a useful study of the Japanese Christian interaction with and participation in the imperial venture see the work on the Protestant Manchurian mission in Kan (1999b).

[7] "Hidden Christians" who did not identify themselves as Roman Catholics represent Japan's most profound case of indigenization—to the point where the widest definitions of "Christianity" appear strained. See Turnbull (1998) on their history and practice.

Fractures soon emerged in the educated elite of Japanese Protestantism also, as a few charismatic leaders broke with transplanted Western denominations to found self-consciously "Japanese" alternatives. The latter commonly involved a radical embrace of some domestic religious traditions, complete with a heavy emphasis on a routine and practical mystical interaction with the spiritual world. Together with the accession of Japanese to leadership posts and the increasing participation in imperial ventures by mainline denominations, this native protest called for and witnessed to a deepening "Japanization" of Christianity. Uchimura Kanzō's famous No-Church movement, which pioneered this process in 1901, remained elitist and bookish, true to its samurai and Puritan roots. However, the subsequent Japanese departures from mainline Protestantism were more populist, syncretic and emotional, in line with the prevailing élan of Japan's "new religions." Shunned by established religionists, secular social activists and officials alike for their "superstitious" deviance, popular success and organizational autonomy, "new religions" were the first religious victims of the renewed Japanese state.

Ironically, this oppressive turn occurred during the ostensible high-point of liberalism, under imperial Japan's only Christian Prime Ministers—the Roman Catholic Hara Takashi (1918 - 1921) and the Protestant Takahashi Korekiyo (1921 - 1922). Amid anti-communist fears in the wake of the Russian Revolution, "new religions" were officially classified as "pseudo-religions" in 1919 and began to suffer periodic interventions by the police—including a few high-profile leadership arrests in the 1920's and a multitude of effective dissolutions since 1935. It was inside this domestic typology of syncretic "evil cults" that such foreign Christian groups as Jehovah's Witnesses, Holiness churches and others faced forcible disbandment since 1940. The officials saw these groups' transgressiveness in terms familiar in the "new religion" context—"superstition," faith healing, eschatological expectations. Christianity had joined both the enervated mainstream and the animated fringe of Japanese religion.[8]

Relatively well-sponsored but slow-growing, Western-affiliated mainline Christianity failed to capture pioneering agency, but was seminal to the modern reconfiguration of Japanese religion. Samurai Confucianism framed in Christian terms was encoded by a Japanese Quaker, Nitobe Inazō, into the famous "Way of the Warrior" (*Bushidō*), widely employed in the construction and inculcation of Japan's national "spiritual" norms. Rude official disestablishment and Christian adversity evoked revitalization and mimicry in Japanese Buddhism, which gained a new global self-awareness as a "world religion," greatly expanded charitable and missionary action, and in some cases even adopted Protestant-style liturgical elements.[9]

Most importantly, Japan's borrowed notion of "religion" assumed Christianity as prototypical, spurring a rejection of the religious label with regard to the native "Way of the gods" (Shintoism). While an early attempt at institutionalizing a new national creed was denied to the Meiji reformers by the Western demand for religious freedom, the Japanese state gradually configured some of the localized Shintoist cults into "state Shintoism"—an obligatory "non-religion" of reverence for ancestors, the imperial lineage, and the state. In an erratic manner, with contradictory official statements on the nature of "state Shintoism" vis-à-vis the avowedly religious "sect Shintoism," the former was codified on the level of ritual and gradually imposed onto the public life of the nation.[10]

[8] Aside from the No-Church movement lead by Japan's most documented Christian leader—Uchimura Kanzō—Christian "new religions" and their typological linkage with some "foreign" groups have long been neglected in academic scholarship. A major work which introduced Christianity "made in Japan" is Mullins (1998). On treatment of the suppression of "unorthodox" religious groups in the context of state-society synergy see Garon (1997), 60-87.

[9] Key works on the Meiji-period refiguration of Buddhism in its tension with Christianity are Thelle (1987) and Ketelaar (1990).

[10] On the elaboration and praxis of state Shintoism see Hardacre (1989).

Ever since the "*lèse majesté* incident" of 1891, when the Protestant teacher Uchimura Kanzō failed to publicly venerate the imperial seal with a full bow, the controversy over the Christian attitude toward state Shintoist ritual divided the concerned opinion. Japan's major Western-derived Christian bodies took until the 1930's to finally accept the rites, even as many of their counterparts in Korea rejected state Shintoism and faced severe repressions.[11] As Japan's fascist movement gained influence and the nation geared for total war, the government finally assumed systemic control of the religious sphere. In 1939 the long-prepared comprehensive Religious Organizations Law institutionally encoded the difference between "state Shintoism" and "religion," providing a mandatory pattern for the legal operation of all Japanese religious groups.[12]

The new regulations in effect empowered the Ministry of Education to dictate the constitution and doctrine of religious bodies before granting them legal recognition. Severance of foreign links, expulsion of foreign leaders, avowals of explicit faith in the global mission of Japan and the transcendent significance of its eternal emperor-centered polity, administrative integration into larger empire-wide groupings—these were the major unwritten "preferences" behind the organizational requirements of the 1939 law. After gradually learning of these demands in 1940, Christian groups were given about a year to comply. Since the large mission-engendered Japanese denominations still depended in some measure on foreign subsidies, their termination came as a blow for all. Yet, on other counts, the Roman Catholics—organizationally united and relatively free of Anglo-American ties—fared better. The Ministry of Education made a special allowance for their continued connection with the Vatican

---

[11]On the tortuous process of coming to terms with Japan's "state Shintoism" see Dōshisha (1996) for Protestants; Minamiki (1985) for Roman Catholics; Kurata (1991) on the situation in Korea.

[12]See the full text of the law in Cabinet (1999), 153-159.

and registered them as a tax exempt "Japan Heavenly Lord Catholic Religious Organization."

Some seventy diverse Protestant groups faced a much harsher dilemma, which defined the stereotypical "Christian" experience of wartime Japan. Their overwhelmingly Anglo-American connections and extensive missionary staffs were suddenly untenable, leading to a multitude of more or less involuntary anti-foreign "coups" inside each body. Even more revolutionary was the official demand for Japan's Protestants to form a single "Japan Christian Religious Organization"—a long-time ecumenical dream which turned into a nightmare for many participants on account of the tremendous compromises entailed. Hastily formed in 1940, this pan-Protestant structure failed to achieve organizational and creedal stability until 1945 once more radically altered the context. In the meantime, the groups which refused the state-imposed merger, including most of Japan's Anglicans, faced schism, endangered extra-legal existence, or else laborious parish-by-parish registration as "associations" (*kessha*)—generic socio-political groups devoid of the many exemptions enjoyed by the "religious organizations" (*kyōdan*). As Japan launched its attack against the Western Allies at the end of 1941, the stifling context soon became crushing—regular services lapsed, believers deserted churches, the handful of remaining Anglo-American missionaries and their Japanese contacts were arrested with increasing frequency, and the expanding radius of "thought crime" compelled many Christians to assert ever more dramatically "Japanese" beliefs and rites. Only the immediacy of life-and-death issues at the close of the war, as Japan sustained destructive US firebombing, communicated a reenergizing humanitarian impulse to what appeared a paralyzed religious scene.[13]

[13]The wartime experience of Japan's Christian groups is amply documented through the prism of Special higher police materials in Dōshisha (1981). For the particularly acute trauma sustained by the Anglicans see Tsukada (1981), Ion (1993). On the expansion of wartime thought policing to Christian eschatological teaching, see Mullins (1994).

Unconditional surrender to the US occupation ushered into a "Christian boom," as many Japanese sought to align with the ascendant "Christian" power and fill the spiritual vacuum resulting from the Americans' summary dismantlement of "state Shintoism." Despite devastated infrastructure (about 500 of the country's 1600 major church buildings destroyed)[14] and decimated personnel, the growth of Christian groups in the radically deregulated religious economy of 1945-1951 was striking. Although American occupation authorities prided themselves on religious impartiality,[15] the occasional flamboyant Christian messianism of the Supreme Commander of the Allied Powers General Douglas MacArthur, the summary arrangement by the US forces for mass-production and distribution of Japanese-language Bibles, and the predominantly Protestant image and composition of the occupation personnel were powerful catalysts. Since missionaries were administratively hampered from returning to Japan at the outset of the occupation, the first fruits of this growth went to Christian new religions and to the Roman Catholics—the latter enjoyed a 7-to-1 advantage over Protestants in missionary forces in Japan as of mid-1947.[16] Although manifestly skewed, a survey from that year revealed a figure of Christian believers unprecedented either in the prior or subsequent annals of Japan—6%.[17] Since Japan's long-suppressed communists were enjoying a similarly unparalleled boom, Americans were keen to boost the Christian dynamic. With MacArthur's famous call for "a thousand Christian missionaries" the floodgates opened: if there were 1401 foreign missionaries in Japan in 1940, in 1949 their number had risen to 1800, while the following three years brought over 1500 more new ones, with the corresponding inflow of foreign funds.[18]

[14]Iglehart (1959) 299.

[15]The standard account of US occupation religious policy is Woodard (1972).

[16]Brumbaugh (1947).

[17]Wada (1981), 2.

[18]Orthodox Messenger (1949.05.15 - № 719), 2; Iglehart (1959) 341.

Yet, as the US occupation ended in 1952 and Japan's speedy reconstruction took off, privation-driven Christian growth began to slacken.[19] By the close of the decade spectacular advance was over, with the 1942 to 1960 net gain for mainline Christians being some 435,000 believers, an increase of 2.5 times compared to an overall population increase of 1.3 times.[20] Impressive as this was, the Christian share of the religious market remained negligible—about 1%, if Christian "new religions" are included. This proportion would remain stable for decades. Japan's "Christian boom" left Christianity numerically and culturally strengthened, but still tied to the stereotype of elite intellectual Western-leaning leftist Protestants, with the Roman Catholic peasant legacy declining in numbers and Christian-related "new religions" growing in syncretism.

The invisibility of the Japanese Orthodox Church in this dominant narrative was not only a factor of size, but also of its being both out of step and out of character with the prevailing dynamic. It squared poorly with the mainline mission-originated bodies because its distinctive missionary approach and theological aspects (like the notion of the emperor's sacredness) reduced tension with the new Japanese "national polity"; its homeland was viewed as a second-class power shorn of the political and cultural magnetism inherent in the appeal (and stigma) of Western Christian denominations; and its overseas support, linkage and personnel remained scarce or non-existent. On the other hand, the Japanese Orthodox Church was not an isolated "new religion"—its believers remained in communion with a vast global network

[19]The Roman Catholics' 1951 new convert rate of 10.4% dropped to 7.9% in 1953; the Protestants reported a 12% fall in attendance between 1955 and 1957. See consecutively Mullins (1998), 23; Iglehart (1959), 331.

[20]The approximate 1942 and 1960 figures for the Japanese home islands were, respectively: some 100,000 and 323,599 for Roman Catholics; some 190,000 and over 400,000 for Protestants, according to Mullins (1998), 23. The total Japanese population between those years went from some 74,000,000 to 94,096,000.

of coreligionists and its formally accepted theology never broke from the shared Orthodox Christian premises. Finally, the historical trajectory of this community ensured that the radical severance of foreign links, which most mainline Churches faced in 1940, occurred already in 1917, while the trials of 1940 revealed a pattern unprecedented in the Japanese wartime empire—at the Imperial Army's behest a Japanese religious body was being subordinated to a Russo-Manchukuoan one. The logic of these idiosyncrasies was rooted in the ironic relationship between two modern heavily Westernized non-Western empires—the Russian and the Japanese.

Elusive common ground of Russo-Japanese relations

It remains underappreciated that the first encounter of Russia and Japan was arranged by the expansionist Counter-Reformation Roman Catholic world—the late 16th century guise of the emerging colonialist West. The first Japanese to enter Russia and inform its authorities about Japan's conditions was an Augustinian by the name of Nicholas, a convert of the booming Jesuit mission in Japan. As a papal diplomat, he walked into the midst of Russia's "Time of Troubles"—an era of unprecedented socio-political instability, when Orthodox Russia's nemesis, the Roman Catholic Polish-Lithuanian state, nearly succeeded in subjugating its prostrate Eastern neighbor.[21] The same years saw Japan's first artistic depiction of the "Grand Prince of Moscow"—an elaborated copy of a Western work in the exoticist genre of Japan's "Christian century" paintings.[22] With the triumph of re-centralization in both Russia and Japan under the new

---

[21] For a useful overview on the story of Nicholas the Augustinian, see Cherevko (1999), 14-23.
[22] Ermakova (2005), 225-233.

dynasties—Romanov and Tokugawa—by the second decade of the 17th century the footholds of the Roman Catholic West were being forcibly eradicated, even as new impulses and seminal borrowings were absorbed. From this time the fear of a religio-political Roman Catholic takeover—ambiguously extrapolated to the fear of Western ways in general—became a culturally encoded bogey-man of the dominant ideologies in both lands.

Yet, the increasing absorption of, with, and by the magnetizing "West" spurred a demonstrative attempt at walling-off and then a decisive opening-up to the apparently inevitable "coming of the West"—a cycle to be repeated in subsequent history of both countries. The mythologized and oft-compared "Great" emperors, Russia's Peter and Japan's Meiji, who presided over the launch of the radical Westernization in their lands at the start of the 1700's and at the close 1860's respectively, rode the crest of a pent-up reformist tide. Extensive corporate memory of the native polity, prior successful borrowing of a digested and compartmentalized foreign civilization, meritocratic service bureaucracy, large and comparatively homogenized population, and relatively high per capita GNP formed the rare combination which permitted these "latecomer" polities to propel themselves successfully into the West-defined race toward "modernization." By Westernizing themselves defensively, Russia and Japan readily embraced technologies, but only partially and controversially accepted underlying belief-systems.

Both Russia and Japan rose to "great power" and "colonizer" status by the start of the 20th century, complete with compelling military-industrial complexes, but remained torn in their quest for self-definition vis-à-vis their great object of authority and anxiety—the "West." This troubled relationship with the same dominant and partially appropriated "other" is the chief common ground in the recent history of Russia and Japan, the root of their modern civilizational dilemma.[23]

At the same time Russia and Japan were also becoming "others" to each other. Gradual extension brought them into contact at the close of the 17th century and showed the Russians the more pro-active party—Russian prodding and Japanese temporizing formed the stuff of over a century of their subtle diplomatic and cultural relationship. It was only after Western military might in mid-1850's humiliated both Japan and Russia sufficiently to spur decisive domestic change—Japan's "Meiji Restoration" and Russia's "Great Reforms"—that the two concluded their first treaties. With their boundaries settled, gradual approach began to transform into imperial competition.[24]

In the next era of the Russo-Japanese political relationship the Japanese seized the initiative. Convinced of Russia's second-class standing vis-à-vis Japan's chosen models—Germany, the UK and the US—leading Japanese ideologists began to construct a triangular identity paradigm which contrasted Russia and Japan: the former was the barbaric "Orient in Europe," the latter—the civilized "West in Asia." The attempt on the life of the Russian Crown Prince Nicholas during his 1891 visit to Japan—the Ōtsu incident—adumbrated the rise of Japan's new anti-Russian sentiment, as the two nations set on a collision course for domination of Northeast Asia.[25] The well-known sequence of ambitious advances into

[23]The basic effort to treat the structural parallels in Russian and Japanese "modernization" is Black et al. (1975), which, however, only skirts cultural issues. Many consequences of this parallelism have been recognized—for instance, Oguma (2002), 330-331, suggested Russia as the closest parallel to Japan in its construction of imperial mixed-nationhood—but the basic implications of resulting cognitive similarities to bilateral relations are only beginning to receive sustained attention; see Bukh (2010).

[24]The basic works on this period of Russo-Japanese mutual approach include Lensen (1959); Wada (1991); Cherevko (1999). The significance of direct encounters and emerging diplomatic ritual for the early image-formation of the two societies is taken up by Ikuta (2008).

[25]See a dissertation on the incident by Shin (1989) and an accessible English language summary in Lensen (1961).

China and Korea resolved into the Russo-Japanese War of 1904-1905, in which Japan showed its informational, technological and logistical superiority over the unprepared, disunited and isolated adversary.[26] Yet, with the geopolitical tension diffused, the political relations warmed nearly as quickly as they had chilled, and cooperation in World War I brought the nations into an alliance sealed by Russo-Japanese convention of 1916. For the first time in the two nations' history, both of these endemically sacralized, factiously bureaucratic and nominally constitutional monarchies entered a relationship that appeared amicable and durable, if only reaction could stem pent-up revolution.[27]

While Japan was consumed by forestalling Western imperialist challenges through the pursuit of "rich country, strong army" and "treaty revision," a greater portion of Russia's energies were channeled into an artistic efflorescence, ensuring that the vector of cultural influence in contemporary Russo-Japanese relations was reversed. Russian literature, first of all the monumental works of Dostoevsky, Tolstoy and Chekhov, made an early and lasting entry into the mainstream of Japan's rich literary tradition, becoming the most important foreign literary influence on modern Japan. By 1908, as Russo-Japanese relations were improving and an increasing trickle

[26]The literature on the Russo-Japanese War is one of two thickest strata in the entire historiography of Russo-Japanese relations. As a much-trumpeted first military victory of an "Asiatic" power over a "European" one; as "World War Zero" which determined the power-balance in the Pacific; as the catalyst of Russia's first modern revolution; as a consolidator of Japan's nationalism and imperialism; as a large-scale destructive military conflict; and as an enduring and versatile cultural signifier, this war monopolizes much attention, with a new outpouring of writings in the wake of its centennial. The cultural implications, particularly significant to the present work, are treated in the collection of Wells & Wilson (1999) as well as many individual writings, including Katayama (2009) on the globalization of Japanese media discourse; Shimazu (2009) and Oku (2007) on the evolution of Japan's popular domestic front, including the juncture between the rise of Japanese national consciousness and anti-Russianism.

[27]This rapprochement is treated best in modern works by Russians, like Shulatov (2008), Baryshev (2007), Molodiakov (2010).

of highly-cultured Russian inquirers began to visit Japan, the number of translations into Japanese from Russian exceeded those from English.[28]   In the related fields of theater and cinema, and less notably music and visual arts, Russia likewise gained Japanese attention and following, highlighting the dilemma of the East-West cultural choice.[29]

The converse Japanese cultural influence on Russia did not produce a comparable tide, although the French current of *Japonisme* and early home-grown enthusiasts like Kitaev combined to provide public prominence to Japanese prints and impregnate some of Russian "Silver age" imagery with Japanese motifs.   Far more important was the role Japan played in stirring Russians to self-searching imaginings about the "East" and their own questionable belonging thereto—a prominent factor in most culturally-resonant Russian evocations of Japan, from Solov'ev's apocalyptic renditions of the "Yellow peril" to the groundless optimism of the revolution-era Eurasianists.[30]   Whether this new wave of rhetorical fascination with the East would have yielded a constructive Russo-Japanese cultural rapprochement cannot be known, because the advent of the Soviet dictatorship soon foreclosed this search inside Russia.[31]

The Russian Revolution of 1917 ushered into the first trial run of militant socialist "alternative modernity," which

---

[28]Ōta (1959), 12.

[29]General overviews of Russian cultural impact on Japan usually focus overwhelmingly on literature, the basic works being Fukuda et al. (1976), Kim (1987); a wider scope focusing on literature and socialism is presented in Nobori & Akamatsu (1981). The inquiry dramatically expanded and diversified since the last years of the Soviet regime, exemplified by a recent wave of micro-histories on Russian émigré cultural legacies in Japan, the better-known treatments belonging to Sawada (2001, 2002) and Podalko (2001).

[30]On the shaping of Russian views of Japan since the second half of the 19th century see the treatment of the politically salient visions in Schimmelpenninck van der Oye (2001) and useful broad sweep of the subject in Simeonova (2007).

[31]Notable article compilations which present a broad perspective on Russo-Japanese cultural interaction are Rimer (1995) and Mikhailova & Steele (2008).

pitted itself against the entire capitalist world and drew Japan into its deepest and most contradictory engagement with Russia—the Siberian Intervention, in which the Japanese experimented in dominating the Russian Far East through support and manipulation of Russia's losing anti-communist Whites.[32] Normalization of Soviet-Japanese relations through the 1925 Treaty of Beijing represented Japan's resigned geopolitical accommodation and a major triumph of Soviet diplomacy. However, neither country retreated from ongoing ideological war—this was made clear by Japan's simultaneous passage of the severe Peace Preservation Law, the country's chief thought-police ordinance aimed primarily against "Red" ideas. With leading Japanese political writers likening the function of communism in contemporary Japan with that of Christianity in the Tokugawa period,[33] Russia had once again become the purveyor of Japan's main officially prescribed "evil creed."

However, the Soviet spectacle of a centrally-planned autarkic non-capitalist rationalization and mobilization allured revolutionaries, reformers and rational planners throughout East Asia. While outright Japanese communists remained a diminutive and harshly persecuted movement,[34] Japan's broader socialist currents provided a receptive milieu for Soviet-derived discourse. Most influentially, the pull of Soviet studies exerted a profound influence on the parallel development of Japan's own "alternative modernity" movement which emerged in the course of the 1930's as an answer to the Great Depression and a synergy of radical officers' terror, utopian intellectuals' theorizing, reformist bureaucrats' activism, and public activists' patriotism. With the establishment of the puppet-state of Manchukuo, Northeast China emerged as the locus where the modern Russo-Japanese

[32]Hara (1989) provides the basic outlines of the intervention process; Izao (2003) problematizes the lightly dismissed rhetoric of the intervention as a "crusade."

[33]For example see Tokutomi (1936), 1-3.

[34]The basic handbook on Japanese Marxism is Hoston (1986).

23

encounter emerged most vividly through the contrast and convergence of colonization patterns, as well as the conflict and collaboration on the ground.[35]

As both regimes reinvented themselves in order to more effectively best the "West," in the later 1930's Soviet Stalinism and Japanese fascism showed signs of convergence. Both were becoming totalitarian militarized police regimes which purveyed a collectivist ethic geared for nationalistic messianism, a utopian resolution of the contradictions between breakneck industrialization and communal agrarianism, and a revolutionary transcendence of the imperialist paradigm. At the same time, Japan and the USSR continued their ostensibly bitter ideological and geopolitical rivalry and tested each other's strength with increasingly serious border battles in 1937-1939. These tests concluded with Japan's resounding defeat at Nomonhan—trumpeted in the USSR and concealed in Japan.[36] This resolution paved the way for a momentary viability in 1940 of the Eurasian "Pact of four" that would unite the Axis powers with the USSR on the basis of pragmatic geopolitical power-sharing—a project taken seriously both in Tokyo and in Moscow, but scuttled in Berlin. The subsequent Japano-Soviet "strange neutrality" and Japan's hopes for Soviet arbitration illustrated the fruits of the painfully elaborated ambiguous balance, dashed by the Soviet entry into World War II in the East on August 9 1945.[37]

---

[35]The early Russian presence in Manchuria garnered relatively little attention, a notable work being Quested (1982). On the other hand, much has been written on the Russian émigré society in post-revolutionary Manchuria, landmark volumes being Stephan (1978), Patrikeeff (2002), Aurilene & Potapova (2004). The recent academic "rediscovery" of Manchukuo as a provocative field of modern identity-construction gave new salience to the subject, exemplified by Young (1998), Yamamuro (2006) and especially Duara (2003).

[36]For the border clashes of 1937-1939 see Coox (1977, 1985).

[37]Important treatments of the diplomatic relationship of the pre-war USSR and Japan are Lensen (1970, 1974); Kobayashi (1985). On the unlikely cycle of wartime rapprochement see Molodiakov (2004); Slavinskii (1995). The finale of Japan's World War II has been convincingly analyzed from an international

USSR's race into war to "cash in" on Japan's defeat, conditioned by the Japanese enemy-images which dominated the Soviet press,[38] imparted two major legacies for the Russo-Japanese relations of the 20th century: the saga of some 600,000 Japanese captives serving forced labor sentences across the war-ravaged Soviet Union[39] and the "Kurillian knot" of borderland issues. The overwhelming socio-political realities worked by US occupation and the quickly articulated Cold War—which went "hot" in Korea already in 1950—assured that the USSR and Japan failed to sign a peace treaty, with Russia remaining Japan's "distant neighbor" to the present.[40]

As this overview shows, the first century of intensive Russo-Japanese relations heavily favored stereotypes of alien enemies, obfuscating constructive junctures. Lasting human communities which might pioneer broadly-grounded cultural dialogue, understanding and synthesis between Russia and Japan remained elusive. The shared vacillating dynamic of anti-Western Westernization remained a structural parallel devoid of notable Russo-Japanese communal embodiment. While inherently tenable, not a single rapprochement in the modern Russo-Japanese political relationship proved lasting. The most prominent fruit of the lopsided cultural interpenetration was probably an elite of Japanese literati and socialists,

perspective which gives due weight to Soviet involvement in Hasegawa (2005).

[38]For a rare treatment of the Soviet propagandist construction of Japan see Mikhailova (2008).

[39]While repatriants to Japan produced much memoiristic material, whose pioneer synthesizer was Wakatsuki (1979), systemic access to primary documents of the camp administration placed post-Soviet Russian researchers in the forefront of this inquiry with such works as Kuznetsov (1994, 1997) and Piankevich (1999).

[40]The post-war burdened relationship between Russia and Japan has produced a vast literature dominated by the territorial dispute. A few representative guides are the introduction to the region and the problem by Stephan (1974); the products of the moment of flexibility in early 1990's like Wada (1990) and Slavinskii (1993); recent representative works by Russian and Japanese historio-political antagonists like Latyshev (2004) and Kimura (2005).

whose potential for effective bicultural bridging activism was usually undermined by the dearth of Russian reciprocity. The convergent practice of wartime "alternative modernity" may have included a common ground of aspiration, method, and even function, but as long as form remained starkly dissimilar the mutually exclusive integrity of the Soviet "Union" and Japanese "Co-Prosperity Sphere" remained a violently affirmed conceptual fixture. The many Russian refugees in Japanese-dominated lands and the even more numerous, though transitory, Japanese captives in the USSR, were mostly forced expatriates, more often cultural resisters rather than intermediaries.

This finally brings us to Japan's Orthodox Christians, who fall out of the paradigm of shattered middle-grounds—they were the single inextricably Russo-Japanese community to have proven itself stable and flexible enough to sustain all the vicissitudes of the volatile Russo-Japanese relationship without reneging the bridging cultural function. The narrative of unfulfilled Russo-Japanese links remains unprepared to integrate their existence precisely because of those factors which allowed the "Church" to remain "in but not of" Russo-Japanese relations.

Arrested Asian reach of Orthodoxy

As a refiguring of Judaism, Christianity inherently carries in itself both a universalist and a particularist strain, a tension between the Gospel to be preached to "all nations" and the exclusive consciousness of the sacred "chosen people," a mission to convert and a duty to preserve. Breaking out from the ethno-political confines of Israel in a dramatic missionary expansion spearheaded by Apostle Paul, the new community—the "Church"—attracted numerous adherents in Jewish diasporic and non-Jewish convert cells scattered as far eastwards as India within a century's time.

Yet, only by partially accepting as normative the ethno-political confines of the Mediterranean "inhabited world" of the Roman Empire did Christianity succeed in forming a coherent civilizational model. By embracing the philosophical, legal and artistic sophistication of the declining Hellenistic cultural sphere, Christians rose to dominate what gradually became after the 4th century the prototype of the Christian polity. In the formulaic ideal vocalized by early 6th century, five peer patriarchs presided over the spiritual and one or more emperors—over the civic spheres of a single Roman imperio-ecclesial condominium, the Church and state being joined in "symphony" as "soul and body." This metamorphosis amplified and politicized the challenges faced by the increasingly "Roman" Church in the non-Roman East—the 4th century persecution ravaged what had been a large Christian population in the competing Persian superpower, the 5th century Nestorian and Monophysite controversies turned geo-political and sliced off most of the Christians on the Southeastern fringes of the empire, the 7th century rise of Islam—arguably Christianity's most distant and most important heresy—imperiled the very survival of the reduced Roman realm.

Indeed, the strain of the ensuing "dark age" disrupted the Roman condominium itself. In the Latin-speaking Western half, where Celtic and Germanic peoples set up new states on the empire's ruins, the regional patriarch—the pope of Rome—was increasingly assuming an activist and political leadership over and against "barbarian" secular rulers around him, thence strengthening his claim to a similar superiority in the global ecclesiastical economy. When the Greek-speaking Eastern half of the empire regained vitality in the 9th century and launched a campaign to convert its threatening northern neighbors, the division between two competing and increasingly dissimilar Roman Christendoms was manifest. By 1054, when formal excommunication announced this divergence, the Constantinople-centered Eastern Roman civilization achieved a missionary breakthrough by attracting the Slavs and staking out for itself a heartland between Ochrid, Novgorod, Tbilisi and Sinai. This region of Orthodox Christian habitation, despite political upheaval, would remain relatively stable until the 16th century—the century which signaled the advent of Protestant Reformation, Western colonialism, and Russian advance to the East.[41]

The essential features of missions helped build up this "Byzantine commonwealth" were, according to the author of the term:

> the eagerness to preach the Gospel to pagan barbarians; the use of vernacular translations of the Scriptures and the liturgy in order to facilitate their conversion; the support, political and economic, given to the mission by the imperial government; the missionaries' efforts to... provide a stable framework for the religious and cultural growth of their community; their willingness to place their technical expertise... at the service of their flock; and the shrewd flexibility of imperial diplomacy.[42]

Such coordinated Church-state ventures, above all that of Sts. Cyril and Methodius to the Slavs, allowed the Eastern Roman civilization to outlive its original incarnation, albeit in a "translated" form. By the 16th century, when other Orthodox lands had been subjugated by Muslims or Roman

---

[41]As handy summary treatments on the history and nature of Eastern Roman Christendom—"Byzantine Orthodoxy"—one might indicate the basic schematic work on the Church in the Eastern Roman empire by Hussey (1986); a recent collection with comprehensive sweep in Angold (2006); interpretive monographs by well-known Orthodox popularizer-theologians—Schmemann (1963) and Kallistos (1997) – and by a more restrained outsider like Binns (2002).

[42]Obolensky ([1971] 2000), 61-62.

Catholics, Moscow-centered Russia donned the mantle of the "Third Rome."[43]

The Russian redaction of the Eastern Roman ecclesio-imperial condominium, which formally endured to the 20th century, was decisively stamped by the ascendant Western secularizing context. The main signpost on the path of governmental "liberation" from and "taming" of the Russian Orthodox Church were the reforms of Emperor Peter I which instituted in the first quarter of the 18th century a "Synodal system" of ecclesiastical governance. This was an adapted Protestant model of a "state Church"—devoid of its own primate, governed by a rotating board (styled the Most Holy Synod), and subordinated to the monarch as the "Supreme Judge."[44] Yet, despite the obvious imbalance in its supposed "symphony," the Russian Church-state relationship remained uncommonly close, making early 20th century Russia the leading Christian nation in the amount of funds centrally allocated by the state to the ecclesiastical apparatus.[45] Consequently, Russian Orthodox eastward missionary expansion likewise occurred overwhelmingly in tandem with and within the confines of the growing Russian Empire, which encompassed a great diversity of tongues and cultures.

[43]A rare attempt at a comprehensive in-house interpretive scheme of Orthodox missionary activity is found in Stamoolis (1986). Baker (2006) might be consulted as an interesting attempt to link later Russian-connected Orthodox missions in East Asia with the understudied background of non-Western Christianity in the region. The principal medieval expansion and transmutation of Eastern Roman Christendom is treated overwhelmingly in civilizational terms, although Orthodoxy figured centrally in each case. One might usefully consult the range of recent scholarship on this subject in Shepard (2007); the basic paradigm of the "commonwealth" in Obolensky ([1971] 2000); the Byzantine role in the rise of Muscovite Russia in Meyendorff (1981); the process of resignification of key elements of the Byzantine cultural package in the Russian context in Uspenskii (1998).

[44]The Petrine religious reforms are treated well, if narrowly, in Cracraft (1971). Tsypin (2006) offers a somewhat sanitized but uniquely comprehensive overview of the modern history of the Russian Orthodox Church from Peter the Great to the post-Soviet period.

[45]Hardacre (1989), 166-167.

An apparent force for assimilation, the Russian Church had in fact repeatedly contributed to the consolidation of distinct ethnicities by giving them new vitality in the ecclesiastical context, as exemplified by the work of Sts. Stephen of Perm', Macarius (Glukharev) of the Altai and Innocent (Veniaminov) of Alaska.[46] Russia's "Great Reforms" spurred a reanimation of missionary ventures with the codification of the "Il'minskii system" which emphasized native-language translation and education. The newly-founded Russian Missionary Society developed a Janus-faced self-presentation—a more nationalist guise for official consumption and a more vernacular religious one for native populations.[47] This allowed the Church to accommodate the occasional political demand for "Russification" with the increasingly universalist mission, which reached China and Korea and created the context for a breakthrough in Japan.[48]

The denouement of World War I transformed the Orthodox landscape more decisively and unexpectedly than the Turkish conquests of the 15th-16th century. On the ruins of empires, Wilsonian remapping of Europe boosted the factious limitrophe states of Southeastern Europe into the powerhouse of the Orthodox world. Kemalist Turkey savaged

---

[46]The activity of the former, well-known in outline, continues to be excavated through folkloric data, as in Limerov (2008). The latter two have been accessibly, although hagiographically, treated in English in Kharlampovich (2001) and Garrett ([1979] 2006) respectively.

[47]Michaelson (1999), 364-365.

[48]The scholarly historiography of the Russian Church's modern missions has long been largely subsumed under secular rubrics, until the post-Soviet access to sources and altered ideological climate showed up greater ambiguity and autonomy of missions. The resulting discussion has been taking shape with such collections as Geraci & Khodarkovsky (2001). Broad coverage is provided by the ample factographic dissertation by Michaelson (1999) on the Russian Missionary Society and by the antiquated but comprehensive monograph by Bolshakoff (1943). Particularly salient for the present work are the treatments of the uniquely well-studied case of Alaskan Orthodoxy— Oleksa (1992); Kan (1999a); Mousalimas (2004), recapped and generalized by Znamenski (1999)—as well as the representative volumes on East Asian missions, Pozdniaev (1998, 1999b) and Bogoliubov & Augustine (1993-2004).

and expelled almost all resident Greeks, nearly effacing the most significant lineal ecclesiastical descendant of Eastern Rome, the traditionally preeminent Church of Constantinople. Most importantly, Leninist Russia turned the paramount contemporary Orthodox Church-state condominium into a field of harsh persecution against yesterday's established religion. Migration replaced mission as the Russian Church's principal outreach mode, since the Russian "exodus"—some two million refugees, mostly military and elite "White" losers of the civil war—set up embittered Russian Orthodox communities around the globe. Diaspora and ecumenical relations became central topics in Orthodox debates, as the tottering Patriarchate of Constantinople attempted to recoup its losses by asserting global jurisdiction over Orthodox expatriates and in dealings with non-Orthodox interlocutors. Aside from Japan, the foreign missions of the Russian Church folded—the Urmian mission among Persia's Assyrians disintegrated amidst the anti-Christian genocide; "American Russia" descended into organizational chaos; continental East Asian establishments reoriented to serve the émigrés. In the conditions when "the center could not hold," global internecine conflicts over legitimacy and jurisdiction in the dislocated Orthodox world left little energy for mission.[49]

World War II compelled Stalin to permit a controlled revival of the Russian Church's activity inside the USSR and inclined him to lean on ecclesiastical channels to court global public opinion and construct a Moscow-centered "Orthodox Vatican," but Western countermeasures soon caused the

[49] Attempts at a comprehensive 20th century history of the Orthodox Church have not advanced beyond edited collections like Chaillot (2009) and Ramet (1988b). Since the modern transformation of the Russian Church was decisive for the worldwide Orthodox communion, the writings of the premier contemporary Russian Orthodox historian with a global perspective—Shkarovskii (2005, 2007, 2009)—bear special significance. Of the general treatments of the Russian Orthodox early and mid-20th century experience the best English-language presentation is still Pospielovsky (1984).

grand scheme to be dramatically scaled down.[50]   By the time the "Iron Curtain" split the Orthodox communion into opposing camps—centered on the enfeebled ecclesiastical headquarters in Moscow and Istanbul, half-heartedly propped up by Soviet and US interests respectively—the Japanese Orthodox Church had matured on its own. It possessed nearly a century of self-conscious history, a resilient native composition and structure, a basis for material, administrative and conceptual stability tested by autonomous self-realization. However, Japan's inscription into the global narrative of Orthodox ecclesiastical history remained precarious.

The clash between Christianity's early missionary expansion and its precipitous Romanization ensured that the first Christians with whom the Japanese may have come in contact as early as the 7th century were not Roman Orthodox, but Syro-Chaldean Nestorians.   The *translatio imperii* from Constantinople to Moscow made Russians into the sole potential Orthodox missionaries to Japan, and the Russians' prevalent mode of mission appeared to rule out an apolitical encounter. Consequently, the diffuse Russian religious impact on the Ainu since the start of the 18th century, the conversion to Orthodoxy of isolated Japanese castaways from the same time, and the 1858 institution of the first Russian Orthodox consular chapel in Japan did not adumbrate a "Japanese Orthodox Church."[51]Only the emer-

[50]Stalin's global ecclesiastical campaign has been introduced in English by Miner (2003). The broad field of Stalin-era ecclesiastical policies is captured, but scarcely analyzed, in the extensive document collection of Volokitina et. al. (2009). Mention might be made of an article collection on the global history of the Orthodox Church in the Cold War in Leustean (2010), which, however, suffers from many mistakes and gaping omissions.

[51]For overviews on the penetration of Orthodoxy among the Ainu see Kostanov (1992) 8-13, 72-73; Kushiro church (1992), 3-13. Research on the formal establishment of Russo-Japanese relations gave detailed coverage to the emergence of the Orthodox consular presence in Hakodate. Early Russian cultural influence in Northern Japan has been accessibly introduced by Lensen (1973), while a dramatized but reasonably accurate collection of Orthodoxy-related sketches on early Hakodate-centered Russo-Japanese interaction is found in Kuriyagawa (1994).

gence on the chaplain's post of a zealous and gifted carrier of the reviving universalist missionary tradition propelled the Japanese Orthodox community into its startling existence. The late 19th century renaissance of Russian mission provided the context for the Japanese Church's deserved prominence before 1917, but the subsequent traumatic history of the Orthodox communion made Japan all but invisible in the "larger picture." The successful autonomous elaboration of ecclesiastical self-consciousness by a young mission inside a different civilizational sphere was unprecedented amidst the chaos and struggle of the Orthodox Church during the age of the World Wars. It is to the history of this Japanese Orthodox body that we turn next.

Chapter 2

A century of Orthodox Christianity in Japan[1]

The 1855 Treaty of Shimoda, which inaugurated diplomatic relations between Russia and Japan, allowed both Japanese in Russia and Russians in Japan to be judged "by the laws of their own country," thus tacitly tolerating the practice of their respective religions. When the first Russian consulate in Japan opened in 1858, it was—according to the obligatory Russian practice—supplied with an Orthodox priest to minister to the consular personnel. Japan's northern-most city of Hakodate thus became the site of the country's first purpose-built Orthodox temple—the Resurrection church of the Russian consulate. The elderly Fr. Basil Makhov, sent to fill the Japanese post, arrived in 1859, only to leave the next

---

[1]The following basic overview traces the well-known outlines of Nicholas' missionary venture—most notably elaborated in Ushimaru (1978) and Nakamura (1996) in Japanese; Sablina (2006) in Russian; Remortel & Chang (2003) in English—and continues the narration to mid-1950's with minimal analytical and bibliographical engagement. The detailed discussions and analytical elaborations of the core issues touched here are presented in Parts II and III.

year due to ill health. In response to the consul's request for a capable replacement, the Russian Church selected the missionary-minded student John Kasatkin, who was ordained as hieromonk under the name of Nicholas and dispatched to Japan in 1860.

Figure 2.1: Archbishop Nicholas (Kasatkin) of Japan (1836–1912).

Nicholas had already read about Japan during his student days and his desire to start a mission there was given a new impetus by St. Innocent (Veniaminov), the veteran Orthodox missionary in Northeast Asia and Alaska, as the two prelates wintered in Nikolaevsk-on-the-Amur.

In 1861 Nicholas arrived in Japan, overcame the initial bout of hopelessness, and threw himself into the task of learning the Japanese language, history, religions and mores. His missionary activity in the proper sense was initiated by the 1865 assassination attempt, as an ultrapatriotic zealot, Shintoist priest and masterless samurai Sawabe Takuma burst into Nicholas' room intending to slay the suspicious foreigner. Nicholas' calm response so astonished the assailant as to make of him a disciple. In 1868 Sawabe and two of his samurai companions requested and received baptism. As Japan's Tokugawa regime had just collapsed in the face of the movement for radical renovation, disorientation, deprivation and dejection were rife especially among the supporters of the defeated shogunate, allowing the Japanese Orthodox converts-turned-preachers to attract to the new teaching a number of disgruntled warriors in Northeast Japan, especially in the city of Sendai. In 1869 Nicholas set off for Russia to procure official sanction and sponsorship for the emerging Orthodox mission in Japan.

On April 18 1870 the Most Holy Synod of the Russian Orthodox Church chartered the Japanese Orthodox Mission according to the ambitious blueprint prepared by Nicholas. He returned to Hakodate in 1871 accompanied by a Russian helper and assured an annual subsidy of 6000 rubles. Facing local Japanese officials' attempts to suppress Christian evangelism and aiming to make a speedy start on building up new headquarters in the capital, in 1872 Nicholas relocated to Tokyo. His exceptional Japanese-language competence made him a valued intermediary in Russo-Japanese diplomatic encounters, and procured both legal and material backing for establishing the mission's compound on a choice spot in Tokyo's Surugadai district. In 1874 Nicholas reacted to the official suspension of anti-Christian persecution by converting the language school, which he had been running to attract pupils, into one dedicated solely to preparing native Orthodox preachers and theologically-trained women—the core personnel for the future community. That year he also convoked the first Council of Japanese Orthodox Church-servitors, which agreed upon a nationwide strategy for mission, nominated the first convert, Paul Sawabe, to the priesthood, and instituted community-wide gatherings as an annual practice. For the first time Japanese Orthodox catechists dispersed to preach across the country.

In 1874 Japanese Orthodox numbered some 900 believers clustered in only three metropolitan areas—about 100 in Tokyo, about 300 in Hakodate, and about 500 in Sendai. In 1878 the reported membership was already 4215 baptized, 3 Russian missionaries, 6 Japanese priests, 27 Japanese catechists and 51 Japanese assistant-catechists preaching in almost 150 locations.[2] Japanese church-workers were being trained

[2] Sablina (2006), 92-93.

in three Tokyo schools—the seminary, the catechist-school and the women's school. The initial Orthodox approach to mission, with Japanese catechists doing the preaching and Nicholas making occasional tours to confirm the converted, was proving more effective in terms of early numerical growth than that of Protestants or Roman Catholics, who relied chiefly on foreign missionaries. Likewise, Nicholas' distinctive view toward converting not just individuals but households, combined with pioneering efforts at women's education, helped create family-based communities, rather than individualistic interest clubs.

However, the material base of the Orthodox mission was much weaker than that of Western counterparts—according to one estimate, the Roman Catholics in this period disposed of twenty-six and the Protestants fifteen times more money for their Japanese missions than the Orthodox.[3] In addition to lower funding from the metropole and a habit of dependence on state subsidies, a significant reason for this gap lay in the different social makeup of the emerging convert community. Whereas Western denominations attracted the forward-looking urban elite, relatively educated and enterprising, a larger portion of Orthodox believers were villagers, including many humble laborers, whose material contributions were meager.[4]

The initial tide of popularity, when Orthodoxy—in line with other Christian denominations—was identified with the package of Western civilization and attracted progressive modernizers, was a quickly passing phenomenon, which Nicholas, at any rate, was not eager to encourage, aiming instead at religiously-motivated conversion. To sustain his work, Nicholas turned to Russian authorities and benefactors with pleas to increase disbursements. His detailed requests

[3]Drummond (1971), 115.
[4]In 1897 Nicholas divided his flock in half between "impoverished gentry" and "laboring folk," in Nicholas (2004), vol. 3 (1897.01.15), 443-444.

and manifest successes soon achieved a major elevation of the mission's standing in Russia.

In 1879 Nicholas was summoned to St. Petersburg where, on April 11 1880, he was ordained bishop. Since bishops alone are capable of ordaining other clergy, through Nicholas' elevation to this highest clerical rank the Japanese Orthodox community was freed of the necessity to summon or seek out Russian bishops each time a new cleric was slated for ordination. On November 2 1879 the Council of the Russian Missionary Society resolved to contribute an annual sum of 23,800 rubles for the mission, while on March 9 1880 Emperor Alexander II allotted another 29,695 rubles annually from the State treasury, increasing the Japanese Orthodox Mission's yearly disbursements ten-fold.[5] Throughout his stay in Russia, Nicholas sought out new patrons and supporters, arranged for the dispatch of Japanese students to Russia, and made special efforts to amass contributions for a stately cathedral to serve as a symbolic center of the fledgling Japanese Church.

Upon Nicholas' return in late 1880, he expanded the Mission's operations in accordance with its new financial basis. Already in December 1880 the Mission began to issue its official journal and a Japanese Orthodox student—Irene Yamashita Rin, the first Japanese woman to study abroad—was sent to study iconography in St. Petersburg. From 1881 on, aided by a converted Confucian scholar Paul Nakai Tsugumaro, Nicholas began to spend four hours a night translating into Japanese Scriptural and liturgical texts for immediate publication. He also made first use of his new capacity to ordain clergy by ordaining Paul (Niitsuma) as a hieromonk, with a view of making him a successor-bishop. 1882 saw the foundation of publishing and translation bureaus staffed with newly-formed Orthodox Japanese literati; opening of a women's seminary; dispatch of the first Japanese students for advanced learning to Russia's theological academies.

[5]Barsov (1885), 242-243.

39

Henceforth expansion of the amount and assortment of translated and original publications, ordinations of new Japanese clergy, and the dispatch of select students to Russia became routine. Together with the expanding network of engaged locations and the rising number of Japanese Church-servitors in the field, the activity of the Japanese Orthodox Mission was generating well over 1000 baptisms a year.

The most spectacular undertaking of the 1880's was the construction of the Tokyo Resurrection cathedral at the missionary headquarters compound. This symbol and center of Japanese Orthodoxy consumed over 300,000 rubles of Russian-donated money and church-furnishings. The construction funds themselves amounted to some ¥240,000 at the time when a ruble was roughly equivalent to a yen, which meant that a huge sum nearing ¥60,000 was invested into the splendid and superabundant furnishings. The sum was so large as to evoke the first notable attempt at opposition to Nicholas on the part of many Japanese believers, who unsuccessfully pleaded to divert these funds toward what they considered more immediate needs.

Work on the grand edifice was commenced in March of 1884 and immediately attracted mass attention—not only the sheer size and peculiarity of the outlandish domed temple, but its towering presence nearby the Imperial palace grounds were cause for curiosity and concern. When the completed cathedral was consecrated on March 8 1891, it had already become an internationally recognized landmark, popularly dubbed the "Nicholas hall" (Nikorai-dō).[6] Indeed, Nicholas' prestige and influence were at their height, since in May of the same year the Japanese government tapped him to intercede on behalf of Japan before the Russian crown prince and future Emperor Nicholas II after the latter had been assaulted by a Japanese nativist fanatic. By the start of 1891

[6]On the cathedral's construction see particularly Sablina (2006), 121-131; Tokyo cathedral (1998), 66-72. An exhaustive treatment of the architectural history of the cathedral is to be found in Suzuki and Takamura (1998).

the Japanese Orthodox community numbered 18,625 believers in 216 localities, served by 18 native priests.[7]

The 1890's saw continued expansion of Orthodox missionary activity. Tokyo headquarters began publishing two more periodicals—Japan's first women's journal *Inner brocade* (*Ura nishiki*) from 1892 and a magazine with a literary-philosophical bent *Spiritual Sea* (*Shinkai*) from 1893. A record number of 15 new Japanese priests were ordained during the decade. However, the 1890's highlighted two major dilemmas inherent in the mission's structure—Nicholas' centrality and Russian linkage.

Nicholas was fundamental to the mission's existence, but his towering presence hampered the formation of a pool of junior leaders around him. In 1892 Hieromonk Paul (Niitsuma), whom Nicholas had been grooming as a successor-bishop, had violated his vows and was defrocked.[8] After sending 18 Japanese Orthodox students to Russia for advanced study, in 1893 Nicholas discontinued this practice, as he witnessed one after another deserting ecclesiastical service for more lucrative and prestigious Russia-related careers in Japanese government, military and academia.[9] As hopes for weaning a generation of Japanese church-leaders faded, Nicholas' troubled relationship with Russian missionaries became an increasingly urgent concern. No less than 26 Russian Church-servitors are known to have served in Japan between 1871 and 1912, but most departed within a few years, if not sooner.[10] In the 1890's Nicholas welcomed two of his most illustrious Russian would-be helpers and successors— the future Patriarch of Moscow Sergius (Stragorodskii) and the future Archbishop of Perm' St. Andronicus (Nikol'skii)— only to see them leave during the same decade. The founder of the Japanese Orthodox Church was unready to cede his

---

[7]Sablina (2006), 127.
[8]Nicholas (2004), vol. 2 (1892.10.19), 636.
[9]Count of students according to Naganawa (2007), 210.
[10]Remortel & Chang (2003), 200-202.

comprehensive and close control over the mission, yet was exceptionally demanding toward close aides. As a result, during Nicholas' half-century in Japan, the only Russian aides who remained at his side for over a decade were those with independent spheres of competence—two choirmasters and two legation priests.

The 1890's also tested another aspect of the mission's structure—namely, its dependence on Russia. The Russian connection had been the mission's lifeline in terms of funding, supplies, and higher theological learning. However, the Japanese popular opinion, already prejudiced against Russia, turned increasingly hostile as Russo-Japanese competition for preeminence in Northeast Asia escalated. The Sino-Japanese War brought a precipitous drop in the already sagging conversion rate of the Japanese Orthodox Church— 1894 brought only 811 baptisms, about half of the annual rate at the turn of that decade. Although during the following years the conversion-rate hovered around 1000, the worsening publicity was taking its toll. Broadly-targeted mass media, not to mention dedicated patriotic and anti-Russian societies, blasted the mission as the den of spies, branded Orthodox Japanese as traitors, and called for Nicholas' death. 1903 brought in a record low of 720 baptisms. Inasmuch as its being was rooted both in Japan and in Russia, the mission faced an existential crisis during the Russo-Japanese war of 1904-1905.

Patriotism, preached and practiced, was central to resolving the predicament. Already in 1903 Nicholas instructed the delegates at the annual Church Council that to fight the nation's adversaries was the duty of all loyal subjects. The task of Japanese Orthodox Christians was to do so with the right motivation—not out of hatred for the enemy, but out of love for one's kin. When war broke out, Nicholas was the sole Russian who remained in Japan—at the request of his flock. However, after issuing a circular which extolled patriotism as a natural and holy feeling, he withdrew from public prayers for the duration of the war, in order to allow Japanese believers to pray for the victory of their nation's arms, even as he prayed for Russia's.

The missionary routine continued as much as the war permitted, but Japanese Orthodox believers undertook special tasks to participate in the war-effort by compiling and donating Russo-Japanese conversation booklets for the Japanese Army, organizing societies to comfort Japanese soldiers at the front and Russian POWs in Japan. Assured of its loyalty, the Japanese government guarded and supported the mission's activities so as to convince Western public opinion that Japan's war was neither anti-Christian nor inhuman. Thus, stringent official rules against anti-Orthodox manifestations, as well as ample police and military protection of the Tokyo mission headquarters, insured that open violence against Japanese Orthodox was limited to a few mob assaults in the province. The state backed and amplified the Orthodox program for Russian POWs, using it to better monitor and control this mass of military men, who in sum numbered nearly 80,000. Japanese Orthodox clergy, with the aid of the secular authorities, served the daily religious needs of this Russian flock, while Nicholas supplied them with books, church-utensils, and pastoral letters. By the end of the war, the Japanese Orthodox Mission emerged with a more secure identity, a broadened network of connections, and impeccable patriotic credentials both in Russia and Japan, numbering 28,920 claimed believers and 39 clerics.

With myths about Russian political ties dispelled, but with the reality of Russian financial subsidies intact, the subsequent decade favored further growth. On April 22 1906 the Most Holy Synod of the Russian Church promoted Nicholas to the dignity of archbishop and formally recognized the Japanese Orthodox community for what it had become—a large and increasingly self-sufficient diocese, an emerging local Church. The annual baptismal rate climbed back up to about 1000. The number of engaged locations edged upward,

Figure 2.2: Page from a pamphlet celebrating Archbishop Nicholas' 50 years in Japan. The display of Japan's Orthodox sacred spaces is centered on the Tokyo cathedral, surrounded (clockwise from top right) by the churches of Kyoto, Sendai, Hakodate, Matsuyama and Osaka. From Nagoya Orthodox church collection.

engaging the length and breadth of the Japanese Empire. Until his last days the terminally ill Nicholas continued his life-time work of translating Scriptural and service texts, equipping the Japanese Church for complete liturgical life in its native language. A new dimension of church life was the construction of imposing church-buildings. Although some had already been built across the country, very few answered the demands of Orthodox Christian architectural tradition. In the wake of the Russo-Japanese war, in part with private funds from Russians wishing to commemorate the war-dead, custom-built Russian-style onion-domed edifices cropped up in Matsuyama in 1908, Osaka in 1910, Shūzenji in 1912, Toyohashi and Shirakawa in 1915, Hakodate in 1916. This work provided on-the-job training for Japan's first Orthodox church-architect, Deacon Moses Kawamura Izō.

Simultaneously, the Japanese Church underwent its first episcopal succession. As Nicholas entered his seventies, his health worsened and the end of his missionary service was at hand. The Japanese believers, the Russian Church and state, Protestant missionary circles, and even some non-Christian Japanese forums, sped to celebrate his work with decorations and recognitions. However, most important for the mission was the arrival in 1908 of a Russian assistant to whom Nicholas began to entrust leadership. This was Bishop Sergius (Tikhomirov), who swiftly mastered Japanese and engaged in continual pastoral travel to introduce himself to the Japanese believers. On Nicholas' decease in 1912 Sergius assumed leadership of a Japanese flock of 34 priests, 7 deacons, 118 catechists, and 33,377 believers listed in 266 locations with 175 houses of prayer.[11]

To be sure, both the "leadership" and the "flock" were less impressive than they appeared. Regardless even of his individual leanings and career background, which were dissimilar on many counts from those of Nicholas, the new

---

[11] Council (1912), appendix.

bishop could not hope to match his charismatic predecessor in terms of the intimate experiential knowledge and consequent influence on the Japanese believers. The latter, in turn, while growing in national consciousness and confidence, were in fact a considerably smaller body than the overall count showed: as Sergius discovered in his thorough tour of the country, the number of actual practitioners involved in ecclesiastical life was about half of the claimed total of the baptized-and-unburied "general believers." Yet, the episcopal transition proved smooth enough owing primarily to stable sponsorship from Russia—by this time, with some 90,000 rubles a year, it covered over 90% of the Church's annual expenses.[12]

The principles of missionary organization bequeathed by Nicholas allowed the Church to continue many routines. The Japanese Church maintained the momentum recaptured after the Russo-Japanese War, with around 1000 annual baptisms and a stable number of active clergy, catechists and communities until the fateful 1917. In line with Sergius' penchant for theological education and closer ties with Russia, the 1910's saw continued expansion of the ecclesiastical publishing, educational and Russo-Japanese exchange activities. World War I buoyed the Russo-Japanese rapprochement and gave the Japanese Church an opportunity to foreground itself as a fixture of the new friendship. Although the flow of Russian supplies to the Japanese Church slackened, the flow of Japanese clergy and seminarians to Russia increased.

The Russian Revolution and its attendant cataclysms was the most important turning point in the history of the Japanese Orthodox Church, both destructive and constitutive; all the more dramatic for having been largely unanticipated in Japan. While the scope of the event was only beginning to be

---

[12]For example, in 1910 some 91% of the Japanese Church's annual budget of ¥94,910 was covered by official Russian sources, compared with only about 3% contributed by Japanese believers, as reported in Orthodox Evangelist (1911.02 - №1-3), 103.

grasped, crushing practical consequences—above all the cessation of Russian subsidies—had to be faced immediately. In the ensuing all-out effort at self-sufficiency, the Japanese Church quickly transformed itself into what its earning and engaged members—between 4 and 5,000 working men[13]—could and would support. As of mid-1918 only 45 of 158 Japanese Church-servitors—and none of the non-parish central ventures—were supported by local donations.[14] Consequently, in the course of the Russian Civil War, between 1918 and 1922, a wave of dissolutions, discharges and desertions left little of the Japanese Orthodox Church aside from a network of parishes—particular local communities centered on a single sacred space with a lone cleric leading the liturgical life of the congregation. All Orthodox schools were suspended—Tokyo's theological seminary, women's seminary and catechist school in 1919, Osaka's catechist school in 1920, Kyoto's women's seminary (turned Kansai women's school) in 1921.[15] The Tokyo foster home survived, but cut its affiliation to the Orthodox Church.[16] Translators and iconographers were out of a job. Incidentally, this cut meant the dismissal of all national-level Orthodox women-leaders, leaving them only the parish-level roles of a cleric's wife, choir-director, and sisterhood officer.

The one field of central activity not evacuated entirely was publication. While central publishing activity shrank from 3-4 regularly issued magazines and up to ten annual unique titles to a single shriveled monthly *Orthodox Messenger*, new initiatives attempted to fill the void with what appear as the first significant grassroots periodicals. *Orthodoxy of the North Seas* (*Hokkai no Seikyō*) from Sapporo lapsed soon after it was established in 1919, but *Yeast* (*Pandane*) from Nagoya went on

---

[13] An early 1919 estimate by Bishop Sergius in Sergius (1919a), 5.
[14] Council (1918), 8.
[15] Japan Christian dictionary (1988), 692; Ushimaru (1985), 19.
[16] Nakamura & Nakamura (2003), 201-202, 428.

to become a nationally significant edition in the course of its existence between 1921 and 1935.[17]

However, the precipitous plunge of all principal statistics of the Church left no doubt as to the gravity of the crisis. In the course of five years after 1917, mission in about one-fifth of the total engaged locations was abandoned, the annual baptismal rate shrank by a half, and the ranks of catechists decreased by two-thirds. As the number of catechists dove below the number of clergy for the first time in the history of the Japanese Orthodox Church, it had become clear that active missionary outreach was over.

For the duration of the Russian Civil War—and the simultaneous Japanese Siberian Intervention—the unsupportable cadre of Japanese Orthodox specialists, with their rare expertise in Russian matters, proved to be a unique Russo-Japanese bridge. Ex-seminarians, ex-catechists and even a few ex-clergy left *en masse* for plentiful secular employment as Russia-hands amid continental intervention. This offered the Japanese Church elite a fateful opportunity to deepen its engagement with the Japanese state, Russia's "Whites" and the colonial venture in Manchuria—of fleeting import for the moment, this linkage proved profoundly significant in two decades' time. With the last shots of the Russian Civil War in Asia the last notable trickles of occasional monetary support from White Russian authorities dried up, leaving the Japanese Church "completely independent" of external financial support.

"Independence" was becoming a reality not only in material terms, but also in organizational and psychological, primarily as independence of the Japanese flock from its Russian bishop, and of the Japanese "Daughter-Church" from

[17]Ushimaru's claim that *Yeast* was established in 1914 is not substantiated by Itō (2010), 24-25. The best overview of Japanese Orthodox periodical publication activity in the post-revolutionary period is Seraphim (2007b - Nº 1401).

Figure 2.3: Amid the wreckage of the Tokyo Resurrection cathedral, September 1 1927. Prayer service at the commencement of the reconstruction.

its Russian "Mother-Church"—the central dilemmas of the new period, which were codified in the ambiguities of the *Constitution of the Japanese Christian Orthodox Church* from June 8 1919. Mounting chaos in the higher administration of the persecuted and dispersed Russian Church militated for dissociation. The arrival to Japan's shores of a small wave of Russian post-revolutionary émigrés did more, at first, to highlight national differences than to stimulate a consciousness of a Russo-Japanese bond, as Russians went on to set up parallel, partially self-segregated congregations in Kobe, Yokohama, Tokyo and Tsuruga. It was on the basis of a new autogenous charter, as a would-be self-sufficient Church, that the reeling Japanese community faced 1923—with 14,447 practicing believers supporting 44 clerics and 38 catechists, while the central headquarters subsisted on approximately ¥21,000 a year, generated chiefly by rented properties.[18]

---

[18]In 1922 ¥17,765.00 of the annual income of ¥21,356.50 was provided by rented properties. See Council (1923), 18-19, appendix.

49

However, before something like a new equilibrium was to arrive, the Church faced one more trial, which helped shake off the lingering shock of collapse and channel collective energies into a grand yet manageable venture. The Great Kantō Earthquake of September 1 1923 and the ensuing fires leveled most of the Tokyo-Yokohama metropolitan area, laying waste to the Tokyo Orthodox headquarters and challenging the community to restore its symbolic center. In what was meant—and appears to have become—a Church-wide movement of religious recommitment and reunification, many believers invested extensive efforts and funds into their central collective exploit of the 1920's, the rebuilding of the Tokyo cathedral. Although on a somewhat diminished scale and with only a bare minimum of necessary church-utensils, the cathedral was completed and consecrated on December 15 1929, just in time to avoid the global Great Depression. The construction costs amounted to ¥170,000 of mostly in-house funds, the first time Japanese Orthodox believers pooled such a sum.

The accompanying boost of morale propelled the Japanese Church to turn a fresh page and begin to resume some suspended activities. The revival of publication dawned in the course of the construction campaign, with Archbishop Sergius' literary-theological magazine *Dawn* (*Akebono*) and Osaka church's *Naniwa Orthodoxy* (*Naniwa Seikyō*) established in 1925, and new Japanese-authored theological treatises issued since 1928. Local communities, inspired by the national success in Tokyo, cooperated in regional fund-raising campaigns to construct new purpose-built temples in what was becoming a Japanese Orthodox "rustic Russian" architectural style—notably the churches in Kushiro in 1932, Kannari in 1934, Yokohama in 1935, Sapporo in 1936. The Church even made efforts at reviving higher theological education by sending hopefuls to the Anglican *Rikkyō* University in 1925, reopening of the attenuated Orthodox Theological College in Tokyo in

1927, and operating the "Enlightenment College" in Toyohashi between 1932 and 1934.[19]

However, although the revival worked by the cathedral reconstruction campaign staved off collapse, the interwar era of the Japanese Orthodox Church saw a measured decline, and certainly no missionary recovery. Nicholas' emphasis on families over individuals as basic building blocks of the Church proved crucial in offsetting the precipitous loss of appeal with the stability of self-perpetuating clans. The offspring of Orthodox families formed the lion's share of the annual harvest of baptisms—averaging slightly below 500 annually until 1936, when 300 became the new wartime norm. The realistic number of "actual" adherents crept ever lower, but some 13,000 believers continued to lead an engaged ecclesiastical life throughout the interwar era. Scattered in the unchanging 184 listed locations, their population shifts registered advancing urbanization, but a major rural presence as well as disproportionate geographical concentration in Japan's less industrially developed Northeast remained fixtures.

The one area in which decline was still veiled but most threatening was the cadre of Church-servitors—trained clergy and catechists—who appeared irreplaceable. For the time being new clerics could be ordained from the ranks of the still-plentiful pre-revolutionary seminarians,[20] but almost no new hopefuls arose—there were barely ten Orthodox seminarians engaged in all interwar attempts at higher theological education combined. In 1926, of 65 active Japanese

[19]The subject of interwar educational attempts has received only passing notes, like in Japan Christian dictionary (1988), 692. For a vivid sketch of Fr. Anthony (Hibi)'s effort to found and run the "Enlightenment college" in Toyohashi—a self-sacrificing venture which cost him his life—see Toyohashi church (1979), 16.

[20]In late 1936 there were no less than 174 active graduates of the Tokyo Orthodox Seminary in touch with the ecclesiastical establishment. See their list in Orthodox Messenger (1936.09.01 - №25-9), 34-37; (1936.10.01 - №25-10), 35.

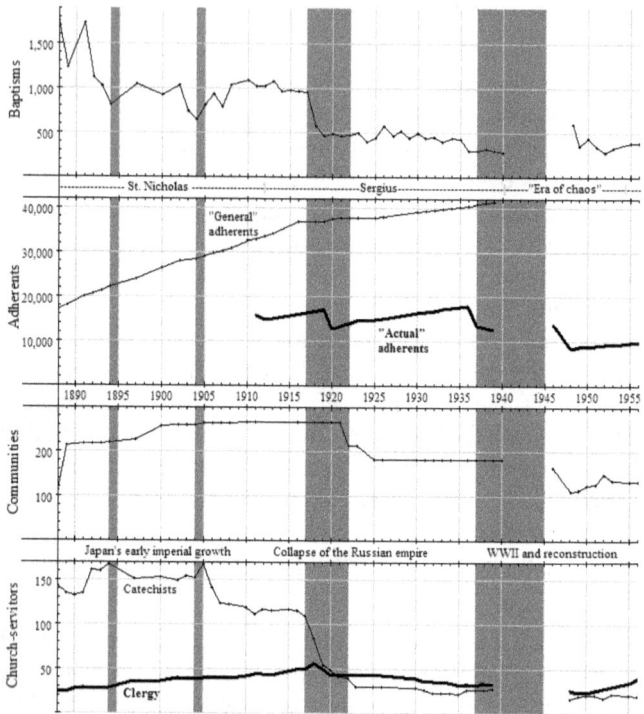

Figure 2.4: Principal statistics of the Japanese Orthodox Church from 1888 to 1956 according to the annual Councils of the Japanese Orthodox Church.

The top section traces the yearly baptism rate—the prime barometer of the Church's vitality. The next section shows the annually reported total membership—the "general" number was arrived at by adding the baptized and subtracting the buried from the overall total; the "actual" number was supposed to count members presently involved in Church life, but it too had to be periodically lowered in attempts to wrestle with wishful bookkeeping. The third section lists the number of localities where the Church strove to maintain a presence, if only via a community in single digits. Last comes the count of active clergy (hierarchs, priests, deacons) and catechists (full-time lay missionaries), with subdeacons and retirees excluded where known. To highlight the impact of major wars—the Sino-Japanese, Russo-Japanese, Russian Civil and World War II—these periods are shaded in gray. Of prior attempts at compiling the statistics of the Japanese Orthodox Church the most notable published work is probably Utsumi (1979), which, however, suffers from many mistakes and gaps.

Orthodox Church-servitors there were 32—less than half—who were 60 or older; by mid-1931 the proportion was already 41 out of 64—nearly two-thirds, counterbalanced by only one person under 30.[21] Japanese longevity postponed the loss of elite cadre, but the stark choice between extinction and ordination of the underqualified became more pressing with each year.

Especially ominous were the successive deaths of the Church's "three founding elders": Frs. Peter Shibayama (1937), Paul Morita (1938) and Symeon Mii (1940). Another irreparable loss was the death of Fr. Moses Kawamura (1940)—one of only two centrally-involved Japanese Church-servitors whom even the strict Archbishop Nicholas had considered "dependable."[22] The loss of these widely respected and capable uniting figures destabilized the Japanese Orthodox community precisely at the moment of new crisis. The rapid 1939 turn toward the "national mobilization" of wartime Japan impacted the Orthodox Church with two unprecedent-edly invasive government campaigns. One emanated from the civil officials of the Ministry of Education, who aimed to fit the Church into the procrustean bed of officially-defined dogmatic and organizational "orthodoxy." Another came from the Japanese Army, which launched a program to organize a united Pan-Asian Orthodox Church as an anti-Soviet mobilization and propaganda tool. These simultaneous and contradictory intrusions stimulated a dramatic resolution of long-standing internal processes which set off what was soon dubbed a "period of chaos" in the Japanese Orthodox Church.

Once opened, the Pandora's box of in-house drives proved no less contradictory than the external stimuli. Dissociation from Moscow, rapprochement with the Russian Church,

---

[21] Japanese Orthodoxy (1931.06.01 - № 1-4), 12-13.
[22] The other was Nicholas' secretary David Fujisawa. Nicholas (2004), vol. 4, (1908.09.10), 444.

nationalist isolation, regional integration, populist democ-racy, hierarchal rule, changing of the guard, and old feuds were being pursued by the Japanese Orthodox at once, some because and some despite of government pressure. Apparently peripheral phenomena in the life of the Japanese Church—continual marginalization of the ruling bishop, East Asia's Russian émigré presence, the resettlement of Japanese Orthodox onto the continent, lapsed international links—revealed themselves to be of central significance. All plotlines of 20th century history of the Japanese Orthodox Church surfaced, making this a singularly complex and dynamic "moment of truth."

The regularly constituted 1940 Council of the Japanese Orthodox Church on July 13-17 proved highly irregular, due to the acknowledged need to obey unofficial orders of the Ministry of Education and the Imperial Army. According to these directives, ties with the Moscow-based Mother-Church were declared completely cut, Metropolitan Sergius predes-tined for retirement, a "Special Committee" empowered to alter the Church's organization, and a new—still unnamed—Japanese bishop scheduled to accept ordination at the hands of Russian hierarchs in Manchukuo, thus joining the Japanese into the Pan-Asian Orthodox organization in the making. The traumatic Council became the scene and the cradle of open opposition, as factions took shape in the following months. Professor Arsenius Iwasawa headed the plenipotentiary Spe-cial Committee and secured for himself a "transfer of all power" from the retiring Metropolitan Sergius on September 4-5. This signaled an open break, as Iwasawa's multiplying opponents contested his aberrant power-grab. His cause was damaged by early use of force—with police assistance, he aborted the Provisional Council of September 22-23 just as it was about to begin proceedings, and had the retired Metropolitan Sergius expelled from the hierarch's quarters at the cathedral compound on December 24. Coalescing anti-Iwasawan opposition of the Tokyo area, driven by youth activists, solidified its ranks in meetings on December 4, 15 and 25. Building on this organization, anti-Iwasawans convoked a nationwide All-Japan Clergy-Laity Conference (reconstituted as a Provisional Council) on January 11-12 1941, at which familiar Church governance structures were restored and the Iwasawan Committee branded illegitimate. Meanwhile, Iwasawans, aided by the Army, established contact with émigré Russian hierarchs and forged ahead with the ordination of the first Japanese to episcopacy. On February 27 1941 Fr. John Ono left Tokyo, on April 6 he was ordained in Harbin as Bishop Nicholas, and on April 12 returned to Japan posing as its sole rightful Orthodox hierarch. Both factions were thus armed with their respective "successes" and unwilling to yield. The struggle of ecclesiastical partisans escalated into violence on Tokyo streets. To quell disorder, secular powers intervened with enforced mediation on May 2, the arrest of 30 leading Japanese Orthodox figures on June 12, an officially-scripted truce on June 23, and a controlled Provisional Council of the Japanese Orthodox Church on July 18. The heavy hand of the state repressed the first outbreak of "chaos."[23]

Official intervention left Iwasawan adherents ascendant, but they represented a mere 10% of all engaged believers, perched precariously atop an antagonized 80% and a disinterested 10%.[24] Such disbalance ensured that factional struggle—although in more subdued forms, like disobedience and litigation—remained a fixture of the wartime life of the Church. Since ongoing strife prevented the Church from being recognized as a unitary "religious organization," the sole path to legalization under the new law was registration

[23]While this sequence of troubles invariably received special attention, its basic facts have often been mislabeled and misdated. The best readily available and generally accurate digest is to be found in the contemporary editions of the *Monthly* of Japan's Special Higher Police, conveniently assembled in Dōshisha (1981), vol. 1, 302-303, 323; vol. 2, 72-76, 107.

[24]An estimate of the ousted Metropolitan Sergius, likely biased against the Iwasawans but not improbable, in Sergius (1944), 2.

of individual "religious associations" officially unconnected with each other. Anti-Iwasawans pioneered by registering their own "religious association" on March 3 1941, leaving each Japanese Orthodox parish to proceed with individual registration.

Independent parish registration contributed to the organizational dysfunction of the Japanese Orthodox Church, deepened by the wartime limitation on travel, breakdown of communications, and mounting fear of arrest on charges of "espionage" or "dangerous thought." Shortages of essentials began to further undercut the routine of ecclesiastical life. Metal furnishings of most churches were confiscated by the authorities amid a desperate drive to marshal Japan's minute reserves. Limitations on paper usage wiped out publishing activity, with the last known wartime edition of the *Orthodox Messenger* issued on June 1 1944. The Divine Liturgy—the chief service which regularly reassembled each congregation—was becoming an impossibility as bread and wine passed into the realm of rare delicacies. Most emphatically, as food shortages and aerial bombardment began to decimate the population and level cities, the physical infrastructure and the elderly core personnel of the Church suffered greatly. The last year of the war brought ruin to some of the most significant urban houses of worship, including those in Tokyo (the Yotsuya church), Yokohama (the Russian prayer house), Osaka, Sendai, Nagoya, Nagasaki, Kobe, Kagoshima, Okazaki, Maebashi and Mito. The long-anticipated wave of cadre extinction became reality starting in April 1944, as key figures—including some 15 senior clergy with the mistreated Metropolitan Sergius among them—died in the course of a little over two years.[25] Atomized and reduced, the Japanese Orthodox Church appeared on the verge of dissolution.

The religious nature of the bond uniting the community helped sustain it despite organizational breakdown. Even

[25] A partial listing of churches and Church-servitors lost at the time is found in Council Provisional (1946), 10-11; Council (1946), 6.

in 1941, arguably a spiritual low-point, Metropolitan Sergius estimated that some 80% of the practicing Japanese believers "have firm faith," and even the remainder are still "better that the former Russian 'intelligentsia'."[26] Japan's wartime privations and its post-war embrace of the American occupation conditioned a brief Christian boom, which the Orthodox Church was ill-prepared to tap for missionary purposes, but which did raise the profile of ecclesiastical service and reactivated lapsed members. As Japan's militarists were being purged and foreign occupiers figured as the nation's new benefactors, the Tokyo-based Orthodox elite set their community on the same track by purging a symbolic handful of Iwasawans and applying to the USSR and the USA for a Russian Orthodox "rescue mission." The choice of ecclesiastical jurisdiction—the Moscow Patriarchate or the "American Metropolia"—was largely out of their hands, a matter for Soviet and American agents to sort out in an early bout of the Cold War. Nor were the Japanese overly concerned, as long as effective aid came their way.

The arrival in early 1947 of a bishop from the American Metropolia, Benjamin (Basalyga) of Pittsburgh, was greeted with exuberance and the hierarch's early activity—pastoral tours and speedy ordination of 10 new clerics—brought an enthusiastic surge. In August 1947 the Church's central mouthpiece—the *Orthodox Messenger*—made its post-war reappearance in the form of a few screen-printed sheets. As students flocked to the Church-run "Nicholas Institute" in Tokyo—a language school with an aspiration of becoming a humanities college—enrollment reached 1,200 by mid-1948, generating more than half of the annual revenue of the Church.[27] In July 1948, although realistic estimates of active believers and extant congregations stood at the lowest marks since the start of the century—below 9,000 and some 110 respectively—the annual count of 595 baptisms superceded

[26]Heavenly Bread (1941—№ 2), 39.
[27]¥120,000 of ¥228,992. Council (1948), 15, 17.

anything on record since the Russian Revolution. The core cadre of the Church—24 clerics and 17 catechists—was thoroughly restaffed, as new faces with little background in ecclesiastical service took up the posts of the deceased. Of the 59 Orthodox Church-servitors in 1939, there were only 22 "survivors" still on active duty and in good standing as of mid-1948.[28]

Yet, the fresh start of the Japanese Orthodox community proved a false one. Although in position to direct and sponsor the Japanese Church, the American Metropolia and its bishop were slow to shoulder these prerogatives, leaving ample room for "chaos" to reemerge in the still unsettled and already disillusioned community. A set of in-house oppositions flared up into schisms, as pro-Soviet Russians refused to accept American ecclesiastical jurisdiction, the two surviving charismatic Japanese senior clerics—Protopriests Samuel Uzawa and Anthony Takai—gave vent to their mutual enmity, Bishop Nicholas (Ono) challenged Benjamin's author-ity, and a group of Tokyo Orthodox activists rebelled against an aloof American hierarch. By mid-1949 the underdogs in all four parallel confrontations converged tenuously into a single opposition front under the aegis of the Moscow Patriarchate, which lent canonical legitimacy and Soviet backing for their cause. The latter fact militated against them in what was a US-dominated country of the Cold War era, but the dissatisfaction in the majority group was such that some parishes and clergy began deserting for Moscow. Even more promising was the newly discovered option of joining the Greek Orthodox Church—a vista opened up by the Greek-American occupation troops and the Greek expeditionary force of the Korean War. Amidst disorienting jurisdictional strife, the restoration effort stalled, baptism rates plunged to a record low of 283 in 1952,[29] and the initial impetus of the "Christian boom" was wasted. Indicatively, some of the first Orthodox parishes to construct

---

[28]Calculated according to Council (1939), 105-108; (1948), 28, 81-94.
[29]Council (1952), (14).

permanent churches in the wake of the war did not belong to the perplexed Japanese majority. Rather, these were the Moscow-aligned Japanese parish in Kamimusa in 1951 and the Russian émigré congregation in Kobe in 1952.[30] Although Japan had launched its reconstruction in earnest with the economic boost of special orders for the Korean War in 1950 and the political coup of the San Francisco Peace Treaty in 1951, the Japanese Orthodox Church had yet to enter its recovery phase.

The decisive turn came with the change of the presiding hierarch in 1953, as an activist Bishop Irenaeus (Bekish) took charge of the situation. He combined an authoritative tone with rare effectiveness in solving the outstanding dilemmas of the Japanese Church. In little over a year he compacted a peace on his own terms with most of the Moscow-aligned opponents, arranged for an increased flow of donations from the US, and opened two routes for Orthodox higher education—study-abroad in America and training at the reopened Tokyo Orthodox Seminary. The timid 1951 revival of publishing activity sped up, churches began to be rebuilt across the country, 11 new clerics were speedily ordained, and the number of baptisms showed a measured increase to 392 in 1955.[31] The imperial age likewise sounded a final note in the same year, as the Japanese Church lost its organizational link with the neighboring Korea, whose Orthodox flock passed under the influence of the Greeks. It was undoubtedly under Irenaeus "the reconstructor"[32] that the Japanese Orthodox Church regained coherence and entered a new "American" phase in its existence, which would last until the major US-USSR ecclesiastical settlement of 1970, and in many cultural trends—until the present. The first century of Orthodoxy in Japan came to an end together with the "period of chaos," as potent external controls and

---

[30]Kikuchi (1986), 10, 29; Kobe church (1983), especially 6-7, 25-27.

[31]Council (1955), B. The number of clerics ordained by Bishop Irenaeus as of March 1956 is according to Orthodox Messenger (1956.12.05 - № 805), 4.

[32]Expression by Shōji (2007), 44.

supports were reintroduced into what was the first native East Asian independent local Orthodox Church between 1910's and 1950's. Its tortuous self-discovery, encrusted by the rugged façade of isolationist survival, is the theme of the writing which follows, starting with the basic exposition on the formal statements of identity—the ecclesiology of the Japanese Church.

Chapter 3

Ecclesiological autograph of Japanese Orthodoxy

Catechism of St. Philaret

The best starting point for apprehending the public self-definition of Japanese Orthodoxy is the famous *Extensive catechism* of Metropolitan St. Philaret (Drozdov) of Moscow, the officially accepted standard catechism of the Russian Orthodox Church from 1827 on.[1]   Despite criticism, it remains the accepted compendium of basic "safe and sound" theological knowledge throughout the Russian Orthodox world. This staple work was first translated into Japanese by Symeon Mii in 1881 and subsequently republished in a variety of redactions, altering both the language register—between the Meiji-period bookish and the post-war colloquial—and

[1] Issued hundreds of times in the original Russian, St. Philaret's catechism is also available in English in Philaret (1971).

the expository format—between the question-and-answer of the original and the narrative retelling by Bishop Basil (Preobrazhenskii) of Mozhaisk.[2] Philaret's catechism was the one Christian handbook a Japanese Orthodox was most likely to own throughout the period under discussion.

Philaret expounded the bulk of the teachings through an extended interpretation of the Niceo-Constantinopolitan Creed and the Ten Commandments—the two principal summations of the Orthodox Christian faith. The catechism takes up the topic of the Church under the 9th paragraph of the Creed: "(I believe) in *one, holy, catholic* and *apostolic* Church." Since these four defining parameters of the Church are supposed to constitute the basis of the corporate identity of Orthodox believers and, therefore, serve as axes of discussion in the present dissertation, it is worth introducing Philaret's basic treatment at some length.

The exposition begins with Philaret's famous definition of the Church—"the Divinely established community of people, joined by the Orthodox faith, the law of God, the hierarchy and the mysteries." Attacked for its narrowness by theologians since the latter 19th century, this formula continued to be replicated globally throughout Russian Orthodox circles well into the 20th. It is followed by a discussion of the visible (earthly) and invisible (heavenly) parts of the Church and an affirmation of continuous action of God's grace inside the Church. Supported by Scriptural and Patristic quotes, as is the case throughout the catechism, the introduction spells out the corporate metaphor for the Church—that is, the Church is the body with Christ as its head—the basic image which dominates the subsequent exposition.

The treatment of the creedal definitions of the Church opens with *oneness*, predicated primarily on the oneness of

---

[2]The following editions are known: Fr. Symeon Mii's translation of the original—in 1881, 1886, 1907; Paul Yoshida's translation of Bishop Basil's retelling—in 1910; deacon Basil Takeoka Takeo's reworking of Yoshida's translation—in 1952. The latter remains on sale in Japanese Orthodox churches to the present.

Christ, the head of the Church. "Jesus Christ is the unique head of the unique Church;" "the Church is one because it is one spiritual body, and has one head—Christ, and is inspired by one Holy Spirit." This corporate metaphor—Church-as-body—takes clear precedence over other Scriptural metaphors for the Church. Thus, another vivid image—that of the Church as a building with Christ as its foundation—is cited only once. Most of the clause on the unity of the Church, however, is devoted to apologetics against classic Roman Catholic and Protestant charges, dealing, respectively, with organizational disunity and prayers to the saints. The multiplicity of the self-governing Orthodox Churches is defended by a reference to overriding spiritual unity—that is, unanimity in the confession of faith and communion in prayers and mysteries. Finally, nearly half of the text deals with the validity and effectiveness of prayers to and by the saints in Heaven.

Next comes a brief discussion of *holiness*. The Church is held holy because it is sanctified by Christ—through His sufferings, teaching, prayer, and through mysteries, of which confession repeatedly sanctifies repentant sinners.

Perhaps the most elusive of the creedal traits of the Church is *catholicity*, from the Greek *cath ola* – "throughout the whole." The catechism dodges terminological difficulties by a facile equation of catholicity with *ecumenicity* and *universality*. The latter, in turn, is deciphered as unboundedness by place, time, or nation, embracing all right-believers. Making an unexpected leap of logic, the catechism then points out that Christ's promises of eternity and infallibility are given to the catholic Church, and, for these reasons, salvation is impossible outside it. Since to belong with the head (Christ) one must be a part of the body (Church), the corporate metaphor once more comes to the fore, but also that of Noah's ark—i.e. to be saved one must be aboard. This somewhat confusing clause ultimately comes close to equating catholicity not only with ecumenicity and universality, but also with oneness.

Then the sequence of creedal definitions breaks, giving way to an interlude, unexpectedly resonant in the Japanese context. In addition to the four attributes spelt out in the Creed, convention has fixed another appellation behind the Orthodox Church—*Eastern*. Initially a geographic label for the Eastern part of the Roman Empire, in Philaret's day it served as the spring-board of pejorative Orientalism among Western Christians and thus evoked the writer's defensive reaction. In this clause the catechism not only provides an apology for, but universalizes the "Easternness" of the Church. The Church is Eastern, Philaret's line goes, because the Biblical "East" was the site of the Paradise, and "Eastern" Judea was the locus of Christ's salvific activity on Earth.

The final section of the catechism's ecclesiological exposition deals with the *apostolicity* of the Church, presented here as the inviolate preservation of the teaching and the grace passed down from Christ's apostles. In this connection the manual notes the most common self-description of the Church's members—*Orthodox*—meaning "right-believing," "right-thinking," or, as the Japanese rendering goes, "right-teaching (*seikyō*)." However, it is the passing down of the apostolic grace of priesthood through the uninterrupted chain of ordinations from one bishop to another which receives more attention. The hierarchs (senior clergy of episcopal rank[3]) are therefore indispensable carriers of that grace and hold power in the Church: hierarchs preside over various parts of the Church, while a general assembly of the world's hierarchs—an Ecumenical Council—extends power over the global Church. A small closing note lists the authoritative texts, which are supposed to be binding upon the Church throughout the world: Holy Scripture and various canonical collections.

[3]While all hierarchs are sometimes collectively called "bishops," they are also distinguished by honorific grades—bishops, archbishops, metropolitans and patriarchs (in ascending order). Consult the "Note on usages" for the annotated table of episcopal ranks.

The last Japanese edition of Philaret's catechism during the period in question was the narrative abridged colloquial version, augmented and paraphrased, issued by the Consistory of the Japanese Church in 1952. By this date the Japanese Orthodox community had weathered nearly forty years of informal independence, and the telling abbreviations and additions throughout the catechism reflected its accumulated experience. The Japanese rendering is generally faithful to the original content, with the chronic omission of citations. While Scriptural quotes are mostly retained, almost all sayings of the Church Fathers are excised, revealing what was both a shortage of citable patristic translations, as well as a Protestant-leaning *Sola Scriptura* ("by Scripture alone") bias. There appears a subtle preference for a "spiritualization" of the original, composed as it was under the residual influence of humanistic Enlightenment.[4] Specifically, the Japanese edition ameliorates the anthropocentrism of Philaret's opening definition of the Church by inserting angels as members of the Church,[5] and disincarnates the imagery by frequently using "spiritual body" or "spiritual organism" instead of simply "body" to refer to the Church—an attempt, perhaps, to distance the "inviolable" Church-as-object-of-faith from their troubled Church-as-earthly-community. Additions to the Japanese text reflect a preoccupation with avoiding schism and the extinction of the hierarchy—the treatment of these calamities, experienced by the Japanese Church, is highlighted by extra citations and clarifications.[6] Expectedly, native to the nation and the time which produced so much rhetoric to idealize "the East," the Japanese Orthodox Church did not fail to elaborate on Philaret's apology of the Eastern quality of the Church. The Japanese edition made this "Oriental clause," addendum-like in the original, appear no less authoritative than the treatment of creedal definitions, by supplying the

---

[4]See that point made in Florovsky ([1937] 1983), 166.
[5]Basil (1952), 54.
[6]For instance Basil (1952), 57, 61, 63.

previously lacking Biblical proof-texts.[7]   Conversely, the universal character of the Church is muted by the omission of the various particular Orthodox Churches, explicitly named in the original.[8] To sum up, this 1952 catechism shows up an Orthodox Church somewhat parochially "Eastern," painfully conscious of schism and extinction of hierarchy, heavily leaning on Scripture and little on the Patristic tradition, favoring the more distant "spiritual" metaphor for the Church over the incarnate one. To gauge this impression, this chapter now turns to the significant ecclesiological monuments of the Japanese Church in the World War era in their diachronic and typological progression.

Constitution of the Japanese Orthodox Church

The first attempt at a definitive corporate self-expression of the Japanese Church, collectively authored by its members, was the *Constitution of the Japanese Christian Orthodox Church*. This document was debated and accepted by clergy and lay delegates at the Church Council on May 1-6, and promulgated on June 8 1919. The *Constitution*, catalyzed by the Russian Revolution and accepted amidst the breakdown of the Russian-financed missionary organization of the Japanese Church, became a monument to two powerful discursive threads— those of national "independence" and popular "democracy," the ecclesiastical refraction of Japan's prevalent public mood. The Japanese Orthodox Church would be governed by this basic statute throughout the imperial period, and only after World War II would the *Constitution* undergo significant modification.[9]

[7]Luke 1:78 and Matt. 24:27 in Basil (1952), 62-63.

[8]Basil (1952), 57.

[9]The pamphlets referred to for this section are Constitution (1919); Council (1919).

Testing and discarding numerous other options, the Japanese drafters consciously chose the weighty and distinctive term "Constitution" (*kempō*), identical to the one used by the secular Meiji Constitution under which Japan was governed. The Orthodox Church had centuries of experience with statutory texts of circumscribed applicability—usually anglicized as "Rule" or "Typicon"—but the drafters from the Consistory of the Japanese Church seem to have spent little time looking for Orthodox precedents. Instead, they drew heavily on secular models, to the extent that Church-state parallelism became codified in the sporadic substitution of the word "country" for "[Japanese Orthodox] Church."[10] The initial draft of the *Constitution* as presented to the conciliar delegates read as a declaration of Japanese ecclesiastical independence, an assertion of power trumping the authority of canons, of foreign ecclesiastical centers, and of the ruling bishop. Schism and heresy alike could be read into its rash wording. Stiff rebukes from Bishop Sergius (Tikhomirov), from the premier Japanese clergyman Protopriest Symeon Mii, and from country parish representatives threatened to quash the draft altogether, but the majority of Council delegates voted to deliberate on the draft paragraph-by-paragraph. After nearly a week of discussions, the Council accepted the modified *Constitution*, together with appended subsidiary regulations for the Council, Consistory, and clergy. The Council minutes convey a reconciled mood by the end of the conciliar process, but the resultant basic statute expressed both ambiguity as well as unanimity.

"The Japanese Orthodox Church of Christ adheres to the dogmas transmitted by the One Holy Catholic and Apostolic Church" begins the *Constitution*.[11] Nowhere in the subsequent clauses is the relationship of Japanese Church to the global Orthodox communion explained in any other way, for to do

[10]See the provision for the Consistory to elect clergy candidates after requesting "the opinion of the active clergy of the whole country." Constitution (1919), 3.

[11]Constitution (1919), 1.

67

so would mean tackling that elephant in the room: Russia. During deliberations Bishop Sergius' main criticism of the first draft of the *Constitution* dealt with its failure to specify the relationship between the Japanese Daughter-Church and the Russian Mother-Church. His adamant assertion of his personal loyalty and responsibility to the Russian patriarch, Synod, and the Russian Missionary Society ruled out the formal assertion of Japanese ecclesiastical independence in the final draft—the Japanese delegates were neither prepared to rebel against their bishop, nor unanimous in their advocacy of complete independence. At the same time, it was clear to the assembled that *de facto* independence of the Japanese Church was both real and urgent: real because direction, aid and communication from Russia ceased; urgent because the Japanese Church faced imminent bankruptcy unless financial self-sufficiency was swiftly achieved. As a result, even Bishop Sergius may have come around to the resigned understanding that leaving unstated the relationship with the Russian Orthodox Church—itself in the midst of an unprecedented upheaval—was perhaps the only possible course.

For similar reasons, studied silence and ambiguity shroud the figure of the bishop in the *Constitution*. Because bishops for the Japanese Church had been sent from Russia, the *Constitution* contains no discussion of the bishop's provenance or of the method of his election. The Council and the Consistory of the Japanese Church are granted power to appoint a cleric to be a *locum tenens* in case of the bishop's absence, but no clues are given as to whence bishops are presumed to appear. Yet appear they must, since the *Constitution* entrusts the ruling bishop with the power to govern the Church. A fundamental tenet of the Orthodox ecclesiastical organization establishes the supreme authority of the hierarch within his diocese, leaving him subject only to the judgment of his fellow bishops. However, avoiding as it did any mention of external agents, the *Constitution* of the Japanese Orthodox Church says nothing about appealing to the court of Russian hierarchs. Instead, seeking to impose some checks on the bishop, it comes close to subjecting the "shepherd" to the power of his "sheep." The *Constitution* holds the bishop to govern "in accordance with the regulations of Scripture, Tradition, canons and this *Constitution*." The bishop holds complete sway in the sacred sphere, but his ability to issue new regulations and manage financial affairs is limited by the necessary "cooperation" and "decision" of the Church Council and Consistory. While the Consistory is set up in name as an advisory organ to the bishop, the management of the Church's income is handed over to this body, giving it more than a merely consultative function.[12]

Instead of the bishop, the *Constitution* stressed the Council as the chief ruling organ of the Church. Not the decisions of the bishop, but those of the Church Council are declared to have "absolute force," albeit with the bishop's blessing. The amendment of the *Constitution* itself was made possible only through the Council. The latter was to be summoned yearly, or else as extraordinary circumstances would dictate. All clergymen of the Japanese Orthodox Church as well as leading laymen could be elected as delegates, as minutely defined in the *Council Regulations* and *Council Delegates Electoral Regulations*, appended to the *Constitution*. At the Council itself, all decisions were subject to popular vote, with the ballot of the bishop or an elder priest weighed the same as that of the youngest lay delegate.[13]

While its studied silences permitted a face-saving balance, the *Constitution of the Japanese Christian Orthodox Church* obfuscated external relations and episcopal prerogatives to the extent of practically effacing them. Instead "independence" and "freedom and democracy"—values which Bishop Sergius himself, despite defending the Russian link and bishop's power, praised at the 1919 Council[14]—were held up as the

[12]Constitution (1919), 1-2, 5-6.
[13]Constitution (1919), 4-5, 7-15.
[14]Council (1919) 26-27; 129-130.

69

institutionally encoded governing principles. A document from Japan's age of "imperial democracy," the *Constitution* transparently reflected the prevalent view of the emperor as a symbolic constitutional monarch, combined with continued popular support for a strong and self-sufficient imperialist realm. Thus, the ruling hierarch—the supposed carrier of irreducible apostolic grace—was limited to the role of a largely symbolic "constitutional bishop," while the catholic quality of the Church was interpreted in line with its "democratic" reach to all believers, rather than with its "universal" extension to all local Orthodox Churches. Apostolicity and catholicity were thus marked out as the two areas in which the basic catechetical definition entered into tension with the preferred practical arrangements.

Figure 3.1: The ruling hierarch and the "three founding elders" (left to right)— Fr. Peter Shibayama, Fr. Symeon Mii, Archbishop Sergius (Tikhomirov), Fr. Paul Morita. Tokyo, September 2 1928. From Andrew Shibayama Masao.

Manuals of the three founding elders

The later 1920's and early 1930's saw the Japanese Orthodox Church regain a measure of optimism and dynamism amidst a revitalization of ecclesiastical life worked by the campaign to restore the Tokyo Resurrection cathedral. As book-publishing became once more financially feasible, the Japanese Church issued a few new catechetical manuals to fill the void of theological literature. The most prominent writers were the "three founding elders" (genrō) of the Japanese Orthodox Church, as they have come to be known by mid-1930's.[15] Nicknamed after Japan's small group of elder statesmen who exercised central integrating and administrative functions in the ostensibly emperor-centered system of Japanese imperial governance, Frs. Symeon Mii, Paul Morita and Peter Shibayama were among the most authoritative and influential unifying figures of the Japanese Church. All of them ordained to priesthood by Archbishop Nicholas and assigned to prominent posts in Tokyo by his successor Sergius, they commanded respect widely throughout the community, combining devotion and practicality, rootedness and internationalism, theological education and pastoral experience. As a choice remnant of former glory days, they were some of the most important bridges between the Russian hierarch and the Japanese flock, between the reform-minded activists on the right and on the left, between the increasingly idealized past and the lackluster present. Their combined efforts paved the way for the beginnings of Japanese Orthodox interwar literary revival.

The most significant writings belonged to the bishop's right-hand man, the most esteemed and highest-ranking clergyman of the Japanese Church in the interwar era—Protopresbyter Symeon Mii Michirō (1858-1940). The youngest of five sons of a samurai from the Nambu domain, he converted to Orthodoxy in the wake of the revolutionary Meiji Restoration. Early acquisition of English competency propelled him to the Tokyo headquarters where Archbishop Nicholas tasked him with translation, then seen as one of the paramount tasks of the Japanese mission. After surmounting

[15]Expression from Orthodox Messenger (1936.05.01 - № 25-5), 36.

the full course at the nascent Tokyo Orthodox Seminary where instruction was conducted in Russian, the star-student Symeon was sponsored to pursue higher studies and spent four years at the Kievan Theological Academy, away from the politics and glitter of the Russian capitals, but close to the springs of Russian Orthodox monasticism and scholasticism. He was one of a handful of Japanese returnees from the Russian theological academies to quickly choose the path of a clergyman, thus ascending a lofty place in the hierarchy of the Church. His unique balance of academic achievement and pastoral experience was crowned with the respect for sentiments and realities of the Japanese and the Russians alike, making him the most sought-out Russo-Japanese bridging figure in the Japanese Church of his time.[16]

Fr. Symeon was responsible for introducing to the Japanese Orthodox believers Philaret's fundamental catechism treated at the start of the chapter. After ordaining him to the priesthood, the usually strict Archbishop Nicholas introduced Fr. Mii with unqualified praise for his translation of the catechism before the assembled delegates at the Japanese Church Council of 1894.[17]   When Fr. Symeon decided to write his own catechism, it proved almost a retelling of Philaret's, condensed and further schematized. Appearing in 1928, the catechism was met with enthusiasm and subsequently centrally reissued in 1935.[18]   When the Orthodox were asked to produce a summary of their

[16]Material on Fr. Symeon Mii is abundant. The most widely available are Naganawa Mitsuo's writings—his main monograph constructed around Fr. Symeon's biography is Naganawa (1989); his English-language digest of Fr. Mii's life-story appeared in Remortel & Chang (2003), 141-149, 174-175. Fr. Symeon's son Justin Mii Yoshito published three autobiographical memoirs of his father in Mii (1982). Fr. Symeon was a frequent contributor to the central periodicals of the Japanese Church and his name appears in most issues of the official *Orthodox Messenger* from early 1890's to late 1930's. Especially valuable data appear in 1940, in connection with Fr. Mii's death, especially Mii (1940).

[17]Naganawa (1989), 153.

[18]Mii ([1928] 1935).

identity and teaching for the series of self-presentations by contemporary Japanese religions, it was once more Fr. Mii who articulated the Church's voice. Published in 1934 but dateable to later 1920's,[19] this exposition to outsiders could not replicate the limiting framework of the catechism and brought out more of the Japanese clergyman's original voice. His opening phrase exemplifies his phraseology and ecclesiological thinking by stating that:

> The Orthodox Church of Christ is a place where Orthodox Christians engage in practicing and transmitting the eternally and universally fixed and unchanging principles of purity and right which should be accepted by all humankind, with established dogmas adhering through formal regulations to certain basic principles immutably instituted by the Savior of the world Jesus Christ from the beginning of distant antiquity—in short, it is the legitimate Christianity.[20]

From this long-winded description one might usefully abstract the perspective on the Church as an all-comprehending "place," inside which salvation is possible. While Fr. Mii's historical description of the Church presents it as a "great religious organization,"[21] in the dogmatic prescription which follows he once more emphasizes the Church to be a kind of spiritual location or object, "a fountain and a treasury of grace."[22] He does not leave out the four creedal definitions, nor the Biblical metaphors for the Church, but Church-as-sacred space seems to dominate Fr. Symeon's vision.

---

[19]The statistics from 1926 are cited as current and the restoration of the Tokyo cathedral—completed in 1929—ongoing. Mii (1934), 9-10.

[20]Mii (1934), 1.

[21]Mii (1934), 3, 4.

[22]Mii (1934), 27.

The spatial approach had a distinctive resonance in the contemporary realities of the Japanese Church. Fr. Mii's exposition devotes much space to recounting the history of the Japanese Orthodox Church around three foci—St. Nicholas, Bishop Sergius and the Tokyo Resurrection cathedral—and ends with a fervent appeal to participate in the effort of rebuilding the Church's chief sacred space ruined by the Great Kantō Earthquake, a task for which "the pure believers of the whole country must contribute greatly and continue to pray deeply."[23]   Fr. Mii's theological perspective links the restoration of the monumental edifice for worship with spiritual regeneration of worshippers, making clear the logic behind calling both believers' communities and their sacred spaces "churches." One might add that, Fr. Symeon himself once resided at the Tokyo cathedral compound and lived through the calamity, his family having lost their home and possessions, making the rebuilding a very personal cause. In contrast, even this most Russian-connected of Japanese Orthodox clerics left unmentioned the Russian Revolution and its debilitating impact on the Japanese Church—the latter is acknowledged as the "child of the Russian Orthodox Church,"[24] but no mention is made of the state of those family ties. Since Fr. Mii's emphasis on the inanimate "spiritualized" Church-as-space sidelined the incarnated visions of the living Church-as-community and Church-as-organism, ecclesiastical separation between Russia and Japan appeared implied in the geographical.

The longest and most detailed exposition of Orthodox teaching among the original Japanese interwar works came from Protopriest Peter Shibayama Junkō (1857-1937).   Although senior by age, he was junior by status among the "three founding elder"—he had the least experience in Russia and in Tokyo, and none at all as an instructor of the seminary or as an editor of the official *Orthodox Messenger*.   After

[23]Mii (1934), 9-10.
[24]Mii (1934), 7.

exchanging a teaching career for a religious one, most of his life as an Orthodox Christian was spent building up and serving a parish in his native Nagoya, until being summoned to Tokyo in 1923 to lead the Consistory and the cathedral reconstruction committee in the wake of the Great Kantō Earthquake.[25]

Fr. Peter may have been chosen to become the first head of the reconstruction committee for his "hands-on" character— his works in Nagoya ranged from cutting and sewing clerical vestments to the assembly (and probably also design) of the iconostasis and the funerary monument. He also had an occasion to serve the Japanese Church by introducing to Japan the production of church candles, which he observed at the Vladivostok Shmakovka monastery in Russia.[26] At the same time, he was an erudite and talented writer and preacher, a savant of the tea ceremony and Japanese antiquities. The pressures of serving at the capital soon saw him retire into a suburban family retreat, but his literary work continued to the end, producing a year before his death a major *Life* of Archbishop Nicholas which became the basis for the staple monograph on Japan's Orthodox apostle, indispensable to this day.[27]

Fr. Shibayama's *Prospect on Orthodoxy* was issued in 1928, from the "Yeast" press in his native Nagoya, which at the time became de-facto the second official publishing center of the Japanese Orthodox Church. This treatise commands attention not only by its breadth of coverage, but for the extensive outline of Orthodox anthropology and an emphasis on the relationship between God and man. In line with this, Fr. Peter's first definition of the Church is of an "organization of believers gained by the shedding of the Savior's blood on the

---

[25]Council Provisional (1923), 1-2 (1st pagination).

[26]Fr. Peter's hand-drawn blue-prints for his various projects are preserved at the family archive of Andrew Shibayama in Koganei.

[27]Consistory (1936). For the biographical profile of Fr. Shibayama see the obituaries in Orthodox Messenger (1937.06.01 - № 26-6), 29, 33-36.

Cross, established and headed by Christ Himself." Yet, already the next sentence echoes Fr. Mii's spatial metaphor, strengthened with a note of exclusivism—"Church is a treasury ever-full of God's grace, unchangeably and eternally preserved by the grace and power of the Divine Holy Spirit, and man has no means of obtaining God's grace except through the Church."[28] The defensive assertion of the Divine and exclusive qualities of the Church is perhaps the chief characteristic of the treatment which follows. Thus, "the name 'Church' is not something which all religions possess... and it is laughable that this name in recent times is used by followers of various alien teachings."[29] The outline of Church history is at pains to claim the centrality of the ecclesiastical "East" vis-à-vis the peripheral Latin Christendom located "far away in the isolated West."[30] A similar insecure emphasis is evident in the repeated affirmations that clergymen, above all bishops, are Divinely placed to lead the Church and are communicated a special grace for the purpose.[31] Indifferentism to the exclusive claims of the Orthodox Church, doubt in the avowed spiritual realities inside incarnate forms, and the resultant disregard for the administrative implications of charismatic gifts claimed by the clergy were the likely phenomena which evoked the priest's vehemence.

Since he participated in the drafting of the ecclesiastical *Constitution*,[32] one might gauge the strength of the prevailing "democratic" sentiment by how little of Fr. Shibayama's vision of clerical preponderance found its way into the final document. His 1928 opus, while emphatic in terms of doctrine and the reality of the "spiritual," safely avoided tackling the historical and contemporary conditions of Orthodox ecclesiastical organization—not even the existence of the Russian or Japanese Churches is mentioned, as the historical

[28] Shibayama (1928), 123-124.
[29] Shibayama (1928), 123.
[30] Shibayama (1928), 129.
[31] Shibayama (1928), 124, 127.
[32] Orthodox Messenger (1937.06.01 - № 26-6), 34-35.

excursus is cut short with an idyllic sketch approximating the formula of the 6th century Church.

The youngest of the "three founding elders," Protopriest Paul Morita Ryō (ca. 1862-1938), also left a mark, however pale, in the bibliography of the Japanese Orthodox Church at this time. A seminarian since the age of 14, his academic capacity was combined with a forthright patriotism, directed in favor of speedy independence of the Japanese Church. The young Morita was the leading voice in formulating the strongly statist Japanese Orthodox criticism of Uchimura Kanzō's "*lèse majesté*" in 1891.[33] His patriotic outspokenness, however, eventually clashed with the views of Nicholas, which resulted in exile from the post of Tokyo seminary lecturer to the humble duty of preaching in the distant north of Kyushu. His ability and good repute among believers eventually brought him back to Tokyo at the time of the personnel reshuffle in the wake of Sergius' succession. Fr. Morita has since remained an indispensable man in a variety of responsible posts, including spending much of the 1916-1919 years as a Red Cross priest and Japanese ecclesiastical emissary in St. Petersburg and the Russian Far East. Adept administrator and pastor, his character had a stern, monastic bent, and Fr. Paul proved an inspiring preacher of the Japanese warrior-spirit.[34]

Fr. Morita's imprimatur stamped the 1931 reworking of an older catechism, an adaptation of a pamphlet once translated from Russian—a simple scripted dialogue meant as a basic introduction for first-time hearers. It explains the Church in global general terms as "an assembly of all Orthodox believers under heaven, akin to a single body, established by Our Lord Jesus Christ Himself," equipped with rituals "whereby people can partake of God's grace."[35] The subsequent section on

[33]Morita (1891).
[34]For biographical details see the obituaries and recollections in Orthodox Messenger (1938.03.01 - № 27-2), 25-27; (1938.03.01 - № 27-3), 3-7, 10-12.
[35]Morita (1931), 15.

the Church is, in fact, an overview of the seven mysteries, available in the Church. The Creed is also included, providing the four parameters of the Church without commentary.

The calamity of the Russian Revolution already subsumed into a new normalcy, and the intense pressure by the Japanese state not yet applied, this period allowed for greatest insulation of theological writing from routine reality during the inter-war period—a fact well-attested by the writings of the "founding elder" clergy. If one is to look for a characteristic leaning in these seemingly neutral formulae by Nicholas-era stalwarts, it would be the "spiritualization" of the notion of the Church—a focus on the Church as a spiritual location or object, source of mystical services or remedies. Rather than belonging together with fellow men, emphasis is upon receiving from God via ecclesiastical channels. Hand-in-hand with chary treatment of the institutional reality of the Church, this "spiritualization" might suggest a weakening of the link between ethereal ecclesiastical attributes and the incarnate corporate daily life of the community.

Treatise of Metropolitan Sergius

Metropolitan Sergius (Tikhomirov), Japan's ruling Orthodox hierarch from 1912 to 1940, was the most important individual in the Japanese Orthodox Church during the interwar period. His position and learning assured his preeminence in formulating the voice of the Japanese Orthodox community at this time. At the same time, the effective severance of most Russo-Japanese links drastically undercut his power and status. Thus, his *magnum-opus* and swan-song, *The Apostolic Twelvesome*, was an ecclesiological statement of a doubly-disempowered leader—a "constitutional bishop" and a stateless alien. Translated and issued in Japanese in 1941, its Russian-language original was published in France in 1935, while significant Japanese-language excerpts became available in the Japanese Church's *Orthodox Messenger* since the early 1930's.[36]

Metropolitan Sergius prefaces his monograph with an ecumenical appeal to unity of all Christian denominations conditioned by his lifelong experience in Japan. As he says, there is "nearly one hundred million pagans" in Japan, and "wasting time, energy and manpower for sectarian struggles is a crime."[37] Lavishing praise on Protestants and professing Christian brotherhood with them, he goes on to bemoan the Roman Catholic interpretation of papal primacy, in which he sees the main stumbling block for Pan-Christian unification. Sergius' stated cause, then, is to remove this obstacle through carefully analyzing the role of Apostle Peter and the idea of primacy in the Scriptures.[38] The monograph then goes on to minutely dissect all references to Apostle Peter and apostles in general, as well as headship and power in the Church, in order to establish the unity and equality of all apostles as servants of the sole head of the Church— Christ. A major feat of linguistic analysis and historical learning in over 600 pages, this treatise dwarfs other works published by the Japanese Orthodox Church at the time. Sergius' ambition likewise appeared grand indeed—to finally settle the issue dividing tripartite Christendom. Devoid of national references to the "Russian" or "Japanese" Church, barely mentioning denominational allegiance, *The Apostolic Twelvesome* is at pains to escape all uncomfortable local issues, instead championing the universality of the Church on the basis of exhaustive Biblical evidence.

Yet, this "universal" Church appears uncannily Protestant. Metropolitan Sergius' treatise strikes a reader accustomed to Orthodox theological literature with a gaping lack

---

[36] See the original Russian in Sergius (1935). The later Japanese edition referenced below, Sergius ([1941] 1971), has been supplied with common Japanese rendition of Christian names and a few appendices.

[37] Sergius ([1941] 1971), 5.

[38] Sergius ([1941] 1971), 6, 10.

of quotes from the Holy Fathers.[39] Such an omission cannot be explained by the inaccessibility of patristic texts to the author—on top of his native Russian, Sergius was fluent in Slavonic, Greek, Hebrew, English, French, German and Japanese. Neither would the Roman Catholic audience be deaf to argumentation based on Church Fathers' authority. It is rather the Protestants, with their teaching of *Sola Scriptura*, who appear to be the chief intended audience of Metropolitan Sergius. In fact, since the initial factor which spurred Sergius to compose his work was a Roman Catholic apologetic by two turncoats—an ex-Orthodox and an ex-Anglican[40]— Sergius appears also as a defender of Anglicanism. Most of the authors whom he cites in his work are contemporary Protestant Anglophones,[41] and it was an American Protestant friend, YMCA's general secretary J. R. Mott, who arranged for the first publication of Sergius' monograph in Paris.[42] Mott was famous as the "father" of the ecumenical movement which sought to overcome denominational differences among all self-identified Christians. It is this aspect of his activity which Sergius stressed, holding up Mott as the epitome of

[39] An anonymous numerical ratio of the Church Fathers' opinions on the interpretation of Mt. 16, 18 and a single quote from Origen (Sergius ([1941] 1971), 131) appear to be the limit of the monograph's engagement with patristic texts.

[40] The ex-Orthodox was the Romanian Vladimir Ghica, who personally called upon Sergius, while the ex-Anglican was the Englishman Vernon Johnson, whose book—Johnson (1929)—Ghica presented to the Metropolitan. See Sergius ([1941] 1971), 18; Senuma (1938), 5.

[41] Metropolitan Sergius does not fully cite his sources, but the bulk appears to be derived from the major collections of Scriptural commentaries by 19th century overwhelmingly Protestant Anglophone luminaries in Nicoll (1897); Eiselen et al. (1929); Dummelow (1926); McNeile, R. J. Knowling, C. H. Irwin, T. V. Bartlet, J. R. Lumby, Rachman, Foakes-Jackson, Peake, Rackham, T. Denney, S. D. F. Salmond, T. Y. Bernard, Lightfoot, Fr. Rendal, Blunt. In contrast, Orthodox works cited appear to include only two Russian monographs—Bulgakov (1926) and Florenskii (1929)—and a single article by Nicholas (1910). To be fair, this dearth is convincingly explained by the author with a reference to the 1923 Great Kantō Earthquake and the subsequent fire, which destroyed the Mission's library. See Sergius ([1941] 1971), 14, 182-3.

[42] Sergius ([1941] 1971), 18.

a modern-day apostle in no uncertain terms. Describing
the missionary conferences organized by Mott, Sergius states
that:

> Denominational differences were quite forgotten
> at these conferences. All breathed one spirit... All
> pray together. Dine together. Spend two or three
> days together. And among some eighty of us,
> always there is the true giant of spirit and action—
> Doctor Mott! [...] He represents all apostles.
> Yet, his thought is always one. That is faith,
> Christianity, unification, the One Pastor. Even
> to think of him as belonging to one or another
> denomination is shameful. Naturally, from his
> heart, he is a Christian. A global Christian.[43]

These words make clear just how powerful was the
magnetism of J. R. Mott and his brand of Christianity
for the isolated and pessimistic Russian bishop in Japan.
Personally sympathetic toward many Protestant leaders, an
admirer of the Protestant-dominated ecumenical movement
for Christian unity, Sergius was also aware of the great
significance of good relations with Protestants, first of all with
Anglicans, for the struggling Orthodox communities outside
of their traditional ken. Seen from this perspective, *The
Apostolic Twelvesome* was not only a book to "rescue believers
from Roman Catholicism," as Sergius himself recommended
it,[44] but also an appeal for membership in the Protestant-
dominated "global Christian" circles. In line with the slogans
of the nascent ecumenical movement, the volume sought to
"hasten the time when all of Christianity will be pastored by
Christ alone and form His one flock,"[45] removing unity and
catholicity into a desired future, instead of affirming the unity
and catholicity of the Orthodox Church here and now.

[43] Sergius ([1941] 1971), 6-7.
[44] Council (1939), 73.
[45] Sergius ([1941] 1971), 10.

Pamphlet of a provincial cleric

By the time Sergius' monograph was finally published in Japanese, the focus of attention for Christians in Japan had decisively shifted away from mission and interdenominational affairs to relations with the invasive state and adaptation to the realities of wartime. The Japanese state required all Christian groups to summarily divest themselves of foreign ties to accord with the "new structure" of the Japanese nation. To make up for Sergius' silences on this vital subject, the Japanese translator of his work, John Senuma Kakusaburō, prefaced the treatise with the then-obligatory avowals of the Asian origin of Christianity and its non-foreign "Japanized" quality.[46] The trauma of wartime Japanization, hidden behind these words, found its reflection in a new series of ecclesiological monuments.

An early example of the wartime defensive nationalist shift in Orthodox discourse was a brochure *About the Christian Orthodox Church*, issued in 1937, the year World War II began in Asia. This publication was issued from the church of Sendai, the heartland of Japanese Orthodoxy. Its author, Priest Ignatius Iwama Yoichi (1883-1945) was a cleric of new formation—that is to say, he entered the ranks of the clergy after Archbishop Nicholas' repose and was ordained a priest following the Russian Revolution. He appears to have never been abroad and spent his life as a Church-servitor mostly in the Northeast of Japan, from 1933 until his death pastoring the congregation of Sendai.[47]

From the outset of his work, a preoccupation with the Church's antiquity is striking. After the opening definition of Christian Orthodox Church as "the Heaven-revealed

---

[46] Sergius ([1941] 1971), 16.

[47] The priestly public aspect Fr. Iwama's life is amply presented in the histories of the respective churches in Northeast Japan where he served. See Sapporo church (1987), 96-117; Tomakomai church (1998), 136-138; Sendai church (2004), 148-183, 261.

religion furnished with the means and method for the eternal salvation of man," he goes on to list its three other "distinctive traits," each supplied with an impressive age. Thus, this "traditional legitimate Church" is erected on "some-7000-year-old historical base," preserving the dogmas and mysteries through "fighting paganism and heresy over the course of 2000 years," and possessed of well-ordered Divine services and distinctive four-part choirs "which developed over the course of 2000 years."[48]

Although Fr. Iwama subsequently does state the conventional view of the Church being founded at the conclusion of Christ's earthly ministry,[49] he is among the earliest Japanese Orthodox authors to stress the Old Testament Jewish tradition to illustrate his community's great age. In this he is most likely responding to the "Era Day" (*kigensetsu*) celebrations of Japan's founding—in 1937 officially considered to have happened 2597 years ago—which were marked with increasing grandeur in wartime years. Fr. Ignatius also echoes the prevalent mood of the time when, after a eulogy to St. Nicholas, he sums up the identity of the Japanese Orthodox Church thus:

> The distinctive trait of the Japanese Christian Orthodox Church has been, from the outset, the principle of the centrality of the Imperial house, as well as the principle that mission throughout Japan should be carried out by the Japanese, according to which even at present, except for the senior cleric Metropolitan Sergius, all clergy are Japanese, and the Japanese Orthodox Church has been entirely financially independent and self-supporting for twenty years now.[50]

His conclusion with an outline of the history of Orthodoxy in Sendai—where believers were subject to incarcerations,

[48]Iwama (1937), 1-2.
[49]Iwama (1937), 7-8.
[50]Iwama (1937), 13.

house-arrests and surveillance as recently as 1872, and whence local Orthodox leaders later dispersed across Japan to "lay the foundation of the present Japanese Orthodox Church"[51]—contained a countercultural confession, but was above all a show of rootedness.

Fr. Ignatius was justified in his claims. His appropriation of seven millennia of history for Orthodoxy referred to the connection between the Old and New Testament periods. The Orthodox Church's Roman imperial legacy made it the one missionary-originated Christian denomination to take most kindly to the "centrality of the Imperial house." Finally, Nicholas' method of sending out Japanese catechists to spread the faith has been widely recognized as a distinctive and successful approach in the annals of Japanese Christianity. Yet, the transparently defensive tone of Fr. Iwama's assertions reveals the pressure mounting on Christians to prove that they belonged in wartime Japan. Perpetual assertion of Japanese authenticity drew apologists ever deeper into the discursive field of the nation-statist culture, substituting antiquity and nativism for engagement with the core creedal definitions of corporate identity.

Manifestoes of lay reformers

If Fr. Ignatius was writing in a climate when state pressure was a likelihood, three years later it became a threatening reality which sparked a resolution of pent-up drives inside the Japanese Orthodox Church. By unilaterally severing all ties with the Moscow-centered Russian Church over Metropolitan Sergius' staunch refusal, the Church Council in July 1940 flung open the doors for radical reform. However, aside from the expulsion of foreign leadership, most of the roadmap to "Japanization" remained uncharted. In these conditions

[51] Iwama (1937), 14-15.

the main editor of the Japanese Church's official *Orthodox Messenger*, Basil Nobori Naotaka (a.k.a. Shōmu, 1878-1958), printed his own manifesto for the "New beginning of the Japanese Orthodox Church" in the August 1 issue.

Nobori was a son of a Russian literature specialist, himself a lay literati popularly known in his day as one of the leading Japanese experts in Russian and Soviet culture. A native of the distant Amami islands on the southern edge of the Japanese archipelago, he converted to the Orthodox faith in his early youth, attended the Tokyo Theological Seminary and was even an instructor there for a brief time. However, his literary bent and expertise in Russian got him out of the seminary and into the military during the Russo-Japanese War. Teaching in army schools and, briefly, at the Waseda University, he went on to make a name for himself as a translator of Russian literature and columnist on things Russian, already in 1907 authoring the first comprehensive overview of Russian literature in Japanese. At the time of Japan's Siberian Intervention he emerged for a time as a consultant to the Japanese cabinet, Home and War Ministries, and was sent by the authorities to inspect Japanese-held Russian territory in 1920 and 1921. He did not abandon his close association with the Orthodox Church, but gravitated toward a circle of nativist liberal reformers, who, as he described, were viewed as "ecclesiastical rebels or revolutionaries" and therefore marginalized from the establishment at the Tokyo Orthodox headquarters.[52] However, as his social stature as a savant of Russia grew, his voice began to sound increasingly powerful in the Church's *Orthodox Messenger*. With the "three founding elders" dead and clergy of later formation endowed with far less education and international experience then the Nicholaevan old guard, the center of the ecclesiastical stage opened up to influential laymen like Nobori.[53]

[52] Nobori (1938a), 3-4.
[53] Nobori Shōmu is well-known, although primarily in his literary capacity. Recent monographs by Tashiro (2009) and Wada (2001) have been dedicated

Nobori's programmatic article celebrates the 1940 Council's proclamation of independence as historic, a moment when "our Church shook off Moscow's control and took its first step as a pure revived Japanese Orthodox Church."[54] Yet, this was to be but a start of a long overdue and complex process of Japanization, which the author had championed in word and print for the past three decades.[55] Nobori forecasts "quite some time and study" before the Church can finally "throw off the antiquated ways transmitted from Russia and be born again as a pure Japanese Orthodox Church in both name and reality."[56] This is not surprising, since he proposes to first cleanse Orthodoxy of all "historical accretions," and only then move on to "Japanization" proper. If the latter, in addition to personnel and organizational independence from outside ecclesiastical control, appears as a matter of "customs and regulations," the former is held to be the wiping-out of Byzantine "other-dependent esotericism" and Russian "mysticism, idealism and bureaucratism."[57] The author proposes to summarily begin investigating reforms by a "plenipotentiary committee," even as he lays out his own view on the matter.

Nobori's basic premise holds that in Russia, and earlier already in the Eastern Roman Empire, the Theanthropic (Divine-human) religion of Christ, the God-man, has become all-too Theocentric, with the human element much diminished. "Above all, the basic and major fault of the Old Orthodox Church is the negation of earthly life and the affirmation of

to him; in English a useful work is Nobori & Akamatsu (1981), where he figures both as subject and author.

[54]Nobori (1940), 1.

[55]Nobori (1940), 1-2. A critique of Russian religiosity for its overemphasis on the Divine at the expense of the human was already expressed by Nobori in the wake of the Russian Revolution in 1917—see Naganawa (1989), 206-207 citing Orthodox Messenger (1917.12.20 - № 6-24). Also, much of Nobori's program appeared in print in Nobori (1931), in a journal of the influential Japanese Orthodox nativist reformers.

[56]Nobori (1940), 1.

[57]Nobori (1940), 2-3.

the heavenly Church."[58] Much of Nobori's piece, in fact, is a tragic vision of a perverse religion leading Old Russia to its doom. The constructive kernel of the article is a confession of Nobori's ecclesiology—"the genuine Church is on earth, is an earthly thing..., is for earthly life..., is something that we have constructed for earthly life."[59] He proposes only a few practical solutions for the reawakening of Orthodox believers into becoming "God-believing realists"—remaking the Divine Liturgy into a dinner-and-discussion on the daily tasks of life,[60] doing away with the hierarchical distinctions among the clergy to be "as popular (minshūteki) and class-transcending as the primitive Church of the apostles"[61]—but the sheer magnitude of his proposed reforms obviates the need for much elaboration. A full-scale Orthodox Reformation was in order.

Nobori's line was not without its caveats. He cautioned against "willful alteration of immutable verities, which would not only lessen the significance of Christianity, but also squander its authority as a world religion."[62] The pathos of his contradictory view lay in the seemingly inescapable dilemma—instead of a Theocentric religion, he proposed an anthropocentric one, even as he proclaimed it to be Theanthropic. In this he not only accepted the Protestant "revivalist" theology, positing a radical discontinuity between the original "primitive" and the medieval "perverted" Church, but also the Buddhist dualism of other-dependence vs. self-dependence.[63] These views were manifestly too extreme to pass for a description of Orthodox ecclesiology. By aptly labeling the Orthodox Church as he knew it the "Old Orthodox

[58]Nobori (1940), 4.
[59]Nobori (1940), 4-5.
[60]Nobori (1940), 5.
[61]Nobori (1940), 1-2.
[62]Nobori (1940), 2.
[63]The latter influence is transparent in his use of the characteristically Buddhist term "other-dependent original vow" (tariki hongan) to describe Byzantine Orthodoxy. Nobori (1940), 3.

Church," he set up discursive space for a "New" one—a new religion to be made in Japan.

The course of reform, however, did not proceed as Nobori had outlined, since the Japanese Orthodox Church entered a divisive succession crisis. The idea of a plenipotentiary reform committee charting the path of the entire community proved uncongenial to most active believers, and, at any rate, there already emerged one such committee, which had another vision for the future. Already in October 1940 Nobori was ousted from the office of the *Orthodox Messenger's* main editor by the ascendant "Iwasawan" faction, joining the ranks of the swelling and inchoate "anti-Iwasawan" majority.[64] In the early spring of 1941, as rival groups congealed and schism threatened to institutionalize itself, the man whose name became the referent of polarized allegiance— Arsenius Iwasawa—took the lead in defining the Church in his "Declaration № 1."[65]

Publicly approved as the "representative" of the Japanese Orthodox Church at the July 1940 Council and stealthily inaugurated as the Church's "general administrator" in September 1940 by the plenipotentiary Special Committee under his own leadership, Professor Arsenius Iwasawa Heikichi (ca. 1863-1943) was at the time the man best qualified to bridge official secular and Orthodox ecclesiastical worlds of Japan. His baptism at 13 followed that of his father. Although the start of his career resembled that of his schoolmate from the Tokyo Orthodox Seminary, Fr. Symeon Mii, Arsenius' years of studying theology in Russia lead him unto a different path. While Mii went to Kiev and thereafter became a priest, Iwasawa studied at the Moscow Theological Seminary and the St. Petersburg Theological Academy—an experience which lead him to consciously choose the life of a layman.[66]

---

[64]Seraphim (2010a), 10.

[65]The situation described in the text of the declaration dates it after March 3, but before April 6 1941.

[66]Even his pen-name was Miriyanin (三里野人)—Russian for "layman,"

An active writer and educator in the Japanese Orthodox Church before the Russian Revolution and a perennial member of its Consistory thereafter, Arsenius began teaching Russian at military schools as early as 1902 and continued in state service until his last years. In the field of Russian language studies in Japan he is notable as a translator of the well-respected Russo-Japanese grammar of Fr. Sergius (Glebov), compiler of a dictionary, and the chief Russian language examiner of the military at the time of the Siberian Intervention. By the latter

Figure 3.2: Arsenius Iwasawa points the way to the "new structure" of Japanese Orthodoxy. From Tokyo Daily (1940.09.10), 2.

1930's he had reached the rank of junior 4th class official in the Imperial Household Ministry, imperially appointed high 3rd class official in the Cabinet, and 4th pay grade official in the Army Ministry, besides having been awarded numerous decorations. Since he categorically refused to become a cleric, Iwasawa's brief and much-contested tenure at the helm of the disunited Japanese Church—in fact, at the helm of a small minority faction—lasted only about a year. His final days were spent in honorable semi-retirement, as a director of the Russian language school at the Tokyo Orthodox cathedral compound.[67]

phonetically spelt in Japanese with Chinese characters. Cf. his testimony on this count in Council (1941), 73.

[67]There is little written on Iwasawa due to his post-war identification with "militarism" and troubles in the Church. See his profiles in Remortel &

Purported to clarify the *Root of Church troubles*,[68] Iwasawa's general epistle is penetrated with a political pathos, boiling down to the choice of a state to serve—the Japanese Empire or the Soviet Union. Iwasawa links this with the choice between two views of Christianity: the "nationalist-statist" view to go with the former and the essentially undifferentiated "socialist-suprastatist" and "communist-antistatist" views to go with the latter. Most of the text is devoted to the critique of the pro-Soviet and ambivalent acts of Metropolitan Sergius and his "three or four confidants," who have for many years obstructed those "sincerely concerned for the Church," a conflict which has now come to a head due to the government's "stimulation." The plans of the "sincerely concerned," with Iwasawa in the lead, are said to include the setting up of an independent Orthodox headquarters in Tokyo, the merger with the Russian Orthodox in Manchuria and China, and the furtherance "of our country's New Order of East Asia, making the Japanese Orthodox Church into one great anti-communist camp." While sounding hollow calls for ecclesiastical independence and reform, Iwasawa in fact prepares his readers for linking-up with Russian émigré hierarchs and fervently appeals to reunite under new leadership. Evidently, this academy-trained theologian was well-aware of the need to assert the Church's normative apostolicity via a properly ordained bishop, its catholicity via adherence to the Mother-Church, and its unity via overcoming the schism. If Iwasawa could establish proper organizational arrangements, he would be in position to assert the legitimacy of his faction's "Orthodoxy," trumping the numerical advantage of his opponents.

Chang (2003), 160-161, and in Naganawa (2007), 213-215. Japanese Orthodox periodicals contain many significant memoiristic and analytical articles by him, while the most notable biographical data on Iwasawa is gathered in Orthodox Messenger (1941.10.01 - № 31-9), frontispiece; (1943.11.01 - № 33-10), 14-15.

[68]The available version of this document—Iwasawa (1941)—is a photocopy of four unnumbered sheets, pasted together into two strips. Holdings of the Sendai Orthodox church.

However, the perspective on the Church expounded by Iwasawa is an attenuated one, wherein basic units of collective identity are family and state. Christianity—as "heavenly revelation"—is in line for harmonization with "the sole earthly revelation," Japan's Imperial way. To underscore his statism, Iwasawa appends the competing articles of faith submitted to the Ministry of Education by his own group and by the opposition. The latter appears to be the voice of the marginalized Orthodox majority—an artless and unassumingly universal paraphrase of the Niceo-Constantinopolitan Creed. On the other hand the Iwasawans' document is a flowery testament to the extent that nativism made its way into the creeds and practices of "official" wartime Japanese Christianity. According to the "Iwasawan Creed," the first three dogmas to be held by the Japanese Orthodox dealt with the Japanese emperor, including the universalization of his role in the Divine economy of salvation. Namely, one was to believe that "the teachings of Jesus Christ can for the first time develop fully only under the rule of His Majesty our brilliant and sagacious Emperor; they can for the first time bring about the salvation to the souls of all mankind only illumined by our spirit of the Imperial Way." Only the last two articles of this Creed, twelfth and thirteenth, mentioned the existence of the Church, "founded and led by apostles," whose authority is "inherited by bishops," but elaborated no further. In a bid for continued state tolerance, the Iwasawan formula left the notion of the Church both opaque and irrelevant.

The wartime crisis of the Japanese Orthodox Church revealed both disintegrative and restorative trends. While squeezed into state-dictated parameters, the reformist corporate agendas and self-definitions which surfaced in the wartime manifestoes were long in gestation, drawing on decades of development. Their eruption into prominence left little of the "one, catholic and apostolic" Orthodox Church in Japan, tending instead toward the many, isolationist and oligarchic bodies. Yet, the dynamic of restorative legitimization simultaneously impelled opinion leaders to reach for authenticity—Iwasawans strove to reconstruct the arrangements of administrative "Orthodoxy," while their opponents, rejecting the excesses of Nobori's reformism, held fast to the formulas of theological "Orthodoxy." Conscious and formal departure from "Orthodoxy" as such did not become an issue.

History of a cradle Christian

After 1945 the Orthodox Church of occupied Japan, threatened by schism, extinction of clergy and destruction of churches, was in no position to maintain the independence it previously claimed and raced to reestablish effective links with the Mother-Church. Although the Japanese community had previously engaged with only two contenders for the pre-revolutionary legacy of the Russian Church—the USSR-based Moscow Patriarchate and globally dispersed Russian Orthodox Church Abroad—American domination of Japan conditioned the entry of a third party, the New York-centered Russian Orthodox "American Metropolia." The internecine conflict which simmered among Japanese Orthodox was redescribed in Cold War terms, which quickly made the US the affiliation of choice. Compared with its Muscovite rival, the New York group was not outspoken about its Russian identity, increasingly hyphenated as it was with an American one. However, whichever link finally won out, a reaffirmation of Russian ecclesiastical legacy was imminent, aptly symbolized by the 1952 republication of St. Philaret's classic catechism treated at the start of this chapter. The self-presentation of the Japanese Orthodox community remained in the hands of native authors, but the Church was now to be headed by hierarchs dispatched and financed from the ascendant America. The task of the Japanese believers was to present themselves to their newly arrived bishops, ignorant of Japan's conditions, but crucial for the wellbeing of the local Church.

The new task called for a new genre—a historical exposition on Japanese Orthodoxy up to the present. At the request of Bishop Irenaeus (Bekish), who wished to make a presentation about his Japanese flock to the Fall 1954 Council of Bishops of the American Metropolia, an assistant professor of the Sendai Northeastern University, layman Symeon Iwama Masamitsu (1915-1984), took up the challenge. Eldest son of the above-mentioned Fr. Ignatius Iwama, Symeon was brought up in and around the church, making him one of the first Japanese "cradle Orthodox" to make his voice heard in the self-presentation of his Church. His qualifications for writing a history of the Japanese Orthodox Church included not only life-time membership and clerical pedigree, but also academic training as a historian. Although a specialist in early modern Europe, his research for the bibliography of Japanese Orthodox historical materials for the Society of Japanese Christian Studies took him to churches throughout Japan and reintroduced him thoroughly to the past and present of his Church. His brief but content-rich framework for the history of the Japanese Church was completed in about three months, on August 10, 1954, and issued the next year by the Consistory of the Japanese Church.[69]

Professor Iwama's essay is much more than a neutral narrative—it is an analysis by a historian, a plan for action by a believer, and an appeal for help by a victim—all three hypostases representing the stance of the Japanese Orthodox Church as it reflected on its past, struggled with the present, and hoped for the future. The victimization narrative would seem particularly salient in the wake of the wartime US

[69]Symeon Iwama is also known inside the Orthodox Church as a choir-director, and outside as an author and translator of monographs on early modern English political history like Iwama (1975, 1979); Sutherland (1969). See Iwama (1955), i; internet communication to the author from Bishop of Sendai Seraphim (Tsujie).

bombardment, but Iwama prudently avoided mentioning this to the American bishop, instead laying the blame for the Church's misfortunes on the link with Russia, inept financial managers, and Japanese state intervention. He defined the Church in the impersonal terms of its unfulfilled infrastructural needs—its financial base, educational facilities and missionary program.

In his description of the "thriving tide" period Church, Professor Iwama enumerates educational institutions and periodicals issued by the Church, wholly omitting St. Nicholas' exceptional charisma and vital theological decisions. Likewise, he identifies the end of the thriving era not with the loss of the saintly founder in 1912, but with the cessation of funds from Russia in the wake of the 1917 Revolution.

Church-as-consumer comes to the fore of Iwama's story. He stresses Nicholas' success in procuring sponsorship in the preparatory stage, the first inklings of subsequent financial hardships after the wake-up call of the 1904-05 Russo-Japanese War, and the primary significance of the quest for financial independence in what he identifies as the third period of Japanese Orthodox Church's history, from 1917 to 1933.[70] Nowhere in his work does he express blame or positively evaluate individual dissenters, except for the crucial matter of handling the 1917 cessation of funds from the Russian Missionary Society, "a calamity which could have been foreseen." At this point he writes:

> The issue of the financial independence of the Japanese Orthodox Church has been vociferously raised earlier by such intelligent people as Ishikawa Kisaburō, Iwada Yōjirō and others, but since there were few people with managerial acumen at the headquarters and, instead, many who were careless in financial matters, the sense of danger only worsened.[71]

[70] Iwama (1955), 3, 6.
[71] Iwama (1955), 7.

His keen attention to monetary matters makes for an uncommonly balanced summary of the successful fundraising campaign for the restoration of the Tokyo cathedral after the Great Kantō Earthquake. While he echoes the celebratory line about the cathedral being "built by Japanese believers," he is one of the few Japanese observers to point out the significance of foreign contributions in this symbolic coming-of-age feat of the Japanese Church.[72] Predictably, among the three main proposals for setting the Japanese Orthodox Church on the path of success, Iwama gives first priority to the stabilization of the financial base.[73]

Defining the Church through its needs, Symeon Iwama gives second place to personnel training. Citing approvingly Nicholas' principle of cultural adaptation and "missionization of Japan by Japanese," he points out, with a touch of local Sendai pride, that the very first "founding elder priests" of Japan were Nambu and Sendai-clan samurai with Confucian warrior upbringing.[74] The second story of the post-revolutionary Japanese Church, then, is a struggle for producing rooted native pastors. In this light the destructiveness of the financial collapse looms larger, considering the mass dismissal of catechists and clergy, as well as the closing of the seminary. The subsequent deaths of well-trained priests during the interwar decades could hardly be made up for by what Iwama calls makeshift "appearances of commissioned education" with Metropolitan Sergius, at Hieromonk Anthony Hibi's catechetical school, or at the Anglican *Rikkyō* University. As a result, at the time of his writing, Iwama noted that most Japanese Orthodox clerics were between 60 and over 70 years of age.[75]

This lack of personnel, according to Iwama, was likewise the reason for the troubles over canonical allegiance to the

[72]Iwama (1955), 8.
[73]Iwama (1955), 12.
[74]Iwama (1955), 3, 12.
[75]Iwama (1955), 8, 12.

Russian Church. He sees the key to administrative stability in "choosing via a proper procedure a bishop from among the natives"—something which Iwama denies to the first Japanese Orthodox bishop, Nicholas (Ono), ordained in wartime "at the hint of the military clique which was planning the advance in Manchuria and Siberia."[76] While celebrating study-abroad,[77] Iwama's exposition was transparently aimed at a long-term reassertion of Japanese ecclesiastical self-reliance, as is clear from his second proposal for the Church: "to revive the seminary to send out young hopefuls as clergy so that a man of high learning and virtue can be chosen bishop from amongst them in order to create an opportunity for administrative independence."[78]

Most muted and opaque is the third tier of Symeon Iwama's vision—mission. Even if he had more definite views, being a layman unaffiliated with the Church's central offices he was all the more reticent to express himself on theology before the ruling bishop. He does not present a history of ups and downs of religious fervor, but simply confesses the contemporary condition of "weakening and formalization of faith" in the "gradually fixated and stagnating Church."[79] He links this with the loss of missionary drive and the consequent predominance of an inherited, presumably dispirited, Orthodoxy: "there are now few 2nd-generation believers in the Japanese Orthodox Church, most are 3rd-generation believers from grandfathers and grandmothers, now shifting into the 4th-generation."[80] While he sees the situation to be urgent, he only vaguely proposes "to consider adapting the externals of the Church structure in response to the advances of the age so that the youth could assimilate to it."[81] It was less reform,

[76] Iwama (1955), 10-12.
[77] Iwama (1955), 4, 13.
[78] Iwama (1955), 12.
[79] Iwama (1955), 10, 12.
[80] Iwama (1955), 10.
[81] Iwama (1955), 12.

than the "need of new energy,"[82] which animated Symeon Iwama's third appeal.

Even as Professor Iwama was defining the Japanese Orthodox Church through its lack in his plaintive essay, Bishop Irenaeus was fulfilling this lack and bringing to a close what Iwama identified as at the fourth period of Japanese Orthodox history, the troubled "pre-&-post-war" from 1933 to the time of his writing. Irenaeus, however, was not only the "reconstructor," but the Americanizer of the Japanese Orthodox Church—it was during his tenure that the "American Metropolia" consolidated its influence upon the Orthodox ecclesiastical situation in Japan, redefining a wide range of communal fixtures from teaching (in the form of Alexander Schmemann's liturgical theology) to grooming (as with the Western clerical collars and lack of facial hair for clergy). Other global centers of the Orthodox Church involved themselves in the shaping of East Asian ecclesiastical identity with new force, while the first native Japanese Orthodox bishop, Nicholas (Ono), passed away in obscurity. The trial run of de facto independence for the Japanese Orthodox Church ended, concluding this earliest experiment of East Asian self-defined Orthodox Christianity.

[82]Iwama (1955), 10.

Chapter 4

Conclusion

The magnetism of Japan's prevailing mode of Christianity, the strain of bridging the sundered Japanese and Russian microcosms, and the isolation from the destabilized global Orthodox scene—the dominant contexts of the Japanese Orthodox community in the era of the World Wars—militated for the Church's dissolution. An outline of its history during these decades illustrates its continued decline. Yet, as the overview of its self-presentations suggests, the logic of its core corporate claims—whether stated or incarnated—possessed a measure of resilience beyond the dictates of the "trends of the times." It is this logic which shaped the distinctive drama of the Japanese Orthodox Church during its period of self-realization.

St. Nicholas, the charismatic founder of the Japanese Orthodox Church, had foreseen and feared this drama. On October 28 1896 he confided to his closest collaborator, the trusted scholar Paul Nakai Tsugumaro, that the Japanese Church "must not break out from under the ecclesiastical protection of its Mother-Church for at least two hundred years, for if it does, the destruction of the Church, schism and extinction will undoubtedly follow."[1]

[1] Nakai (1940), 9.

Figure 4.1: St. Nicholas and his aide, translator Paul Nakai, Meiji-period architects of the Japanese Orthodox liturgical language and consciousness. What became of their work?

Eight years later, speaking at the time of the Russo-Japanese War to a broadly representative informal gathering of Japanese clergy, seminary instructors and writers on July 20 1904, Nicholas shrank the time of projected Russian guidance to "no less than a hundred years." However, he warned that, unless the Japanese obey "strictly and unconditionally" the bishops sent from Russia, the Japanese Church "will spoil itself and become something like a Protestant sect," instead of a "branch of the one catholic apostolic Church."[2]

To clarify what Nicholas likely meant under "Protestant sect" it is useful to turn to the classic Orthodox critique of Protestantism voiced by his younger contemporary, St. Hilarion (Troitskii). In his famous 1912 opus, *Christianity or the Church?*, he considers the defining trait of Protestantism to be the abolition of the notion of the Church, because:

> [*according to Protestantism*]... truth and salvation are open to each separate individual, independently of the Church. Every individual was thus promoted into to the rank of infallible Pope... the theoretical side of Protestantism appealed to human self-love and self-will of all varieties, for self-love and self-will received a sort of

[2]Nicholas (2004), vol. 5 (1904.07.20), 114-115.

sanctification and blessing from Protestantism. This fact is revealed today in the endless dividing and factionalism of Protestantism itself.[3]

Understood in this sense, the label of "Protestantism" might be applied equally to the Western mainline and native "new religious" Christian groups of Japan—that is, to the defining majority of the Japanese Christian scene. Without the authoritative and authoritarian leader, backed by the prestige and power of imperial Russia and the entire Orthodox world, Nicholas expected mutation and disintegration of the core structure of the Church.

With Nicholas' feared circumstances in place, the process was under way. Apostolicity was summarily threatened by the disempowerment of the bishop, catholicity by isolationism, and by 1940 even oneness gave way to factionalism. Yet, it was something more than the post-war Russian-American "reimposition of Orthodoxy" which prevented the Japanese Orthodox Church from becoming a *sui generis* "Christianity made in Japan" which Nicholas had feared. What he had pessimistically written off as the inevitable "destruction of the Church" proved to be a self-searching struggle, self-realization—a process of trying to break or change core relationships and institutional structures only to find out that they are obligatory to one's identity as Orthodox. How the Japanese believers went about discovering themselves to be members of the "branch of the one catholic apostolic Church" is discussed in the subsequent exposition through the prism of the most contested parameters—apostolicity and catholicity.

[3]Hilarion (1997), 26-27.

Part II

Apostolicity in the post-apostolic age

Introduction:
Blueprints for bishops

Part II aims to discern how the Japanese Orthodox Church grappled with the institutional and personal reality of its bishops. While diverse theological interpretations of the term *apostolicity* exist, this defining characteristic of the Orthodox Church has been transmitted and understood in early 20th century Japanese Orthodox circles as having to do above all with the unique charisma and authority of bishops. In this view bishops are held to be descendants, through an unbroken chain of instruction and ordinations, of the authentic teaching and special Divine grace of the apostles, who were taught and empowered by Christ. Therefore bishops are entrusted with the task of teaching, performing sacred functions and governing the Church.[1] They can partially delegate some of these functions, but not those considered sacramental— such as, crucially, the ordination of priests. Nor can bishops wholly surrender their tasks, due to the irreducible quality of apostolic grace they are supposed to receive at ordination. The terms for "bishop," as rendered in the Japanese Orthodox Church, make explicit his crucial role: 主教 (*shukyō*: "chief teacher"), 使徒 (*shito*: "apostle", literally [God's] "emissary"),

---

[1] So goes the common interpretation of Christ's instruction to the apostles in Matt. 28:19-20.

105

監督 (*kantoku*: "overseer"). While a modern local Church is usually composed of multiple dioceses united via some form of higher administration, the nascent Japanese Church was in fact a single diocese, and therefore possessed only one ruling bishop. Thus, he figured as a central institution of the ecclesiastical organization, a plenipotentiary head of the local Church, and an indispensable attribute of Orthodoxy. However, in the realities of the Japanese Orthodox Church in the era of the World Wars there were many other blueprints for the role of the bishop, most of which meshed poorly with the above totalizing model. This introduction aims to outline these basic blueprints, while the following chapters offer a study of their interaction and integration into a vision and practice of apostolicity.

To establish the solely normative paradigm of ecclesiastical administration, the founder of the Japanese Church, Archbishop Nicholas, took special care to speedily translate and widely publicize the prescriptive canonical texts of the Orthodox Church in Japanese.[2] The canons of ancient Ecumenical Councils and select Church Fathers, employed by the Orthodox Church as a set of universal norms, are unambiguous about a bishop's centrality to any given territory under his jurisdiction—in fact, they barely go beyond the person of the bishop in discussing diocesan administration. The canons do not rule out popular participation in the election of a bishop, but, once properly ordained and installed, he is not subject to judgment by his diocesan clergy and laity, but only by a Council of fellow bishops, with plaintiffs required to have unquestioned respectability and Orthodoxy.[3] Factionalism and plotting by clergy and laity against bishops or other clergy is subject to harsh discipline.[4] Nor is the ruling hierarch required to share any administrative prerogative with his

---

[2] The canonical corpus of the Orthodox Church had been published in the main organ of the Japanese Church, *Orthodox Herald* (*Seikyō Shimpō*) since its inception at the end of 1880.

[3] II Ecumenical Council, Canon 6; IV Ecumenical Council, Canon 21.

[4] IV Ecumenical Council, Canon 18; VI Ecumenical Council, Canon 34.

flock, or organize any advisory bodies at his side, although he is charged with keeping a treasurer as an aide.[5] While a bishop is a "brother" unto fellow bishops, he is both "teacher" and "master," the image of Christ Himself, unto clerics and laity within his diocese.

Disentangled in the form of neat compendia from the ecclesiastical realities of the Eastern Roman Empire of the 4-8th century, the above canonical norms did not, in fact, operate fully in any of the 19th century Orthodox contexts. While the Greek and Balkan Orthodox Churches offered alternative patterns, the Japanese contact occurred over-whelmingly with the Russian Orthodox Church, its various guises and successors. A diocesan bishop in this setting, although in principle endowed with the plenitude of power and function that ancient canons outlined, was in fact severely circumscribed in his role. He usually hailed from a narrow and socially segregated class of hereditary clerics, further removed from the life of his flock by being a monastic with elite theological schooling. Circulated from one diocese to another on the basis of merit, ambition, circumstance and politics, bishops had to readjust repeatedly to new populations, each time losing the precious capital of prior personal connections. The size of an average diocese was far too large for a single bishop to form relationships of personal spiritual intimacy with much of his flock. Bureaucratization required bishops to process a vast flow of official paper-work, further reducing their effectiveness. Perhaps most importantly, delegation of "advisory" power put the bishop's administrative assistants—the Consistory with its Chancery, and, occasionally, subordinate local Directorates—effectively in charge of most routine diocesan functions.[6]

Yet, a disengaged bishop did not mean a broadly empow-ered flock. Indeed, such practices as regular diocese-wide

---

[5] IV Ecumenical Council, Canon 26.
[6] For the functions and makeup of Synodal-era Russian Consistories see Barsov (1885), 126-155.

congresses or elected clergy were but a reformers' dream, ruled out in most cases by apprehensive inertia, political oppression or social instability. This Consistory-centered model routinized—or rather substituted for—the requisite episcopal authority and general participation. At the close of Russia's imperial age this increasingly dysfunctional paradigm was heavily under fire from all sides, with bishops among its premier critics.[7] However, although it did break down amid violent persecution and global dispersion, the Consistory-centered model remained the chief reference point for the reality of Russian episcopacy.

Since experience with foreign ecclesiastical settings was limited and canons usually dormant until engaged by emergencies, more familiar Japanese conceptions of leadership often came to the fore in determining the vector of majority thinking and action with regard to Japanese Orthodox episcopacy. The five basic categories of Japanese leadership—hereditary, organization-founder, ideological-charismatic, lieutenant-turned-leader, and the steady climber of the bureaucratic ladder[8]—could all be found in Japan's religious institutions. The second and third types usually blend into one, aptly symbolized by Archbishop Nicholas himself, while the successors of the charismatic founder normally belong to one of the other three. It is these latter—post-founder—types which fit well into the quintessential pattern of a Japanese leader, who has been influentially described by Nakane. Such a figure is thoroughly inside, rather than above, his organization; a senior man in the group acting the part of an emotional "parent" to his

---

[7] The most powerful statement of the collective protest of the episcopacy against contemporary Russian diocesan governance is contained in the 1905-1906 collection of bishops' reform proposals to be discussed at the envisioned Church Council, published in Responses (2004).

[8] As classified by Craig (1970), 25-27.

"children";[9] limited in the sphere of his personal freedom and obliged to tread in step with the desires of the majority; highly dependant on his ability to personally charm and manage the impulses of his subordinates, who are frequently more capable and more powerful than he.[10]

While retaining symbolic primacy as a guarantor of unity, this leader is thus embedded in a vaguely defined leadership milieu, and held up as a "Portable Shrine." According to Maruyama's powerful analysis of Japan's wartime political leadership,

> the Shrine is often a mere robot who affects other people by 'doing nothing'... The force that 'holds aloft' the Shrine and that wields the real power is the Official... He in turn is being prodded from behind by the Outlaw.

These three types of leading personalities are so arranged that "movement starts from the Outlaw and gradually works upwards." At the apex of this "system of irresponsibilities" was, of course, the Japanese emperor—the omnipotent ruler who was presumed to make no decisive political acts.[11] Although representing modes of behavior, rather than fixed categories, these tropes find surprisingly fitting parallels in the Japanese ecclesiastical context. Ex-seminarian activists with sometimes radical theological and organizational ideas appear as "Outlaws," esteemed priests at the Tokyo Consistory as "Officials," suggesting that Japanese Orthodox bishops were expected to act as "Portable Shrines."

The Japanese Orthodox discourse on leadership was invariably shaped by the political conjuncture of each moment.

[9] The attendant nurturing and benevolent sentimentalism is often described as too feminine to be "fatherly," drawing on the centrality of the mother in the Japanese family. See for instance Bellah (2003), 176-183.

[10] Nakane (1970), 63-80.

[11] Maruyama (1963), 128-129.

The unfolding ecclesiastical dialogue—which invoked "democracy" (also "parliamentarism," "freedom") and "autocracy" (or else "dictatorship," "tyranny"), as applicable in Church governance—was impacted profoundly by the perceived political climate. The new Japanese popular consciousness of belonging to a "nation" called to life a desire to participate in the fate of that nation and hence a broadening democratic movement since the early 1900's. Similarly, a consciousness of membership in a "Church" resulted in a drive for some measure of ecclesiastical democracy. Japan's imperialist triumphs and increasing confidence on the international stage made of this democratic movement also a nativist one—both in the society at large and inside the Orthodox Church in particular. This thread was the single most visible linkage between Orthodox ecclesiastical order and political ideas, confirming Gordon's formulation of "imperial democracy" as the central socio-political phenomenon of interwar Japan,[12] and highlighting the centrality of the state as an archetypal organization in the discourse of contemporary Japanese. Bolstered by liberal and leftist thought from late imperial Russia, the vision of Church as participatory polity was becoming more pronounced than that of Church as patriarchal family, despite the universal terminology of "brotherhood" of believers, "fatherhood" of clergy, and "kingship" of Christ. Repeated direct interventions by various state agents between 1939 and 1953 had derailed the development of this discourse, but had not substituted it with any other vision of Church as polity.

Finally, each bishop is also a single man, whose person—with all its theological, intellectual, ethnic, regional, social and political attachments, physical traits and psychological idiosyncrasies, strengths and weaknesses—becomes magnified through and projected onto the entire community of believers. The personal reality of bishops was another defining factor in the evolution of the Japanese Orthodox praxis of

[12] See Gordon (1991), especially the overview in 13-25.

episcopacy. For this reason the outstanding personality of Japan's Orthodox apostle, Archbishop Nicholas, was all the more significant in setting the standard against which his successors would be invariably appraised in this light. In other words, between 1912 and 1956 Sergius (Tikhomirov), Nicholas (Ono), Benjamin (Basalyga) and Irenaeus (Bekish) became bishops of the Japanese Orthodox Church in the "age after" Japan's towering "apostle." As Mullins has shown, this type of a charismatic founder stands at the basis of every indigenous Japanese Christian movement, but is usually lacking in the transplanted Western Christian denominations. This characteristically makes Japanese Orthodoxy appear as more akin to a Japanese "new religion" than a Western transplant. However, the native movements Mullins described all but universally fell back on the hereditary mode of succession, with blood or fictive relatives of the founder succeeding to his mantle.[13] In the Japanese Orthodox Church, governed by monastics appointed from abroad, that was not an option. Yet, a powerful current of sentiment tended to "canonize"— literally, make a rule out of—Nicholas' exceptionally strong personality and inimitable successes, to the extent that the characters and achievements of his successors would be appraised in this invariably unfavorable light. The resulting sense of lack stimulated further search for the proper meaning and mode of episcopacy in the Japanese Orthodox context.

As follows from the above overview, the mode of strong and charismatic primacy which Nicholas had enacted in the Japanese Orthodox Church basing himself on canonical proof-texts was at odds with the practice of bureaucratized Russian episcopacy, the Japanese propensity for nominal heads dis-solved in broad leadership milieus, the rhetorical ascendancy of imperial democracy, and the perceived weakness of his successors. This was not a classic narrative of "Western" missionaries and models clashing with "Eastern" believers and culture, found in many treatments of Christian ventures

[13]Mullins (1998), 43-47, 187-189.

in Asia. Instead, this was a case where an original prototype had managed to incarnate itself on the crossroads of two civilizations *despite both* Russian and Japanese realities and trends. The Japanese Orthodox apprehension and enactment of "apostolicity" in the age after its "apostle" would be a tortuous process, whereby an array of actors, impelled by these realities and trends, bore down upon the prototype with united force, until a sudden crisis revealed that they had been sawing off the very branch on which they nested.

Chapter 5

The saint and the successor

Archbishop Nicholas was born John Dmitrievich Kasatkin in 1836, in a deacon's family at a small village in the Smolensk region of Russia, graduated from the St. Petersburg Theological Academy, and arrived in Japan in 1861 to stay there for the rest of his life. He was a subject of eulogistic and outright fantastic stories already in later 1870's—one, notably, held him to be half-Japanese, fathered by a Japanese castaway to Russia.[1] By the time of his demise in 1912 the bibliography of accounts about him grew to hundreds of articles and has continued to expand at a rapid rate, with peaks in the wake of his death, around the time of his official glorification as a saint in 1970, and after the fall of the atheistic regime in the former USSR.[2] Since 1930 a number of biographical monographs have

[1]Reported in Orthodox Review (1880 - №8), 714-715. See also Abramius ([1956] 1998), 205.
[2]To list even the most significant biographical articles and memoirs would require dozens of entries. The more up-to-date and valuable research pieces include the broad collections in Remortel & Chang (2003) as well as Bogoliubov & Augustine (1993-2004 - vol. 2); an introduction to Nicholas'

been devoted to St. Nicholas.[3] The rediscovery, deciphering and publication of his extensive private diaries, spanning most of the half-century that he spent as a missionary in Japan, has greatly augmented the available store of information and stimulated the study of this outstanding figure.[4] Finally, an ongoing publication of fragments from Nicholas' vast epistolary legacy continues to fuel the inquiry.[5] His stature as a bridge between Russia and Japan, his achievements as a mentor and scholar, and above all his stunning successes as a Christian preacher and pastor, ensure continued dynamism of Nicholaevan studies. Given the wealth of available material and the scope of the present work, the following treatment seeks only to provide a limited sketch of Nicholas' role in the fabric of the Japanese Orthodox Church, necessary for contextualizing subsequent developments.

Many aspects of Archbishop Nicholas' activity and its results place him into the ranks of Japanese religious charis-

diaries by Steiner (1995); Nicholas' psychological sketch in Trukhin (2005); a summary of Nicholas' outlook on Japan's non-Christian religions in Larionov (2006); a series of articles contrasting Archbishop Nicholas and his successor, Metropolitan Sergius, in Seraphim (2008-2010 - №№ 1413-1417).

[3] The first attempt at a large-scale hagiographical monograph was led by Fr. Peter Shibayama and resulted in the still-valuable compilation issued as Consistory (1936). Significant hagiographical biographies have been compiled by catechist Peter Mochizuki Tominosuke in Mochizuki (1930, 1951). The next major contribution came from the premier Japanese Orthodox in-house historian, Fr. Proclus Ushimaru, followed by another cleric, Fr. John Takahashi, the chief volumes being Ushimaru (1969, 1978) and Takahashi (2000). After the fall of the USSR professional academic historians also began to focus their energies on St. Nicholas, foremost works being Nakamura (1996) and Sablina (2006).

[4] After the diaries have been forwarded to Russia in the wake of Nicholas' death, they have passed into oblivion and had been assumed lost until Nakamura Kennosuke stumbled upon them at the Central State Historical Archive of Leningrad in 1979. Significant excerpts from the diaries have been published first by the Hokkaido University Press in 1994, then in other publications in Russia and Japan. The complete edition has been issued in 2004 in the original and in 2007 in Japanese translation. See Nicholas (1994, 2004, 2007).

[5] These publications form most of Sablina (2006), 199-509; Guzanov (2002, 2003a, 2003b).

matic founders—originators of new Buddhist or Shintoist sects, whose names became firmly attached to the communities of their followers. For a time Orthodox Christianity was widely known in Japan as *Nikorai-shū* —the "Nicholas sect" of Christianity—mirroring the appellation of the Nichiren sect of Buddhism.[6] The grand cathedral in honor of the Resurrection of Christ at the Japanese Orthodox headquarters, Nicholas' costly favorite project, became one of Tokyo's landmarks even before its 1891 completion and has since held the popular soubriquet of *Nikorai-dō*—the "Nicholas hall."[7] Nicholas' next great task, to which he devoted much of the rest of his life, has been the translation of ecclesiastical texts, which created an Orthodox Japanese linguistic register with its own vocabulary and style, embodied most famously in the precise and distinctive wording of what is known as the *Nikorai-yaku*—the "Nicholas translation" of the New Testament.[8] The archbishop was consciously setting the pattern that, in his estimation, "would be memorable, studied, imitated... for centuries,"[9] establishing precedents from which "traditions, habits, examples begin in the Church."[10] Indeed, the notion that the creation of the Japanese Orthodox Church was "in essence—a one-man feat" of Nicholas remains a truism among most researchers.[11]

Nicholas was no rebel with regard to the religion of his upbringing, but rather a "minor founder"—a sociological term coined for Apostle Paul as a pioneer within a preexisting subculture.[12] Nicholas' official canonization by the Russian

---

[6] Nakamura (2007), 45.

[7] For the most detailed treatment of the Orthodox Tokyo Resurrection cathedral see Tokyo cathedral (1998).

[8] Ebisawa (1989), 370-375. For a detailed textual comparison of the "Nicholas translation" with other current Japanese-language renderings of the Bible see Besstremiannaia (2006), 193-210.

[9] PTsV (1905 - № 15), 636.

[10] Nicholas' words in a Synodal report from December 1878, cited in Anthony (1974), 38.

[11] Expression in Trukhin (2005), 27.

[12] Stark (1970), 4:84.

Orthodox Church in 1970, by assigning to him the title "Equal-to-the-Apostles," confirmed his name in the short list of persons like St. Nina of Georgia and Sts. Cyril and Methodius of the Slavs, venerated en-par with Christ's direct disciples for being chief transmitters and adapters of the entire ecclesiastical mode of life to previously non-Christian peoples. Characteristically, in addition to direct appeals to God, Nicholas' diaries reveal Apostle Paul and Sts. Cyril and Methodius as persons to whom the Japanese missionary turned in prayer.[13]

As a "minor founder" Nicholas was a child of Russia's "Great Reforms," marked by broad and proactive openness to innovation, yet—for the majority—conceived within the limits of established order. While the contemporary Russian clerical elite produced some of the most revolutionary apostate *intelligentsia*—like Nicholas Dobroliubov and Nicholas Chernyshevskii[14]—it had been more common for idealistic enthusiasm to incarnate itself in a rededication to faith, which gave impetus to the renaissance of missionary ventures. When he first envisioned evangelizing Japan, at the close of 1850's, John Kasatkin did not conceive something principally new—in fact, stories about the Chinese Orthodox Mission influenced his decision. When his interest turned to Japan, thanks to the sympathetic account of that country by the Russian emissary-turned-Japanese prisoner Golovnin, Kasatkin once again found himself in the context of a "continuer," because the vivid example of the once-successful Jesuit mission made contemporary Russians conceive of the general "resurrection of Christianity," rather than first-time implantation of Orthodoxy, in Japan.[15]

---

[13] Nicholas (2004), vol. 2 (1888.03.16), 293.

[14] On the dynamic of radicalization and secularization in the "reform" generation of Russia's clerical families see Manchester (2008).

[15] Thus, the first Russian consul in Japan, Joseph Goshkevich, named the Orthodox chapel at the Hakodate consulate in honor of Resurrection of Christ, referring to the restoration in Japan of the once suppressed (Roman Catholic) Christian faith. See the Letter from Hieromonk Nicholas (Kasatkin) to the

What was indeed uncommon about the young cleric was the energy he invested in cultivating a single-minded devotion to this goal, hammering into himself that "my only aim and joy in life is the enlightenment of Japan with Orthodoxy."[16] Repeatedly affirming in his private diaries, despite his own gnawing apprehensions, the belief in the eventual triumph of Orthodox Christianity in Japan, Nicholas often spoke of himself as an inanimate tool—a "nail," a "match" or a "plough"—wielded by God in the inexorable spread of the Church.[17] Such intensity appears to have been initially sparked by the wide discussion of Goncharov's famous novel, *Oblomov*, which stirred the Russian reading public to embrace "action" amidst officially sponsored "reform." It was thus three basic Russian impulses—ecclesiastical external missionary tradition, official push to establish relations with Japan, and nationwide mobilization effected by the "Great Reforms"—which conditioned Nicholas' emergence.[18]

However, there was a way in which Nicholas became a genuine Japanese character in the cast of "men of Meiji"— revolutionary reformers who refashioned their realm under the rubric of "Meiji Restoration." On the background of the shared Western challenge, which dictated the simultaneity and similarity of Russia's and Japan's new round of precipitous modernization, Nicholas' personal effort at integration had been exceptional. Through some eight years of devoted study of the Japanese language, history and religions, through subsequent journeys across the country, and through an extraordinarily expansive network of interlocutors and correspondents, the missionary eventually became intimately

Over-Procurator of the Most Holy Synod Alexis Akhmatov from August 21 1863, cited in Nakamura (1996), 8-9.

[16]Nicholas (2004), vol. 2 (1889.01.10), 299.

[17]On self-searching assertions about the future of the Orthodox Church see for example Nicholas (2004), vol. 2 (1886.11.30), 287-288; (1889.01.11), 299. For comparisons with the nail, match and plough see consecutively Nicholas (2004), vol. 1 (1880.02.16), 165; vol. 4 (1900.04.26), 242; Sergius (1913), 48.

[18]The most important witness to these three impulses being formative to his activity is Nicholas (2004), vol. 5 (1907.11.03), 338.

familiar with the conditions of Japan, forming a realistic and generally positive image of the Japanese character. Meanwhile, somewhat limited in his personal experience of ecclesiastical life outside Japan—youthful years and two later visits to Russia, a brief observation of the condition of the Orthodox Church in the Near East, and a ride across the United States—Nicholas was uninhibited by the impulse for slavish imitation. He drew his notion of an ideal Church primarily from the advice of mentors, above all from the pioneer missionary St. Innocent (Veniaminov),[19] and from Orthodox prescriptive texts, like the Scriptures, service books, dogmatic and canonical manuals. To embody this exacting ideal in the given reality of Japan, rather than to transplant the extant Russian package wholesale onto new shores, became Nicholas' driving principle. As a result, Nicholas' transmission of Orthodoxy to Japan was in many ways a new—and native— foundation.

The *Statute* for the Orthodox Mission in Japan and the *Instruction* for its head, compiled by Nicholas and approved by the Russian Church's Most Holy Synod in 1871, charged the Mission's plenipotentiary head with responsibility for directing each aspect of the Mission's activity.[20] Nicholas' ordination to episcopacy in 1880 provided him with the capacity to ordain priests and confirmed his primacy in the nascent Japanese Orthodox community, but did not alter the essential praxis of his leadership. For most of his life he remained not only the visionary leader of the Japanese Church, but also its chief fund-raiser and financial manager, the rector of most of its educational institutions, its principal translator of Scriptural and service texts, the definer of its aesthetic expression, and the sole channel for its inter-institutional, inter-religious and Church-state relations. Yet, managing the Church meant above all managing people, so

---

[19]Garrett ([1979] 2006), 266-270.

[20]For the complete text see Sablina (2006), 307-315, reproducing the archival holdings of АВПРИ, ф. Японский стол, оп. 493, д. 1056, л. 27-35.

Nicholas became a deeply involved and emotionally invested spiritual father to many believers, especially the active elite in the employ of the Mission. Most Japanese Orthodox seminarians, translators, writers, catechists, and, of course, clergy, were Nicholas' personal disciples. He, in turn, studied their characters, planned out their personal life, and grieved intensely over both their faults and hardships.[21] Some Japanese disciples would recall the profound sense of attachment and union which enveloped them, when the normally stern archbishop showed them his care and affection—at such moments they "experienced a feeling of reality, in which I am Nicholas' and Nicholas is mine."[22] Indeed, Nicholas not only ran, but appears to have tried to incarnate the Japanese Church in person, according to his belief in the incarnate God and embodied Church. On his deathbed, Nicholas privately confided to his successor, that:

> Throughout my 50-year-long life in Japan I have tried to appropriate everything, which pervades the Japanese: language, customs, food, clothing, daily regimen, etc. And always felt that I still cannot perfectly become a Japanese, still remain a Russian. But now, when I should die, I should be buried on Japanese land, covered with Japanese dust, in a few years I should dissolve into Japanese soil, and finally become perfectly Japanese.[23]

In sum, Nicholas' leadership was all-embracing and self-effacing, autocratic and intensely personal.

[21]Nicholas' diary is ample proof of that. Steiner's review of the diaries is useful in exposing Nicholas' displeasure with the shortcomings of his Japanese collaborators, see especially Steiner (1995), 544-547. For examples of his advice regarding personal life, like choice of marriage partners and acceptance of monasticism, see Nicholas (2004), vol. 5 (1904.03.02), 31; vol. 5 (1904.07.05), 104-105; Kaneishi (1993), 166-167.

[22]Kaneishi (1993), 179, citing Orthodox Messenger (1934.03.01 - №23-3).

[23]Cited in Leontius (1946b), 59.

Such charismatic primacy made for slow institutionalization of the Japanese Orthodox Church. Nicholas' demands
for himself and his coworkers were stiff, conforming, once
again, more to the ideal than to the average practice of
contemporary ecclesiastical life. By asking even more from his
Russian coworkers than from his Japanese spiritual progeny,[24]
Nicholas involuntarily ensured that the officially chartered
"Russian Spiritual Mission in Japan" would remain bereft of
any sizeable presence of Russians, who usually abandoned the
field soon after being faced with Nicholas' requirements.[25]
In his quest to erect a local religious body, Nicholas from
the outset of his activity began to use the term "Japanese
Orthodox Church" to designate the nascent community of
Japanese Orthodox believers. The sole institution of this
new grouping, aside from its omnipotent head, was the
annual "Council," which assembled regularly from 1874.
Borrowing the name from the top governing organ in the
Orthodox Church, usually made up of bishops deliberating
all questions facing the global or local Church, the Japanese
version was in fact a clergy-laity congress with elected lay
representatives and the entire staff of clerics, presided over by
Nicholas. This Council deliberated on the Japanese Church's
internal issues, particularly personnel management, and held
the vital capacity to elect and approve new candidates for
ordination. Although Nicholas authoritatively steered the
course of Councils, he held up the decisions, once taken, as
the "desire of the Church," which thus became binding *en par*
with his own will. The first Council of 1874 also approved
the *Missionary regulations* which set up a nationwide network
of catechists subordinated to a central entity—the "Tokyo
Orthodox church," a euphemism for Nicholas himself, whose
role remained unencoded by any intra-Japanese ecclesiastical

[24]For example, while Japanese clergy received their pay for inalienable
personal use, Nicholas demanded that Russian missionaries surrender at least
half of their salaries for the needs of the Mission. Sablina (2006), 48.

[25]For a useful extract from the diaries on the issue of the Russian staff see
Steiner (1995), 541-543.

statute.[26]

After over thirty years of operation on this basis, as the Church accumulated real estate, the lack of legal recognition from the Japanese state became increasingly worrisome. In 1908 this finally impelled the official registration of the Property-Holding Society of the Japanese Orthodox Church, a shareholder society which became the first Japanese Orthodox legal entity. Yet, the Japanese Orthodox Church as such received neither an internal explicit institutional ordering, nor an external formal acknowledgement from Orthodox ecclesiastical authorities. Only ancient general canons, evolving local tradition, and the twin pillars of the ruling bishop and the deliberative Council anchored the organizational reality of a 30,000-strong body of believers by the time of Nicholas' death in 1912.

Lacking Russia's long-held habits of ecclesiastical life and its mediating diocesan bureaucracy, the first-generation Japanese Orthodox Church had no ready-made mechanism to sublimate the energy of its members and, above all, to replace Nicholas' colossal charisma. A succession crisis was set to ensue in 1912, although there were no doubts as to who would be the next bishop to head the Japanese flock. Since his arrival in Japan in 1908 as the Vicar of Kyoto, Sergius (Tikhomirov) had been the evident successor, presented and prepared as such by the aging archbishop. But it was likewise evident that Sergius, or anyone else, would be unable to fill Nicholas' shoes. As Nicholas opined privately in 1896:

> There are not a few elder clerics and catechists in the Japanese Orthodox Church, and governing them is no easy task. Unworthy as I am, because I have been here for many years, thankfully, I have

---

[26]On the inaugural Council, which set the pattern for subsequent ones, and the complete text of the *Missionary regulations* see Consistory (1936), 52-57; Sablina (2006), 58-59.

> gained the obedience of the people. However, it
> is certain that someone freshly come from abroad
> would be unable to rule the same way.[27]

Already at that time the archbishop had hoped to keep his groomed successor at his side for at least a decade before gradually transferring to him the reins of power, but subsequent developments showed that the future bishop's standing would be even more precarious than had seemed in 1896. By 1904, as the early successes of the Russo-Japanese War stoked the flames of national pride among Japanese believers, Nicholas' position, despite his colossal authority and total control over the Church's finances, was being challenged openly at the annual Council by the "notoriously" progressive congregation of the Kōji-machi district of Tokyo—the vanguard of Japans' "imperial democracy" movement. Their petition called for "the governance of the Church to be reformed in accordance with the contemporary enlightened condition of Japan." What this meant in more detail was enunciated in a private discussion between the parish representative Matthew Niwa and the archbishop, which starkly bared most ideological issues involved:

> Niwa: Everyone in Japan calls our Church "Nicholaevan"... because You alone govern the Church, without the participation of others.
>
> Nicholas: This is not true... in no parish do I decide anything without advance consultation with the priest, charged with oversight of that parish. And the most important affairs are decided with the participation of all Church servitors, for which we have a Council.
>
> Niwa: But it is necessary that there be a permanent cabinet at Your side, made up not only of priests, but also of laymen.

[27] Nakai (1940), 9.

Nicholas: Laymen are admitted to participation in the affairs of ecclesiastical governance when it is necessary...

Niwa: In Japan there was earlier rule by the emperor, but the emperor has yielded his power to the people. A similar thing must happen in our Church.

Nicholas: Ecclesiastical governance is based on immutable Church canons; we have no right to depart from them, otherwise we shall not be members of the Orthodox Ecumenical Church.[28]

As this exchange made clear, the vision of a participatory polity with a nominal emperor submerged in a governing cabinet faced off against the minimally institutionalized and canonically grounded Church, firmly ruled by the bishop.

The tide of imperial democracy was mounting swiftly. In July of 1909, a year after Bishop Sergius' arrival, the impending episcopal succession was greeted with a barrage of assertive demands from the representatives of the Japanese Orthodox believers at the specially convoked All-Japan Laity Confer- ence. The *leitmotif* of the conference was "independence"— of the Japanese Orthodox Church from the Russian, of the Council from the bishop, of laity from the "whims" of the clergy.[29] This independence was chiefly envisioned by its lay advocates as a matter of institutionalization—they called for instituting an ecclesiastical court, appointing special inspector priests, and forming a central administrative organ of the Church.[30]

In support of their demands, the laymen cited not only the political "advancement" of Japan, whose "nationals are already used to constitutionality and self-government"

---

[28]Nicholas (2004), vol. 5 (1904.07.13), 109; vol. 5 (1904.07.16), 111.
[29]See the agenda summarized in Yahagi (1909), 23-29 (1st pagination).
[30]Yahagi (1909), 28-29, 57-58 (1st pagination); 8 (2nd pagination).

as opposed to the "despotic autocracy" of Russia,[31] but also the long-established—and very "Russian"—institution of Consistories. Nicholas' reply, as usual, attempted to remove the discussion onto another plain—it emphasized internal independence of the Japanese Church as a diocese ruled according to the universal ancient canons, and pointed out that the tasks which would be handled by the proposed Consistory are already being debated at annual Councils.[32] The Japanese clergy responded with a sterner rebuke to the laity, stating that the Japanese Church, inasmuch as it had a Russian bishop, was a diocese of the Russian Orthodox Church, administratively an "episcopal autocracy," with the Council as merely a "consultative body" to the bishop.[33]

Yet, as the archbishop's health weakened, Nicholas' heavy-handed leadership was becoming a subject of vocalized criticism even among the clergy. As the top Japanese Orthodox clergyman, Protopriest Symeon Mii, confided his displeasure with Nicholas' "autocratic" leadership to the newly-arrived Sergius, he was transparently suggesting that the new bishop assume a more "democratic" stance.[34] Bishop Sergius' succession portended a power-sharing pact with the leading native personalities of the Japanese Church.

Nonetheless, in the end Nicholas' presence proved irre-placeable and was refigured as a permanent fixture in the fabric of the Japanese Orthodox community. His funeral rites and necrologies, pushing arguments over ecclesiastical administration into the background, began to chart Nicholas' postmortem position among his still-living pupils. In Japanese history 1912 is remembered chiefly as the end of the Meiji period, marked by the nationwide spectacle of Meiji Emperor's

[31]Yahagi (1909), 46. Note the strength of the "autocratic Russia" vs. "democratic Japan" trope. In fact, at that time both Japan and Russia were constitutional monarchies.

[32]Yahagi (1909), 9-10, 33-36 (2nd pagination).

[33]Yahagi (1909), 138-139.

[34]Seraphim (2008-2010 - № 1418), 18, citing Orthodox Messenger (1940.02.01 - № 29-2).

grand archaized funerary rites on September 13-14 and underscored by the ritual suicide of General Nogi Maresuke, who chose to follow his sovereign in the spirit of samurai loyalty.[35]

Nicholas' death on February 16 and the attendant obsequies prefaced this sequence of fatalities, contributing to the acute sense of the passing of an epoch. The following morning Japanese and Russian newspapers, including those normally hostile to the Orthodox mission, began to publish eulogistic obituaries. Nicholas' demise brought to Tokyo believers from the furthest reaches of the empire, including Korea, representing the entire "imperial Church" at the imperial capital. A wide variety of Japanese state, social and religious leaders also expressed condolences, testifying that Nicholas' network of connections was both broad and confessionally skewed in favor of Protestants, with a gaping lack of Roman Catholics. Devotees organized nightly wakes by the mentor's coffin, while Sergius, thwarted by Japanese laws from burying the body inside the Tokyo cathedral, purchased a plot adjoining the prestigious Yanaka cemetery and envisioned building a church over Nicholas' grave.

On 22 February, a magnificent interment ceremony followed. Over half-a-kilometer-long procession included most Orthodox clergy of the Japanese Empire (1 hierarch, 34 priests, 5 deacons);[36] a host of catechists and seminarians; diplomatic representatives of Russia, Great Britain, United States, France and Italy; leaders of numerous Protestant bodies; no less than three Cabinet ministers, four generals and one governor; and thousands of Orthodox and non-Orthodox well-wishers.

---

[35]For an evocative treatment of Emperor Meiji's last days and funeral, including contemporary reactions, see Keene (2002), 701-715. Compare this with the emphasis on techniques of symbolic manipulation in Fujitani (1996), 145-154.

[36]In addition to the clergy of the Japanese Orthodox Church, of whom at most three were absent, other institutions of the Russian Orthodox Church were represented by the chief of the Korean Orthodox Mission Paul (Ivanovskii) and the Russian embassy priest Peter Bulgakov.

Figure 5.1: Tokyo, February 22 1912. St. Nicholas' funeral begins as the imperial flower wreath is borne out of the cathedral grounds at the head of the procession. From Mizutani (1912), 18.

Amid a multitude of memorial wreaths, one from the Japanese emperor compelled the onlookers—who are said to have lined the streets in "hundreds of thousands"—to bow particularly low. Unlike statesmen's funerals, Japanese authorities did little to orchestrate Nicholas' obsequies, which made their scale all the more remarkable. As a Japanese newspaper noted, the scale of Nicholas' funeral compared with that of the Prime Minister Itō Hirobumi, assassinated by a Korean patriot in 1909, but then "many people were present out of obligation, whereas here were assembled tens of thousands out of heartfelt longing to say farewell."[37]

The magnitude of Nicholas' funerary rites and their conceptual pairing with the demise of the Meiji Emperor—due

[37] A detailed contemporary treatment of the funeral concludes Bishop Sergius's description of St. Nicholas' last days in Sergius (1913), 63-76. The final quote is reproduced from an overview of the funeral in Remortel & Chang (2003), 194.

both to their chronological proximity and Church-state parallelism in Orthodox thinking—shaped emergent veneration. Shortly after the deaths of the emperor and General Nogi, both men were formally apotheosized as Shintoist deities, with shrines erected to honor and invoke them and even Orthodox Japanese casually using such designations as "war-god Nogi" in ecclesiastical press.[38] While such celebration has always been a rare distinction, private veneration of ancestors' spirits remained a pervasive Japanese practice at the time, whether expressed in the Shintoist or Buddhist metaphor. Christians of all denominations in Japan were thus culturally conditioned to pray to, rather than to pray for, their departed close ones, and Nicholas' iconic status made his glorification among Japanese believers almost a given. Shortly after his repose, his photographs were being adored and the shavings of his coffin distributed like relics.

It was, however, authoritative voices from Russia which legitimized this veneration. The Most Holy Synod of the Russian Church summarily dispatched an official telegram to Bishop Sergius, invoking the "prayers of Archbishop Nicholas," who had been "translated unto the Lord."[39] Sergius himself publicly affirmed his assurance of Nicholas' holiness at the funeral, calling his predecessor "Equal-to-the-Apostles."[40] In July of 1912 he reported to the Council of the Japanese Church a weighty confirmation—a report of a miraculous healing of a certain priest Peter in the Riazan' region of Russia after an appearance to him of Archbishop Nicholas in a dream.[41] The Council decided to leave a vacant seat to symbolize the continued invisible presence of Nicholas' spirit.[42] Nicholas' formal canonization did not immediately follow, since unwritten tradition required a period of stabilization of emergent veneration, but the stage was set for a cult of "Saint

[38] Nobori (1938a), 4.
[39] Cited in Sergius (1913), 66.
[40] Sergius (1913), 76.
[41] Council (1912), 3-4.
[42] Council (1912), 1912, 5.

Nicholas of Japan" to take hold. If at the time of his funeral "Archbishop Nicolas... preached much stronger from his grave than at any time during his life... ,"[43] this was by no means his last word, albeit henceforth his voice would be projected by others. Invocation of the saintly archbishop became a mighty weapon in Japanese intra-ecclesiastical debate, his figure—a contested standard for apprehending apostolicity in what now appeared as a post-apostolic age.

Sergius (Tikhomirov) entered the Japanese scene ostensibly as Nicholas' apprentice, but was already a fully formed Orthodox bishop appointed to inherit a fully formed indigenous Church. His 37 years in Russia molded his character according to a set of enduring patterns, which structured his subsequent 37 years in Japan. Born on June 28 1871 in a notable priestly family in the village of Guzi near Novgorod, George Alekseevich Tikhomirov successfully pursued the beaten track of a hereditary Russian cleric graduating in 1886 from the Novgorod Spiritual School, in 1892 from the Novgorod Seminary, and in 1896 from the St. Petersburg Theological Academy. At this point the track forked—most chose marriage, but a few of the more pious or more careerist chose monasticism. Electing to accept tonsure, the newly-renamed monk Sergius became a hieromonk and saw a speedy elevation to the dignity of an archimandrite in 1899, and to the ultimate ecclesiastical rank of bishop on November 19 1905. This ascent was not only uncommonly quick, but all the more stellar for occurring in the imperial capital. Here the young Sergius taught and administered at St. Petersburg's elite ecclesiastical schools, renowned for high academic standards and liberality. One of the decisive factors had been the young monastic's favor with the tsar's own confessor-priest, whose high evaluation ensured Sergius'

[43] Sergius (1913), 76.

episcopacy.[44] As bishop he was styled the Vicar of Iamburg, but in fact headed the St. Petersburg Theological Academy as its rector, remaining close to court, at the epicenter of the empire's turbulent life. Suddenly, in 1908, came the appointment to Japan.[45]

Despite the gradual rise in the prestige of missions, the Russian clergy of the pre-revolutionary period often saw a missionary dispatch to a foreign land as exile.[46] In any case, a transfer away from a high-profile post in St. Petersburg was a very ambiguous promotion. Besides, not only the achievements, but also the demands of Nicholas of Japan had become legendary in Russian ecclesiastical circless, as one after another his prospective successors returned home with stories of his possessiveness.[47] Therefore, unless he harbored a hidden desire to devote his life to mission, Sergius' appointment signified a fall from favor.

As for Sergius' inclinations, they do not seem to have included evangelizing unbelievers, let alone migrating abroad to do so. His deep attachment not only to Russia, but specifically to his native Novgorod region, is apparent in his numerous academic theses, dealing largely with the administrative minutia of Novgorodian ecclesiastical history of the 15th-16th centuries.[48] Sergius the linguist mastered Greek, Latin, Ancient Hebrew, English, French and German and

[44]Koike (n/d), 19-20 citing Orthodox Messenger (1961.10.10 - № 863). Ushimaru's claim that Sergius himself emerged as the tsar's confessor is highly improbable. Ushimaru (1978b), 115.

[45]The best overviews of Sergius' Russian years remain those by Ushimaru (1978b), 113-114; (1985), 2-7, mostly culled from Consistory (1933), 1-10. Sergius' official *curriculum vita* for the first half of his life is preserved in РГИА, ф. 756, оп. 189 (1908 г.), д. 8043, л. 8, and has been verified by Naganawa Mitsuo. See Naganawa (1995), 410-411, 428.

[46]For a symptomatic contemporary example, consider the unwilling head of the Korean Orthodox Mission in 1912-1914, Irenarchus (Shemanovskii), who dreamed of imminent recall home. Theodosius ([1926] 1999), 251-256.

[47]Iwasawa (1938), 10; Seryshev (1952-1968), 35-36.

[48]Besides his Candidate's dissertation, these included the individually published works like Sergius (1905a, 1905b, 1907).

showed an aptitude for critical Biblical scholarship, but was probably most inclined to moral theology, remaining deeply concerned with the socio-political course of contemporary Russia. He had come to like sermonizing to common people and organized preaching tours in Novgorodian villages as well as St. Petersburg factories and hostels already as a student.[49] Having come of age under the patronage of Metropolitan Anthony (Vadkovskii)—known for his liberal views, protection of radicals, outreach to the urbanites, and a studiedly calm demeanor—Sergius sought to imitate many qualities of his mentor.[50] Thus, Anthony's inspiration might be read into Sergius' extensive preaching at St. Petersburg factories in the wake and during the 1905 Revolution.[51] The young bishop supported the contemporary effort, spearheaded by Anthony, to overturn secular domination of ecclesiastical administration and restore autonomy to Church governance. The repeated refusal of Emperor Nicholas II to initiate such reform was seen by Sergius in terms uncommonly bitter for a hierarch—as a symbol of the regime which perpetuated the captivity of the Church.[52] Through this lens Sergius idealized his Novgorodian predecessors as representatives of Russia's medieval tradition of righteous disobedience to oppressive authorities.[53] Despite a Synodal interdict, in March of 1906 Sergius celebrated a memorial for the recently executed

[49] Saikaishi (1931b), 10.

[50] The contemporary official ecclesiastical profile of Metropolitan Anthony minimizes the "liberal" label—see Orthodox Encyclopedia (2000-), vol. 2, 621-623. A useful counter-narrative, which details the liberal reform movement with Anthony as the central figure, is Cunningham (1981).

[51] In addition to numerous individually issued sermon collections since at least 1902, Sergius' sermons and articles were published in the organ of the St. Petersburg Theological Academy, *Christian Reading (Khristianskoe chtenie)*; the official Synodal *Church Messenger (Tserkovnyi vestnik)*; and the St. Petersburg diocesan *St. Petersburg Church Messenger (Sankt-Peterburgskii tserkovnyi vestnik)*. See Consistory (1933), 7-9. For a partial bibliography see Manuel (1979-1989), vol. 6, 192-193.

[52] Sergius would harbor and restate this disappointment for decades, as seen in Sergius (1931b), 5-9, 29-30; Leontius (1946b), 60.

[53] Cited in Leontius (1946b), 60.

Lieutenant Peter Schmidt, a rebel who symbolized the pathos of Russia's 1905 Revolution. Although Sergius is said to have been "compelled" to conduct the memorial service by the revolutionary-minded St. Petersburg seminarians,[54] there was no doubt a measure of conscious protest in his defiance of the polity.

By his alignment with Metropolitan Anthony of St. Petersburg, the direction of his criticism of the state, and above all by the widely discussed memorial service for Schmidt, Bishop Sergius unequivocally placed himself on the political left at the time when revolution exacerbated tensions polarizing the Russian society and Church. Opponents from the right, campaigning for the removal of leftists from key ecclesiastical posts, included him on the black list. Influentially, the founder of the militant Union of the Russian People, Alexander Dubrovin, in his open letter to Metropolitan Anthony pointed to the continued activity of the two vicars of the St. Petersburg diocese, Antoninus (Granovskii) and Sergius (Tikhomirov), as proof of Anthony's favoritism toward revolutionaries:

> Patriots have been chased out [of ecclesiastical leadership posts - INK], but Antoninus is there, Sergius, who served for the plotters a sacrilegious memorial service for the rebel Schmidt, is there, and You defended him, even when a theft of money was discovered in his academy, You supplied this money.[55]

Indeed, Metropolitan Anthony exerted many efforts to cover Bishop Antoninus, arguably the most learned, but also the most openly revolutionary hierarch of the Russian Church at the time.[56] Sergius also benefited from his mentor's

---

[54]Bogdanovich (1990), 376.

[55]Dubrovin (1906).

[56]In the wake of the 1917 revolution Antoninus went on to head, with the backing of antireligious state authorities, the radical schismatic "Renovationist" movement in the Russian Orthodox Church. For his general profile see Orthodox Encyclopedia (2000-), vol. 2, 682-684.

patronage, and for some time his milder liberalism and bad bookkeeping at the St. Petersburg Academy did not catch up to him. However, the gradual purge of free-thinkers from theological academies, seen as radically leftist and secularized, incrementally increased the pressure on Anthony to let go of his "revolutionary vicars". In the case of Bishop Sergius, there were also mounting issues of outstanding personal debts and financial malfeasance at the academy. In the beginning of 1908 Antoninus went into retirement "for health reasons," while in March Metropolitan Anthony sent a telegram to Archbishop Nicholas of Japan to the effect that Sergius was "zealously requesting permission" to join the Japanese Mission. On Nicholas' acceptance, appointment was formalized, with Sergius becoming Vicar of Kyoto on April 3.[57]

To be sure, this "banishment" had positive aspects, which might have inclined Sergius to volunteer. His position in St. Petersburg ever more precarious, he had reasons to expect a demotion at any time. Meanwhile, Nicholas was already in his 70's and his successor would soon stand alone at the helm of a Church that was free from those "many sins"[58]— primarily, the subservience to the state—which so distressed Sergius in his contemporary Russian Orthodox Church. The peculiarity of the Japanese Orthodox Church and its course toward independence was well understood in Russia, as Sergius was sent off to be "the last Russian bishop in Japan," proleptically tasked by Metropolitan Anthony and others to "prepare a successor from among the Japanese."[59] With this degree of operational freedom, Sergius could look forward to shaping the Church according to his ideas, and seems to have embraced the new task with enthusiasm.

On arrival to Tokyo on June 27 1908, he vowed before Nicholas to devote his life to mission in Japan[60] and threw

---

[57] Diaries (2004), vol. 5 (1908.03.17), 365; Ushimaru (1985), 13.
[58] Sergius (1931b), 5.
[59] Council (1931), 50; Heavenly Bread (1941 - № 2), 38.
[60] Nakai (1913), 58.

himself at pastoral travel and language-study. Initially Sergius was assisted by Protopriest Symeon Mii as his interpreter, but in a year's time the new bishop of Kyoto was able to journey, converse and even preach to a general Japanese public unaided.[61] Incessant peregrinations during his first four years in Japan from one Orthodox household to another throughout the Japanese Empire took the new bishop to well over 300 locations and personally introduced him to most members of his flock,[62] while the remaining time was devoted to issues of central governance in Tokyo at the side of Archbishop Nicholas.

Nicholas penned glowing reports about his vicar to the Most Holy Synod, praising Sergius' quick progress with the language, apparent zeal for preaching and firmness in faith.[63] While the archbishop's personal notes and correspondence reveal his misgivings about Sergius' excessive "open-heartedness" with money, Nicholas' overall assessment of his successor was optimistic.[64] Although the archbishop was extensively forewarned by well-wishers and personally witnessed the extent of Sergius' accumulated debts,[65] Nicholas became convinced of his vicar's honesty. The the archbishop

[61] Sergius is recorded as delivering a sermon in Japanese before a 300-strong audience already on September 11, 1909. Consistory (1933), 103.

[62] Most of Sergius' time in 1908-1911 was spent in travel. In addition to pastoral journeys meticulously chronicled in Consistory (1933), 87-144, Sergius also visited Korea in 1909, for which see Theodosius ([1926] 1999), 301-302. The only major regions of the Japanese Empire Sergius neglected to visit were its southern reaches beyond Kyushu.

[63] For the pertinent part of his 1909 report see Orthodox Evangelist (1910.01 - № 1-2), 52-53.

[64] Nicholas' diaries show his initially gloomy expectations for Sergius changing to increasingly positive assessments. However, the Archbishop's belief that Sergius was unfit to manage money did not alter. See Nicholas (2004), vol. 5 (1908.06.28), 399; vol. 5 (1908.09.10), 433; vol. 5 (1908.11.15), 459-460; vol. 5 (1909.01.13), 482-483. See also the letter from Nicholas to Protopriest Alexis Petrovich Mal'tsev introduced in Naganawa (1995), 417-418. The original is in РГИА, ф. 834, оп. 4, ед. хр. 1206, л. 2-3.

[65] For instance, in early November 1908 the Most Holy Synod billed Sergius for 4772 rubles of outstanding personal debt. As late as December of 1910, Sergius was using up half of his monthly allowance to pay off old Russian

would present Sergius as a selfless laborer, who had sacrificed a stellar career in Russia for the sake of service to Japan.[66] Contrast of character between the Russian hierarchs in Japan did not preordain conflict—in fact, the two sometimes effectively used the "bad cop-good cop" approach in governing the Church.[67]

Yet, among the differences in sentiment between Nicholas and Sergius, there was one which deeply disturbed the old missionary. Nicholas had never lost love for his homeland, but repeatedly exhorted himself in his diaries to devote unreservedly his entire being to Japan.[68] Meanwhile, Sergius' attachment to Russia was apparent—during his early years in Japan he continued to publish extensively in the Russian religious press, revealing a mixture of fresh enthusiasm for Japan and nostalgia for Russia.[69] In 1909-1911 Sergius lavished a great deal of attention on the isolated "Japanese Russia," the recently annexed South Sakhalin with its remainders of Russian population—he came here more often than to any other region of Japan and penned extensive plaintive accounts on the situation in the Russian papers.[70] Archbishop Nicholas occasionally even decried what he saw as Sergius' attempts at "Russification" of the Japanese Church, as in their argument over the proposed iconography of the Tokyo Resurrection

debts. On these issues and Nicholas' evaluation of them see Nicholas (2004), vol. 5 (1908.04.30), 379; vol. 5 (1908.05.09), 385; vol. 5 (1908.11.07), 457; vol. 5 (1908.11.15), 459; vol. 5 (1910.12.04), 709.

[66] For instance see Yahagi (1909), 37 (2nd pagination).

[67] Witness the sequence of a harsh rebuke by Nicholas and the soft persuasion by Sergius in ensuring the continued allegiance of three catechists. Nicholas (2004), vol. 5 (1910.07.03), 665.

[68] Nicholas particularly exerted himself at this during his earlier years in Japan, as seen in Nicholas (2004), vol. 1 (1879.09.28), 96-97; vol. 1 (1879.09.29), 98-99; vol. 1 (1880.01.12), 135.

[69] See the cycle of articles about his first pastoral journey in Sergius (1908-1909).

[70] Sergius' extensive writings on his three trips to South Sakhalin were initially published in the secular *Moscow Inquirer* (*Moskovskie vedomosti*), but in 1914 reissued in the *Orthodox Evangelist* as well as in book form as Sergius (1914).

cathedral. Sergius opined that the cathedral's walls should be frescoed with images of Russian saints like Sts. Vladimir, Olga, Boris and Gleb, illustrating Japanese Church's Russian lineage. The archbishop cut him off, exclaiming that "one could hardly imagine a dimmer future" for Japanese Orthodoxy, which should hearken to the memory of "ancient Christian saints, common to the entire undivided Church," rather than specifically "our Russian ones."[71] Attempting to instill in his vicar his own attitude, Nicholas instructed that "no matter how attractive an office should appear in Russia, pray to the Lord God that even for the sake of that office you should never depart Japan," "become dead to work in the home country and think only of the Japanese Church."[72] Yet, although Sergius may have convinced Nicholas of his resolution to be "faithful (to Japan) even unto the grave,"[73] it is not clear whether he convinced himself—around 1918 he would privately confess that an imitation of Nicholas' apostolic feat "was not for me."[74]

Although the public presentation of the new bishop to the Japanese believers could not be anything but that of a missionary preacher, Sergius projected a markedly different persona from the rough and charismatic St. Nicholas. By comparison, he struck the Japanese as polished and beautiful, learned and thoughtful. Sergius' "magnificent elegance, complete with his graceful hairstyle," recalled to the man who would go on to become the leading Japanese Orthodox choirmaster "an angel of God" when the bishop celebrated the liturgy in Toyohashi on February 27 1913.[75] Even the

[71]Cited in Leontius (1946b), 59. Cf. Nicholas' omission of the service to St. Alexander Nevsky from the *Festal Menaion* collection of prayers because "it is too particularly related to Russians." Nicholas (2004), vol. 5 (1910.02.16), 623.

[72]The first quote is from Nicholas' autobiographical letter of exhortation to Sergius dated March 12 1909, published in Nicholas (1913), 4; the second—from Nicholas' instruction to his successor on February 8 1912, a week before his death, recorded in Consistory (1936), 86.

[73]Nicholas (2004), vol. 5 (1911.09.24), 796.

[74]Cited in Leontius (1946b), 60.

[75]Katō (1985), 1.

less aesthetically inclined Japanese remarked Sergius' flowing pronunciation and eloquence in both Japanese and Russian, his elegant Russian writing style, his thought-out sermons, his graceful conduct of services.[76] He apparently lacked Nicholas' fervor in explicating doctrine, but lavished attention on ritual.[77] The new bishop had a keen sense for soulful church singing and for a mystical aura of the church's interior, personally tuning the main Tokyo Orthodox choir and ensuring that the central Japanese cathedral was devoid of electrical lighting—"because the soul loves to pray in the half-light of vigil-lamps, and sing hymns with a waxen candle in hand."[78] This professor from St. Petersburg was no obscurantist, but his favored tools for building up Church life were theological philosophy, aesthetic appeal and moral exhortation, as opposed to Nicholas' emphasis on precise dogmatic instruction and restless mission. Together with his liberal inclinations, his attachment to Russia, his lack of financial acumen, the brevity of his Japanese experience and the brewing Japanese discontent over ecclesiastical governance, Sergius' personality played a significant part in the major reconfiguration of organizational forms and internal relations of the Japanese Orthodox Church upon his accession to primacy.

[76]Takeoka (1989) 28-29; Mochizuki (1930), 33.
[77]Katō (1947).
[78]Sergius (1930), 15.

Chapter 6

Constitutional episcopacy

At the first Council after Nicholas' demise, in July 1912, Sergius unveiled an array of innovations. Although ostensibly emanating from the ruling hierarch, they were reflective not only of his own inclinations and realizations, but also of the interests of chief Japanese actors behind the scenes, which had been voiced for years. The Japanese Church was now to have such positions as inspector priest, dean of the cathedral, confessor priests, as well as a standing Conference with extensive administrative, judicial and financial powers. These and other ecclesiastical servitors were provided with written codes of conduct, specifying their obligations, qualifications and rights. Annual written reports with up-to-date numbers of active parishioners were also made a requirement.[1] This amounted to a major structural "Russification," transplanting to Japan the bureaucratic forms of Russian diocesan and seminary governance with which Bishop Sergius was familiar. It was likewise a major managerial "Japanization," inasmuch

[1]Council (1912), 7, 9-11, 44-45, 137-164.

as newly-instituted posts would be staffed by Japanese, to whom passed most of the routine governance of the Church. Thirdly, it was a "politization" of the Church, with rigid legal codes and institutional structures replacing the demanding flexibility of personal mentorship and oversight by the bishop.

Above all, this was a massive delegation of episcopal prerogatives previously held by Nicholas. Keeping an eye on clergy and parishes was henceforth the task of the inspector priest, managing the extensive possessions of the Tokyo cathedral compound would be done by the cathedral dean, hearing clerics' confessions and providing spiritual guidance to them was up to clerics themselves, managing most other ecclesiastical administrative affairs lay in the purview of the Conference. Sergius was freeing up his time for favored pursuits and removing much responsibility from his shoulders. While he would present himself as "sowing the seeds of democracy,"[2] Sergius' actions in fact engendered an oligarchy—the Japanese ecclesiastical elite was invited to form a leadership milieu of professional managers to run the Church. An anonymous article in the November 1912 Japanese official *Orthodox Messenger* lauded ecclesiastical institutionalization and staked out for the newly-created Conference a sphere of action beyond that of a Russian diocesan Consistory. With its telling proviso that this office was "not, initially, an alter-ego of episcopal power," the article appeared to hint at a subsequent development of just such an alter-ego.[3] The shaping of the limited— "constitutional"—episcopacy, to complement contemporary constitutional monarchy, was in the offing.

However, for the time being the bishop was neither willing nor compelled to relinquish his power altogether. As Japan's sole hierarch, Sergius was capable of intervention into any matter, his seal was required to make any directive

[2] Seraphim (2008-2010 - № 1418), 18, citing Orthodox Messenger (1940.02.01 - № 29-2).

[3] Ihaho (1912), 18-19.

operational, and he retained personal oversight over his favored field of academic policy and the all-important sphere of external relations. The latter meant that he alone decided how to spend annual disbursements from Russia, which accounted for over 90% of the Church's proceeds. In this way, until the 1917 Russian Revolution, Bishop Sergius occupied a removed yet unassailable position, from which he could choose projects to engage. In addition to initial institutionalization and a series of symbolic changes, called upon to signify the coming of a new age for the Japanese Church,[4] he summarily conducted a large-scale personnel reshuffle, bringing administratively-gifted clerics to key posts in Tokyo, while sending to obscure small parishes some of the less refined and even-tempered clerics, once patiently tutored by Nicholas.[5] Nicholas' cherished translation projects of liturgical and Scriptural texts halted, the Church's Translation bureau was abolished.[6] Instead, Sergius inaugurated a philosophical-theological magazine *Trends of Orthodox Thought* (*Seikyō Shichō*) which purveyed translations of Russia's Silver Age thinkers "to educate Japanese priests and catechists with the best fruits of Russia's Orthodox theological and philosophical thought."[7]

The bishop's care for raising the educational level of his flock is evident in such contemporary measures as restructuring the courses at the seminary, requiring libraries at each church, guaranteeing free seminary education for children of church servitors, and opening a new catechist

[4]Two of these were the alteration of the name of Church's official organ from *Orthodox News* to *Orthodox Messenger* (*Seikyō Jihō*) and the shift of the date for annual Church Councils.

[5]In addition to the differences in character and a desire to form a new team in place of "Nicholas' men," remarked by Kaneishi (1993), 180, and Naganawa (1995), 414, one must point out to the chronic difficulties both of the "banished" Frs. Sergius Kyūhachi and Basil Usui had in getting along with their parishioners, reflected in Nicholas (2004), vol. 5 (1908.02.23), 360; vol. 5 (1911.08.16), 786.

[6]Orthodox Messenger (1912.11.10 - №1-1), unnumbered (55).

[7]Orthodox Evangelist (1914.03 - №1-3), 183.

school in Osaka.[8] Sergius continued to write and publish extensively, both in the moralizing and narrative styles, but especially for a scholarly audience—and did so mostly in Russian, ordering from Moscow archives expensive copies of historical materials on the local administration of 15th-17th century Northwest Russia.[9] A missionary by obligation, the new Japanese hierarch faithfully toured Japan with pastoral visitations and exhortatory sermons, but found it congenial to also continue along the course of a learned Russian theologian.

For the time being open criticism of the ruling hierarch remained mostly a fringe reaction of discontented ex-seminarian "outlaws" in tabloid press, fueled chiefly by personal disagreements with other ecclesiastical notables, much like in the days of Nicholas.[10] However, the emergent dialogue about ideal episcopacy was shaped by the way in which Nicholas was being remembered. While Sergius cultivated his Russian links, the official Japanese Orthodox press recalled the exclusive devotion to Japanese mission which characterized the late archbishop, who turned down both scholarly work and superior posts in Russia as temptations in the way of his singular purpose.[11] In what was likely Sergius' alternative vision of episcopal ideal, the Japanese *Orthodox Messenger* then printed an extended necrology of Metropolitan Anthony of St. Petersburg, where the latter was praised chiefly as a professor, pastor, ecumenical figure and scholar.[12] Muted tension between perspectives on apostolicity may

---

[8]Council (1912), 70, 156, 163; Orthodox Messenger (1947.08.15 - № "765"), 2; Ushimaru (1985), 19.

[9]Sergius (1930), 8.

[10]Sergius was criticized in the short-lived *New Orthodoxy* (*Shin Seikyō*) in 1913 by Aquila Kajima Akira, similar to the way Paul Yamada Toyohiko and others vented at Nicholas in late Meiji years. For an overview of Kajima's publication see Naganawa (1995), 415-416. For similar activities of one Paul Yamada in Nicholas' day see Nicholas (2004), vol. 5 (1908.11.21), 461; vol. 5 (1909.02.24), 498; vol. 5 (1909.03.02), 500; vol. 5 (1909.04.22), 516.

[11]Iwasawa (1912); Orthodox Messenger (1916.01.20 - №5-2), 19.

[12]Orthodox Messenger (1912.12.05 - №1-3), 41-44.

have yielded creative dialogue, but revolutionary events soon worked yet another redefinition of episcopal authority.

Since Nicholas never trusted his vicar with funds, Sergius had only begun to make sense of the Church's finances from 1912.[13] As he carried out his early expensive initiatives, the Russian financial basis of the Japanese Church began to totter, especially after the outbreak of World War I. Meanwhile, the Japanese Church had barely begun to introduce financial self-support in a handful of parishes in the last years of Nicholas' episcopacy.[14] Sergius' brainchild—arcane even for the more educated Japanese Orthodox, who dubbed it an "artwork"—the journal *Trends of Orthodox Thought* predictably folded already in March 1915, one of the first victims of the wartime shortage of funds.[15] Yet, as late as in July 1917, during the "liberal" phase of the 1917 Russian Revolution which had been welcomed in the Japanese Church just as among the overwhelming majority of Russia's hierarchs and diocesan assemblies, the annual Council was merely projecting a survey for the Japanese Church's financial self-sufficiency.[16]   A rude awakening came later that year, as Bolsheviks seized power in St. Petersburg, the Russian Missionary Society dissolved, and for the first time in Japanese Church's history the annual grant from Russia did not come.[17] The chief prop of episcopal authority was thus removed in one fell swoop, and the Japanese administrative elite began to finalize the arrangements for a disempowered episcopacy.

At the next annual Council in July 1918, the assembled delegates began to reform ecclesiastical structures beyond

[13]Council (1912), 75-76.

[14]Nicholas (2004), vol. 5 (1910.09.13), 685; vol. 5 (1910.10.15), 694.

[15]Orthodox Messenger (1915.03.05 - №4-5), 40; (1947.08.15 - № "765"), 2. For a brief exposition on this journal see Naganawa (1995), 414-415.

[16]Council (1917), 73-76. On the overwhelmingly positive reaction of Russia's ecclesiastical elite and governing structures to the early phase of the 1917 Revolution see Babkin (2006).

[17]On the swift folding of the Missionary Society see Michaelson (1999), 354-355.

Sergius' comfort zone. New administrative departments—Educational and Financial—were formed to further "relieve" the bishop of his tasks, a committee of Japanese clergy began to play the part of a ruler by charging their supposedly "ruling" bishop with fundraising trips among Russians, and another committee was tasked with selecting new clerics. Bishop Sergius had to defend what he saw as proper procedure by insisting that fundraising be done primarily among Japanese believers, and that clergy be elected only at annual Councils, with his own participation. Sergius' appeal to the idea of "Japanese independence" and to the time-honored conciliar authority proved convincing, and the Japanese clergy decided that the best way to ensure the generosity of Japanese faithful would be to call upon the already-revered name of the saintly archbishop, inaugurating a "Nicholas memorial fundraising campaign."[18] Thus, as new organs of ecclesiastical governance edged out the current bishop, his idealized predecessor was evoked with renewed emphasis—much like how the image of the deceased Emperor Meiji towered over his sickly "reigning" son.

Sergius obeyed the conciliar directive and turned to fundraising among Russians—his plaintive missives to the provisional government in Omsk and to the Russian archbishop in New York, but especially his March 1919 trip to the Russian Maritime Region and Northern Manchuria, which brought in 151,060 rubles from Russians and 4400 rubles from expatriate Japanese, helped the Japanese Church avoid imminent bankruptcy.[19] However, this last burst of Russian generosity did not safeguard the bishop's position, but impelled the reassured Japanese believers to proceed with the reordering of their Church. Soon after Sergius' return, the 1919 Council passed the *Constitution of the Japanese Christian Orthodox Church*, which formalized the bishop's subjection to

---

[18]Council (1918), 42-45, 67, 78-79.

[19]The March 1919 trip is detailed in Senuma (1919) and Sergius (1919a). On Sergius' relations with Omsk and New York at that time see Seryshev (1952-1968), 49-50, 58.

the said Constitution, to the Church Council, and to the newly-instituted Consistory. The termination of the Tokyo Women's Seminary around September of that year and a sharp decrease in the volume and print quality of the *Orthodox Messenger* from November signified that even Sergius' favored fields of education and mass-media passed out of his hands.[20] This was the fulfillment of a fifteen-year-old trend of "imperial democracy," an implicit declaration of independence of the Japanese Orthodox Church.

Having thus become a limited, "constitutional," bishop, Sergius was not thereby ousted from formal primacy, nor did he suddenly become irrelevant to the mainstream of Japanese Church's life. At the very least, since the resumption of monetary help from Russia was still faintly imaginable in 1919, he served as "a doorplate for receiving money from over there... necessary because a name on the doorplate is necessary."[21] Additionally, his cooperation and expertise was sought out on daunting issues, and when he tapped into extra-systemic ways to engage the Church, he could reemerge as a popular leader.

The latter occurred as he took charge of the restoration campaign in the wake of the 1923 Great Kantō Earthquake. The calamity, which ravaged the Tokyo metropolitan area, destroyed the material infrastructure of the Japanese Church's headquarters—the vast library, most subsidiary buildings which housed schools and offices, and the grand cathedral became burned-out ruins. Overcoming the trauma of loss and the skepticism vocalized in the "no Russia—no cathedral" formula of the detractors,[22] Sergius mustered the resolve for restoration. At the extraordinary Council called to deal with this emergency, his uncommonly forceful and visionary speech inspired the assembly to rebuild the cathedral "not with foreign, but with Japanese strength," and reinvigorate

[20]Orthodox Messenger (1919.10.15 - № 8-12), 17; (1919.11.15 - № 8-13), 1.
[21]Sergius (1919b), 21.
[22]Sergius (1930), 9.

143

the flagging vitality of the Church in a nationwide revival campaign.[23]

The hierarch spearheaded the daunting fundraising effort, spending much of the remaining 1920's visiting believers from house to house throughout the Empire.[24] His ability to inspire sacrificial generosity outdid the expectations of experienced Japanese clerics. In one instance, overriding the warnings of the priests—who predicted in late 1928 that exhausted parishes needed a 2-3 year break to regain funds—the bishop gathered ¥57,000 of donations in the course of 1929.[25]

Figure 6.1: Cards commemorating the restoration of the Tokyo Resurrection cathedral. From Osaka Orthodox church collection.

Sergius likewise used his global connections to gain assistance from abroad.

The consecration of the restored cathedral on December 15 1929 became a triumph of the Japanese Orthodox Church with Sergius prominently at its head. A pair of commemorative prints for the event showed just how high Sergius' prestige rose by favorably juxtaposing him with Nicholas. The old archbishop was depicted overlooking a photo of the old cathedral and a silhouette of its ruins, while the new one (in the meantime Sergius too became an archbishop) calmly gazed at the

[23] See Sergius' speech in Council Provisional (1923), 5-14

[24] In these journeys Sergius visited some 2700 households, omitting only three locations where Japanese Orthodox believers were known to reside in noticeable numbers—the islands of Taiwan and Shikotan, as well as Suka in Chiba Prefecture. For a day-by-day chronicle of these travels see Consistory (1933), 145-201.

[25] Sergius (1935b).

freshly rebuilt edifice. Sergius personally reconnected with most Japanese faithful and led them in creating a new symbol of self-reliance in what figured as an epochal venture in all subsequent treatments of the Japanese Orthodox Church.[26] This ushered in a "honeymoon" between the bishop and his flock, still evident in the 1931 festivities to mark Sergius' elevation to the dignity of metropolitan and in the 1933 celebration of the quarter-century anniversary since his arrival in Japan.[27]

A positive comparison of Sergius with Nicholas, possible at the peak of this "honeymoon," was an exceptional event, since the Japanese Orthodox discourse—bolstered by the persistent popular Japanese label of "Nicholaevan Orthodoxy" (even the police used this designation, as differentiated from "Christianity")[28]—left no doubt as to Nicholas' avowed centrality to corporate identity. The initial effusion of postmortem praise for the late archbishop was epitomized in the thick issue of the *Orthodox Messenger* which commemorated the first anniversary of Nicholas' demise with laudatory articles both by leading Orthodox figures and by other national luminaries, the likes of statesmen Ōkuma Shigenobu and Gotō Shimpei, together with the leading Protestant thinker Uchimura Kanzō.[29] There was only one foreign voice in this Japanese chorus, and it did not belong to Bishop Sergius, whose appraisals of

[26]The centrality of the cathedral restoration campaign to the life of the Japanese Orthodox Church in 1923-1929 ensured its extensive documentation and publicity. Most of the local reportage in the contemporary editions of the Church's official organ, *Orthodox Messenger*, dealt with the rebuilding effort. Bishop Sergius himself wrote a highly readable, if selective, contemporary brochure on the subject—Sergius (1930). Of the subsequent treatments, one which best combines a scholarly vantage-point and thoroughness is Naganawa (2001).

[27]For much detail on these celebrations refer especially to Orthodox Messenger (1931.05.20 - № 20-5); (1933.07.20 - № 22-7) and to the commemorative booklet—Consistory (1933).

[28]Maruyama (1930).

[29]Orthodox Messenger (1913.02.10 - № 2-4).

Nicholas vacillated dramatically.[30]   Veneration of Nicholas was therefore largely carried out by Japanese believers, at times despite, or even at the expense of their ruling bishop.

Nor were the united efforts of Japanese ecclesiastical administrators always able to steer this veneration in their desired direction.   For instance, when in 1928-1930 the governing elite of the Church attempted to reform distinctive Orthodox terminology in line with the usage of other Christian denominations in Japan, successful defense by provincial champions of Nicholas' "perfect and flawless" translation showed that the saint's appeal could mobilize sufficient popular support to upset unwanted impositions from Tokyo.[31] Veneration for their founder was manifested in the erection of a monument over Nicholas' grave[32] and insertion of his commemoration into the annual cycle of Church services.[33] The 1936 Council initiated an array of undertakings to mark the centennial of Nicholas' birth—a memorial bronze statue, missionary fund, library, museum, and clergy retirement home were in the works.[34]   That year also marked the compilation of Nicholas' official *Life*, a project announced already in 1912, when it was decided to use this text as a

[30]The non-Japanese voice was that of the famous Russian missionary, St. John Vostorgov. For the 1922 lecture, the most strident known example of Sergius' criticism of Nicholas see Seryshev (1952-1968), 31-37. Sergius' call for Nicholas' formal canonization was made during his sermon on February 16 1938 and was reproduced in Orthodox Messenger (1938.03.01 - № 27-3), 5.

[31]A rare case of local opposition trumping Tokyo centralism at the national level, the affair was glossed over by the official *Orthodox Messenger*, but amply treated by the Japanese Church's leading unofficial periodical of the time—the Nagoya-based *Yeast (Pandane)*. See the overview in Itō (2010), 25. Cf. Orthodox Messenger (1928.08.10 - № 17-8), 20.

[32]For its description and appeal for donations see Orthodox Messenger (1923.01.15 - № 12-1), insert.

[33]Memorials on February 16 were served and reported starting from the first anniversary in 1913.   By at least 1928 they were inscribed into the routine reports in the fashion of other celebrations of the ecclesiastical year. Orthodox Messenger (1913.03.05 - № 2-5), 34; (1928.03.10 - № 17-3), 26.

[34]Orthodox Messenger (1936.08.01 - № 25-8), 25.

catechetical aid.[35] Usually described as "great," "larger-than-life," and an "apostle," throughout the years in question Nicholas was the subject of numerous articles in the Japanese *Orthodox Messenger*.[36] Although their official press organ provided Japanese believers with plentiful reportage on the activities of their current hierarch and cursory notes on senior Orthodox figures worldwide, only a handful of bishops were accorded treatment in narrative articles—these were ancient saints, a few outstanding Russian hierarchs,[37] but above all Nicholas. Not only did he figure as the "father" of the Japanese Church, but the Japanese Church appeared as his "avatar" (*keshin*).[38] To criticize Nicholas' endeavor, as had been done in the *Orthodox Messenger* during the crisis of 1919, meant to criticize the entire Japanese Orthodox Church—in the event, to call it "a malformed child."[39]

There was, however, one aspect of Nicholas' activity and character which remained divisive, with many high-placed voices openly celebrating the fact that it has been relegated to the past—strong episcopal authority. In the unique issue of the *Orthodox Messenger* devoted to celebrating Sergius—the July 1933 edition in honor of his 25 years in Japan—the lead article by the paper's leftist main editor Basil Nobori praised the successor for abandoning the saint's "dictatorial Church administration" and replacing it with the "institutions of autonomy" like the Constitution and the Consistory.[40] A liberal churchman of Russia's revolutionary generation, Sergius himself eagerly contrasted his own "democracy"

[35]Consistory (1936). For the early plan of the *Life* see Orthodox Messenger (1913.01.05 - № 2-1), 31-32.
[36]Leaving aside dozens of individual articles, more concentrated in the February issues of the *Orthodox Messenger*, particular mention may be made of special commemorative issues dealing primarily with St. Nicholas: Orthodox Messenger (1913.02.10 - № 2-4); (1936.08.01 - №25-8); (1938.02.01 - № 27-2).
[37]Especially the subsequently canonized Moscow hierarchs Philaret (Drozdov) and Tikhon (Bellavin). See on them Mii (1925); Mii (1931); Iwasawa (1925).
[38]Expression from Yoshimura (1938), 19.
[39]Mokushi-sei (1919), 16.
[40]Nobori (1933), 1.

with Nicholas' "autocracy," affirming that, in ecclesiastical matters, "there is freedom and democracy for all of us."[41] Inasmuch as he had agency, he may have viewed this empowerment of the Japanese as leading up to the elevation of a native successor-bishop,[42] but many key Japanese figures were eager for liberation from the "despotic" power of bishops as such. A common identification between Russia and despotism meant that when Sergius was seen to be neglecting proper "consultation" with the Consistory and the Council, he might be faulted for "Russian-style behavior," which needed to give way to the Japanese cooperative ways of "pure Orthodoxy."[43]

Meanwhile, dissatisfaction with Sergius on the part of right-leaning elements, who throughout the 1930's criticized his "unpraiseworthy" and "fast-changing" character, "private attitude toward life," but above all his sympathy for a socialist Russia, robbed the incumbent bishop of influential advocates.[44]   Thus, the conservative Professor Arsenius Iwasawa symptomatically combined opposition to Sergius, vocal support for a speedy election of a Japanese native to epis-copacy, and defense for what even he admitted was Nicholas' "high-handed despotism." Arguing from the vantage point of his extensive Russian experience and theological education, in 1938 Iwasawa voiced the conviction that the very nature of "episcopal authority renders one into a despot."[45] Herein lay the dilemma of apostolicity in the Japanese Orthodox context, as the autocratic model of episcopacy, established by the canons and the example of their revered founder, had been all but rejected by the native leaders of the Japanese

[41]Council (1919), 26-27; Seraphim (2008-2010 - № 1418), 18, citing Orthodox Messenger (1940.02.01 - № 29-2).

[42]Such was Sergius' explanation in 1940, reported in Heavenly Bread (1941 - № 2), 38.

[43]Council (1930), 105.

[44]For various expressions of dissatisfaction with Sergius see the 1931 wave of anti-Soviet criticisms summarized in Seraphim (2008-2010 - № 1425), 16-19; as well as later statements in Iwasawa (1941); Manabe (1996), 6.

[45]Iwasawa (1938), 10.

Church. This rendered the cathedral restoration campaign all the more notable as an exceptional manifestation of episcopal leadership during Sergius' tenure.

As the Japanese Orthodox managerial elite assumed core tasks of ecclesiastical governance, only external relations remained a sphere of Sergius' routine responsibility. This bespoke both the disinterest of Japanese clergy, as well as the bishop's expertise and desire for dealing with non-Japanese agents. The 1917 Russian Revolution transformed Sergius' domestic connections into international ones, as former subjects of the tsarist empire found themselves in newly independent states on the periphery of the USSR, while others dispersed in the first global wave of Russian emigration. The Japanese hierarch corresponded with Finland, Estonia, Latvia, Lithuania, Poland, Bulgaria, Greece, France, the USA, and above all China.[46] His most treasured links remained those with the increasingly mysterious USSR, wherein sat his largely nominal ecclesiastical superiors. Sergius also made some extra-ecclesiastical connections in Japan.

The most prominent side of his local external engagement had been his complex relations with Russian refugees— "insiders" since they were Orthodox and acknowledged Sergius' episcopal authority, but "outsiders" to the Japanese Orthodox Church in language, sentiment and organization. In 1918-1922, as post-revolutionary Russian émigrés arrived on Japanese shores, the struggling native Orthodox Church ruled out extensive support for them. Sergius, active in organizing and heading the potentially profitable "Russian Society in Japan" for elite émigrés and dubious but well-funded "officials" of Russian anti-Bolshevik regimes, was more than chary in doling out support for needy refugees. Even in the case of fellow clergy, he initially denied hospitality to at least two displaced hierarchs, and when he did grant

[46] Sergius (1939).

humble quarters to a priest, Sergius was summarily faulted and overruled by the Japanese Consistory.[47]

His course of action—which cost Sergius many derailed relationships in the Russian diaspora—was not only a reflection of external limitations, but also internal crisis: the bishop would lose his temper more often, harp on his illness and impending death, his hair and beard abruptly turned gray. However, by the end of 1920's the number of Russians in Japan stood below 2,500, while Sergius, buoyed by the cathedral restoration campaign, regained the confidence to manage some 200-300 active parishioners among them.[48] Scattered émigrés gravitated toward local Japanese Orthodox parishes, but in Tokyo, Kobe, Yokohama and Nagasaki Russians were sufficiently numerous to maintain their own communities. In 1931 there were at least four Russian clerics serving under Sergius, and he was actively working to attract more from abroad.[49] Almost all of these communities and clerics operated under the bishop's personal leadership, outside the bureaucratic and budgetary bounds of the Japanese Orthodox Church. The same was true of the diminutive Korean Orthodox Mission, which had been effectively subordinated to Sergius since 1923. Both by design and demand, Sergius was setting up "his own" parallel mini-Church.

[47]The hierarchs in question were Archbishop of Orenburg Methodius (Gerasimov) and Bishop of Kamchatka Nestor (Anisimov). For the experience of the unfortunate priest, Fr. Innocent Seryshev, see his vivid memoirs, especially Seryshev (1952-1968), 1-2, 8-17, 30-61.

[48]The League of Nations appraisal dated August 30 1930, placed the number of Russians in Japan at 2,356, as reported in Huntington (1933), 299, but Japan's 1930 Census registered 3,587 Russians in Census (1930), 135, 137. The realistic estimate of active parishioners is according to Sergius (1931b), 10.

[49]Russian clerics serving under Sergius in 1931 were Archimandrite Theodosius (Perevalov), Protopriest Alexander Bobrov, Priest Alexander Chistiakov, Protodeacon Procopius Makoveev. One Protopriest Innocent is also mentioned serving in Tokyo in December 1930. Sergius was likewise able to convince Bishop Benjamin (Fedchenkov) to trade exile in France for the Japanese Empire, but Moscow's ecclesiastical authorities had other plans for Benjamin. See Orthodox Messenger (1931.01.20 - № 20-1), 13; (1931.04.20 - № 20-4), 18; (1931.12.20 - № 20-12), 15; Benjamin (2000).

This mini-church was a symptom of Sergius' devotion and nostalgia for the Russian Church, as well as the combination of voluntary withdrawal and tacit expulsion from the core affairs of the Japanese flock. As a gesture of self-assertion vis-à-vis the Japanese, Sergius indulged in claiming a free hand in dealings with expatriate Russians—he pronounced himself "the independent head of the independent" Russian Spiritual Mission in Japan,[50] and repeatedly stated that "[Japan's] Church of the Russians has no connection to the Japanese Church."[51]   Yet, the Russian hierarch hardly felt at home among Russian émigrés, because a decisive gap in their otherwise shared experience translated into sharp opposition in politics. Since Sergius never experienced first-hand the ravages of the Russian Civil War, the prism of his 1905-brand liberalism proved stronger in shaping his views than the post-1917 impressions which stamped the identities of refugees. While para-ecclesiastical émigré circles were dominated by the rhetoric of militant anti-Bolshevism and nostalgia for "Old Russia," Sergius viewed the newly organized USSR as his "Motherland," the sole locus of Russian national and therefore ecclesiastical life.[52] Occasional mailings and telegrams which reached Sergius from the Soviet Union cultivated his inclination to distrust reports about anti-religious persecutions in the USSR,[53] and increasingly placed him at odds with his entire environment.

Through the 1920's, Tokyo-based Russians became intimately familiar with the views of their bishop, who would deliver to them special lectures and sermons. One such sermon followed on March 29 1931 and related Sergius' favorable impression of local church life in the Novgorod

[50] Sergius (1919b), 21.

[51] Takai (1956), i.

[52] Sergius (1931b), 12, 21-24.

[53] After the resumption of correspondence in September of 1927, Sergius records 8 exchanges of letters or telegrams with the USSR by the close of 1929, not counting the dispatch of the official *Journal of the Moscow Patriarchy*. Sergius (1930), 26; (1931b), 3, 9-10.

region based on a reassuring letter from his native village of Guzi he had recently received. The hierarch ended his sermon with a pronouncement that, since Russian people do not rebel, "things are not bad in Russia" and that the assembled refugees would soon be "heading home to your Motherland."[54] As if in reward for these words, on the fourth day after the sermon Sergius was elevated by the Moscow Patriarchate to the exalted rank of Metropolitan. While a number of Tokyo Russians did participate in subsequent festive congratulations for their hierarch,[55] furor against the "Bolshevik" bishop swept the diaspora, with damning articles in émigré periodicals throughout the world,[56] a formal termination of communion on behalf of the Russian Orthodox Church Abroad,[57] and a full-fledged secession movement in Russian ecclesiastical circles in Japan. Under the leadership of the anti-communist activist George Chertkov, a committee for reordering ecclesiastical life of the Russian emigration in Japan succeeded in being accepted under the jurisdiction of the neighboring Harbin diocese of the refugee-dominated Russian Church Abroad. Although the diffuseness and minuteness of the Russian diaspora in Japan meant a parallel anti-Sergian parish was formed only in Kobe, the response of Russian discontents was unambiguous—outright rejection of the bishop as illegitimate on political grounds.[58]

Although some clergy of the Japanese Church were alerted by the Russian schism, for most Japanese believers at the

[54]Sergius provides the text of the letter from his brother, a village deacon, in Sergius (1931b), 2-3. A summary of the letter has also been published in Japanese in Orthodox Messenger (1931.04.20 - № 20-4), 16-17. For the transcript of the sermon see Sergius (1931a).

[55]Orthodox Messenger (1931.05.20—№ 20-5), 15.

[56]Some of the periodicals which expressed outrage over the incident at the time were New Dawn (Novaia Zaria) in Harbin, Word (Slovo) in Shanghai, Rudder (Rul') in Berlin, Russian Voice (Russkii Golos) in Belgrade.

[57]In the autumn of that year. See Naitō (1943), 7.

[58]For the most detailed coverage of the 1931 Russian schism in Japan see Naganawa (2003), 154-159 which relies primarily on the materials of the Japanese Foreign Ministry contained in Oka (1931).

time the very reminder of continuing ties with the Moscow Patriarchate proved more significant. Association with Russia has rarely been appreciated as an asset for the Japanese Orthodox Church, and, as Russia's image blended with the ideology of its communist rulers, external and internal pressure mounted for the Church to dissociate itself altogether from Soviet connections. This pressure was bolstered by Japan's ideological drift to the right and by its expansion in Manchuria, which caused increasing integration of Japanese believers into the predominantly anti-Muscovite conservative ecclesiastical milieu of Russian émigrés in East Asia. Already at the 1923 Council three middling church servitors petitioned for Japanese "independence," a call rather easily deflected by Sergius' discussion of the state of the Russian Church and diverse modes of "independence" in the ecclesiastical context.[59] At the 1930 Council the matter of having "no relations" with the Soviet Russian Church was already put forcefully by none other than the premier Japanese clergymen Fr. Mii and Fr. Shibayama, among others, but Sergius was able to push through an ambiguous resolution which held there to be "no connection" between the Japanese Church and Moscow Patriarchate "except for matters of dogma" and the fact that the former was "a branch" of the latter.[60] Since the resolution did not settle the issue, the buildup of tension climaxed in the heated proceedings of the 1940 Council. At that time Sergius and his few Japanese supporters were shouted down by the majority, after which the declaration of total "severance of ties" with Moscow's ecclesiastical authorities, "as incongruent with our national condition," received "unanimous" endorsement through intimidation.[61] The current of nativist sentiment, stimulated by politicized division inside the Russian Church, gradually led the Japanese to follow in the footsteps of Russian coreligionists and rebel against their bishop's views.

[59]Council (1923), 4-12.
[60]Council (1930), 62-80, 108-111, 115-116.
[61]Council (1941), 84-95.

While rooted in the Japanese Church's internal evolution, the declaration of 1940 came when it did on account of the intensified state pressure in the wake of the passage of the Religious Organizations Law, which required religious bodies to register their charters with the Ministry of Education. After receiving from the Ministry a set of sample regulations at the beginning of September 1939, a sizeable commission of Japanese Orthodox administrators and activists compiled the first draft of such a charter. Submitted to the Ministry on the April 1 1940 deadline, it was soon returned significantly altered, as the Japanese officials set about conforming the Orthodox Church to their own "orthodoxy." The cycle repeated itself after an updated draft was submitted on June 5. The officials' "ecclesiology" required that the head of a religious body, termed "general administrator" (*tōrisha*), be the ruling bishop invested with complete responsibility and subject to effective "appointment" by the Ministry.[62] Most saliently, "according to what they say about the Religious Organizations Law, the Ministry of Education will not allow foreigners as administrators of religious organizations."[63] Indeed, far more significant than the stipulations of the law itself were the vastly greater unwritten requirements emanating from the state. Delegates of the 1940 Japanese Church Council spoke in emergency terms of "existence or extinction" and were understandably at pains to accurately surmise and fulfill the desires of the Ministry—a task complicated not only by the believers' conscience, but also by the cacophony of officials' voices.[64] Although it remained muted, Sergius faced an urgent demand to retire altogether.

While the Religious Organizations Law applied to all

[62]Council (1941), 47, 51. References to "appointment" of bishops from the Ministry of Education come from the record of Sergius' words in Heavenly Bread (1941 - № 2), 37, while the draft of regulations publicized in Orthodox Messenger (1940.08.01 - № 30-8), 7-18, speaks of "approbation" from the Ministry.

[63]Council (1941), 50.

[64]Council (1941), 46, 50-52, 72, 92.

Japanese religious bodies, the Japanese Orthodox Church was unique in facing another force of official intervention calling for Sergius' removal. From 1939 on, in the wake of the resounding Japanese defeat by the Soviets at Nomonhan, a policy proceeding from the General Staff of the Imperial Army aimed at reordering all Orthodox Christian organizations in East Asia into a single Pan-Asian Orthodox Church which would play a key ideological function in the potential all-out war with the Soviet Union. Association with the ideologically acceptable anti-communist Russian Orthodox Church Abroad, which held the allegiance of the overwhelming majority of Russian émigrés in East Asia, was for the time being acceptable to the Japanese Army planners, but Sergius' alignment with the USSR-based Moscow Patriarchate was not. For his part, the Japanese hierarch had long as ruled out administrative merger with the conservative Russian ecclesiastical circles of Manchukuo.[65] Nevertheless, with the "assent of Harbin's military authorities," in 1940 Sergius did receive an offer to participate in and even nominally head this ecclesiastical "new order," if only he moved to Harbin and severed ties with Moscow. Sergius' predictable refusal was no obstacle for the delegates at the 1940 Council, who, having been generally informed of the Army's desires, resolved to finally elect a Japanese to episcopacy and have him ordained at the hands of Harbin's hierarchs.[66]

His desires and principles rejected by the mass of the Japanese Church, albeit in the face of menacing state pressure, Sergius, according to his later statement, resolved to retire already at the July 1940 Council.[67] Long sidelined by the all-embracing Consistory, after the Council the Japanese hierarch was also tacitly subordinated to the Church's "Special Committee on the Religious Organizations Law and Episcopal Election." Although various committees had been formed

[65]Council (1934), 84.
[66]Council (1941), 69, 75, 91-92.
[67]Heavenly Bread (1941 - № 2), 37.

by Japanese Councils in years past to deal with specific tasks, the 1940 Council took the unprecedented step of investing the above Committee with "all powers" regarding matters within its purview, since real-time interaction with secular authorities required a functioning plenipotentiary agency to represent the Church.[68]   Since the bishop, who was supposed to be just such an agency, was no longer counted with, it was this 25-man group which went on to take momentous decisions with regard to Japanese Church's leadership in the course of the following month.   The Committee decided that the Church's "general administrator" and "founder" registered with the Ministry of Education must be a Japanese; rejected the conciliarly approved candidate to episcopacy, Protopriest John Kodera, because of his support of Sergius; divorced the previously twinned positions of "general administrator" and ruling bishop; elected the Committee head, Professor Arsenius Iwasawa, to be the Church's "general administrator"; and finally confronted Sergius with a demand to give up his authority to Iwasawa on September 4 1940.   The hierarch gave in, surrendering his seal, properties held in his name, and "all power invested in me as Metropolitan, general administrator and president" of the Japanese Orthodox Church.[69]   Henceforth, Sergius declared, he would remain only a "Russian" bishop—head of the one-man Russian Spiritual Mission in Japan, pastor of those Russian émigrés who would have him, and writer of Russian-language historical and theological volumes which he had been penning in years past, including the monumental *History of Orthodox mission in Japan for 80 years*.[70]

With Sergius' retirement chaos began immediately, since the two acting administrative bodies of the Church—the plenipotentiary Committee and the Consistory—both claimed provisional primacy and engaged in open confrontation.

[68] Council (1941), 84.

[69] Council (1941), 109-122.

[70] At the end of 1940 the latter volume was said to be 2500 pages long, with some 1000 pages more to go, according to Heavenly Bread (1941 - № 2), 40.

Already at the August 28 sitting of the Committee a strongly worded resolution warned the Consistory "not to infringe upon the sphere of powers of this Committee."[71] At the first sitting after Sergius' retirement, on September 8, a heated disagreement over the extent of Iwasawa's newly gained prerogatives ensued. This conflict quickly degenerated into a standoff between the Consistory under Kodera and the Committee under Iwasawa, issuing into some fifteen years of recrimination, violence, fragmentation and self-discovery which engulfed the entire Japanese Orthodox Church. The removal of the bishop, whose marginality has long been manifest, whose unpopular opinions made him odious, whose retirement had been seen as necessary, proved to be the undoing of internal order in the commnuity which seemed to have done reasonably well under an oligarchic constitutional regime for years. Pressure by Japanese state agents prodded the Church to take the final step in its "democratic" journey— to assert ultimate power of the community over episcopacy by removing its bishop and replacing him with a provisional surrogate body. Although occurring in the context of wartime radical nativism, this had been the culmination of both "Russian" currents of ecclesiastical bureaucratization and revolutionary liberalism as well as "Japanese" demands for leadership diffusion and participatory politization. The long-standing parallel between the bishop and the emperor meant, uncannily, that in 1940 the believers toppled their "emperor" and gave the "power to the people." Devoid of its neglected apostle, the Japanese Orthodox Church was suddenly con-fronted with comprehending and restoring apostolicity, upon which—in the form of ecclesiastical canons and the legacy of St. Nicholas—its existence had been predicated all along.

[71]Council (1941), 116.

Chapter 7

"Without a bishop there is no Church"

With the above words Metropolitan Sergius concluded his defense at the 1940 Church Council, threatening immediate retirement unless proper procedure was followed in applying for Japanese ecclesiastical independence with the Moscow Patriarchate.[1] Most Japanese delegates at the time appeared unfazed by this pronouncement, and although Sergius did not summarily follow through with his promise, the members of the Church's plenipotentiary Committee did it for him. Yet, in the wake of Sergius' removal, as news and rumors about the breakdown of order in the Japanese Church spread throughout the global Russian Orthodox diaspora, the Church's "general administrator" Arsenius Iwasawa received a powerful statement on apostolicity from unexpected quarters. The primate of the Russian Orthodox Church Abroad Metropolitan Anastasius (Gribanovskii), had broken the nearly ten-year-old pause in official communication, and directed a missive to the Japanese Orthodox Church in January

---

[1] Council (1941), 88.

of 1941. In it he affirmed that an Orthodox Church cannot exist without a bishop, and urged immediate selection of a candidate, whose ordination he would then help arrange in Harbin.[2] As Iwasawa with his adherents found themselves outmaneuvered by the mushrooming opposition, they seized upon this letter as a basis for restoring order on their terms and rushed to publicize and realize Anastasius' directive. Henceforth, the issue of episcopacy emerged as one of the most visible strands of Orthodox ecclesiastical activity and discourse in Japan for years.

The prospect of ordaining a Japanese to episcopacy was as old as the notion of the Japanese Orthodox Church itself. The very first Japanese cleric to be ordained by Archbishop Nicholas was Hieromonk Paul (Niitsuma) in 1881, groomed as a future bishop until he recanted from monasticism, abandoned priesthood and married—a traumatic experience which left Nicholas doubly cautious of allowing Japanese to accept monasticism, let alone episcopacy. Sergius was more hopeful—in mid-1910's one of his projects had been the foundation in Japan of a crafts-and-mission-oriented monastery on the model of Holy Trinity Shmakovka monastery near Vladivostok, and in 1915 he succeeded in implanting the first Japanese novice, Ambrose Hibi, into that brotherhood.[3] However, as the role of the bishop was being depreciated amid post-revolutionary crisis, the 1919 *Constitution* of the Japanese Church sidestepped the issue of procuring bishops, although it did provide for a situation wherein multiple hierarchs

[2]Various contemporary sources summarize this crucial letter, including Orthodox Messenger (1941.03.01 - № 31-3), 2; Asahi (1941.03.02); Endō (1941), 13; Council (1941), 13. The last prior communication directed from the Russian Orthodox Church Abroad to the Japanese Orthodox Church was probably the ultimatum from Metropolitan Anthony (Khrapovitskii), received by Metropolitan Sergius of Japan on July 15 1931, offering the latter a final choice between adhering to the Church Abroad or to the Moscow Patriarchate—see Sergius (2000), 322. Rumors about Iwasawa and Anastasius being schoolmates, or even classmates, current to this day in the Japanese Orthodox Church, appear to be baseless.

[3]Orthodox Messenger (1915.07.20 - № 4-14), 34.

would be subordinated to a single "head-bishop." The issue of the native episcopate resurfaced in 1923, when stateless Russian émigrés were being offered Soviet citizenship and Japanese Anglicans ordained their first two native bishops. At that year's Council Sergius was prompted to accept Japanese citizenship and appears to have consented—an intention he went on to repeat more emphatically in 1925 and 1933 without ever carrying out.[4]   Meanwhile, since the 1930 Council,[5] the issue of ordaining a Japanese to episcopacy has been on each year's agenda and an Episcopal Election Committee had functioned since 1934.[6]   However, after the sole Japanese monastic priest, the Shmakovka-trained Fr. Anthony (Hibi), came down terminally ill with pleurisy in early 1933, the matter stalled.[7]

Despite the rhetoric on the necessity of a Japanese bishop emanating from Japanese ecclesiastical administrators and Sergius alike, neither the formulation of episcopal prerogatives nor the person to fill the office could be agreed upon. Japanese administrators were not keen to explicitly define the limits of episcopal authority, for that would mean tampering with the half-articulated arrangements, which relegated the "ruling" hierarch to the periphery.   When Sergius poignantly reminded, that Nicholas' assistant bishops had found work in Japan so difficult because "they had no power," and challenged the administrators to spell out episcopal prerogatives in the *Constitution*,[8] Fr. Paul Morita parried with the popular Confucian formula of fraternal inequality: "Something like fighting over rights is wholly undesirable in our country. All should be like true brothers, the elder brother standing in a place fitting for an elder

[4]Council (1923), 78-80; Suzuki (1925); Orthodox Messenger (1933.07.20 - № 22-7), 23.

[5]Council (1930), 36.

[6]See the Committee's first step-by-step plan for ordaining Japanese bishops in Council (1934), 22-23.

[7]Toyohashi church (1979), 32.

[8]Council (1933), 47-48; Council (1934), 61-63.

brother, the younger brother standing in a place fitting for a younger brother."[9] In a uniquely frank 1933 revelation from a would-be bishop-maker Iwasawa, he admitted that persons in leadership positions tended to be either "tyrants" or "robots," and the Japanese Church's new bishop should best be the latter.[10] In light of the vague and doubly disempowered role thus meted out to the prospective "younger brother" "robot" bishop, premier Japanese clerics balked at this thankless task. When the Moscow Patriarchate nominated Frs. Symeon Mii and Paul Morita to episcopacy in 1936, the former summarily refused, while the latter was too ill to accept.[11] As long as present-day issues militating for a native bishop were limited to the "loss of face" before other Christians who already had them, senior administrators of the Japanese Church would not be enticed into episcopacy.

After the native episcopate became one of the perceived prerequisites for successful government registration in 1939, the Church's Special Committee on the Religious Organizations Law and Episcopal Election set to work with increased urgency. The method chosen for electing candidates had been to solicit the votes of each significant congregation in Japan and present the top-scoring candidates for the decision of the Council. Vocalized qualifications for a bishop included only the broadest formulas—a sound knowledge of the dogmas, adherence to the faith, no forbidding defects of personality and health—as well as a requirement to be single. However, the latter point, though universal in Orthodox Christian practice since the 6th century, had been vociferously rejected in the *Orthodox Messenger*, with reference both to the Biblical precedent of married bishops and to the special circumstances of the Japanese Church. On the background of this explicit loosening of standards, there were, however, at least two unstated parameters which reflected themselves in the final

[9]Council (1934), 64.
[10]Iwasawa (1933), 13.
[11]Council (1936), 6, 64.

foursome: Protopresbyter Symeon Mii, lay Professor Arsenius Iwasawa, lay Professor John Senuma and Protopriest John Kodera. Since all were past 70 years of age, and had been perennial members of the Church's administrative elite, it may be surmised that neither a youthful prodigy, nor a provincial stalwart fit the Japanese Orthodox image of the bishop. At the 1940 Council, the delegates confirmed Iwasawa and Fr. Kodera as candidates and set about imploring their consent.

This proved predictably difficult—Arsenius Iwasawa adamantly turned down all pleas, while Fr. John Kodera required more than a month of coaxing to come up with a list of terms, on which he would be prepared to receive ordination, only to be refused by the plenipotentiary Committee.[12] By September 5 1940, with Sergius resigned, Iwasawa unordained and Kodera rejected, the Japanese Church went from one ruling bishop to three "not-quite bishops" each with his own limited claim to legitimacy. With Iwasawan and anti-Iwasawan activists facing off amid breakdown of ecclesiastical order, one of the earliest Japanese Orthodox "partisan" documents—the "Declaration" of the anti-Iwasawan Conference of Orthodox believers dated December 15—grasped the core issue, explaining the present "unprecendented dark age" of the Japanese Orthodox Church by the "lack of the central ecclesiastical administrative organ" which would enjoy general recognition among believers.[13] Both factions sped to remedy this lack, but along divergent routes.

Anti-Iwasawan activists tapped the established "demo-cratic" channels of ecclesiastical governance—they pushed for the aborted Provisional Council in September 1940; organized a series of Tokyo-based Conferences of Orthodox believers in December, and gathered a numerous and representative All-Japan Clergy-Laity Conference in January 1941. This

[12]Council (1941), 42-46, 69-74, 114-115.
[13]Special Higher Monthly (1940 - № 12), 29.

gathering, the biggest Orthodox assembly in Japan since 1919, went on to rename itself as a Provisional Council and erect a complete set of ecclesiastical governing structures—the Consistory, a number of Committees, and an "episcopal *locum tenens*" to act as the Church's "general administrator." Priding themselves on the "foundational spirit of Council-centrism," which emphasized "unselfish public righteousness," broad popular participation, careful consideration of the constituents' desires and existing regulations, the delegates succeeded in presenting a stark contrast to "lawless," "selfish," "aberrant" and "voluntarist" actions of the handful of Iwasawans. Sergius, although uninvited, was enthusiastic about the anti-Iwasawan gathering, "withdrawing" his transfer of authority to Iwasawa and granting "all powers" to the "episcopal *locum tenens*" Protopriest James Tōhei, as one elected by the "general will of clergy and believers." The assembled clergy, for their part, granted to their chosen would-be bishop an episcopal miter.

With a plurality of significant parishes and clerics vocally on their side, all familiar ecclesiastical organs reconstituted, and a blessing from Sergius, at the start of 1941 anti-Iwasawans appeared to be in position to unite the Church and subject the few opponents to the "appropriate disciplinary action" of the majority.[14] The attempts to invest an "episcopal *locum tenens*" with legitimacy on the part of the Council, the retired hierarch and the assembled clergy were vulnerable to criticism on canonical grounds, but it mattered little as long as the will of the majority was held supreme.

Iwasawa and his capital-based adherents, albeit retaining a presence at the crucial Tokyo cathedral compound and a monopoly on the official *Orthodox Messenger*, lost initiative in the nationwide mobilization of believers. Since the *Orthodox Messenger* passed into their hands from the October 1940 issue,

---

[14]Council Provisional (1941a), especially 9-11, 15-16, 26-27, 32-37, 40. The subsequently published portion of the transcript—Council Provisional (1941b)—has been severely abbreviated and censored.

it became chiefly a polemical organ, in which Iwasawans
emphasized their faithfulness to Nicholas' legacy and to
Japan's wartime "new national structure," while deriding
their ecclesiastical opponents with such abandon as to be
labeled the "voice of the devil."[15] The unprovoked violence
with which Iwasawans evicted the retired Metropolitan
Sergius from the cathedral compound at the end of the year
bespoke growing apprehension in their camp, as they hurried
to seal off the headquarters from the opposition.[16] Ultimately,
it was their unlikely appeal to the unpopular and deactivated
"autocratic" aspect of apostolic authority which assured that
Iwasawa's backers would not be overwhelmed by the swelling
tide of nationwide criticism in 1941.   Having previously
been vulnerable to attacks on the grounds that their chosen
"general administrator" was not even a cleric,[17] they made
use of Iwasawa's connections with the Army and the Russian
Orthodox Church Abroad to validly ordain Protopriest John
Ono as Bishop Nicholas of Tokyo and Japan. This showed up
the brittleness of their opponents' ostensible dominance in
the face of the rhetoric and reality of apostolicity.

Bishop Nicholas (Ono)—whose monastic name had probably been dictated by an appeal to Japan's first apostle[18]—
was the sole Japanese Orthodox cleric tied by a bond of local
loyalty to Iwasawa, both being natives of the Izu peninsula.[19]
Born in 1872 in the family of a former samurai retainer, and

---

[15]Council Provisional (1941a), 26. For the trend-setting article linking
Nicholas' legacy and the "new national structure", see Endō (1940). For one
of the most intemperate denunciations of opponents see Yoshimura (1941a).

[16]For the most vivid account of the incident see Lensen (1966), 271-272. See
also Council Provisional (1941a), 24.

[17]The very first charge against Iwasawa enunciated at the opposition's 1941
Council, as recorded in Council Provisional (1941a), 9.

[18]Just like St. Nicholas of Japan, the new bishop went from the lay name of
John to the monastic name of Nicholas.

[19]Bishop Nicholas was from the village of Kuwahara (now a part of town
of Kannami), while Iwasawa was from the village of Hontachino (now part of
the city of Izu), both in the Shizuoka Prefecture. For a detailed study on the
spread of Orthodoxy on the Izu Peninsula, including the biographical profiles
of Orthodox families and their chief representatives, see Higuchi (1996).

married to the daughter of one of Japan's first three Orthodox clerics, Fr. John Sakai, he combined the desirable attributes of venerable age[20] and elite pedigree in both the secular and ecclesiastical realms. He had received his education under Archbishop Nicholas' guidance at the Tokyo Theological Seminary during its heyday in 1886-1892, mastered Russian, and was among the first three Japanese priests to be ordained in early 1905 specifically to pastor Russian POWs throughout Japan, for which he was subsequently awarded by the Russian Emperor Nicholas II and the Most Holy Synod—a fact used in the 1940's to promote the new bishop among Russian émigrés.[21]

However, perhaps the chief distinction of the new bishop was his nondescript and unassuming conduct—his entire career after the repatriation of Russian POWs until 1939 passed at the helm of a provincial community in Takasaki, with only a handful of publications[22] and studied silence at annual Church Councils to recommend him to the broader public. His sudden emergence as a priest of the quarrel-torn Yokohama parish in 1939, and then as Iwasawa's substitute for the ousted Kodera at the post of the Iwasawan Consistory, likely owed as much to his reticence as it did to his positive qualifications. He was certainly no enemy of Sergius—when the latter was being forcibly removed from the cathedral compound by Iwasawan activists, Fr. Ono found his door chained from the outside, preventing him from coming to the hierarch's aid.[23] This supports the opponents' words that the elder priest was being constrained to remain in the Iwasawan camp against his desires,[24] but it is likewise evident that he

[20] In 1941 Fr. Ono was the second oldest priest of the Japanese Orthodox Church, a factor explicitly cited as a significant qualification for episcopacy. Yoshimura (1941b), 9.

[21] Heavenly Bread (1941 - № 5), 70; Kyō-wa-kai (1942), 263.

[22] In addition to a few translations of St. John Chrysostom's writings in the *Orthodox Messenger*, Fr. Ono published a biography of his distinguished father-in-law, Priest John Sakai, available as Nicholas ([1934] 1976).

[23] Kaminaga (2000), v.

[24] Mori (1941), 7; Manabe (1941), 27.

was unprepared for an open break with Iwasawa, let alone on a matter as significant as episcopal ordination. The fact that he was persuaded not only to accept episcopacy, but to do so at the expense of the twilight years of his married life by separating from his spouse, only confirms the pliability of Fr. Ono's character. He was not only the first Japanese national to become an Orthodox bishop, but the first to accept as a given the distinctive disempowered episcopacy as it had evolved in the Japanese context—the post of a "Portable Shrine" with supreme corporate responsibility and minimal routinely exercisable powers.[25]

Armed with the favorable cooperation of the Japanese Army, which elected them as the vehicle of its plan for a Pan-Asian Orthodox Church, Iwasawans initiated a vociferous campaign against their opponents, advancing to the fore the dormant issue of episcopal authority. Already on March 1, before the Japanese would-be bishop had arrived in Harbin to face the examination committee of Manchukuo's Orthodox hierarchs,[26] the new issue of the *Orthodox Messenger* radically refocused Iwasawan rhetoric. The lead article described Fr. Ono's embarkation in terms of carrying the cross unto Golgotha for the sake of the salvation of the Japanese church. Another piece recentered all post-Nicholaevan Japanese Orthodox history on the figure of the bishop—the marginalized Metropolitan Sergius was suddenly transformed into an archvillain, who had foisted philo-communism upon the believers and caused contemporary troubles. Preaching episcopal indispensability to ecclesiastical life, the writers of other contributions cobbled together pro-Soviet statements of Sergius and pro-Sergian acts of the anti-Iwasawan

[25] Biographical writings about the pre-episcopal period of Bishop Nicholas (Ono)'s life have not delved much deeper, than his own overview in Orthodox Messenger (1941.06.01 - № 31-5), 1-2. Compare Ushimaru (1985), 39-43; Higuchi (1996), 12-13.

[26] Fr. John Ono arrived in Harbin on March 2 according to Endō (1941), 13.

Figure 7.1: Harbin St. Nicholas cathedral, April 6 1941. Manchukuo's hierarchs tower over Nicholas (Ono), whom they have ordained as bishop. Russian bishops hold staffs, symbols of their power; their junior Japanese peer clutches written proof of his legitimacy.

party, thus linking their opposition through Sergius with the dreaded USSR.[27]

Bishop Nicholas' successful ordination on April 6 placed Iwasawans in position to puncture the decades-old discourse of Japanese Church's "independence" and "democracy" with a bishop-centered analysis. The *Orthodox Messenger* affirmed that no gatherings, however representative and democratic, were valid without a bishop's will. Instead, blessing of the Church's presiding hierarch, approval of state authorities, examination by a panel of bishops, innate qualifications of the candidate, and above all valid ordination at the hands

[27]Orthodox Messenger (1941.03.01 - № 31-3)—see especially 2-4; Nicholas (1941); Yoshimura (1941a); Yamauchi (1941).

of at least three hierarchs—which alone imparted the Divine grace of episcopacy—were upheld as seminal to a bishop's legitimacy.[28]   Because it was unable to ordain its own bishops, the Japanese Church was declared to have been merely an "extension of the Russian Orthodox Church" all along, its *Constitution* a pompous name for a set of diocesan regulations.[29] Instead of the parochial Japanese *Constitution*, universally valid Biblical citations, quotes from the Holy Fathers, and canonical regulations were mustered to support this apology for apostolicity.   Perennial calls to do away with alien Russian ways, symptomatic of this nationalistic era, were uncannily drowned out by effusive admiration for Manchukuo's Russian bishops who had empowered their Japanese peer. This, Bishop Juvenal (Kilin) "appeared at a glance to have Asiatic features and emanated the sense of a venerable Zen ascetic who had reached enlightenment," Bishop Demetrius (Voznesenskii)'s voice turned out to be the very voice that Deacon Nicon Endō had heard in an earlier prophetic dream, while Metropolitan Meletius (Zaborovskii) "possessed the countenance and actions of the model man of virtue, bespeaking of holiness."[30] After decades of obscurity, the notion of apostolicity suddenly surfaced as the main lever of change in the Japanese Orthodox Church.

Anti-Iwasawan activists were on the defensive. Unable to gainsay their opponents' arguments about the centrality of the bishop to ecclesiastical life, and unwilling to risk open association with the Moscow-oriented Sergius, their first countermove involved yet another mass mobilization to disrupt the prospective ordination. Scores of letters and telegrams from Japanese clergy and believers, as well as resident Russian refugees, streamed to Harbin's ecclesiastical elite. These messages related the events which had taken place in the Japanese Church, rejected the candidacy of

[28] Yoshimura (1941b), 8-9.
[29] Saitō (1941), 8.
[30] Endō (1941), 15, 18; (1942), 28.

Fr. Ono, who was said to have "nothing to do with the Japanese Orthodox Church," and implored Manchukuo's hierarchs to abort the ordination.[31] These pleas slowed the proceedings in Harbin sufficiently for anti-Iwasawans to secure separate registration as a religious association and thus acquire formal proof that the newly-ordained bishop was indeed unconnected with *their own* Japanese Orthodox Church.

An anti-Iwasawan pamphlet issued nine days after the ordination, while continuing to argue along the lines of majoritarian "Council-centrism" vs. unilateral "dictatorship," manifested a defensive shift in rhetoric. Argumentation on the basis of ecclesiastical law, which Iwasawans had turned to their advantage, was substituted with specific charges of opponents' extreme and despotic "social revolutionary" acts. The pamphlet called believers to stand firm in their non-recognition of the "in effect excommunicated" Bishop Nicholas, and augured an "unsightly" and "trying track," before a "spectacular breakthrough" would be achieved.[32] Indeed, the conflict inside the Japanese Church had already become physical. Bishop Nicholas' attempt to celebrate the Easter service at the Tokyo cathedral on April 19 faced a lockout by the anti-Iwasawan Consistory, who maintained control of the cathedral compound until the bishop broke in at last on May 31.[33] Radicalization of anti-Iwasawans' defense and the shrillness of their denunciations of the opponents' "robot bishop, tactical bishop, make-it-yourself bishop, fill-in-the-blank bishop"[34] showed that the issue of episcopacy moved to the center of the struggle for legitimacy.

As confrontation escalated to street fights, secular authorities stepped in to regulate unruly believers, concocting in June a compromise which envisioned episcopal ordination of anti-Iwasawans' Fr. Tōhei, and subsequent alternating

[31] Yoshimura (1941a), 16; (1941b), 9-10; Endō (1941), 14-15.
[32] Kitamura (1941).
[33] Kamada (1941), 44; Sergius (1944), 3; Satō (1946), 39.
[34] Manabe (1941), 27.

administration of the Church by each bishop half a year at a time.[35] Unprecedented in the annals of Church tradition, this arrangement was the joint handiwork of the Army, the Military Police, the Police Department and the Ministry of Education, whose representatives "allowing neither protests nor discussions, read out their memorandum for execution" before the forcibly assembled leaders of Orthodox factions.[36] On July 18 1941, a Provisional Council brought together over a hundred Orthodox delegates to rubber-stamp the agreements with active participation of "pertinent authorities." Indicatively, in the quest to present broad "democratic" participation, the sponsors of the Council arranged for a sizeable presence of women-delegates—a characteristic wartime innovation unprecedented at prior Councils of the Japanese Orthodox Church. Yet, even under the stifling official oversight, with Bishop Nicholas recognized and Fr. Tōhei slated for ordination, latent confrontation evidenced itself around the issue of episcopacy, with both "tyranny" and "democracy" used as accusations.[37]

Brittle compromise hinged on anti-Iwasawans' hope for Fr. Tōhei to occupy a position of parity with Nicholas, but within months this hope was dashed. On December 1 the Harbin Episcopal Conference directed Tōhei to be a mere vicar (i.e. assistant) bishop, since alternating episcopacy was unconscionable to Russian hierarchs. On January 17 1942, as the Army's plans for a unified Pan-Asian Orthodox Church were being scaled down, the curator of the "Orthodox question" Colonel Yabe Chūta declared that ordination was postponed "until the general outlook of the Great East Asian

---

[35] See the full text of the May 2 agreement in Kamada (1941), 44-45; June 12 and June 23 agreements in Orthodox Messenger (1941.07.01 - № 31-6), 28-29, 14.

[36] Sergius (1944), 4.

[37] Council Provisional (1941c), 6, 21-22, 25-26.

War should become clearer."[38] With no bishop to lead them, anti-Iwasawans lost cohesion and confidence to coordinate resistance. Individual withdrawal from public Church life, parishes ignoring Tokyo's directives, and, from June 1942, a drawn-out court case in which the discontents sued with some success the Iwasawan administrative elite over the management of ecclesiastical property[39]—all this indicated the breadth and depth of smoldering opposition. Yet, the minority was now firmly ascendant, thanks in large measure to its monopolization of the discourse of apostolicity.

Having accepted a disempowered episcopacy out of weakness, Bishop Nicholas found himself constrained to act the part of a strong bishop both more assertive and authoritarian than his Russian predecessors. Professor Iwasawa gradually distanced himself from decision-making and died on October 23 1943,[40] taking his priceless connections in the Army with him. This left the bishop at the helm of what had been the Iwasawan camp, obliged to overcome the alienation of the majority, even as exigencies of wartime required increasingly autonomous and peremptory acts on his part. Thus, with annual Councils ruled out by secular authorities, Nicholas proceeded to ordain and reward clerics on his own, well within bounds of canonical normalcy, but bewildering to Japanese believers, since Russian hierarchs in Japan had decided such matters via conciliar deliberations.[41] Severe official limitation on travel compelled Nicholas to unilaterally restaff the Consistory with Tokyoites.[42] Most damagingly, rapid impoverishment caused the bishop to condone unpalatable

[38]Orthodox Messenger (1942.03.01 - № 32-3), 27; Sapporo church (1987), 143-144. The latter account is based on the brochure—Consistory (1942)—from the collection of Fr. John Kuriyagawa Isamu.

[39]Sergius (1944), 4; Satō (1946), 41; Protopriests' Conference (1943), 8.

[40]Orthodox Messenger (1943.11.01 - № 33-10), 14-15.

[41]Satō (1946), 41; Council Provisional (1946), 36.

[42]Nicholas (1944b).

money-making schemes which dragged him into court.[43] All the same, Nicholas endeavored to carry on the routine which the Japanese Orthodox had come to expect of their bishop— regular services at the cathedral, memorial rites upon the deaths of prominent believers, and pastoral travel across the country, extending as far as the northern-most parish on Shikotan in the autumn of 1942.[44]

Nor was the discourse of episcopal authority allowed to lapse—the bishop and his collaborators continued to uphold the global episcopal network over and above Japanese majoritarian separatism, referring believers to the canons and Russian émigré hierarchs.[45] The Protopriests' Conference— a gathering of senior clerics on August 17-18 1943—showed that the clerical elite was sufficiently reconciled to act in concert under episcopal leadership. At the conference three prospective vicar bishops were elected by means of the ancient custom of drawing lots, which underscored Divine agency, rather than the will of the majority.[46] After Sergius' "constitutional" era, a new equilibrium of ecclesiastical life, tipped in favor of episcopal "autocracy," could be glimpsed in these proceedings.

The above arrangement included a decisive break with the Moscow Patriarchate, reiterated in the November 1943 issue of the *Orthodox Messenger*.[47] However, as news of USSR's military successes and simultaneous rehabilitation of the Orthodox Church inside the Soviet Union seeped through Japan's information cordons, attention refocused on the resident representative of the Moscow Patriarchate. Deprived of his pension by ascendant Iwasawans since July

[43]Satō (1946), 41-42; Council Provisional (1946), 36. In 1944 Metropolitan Sergius opined that Bishop Nicholas was surviving only with the help of his children—see Sergius (1944), 4.

[44]Nicholas (1943).

[45]Orthodox Messenger (1942.04.01 - № 32-4), 3-5; Meletius et. al. (1942); Protopriests' Conference (1943), 24-25.

[46]Protopriests' Conference (1943), 24, 27.

[47]Naitō (1943), 3-8.

1941, Metropolitan Sergius at first "lived in penury and was literally starving,"[48] but gradually began to receive help from well-wishers, at first Russian, but increasingly also Japanese, with erstwhile enemies seeking to make peace and entire parishes sending collective donations.[49] His humble routine of serving a predominantly Russian émigré congregation at a makeshift home chapel was interrupted in mid-May of 1944 by Soviet embassy workers, who offered Sergius to resume communication with Soviet hierarchs via embassy mail, which he did at once.[50] Together with Russian émigrés and Orthodox ecclesiastics the world over, Sergius became a target of a concerted Soviet public relations campaign, proceeded to secretly accept Soviet citizenship and express a desire to return to the USSR.[51]

Yet his was a guarded enthusiasm—from the outset he concealed his compromising Civil War-era visits into White-held parts of Russia,[52] and, although prodded repeatedly, cited health reasons for refusing to enter the Soviet Union. Soviet embassy personnel underestimated Sergius' caution and overestimated Japanese counterespionage, supposing that the Japanese had learned of the hierarch's desire to reemigrate and attempted to lure him with an offer of reinstatement at the helm of the Japanese Orthodox Church.[53] In fact, the Japanese judiciary was oblivious to Sergius' newly-acquired Soviet citizenship—he was indeed detained

[48] Sergius (2007), 51.

[49] Even George Chertkov, who had mobilized Russians against Sergius' pro-Soviet line in 1931, was reconciled with the aged hierarch at this time. Among congregations which materially aided Sergius were parishes in Nagoya, Sendai, Shitaya, Yotsuya, Kanda, Odawara, Shizuoka and others. Help also came from individual believers in Kyoto, Himeji and other locations. See Chertkov (1977), 2; Sergius (2007), 52; Polycarp (1946), 174.

[50] Sergius (1944), 2.

[51] ГАРФ, ф. 6991, оп. 1, д. 23, л. 13.

[52] Sergius reported having been to Russia "only once" since his appointment to Japan—in 1910, for the Missionary Conference in Irkutsk. See Sergius (1944), 5.

[53] ГАРФ, ф. 6991, оп. 1, д. 23, л. 13.

for questioning in mid-May of 1945, but released on June 16 with suspicions of espionage cleared.[54] It was the Japanese Orthodox Church itself, after the court empowered the Consistory to reform itself in early 1945 under the forward-looking and well-informed Protopriest Samuel Uzawa of anti-Iwasawan sympathies,[55] which began to rebuild bridges with Sergius by resuming payment of the hierarch's long-suspended pension.[56] The Allies ascendant, the fragmented opposition of the Japanese Church was once again groping for a coordinating center, with Sergius a prime candidate. His death of heart failure on August 10 1945, a mere five days before Japan's surrender, and the apocalyptic spectacle of Sergius' barely-attended funeral amid bombed-out Tokyo, were immediately taken up as symbolic of the suffering which the Japanese Orthodox Church has had to endure from schism, militarists, and war. Sergius' tragic demise, often blamed on alleged tortures by the thought police, elevated his name overnight to the dignity of a "holy apostle" only somewhat below Archbishop Nicholas.[57]

If Sergius had faced a demand for the structural con-

[54]The documents of the Thought Section of the Criminal Department of Japan's Supreme Court classify Sergius as "Stateless (White Russian)." See Thought Section (1945), especially 5, 34.

[55]Fr. Uzawa was among the first Consistory members to openly oppose Iwasawa in September 1940, dialogued in early 1942 with the powerful Colonel Yabe Chūta in Harbin about the episcopal ordination of Fr. Tōhei, and warned the 1943 Protopriests' Conference that "there is no telling how international relations might turn next." See Council (1941), 124; Sapporo church (1987), 143; Protopriests' Conference (1943), 25.

[56]Seraphim (2008-2010 - № 1434), 21, citing 『総代会会議録』 of the Sendai Orthodox church from June 3 1945, Sendai Orthodox church collection.

[57]Panegyric commemorations of Sergius began to appear as soon as Japanese Orthodox publishing activity resumed, starting with Council Provisional (1946), 11, and Orthodox Messenger (1947.08.15 - № "765"), 2. Allegations of torture or poisoning, which are yet to be supported or dispelled, were current from the time of Sergius' death. The voluminous material about Sergius' last years which has built up thanks to the publication of memoirs and ongoing research has been summarized best in a recent series of articles by Bishop Seraphim (Tsujie), especially Seraphim (2007a, 2007-2008). A notable source missed by the above series is Lensen (1966), 270-272.

striction of episcopal power upon the decease of his predecessor, after Sergius' own death Bishop Nicholas (Ono)
was confronted with a purge of his person, saddled as
he was with supreme corporate responsibility at the time
when American SCAP authorities initiated and encouraged
such purges in all Japanese organizations. Scapegoated for
financial malfeasance and association with "militarists," at
the April 1946 Provisional Council the minority bishop was
called upon to "beg forgiveness before the spirit of the
deceased Archbishop Nicholas" and, together with two other
clerics, compelled to accept "temporary retirement" by the
confident majority. Yet, this assertion of anti-Iwasawan
dominance was a token of collective recantation from wartime
sins to be presented to Americans,[58] not a rebellion against
the principle of apostolic authority. Even as it chased
out Nicholas, this Council amended the Church *Constitution*
to remove some constraints on episcopal power, explicitly
defined the Consistory's prerogatives as deriving from the
bishop, and cited the decision of Harbin's hierarchs—who had
shifted allegiance to the Moscow Patriarchate—as requiring
the Japanese Church to follow suit.

Taught by recent experience of "bishoplessness", conciliar
delegates sped to request a "Russian bishop from America"
while restoring ties with the Moscow Patriarchate and co-
operating with American occupation authorities to order
ecclesiastical life.[59] Within months a more representative
Council was called to confirm these decisions, and the jarring
mixture of unreflective nativism, nascent Cold War rhetoric,
and utter ignorance of ecclesiastical order mouthed by inex-
perienced delegates showed up the precipitous generational
change worked by the war. The tremendous death toll of
1945-1946 made imminent extinction of Japanese Orthodox
clergy a plausible possibility, rendering the urgent need for a

[58]The American occupation authorities were cited as "extremely satisfied"
with the report of the peaceful removal of Bishop Nicholas. Council (1946), 29.

[59]Council Provisional (1946), especially 6, 16, 33-34, 36, 39-40, 47, 51-52.

bishop evident to most—as the final resolution encapsulated, this was an issue of "inviting a bishop to ordain candidates for priesthood and deaconate."[60] Of necessity, the Japanese Consistory opened up to any opportunity to lure a bishop—receptive to Soviet promises of bishops from the USSR, it also invited the Moscow-aligned Metropolitan Benjamin (Fedchenkov) of America, seeking out in the meantime the assistance of General MacArthur's staff. The presence in the latter of Colonel Boris Pash, the fervently anti-Soviet Russian-American son of Metropolitan Theophilus (Pashkovskii), who in turn headed the anti-Moscow Russian Orthodox Metropolia of North America, decided the outcome of the episcopal race.[61] Although Moscow Patriarchate's Bishops Boris (Vik) and Sergius (Larin) enjoyed full backing of Soviet personnel in Japan and would have arrived first, American occupation authorities refused them entry visas, meanwhile officially "requesting" and welcoming the American contender—Bishop Benjamin (Basalyga).[62]

Bishop Benjamin was indeed as American as an Orthodox bishop could be in 1946. From the family of humble Russian immigrants—his father was a coalminer supporting an eight-child family—he was born in 1887 in Olyphant, Pennsylvania, and spent his entire life on the American continent, becoming its first native to assume episcopacy in the Orthodox Church. His theological training did not extend beyond the seminary level, and he matured in the field—as a nomadic hieromonk, reassigned almost annually to localities throughout the US and Canada until his ordination to episcopacy in 1933.

[60]Council (1946), 40-41, 65-68.

[61]In addition to Pash's own description of the events, his confidential correspondence with his father demonstrates his centrality in directing the affairs. See Pash (1958) and some of Pash's letters in Shōji (2007), 62-69.

[62]On November 23 the Patriarch of Moscow telegraphed the Japanese Consistory that the Soviet bishops were already "dispatched" and were soon reported in Vladivostok, awaiting permission to enter Japan. Meanwhile, Bishop Benjamin set off from Seattle on a steamer only on December 23 and arrived in Japan on January 7 1947. See Manabe (1996), 11; RAOM (1946.11 - № 11), 163; (1947.02 - № 2), 30-31.

Amid the unsettled life of the uprooted, untutored and undaunted Russian Orthodox in North America, abounding in religious charlatans, endemic schisms, and matter-of-fact rebellions against higher ecclesiastical authorities, Benjamin had become accustomed to shouting matches, fights, police intervention and arrests being used to settle disputes among fellow Orthodox. Disobedience had been the norm in his pastoral experience—two years into his tenure as bishop of Pittsburgh he was still imploring his supposedly subordinate clergy to provide him with a residence, cease moving from parish to parish of their own accord, and stop "playing the role of American gangsters" among the Depression-crushed flock.[63] American Orthodox environment taught him that, in general, "Orthodox people fundamentally like schism."[64]

A fervent believer, having embraced monasticism at a time of severe illness, Benjamin structured his persona in protest to his unruly surroundings, with ecclesiastical order and loyalty as supreme private virtues. An emergency substitute *par excellence*, he had shown unswerving devotion to the leaders of the increasingly isolated American Metropolia, manifesting no inclination to desert for a competing jurisdiction. This steadfastness was likely chief among qualities which earned him an episcopal ordination, but his distinguishing traits also included unassuming humbleness in daily life and sentimentality—reflected in his propensity for music, tears and alcohol.[65] Thus, Bishop Benjamin was selected to undertake the Japanese assignment neither as an adaptable missionary, nor as a gifted pastor, but as a dependable guardian with high tolerance for discomfort and disorder.[66]

[63]Benjamin (1935).

[64]Council (1950), 6.

[65]Note especially the three aspects of Benjamin's sentimentality subtly evoked in Takeoka (1989), 2-5.

[66]The sole notable account about Archbishop Benjamin (Basalyga) and the source of the otherwise undocumented biographical information in the above paragraph is the commemorative brochure—Golden Jubilee Committee (1961). Some observations were confirmed in the author's interview with

Apprehensive US occupation authorities affirmed their support for Benjamin by directing American Orthodox servicemen to attend *en masse* his first liturgy in Tokyo, on Julian calendar Christmas of 1947.[67] These worries were misplaced, as the Japanese Council of that year eagerly welcomed Benjamin as their hierarch and pleaded with him to remain in Japan permanently, proclaiming that "without a bishop there is no Church."[68] This formula, which had been used by Metropolitan Sergius to assert episcopal authority at the 1940 Council, was now wielded by the Japanese delegates to entice a new hierarch, placing in him hopes for replenishing clergy, reenergizing the Church, and refueling it with foreign aid. Ironically, just as the Japanese delegates in 1940 had ignored their bishop's warning, so did the new bishop ignore this appeal for deeper engagement with the Japanese Church. Benjamin saw himself in his familiar capacity of a stop-gap warden against disorder and schism. Retaining his American title as bishop of Pittsburgh, he had been made to think that his stay abroad would last only half a year.[69] During those six months he proceeded to ordain preselected candidates, tour some parishes, and begin reorganizing Sunday schools, earning himself a promotion to the grade of archbishop.[70]

In some locales crowds flocked to the American hierarch, producing such grand manifestations as the May 19 1947 memorial service for the victims of the war in the Toyohashi City Hall, with over 2000 in attendance.[71] However, by the summer of 1947 Benjamin viewed his "mission of visitation to Japan mostly completed"[72] and retreated into passivity, awaiting a summary recall home—which came only six years

the Archbishop's nephew, John Basalyga, at the St. Nicholas cathedral in Washington, D.C., of the Orthodox Church of America, on May 16 2005.

[67]Pash (1958), 43.

[68]Council Provisional (1947), 10.

[69]Council Provisional (1947), 16; RAOM (1947.05 - № 5), 78.

[70]Council (1947), 6-9.

[71]See the description of this event in Toyohashi church (1979), 21-22.

[72]Benjamin (1947).

Figure 7.2: Missed opportunities of the "Christian boom." Bishop Benjamin, Japanese Orthodox clergy, and many hundreds assembled in front of the Toyohashi City Hall, May 19 1947, after the memorial service for the war-dead. From John Shōji Masatoshi.

later. In the meantime, as of mid-1950 he had yet to visit a Japanese believers' household, limited his participation at annual Councils to opening and closing speeches, and refrained from learning Japanese, considering liturgical service to be the principal method of influencing believers available for him.[73]

His infrequent appeals to the American Orthodox for material help had given meager results, which he considered natural, for the US immigrant flock, as he well knew, "barely supports its own bishops and priests."[74] In line with his prior experience, the few areas in which Benjamin showed himself proactive were pastoring the numerous American Orthodox military flock and combating competing Orthodox jurisdictions.[75] While most other Japanese Christian groups capitalized on the post-war "Christian boom" with overseas missionary aid, the Orthodox were left largely on their own, with Benjamin preaching the value of "independent self-respecting spirit,"[76] and Colonel Boris Pash taking over some functions as fundraiser with the American Metropolia.[77]

Confronted with the very opposite of a "despot" as bishop, the erstwhile Japanese Orthodox quest for liberation from episcopal authority had come full circle, a newly-found desire for a stronger hierarch boiling over into frustration, confrontation, rioting and schism. Due to the bishop's non-intervention, factionalism swiftly reincarnated itself in new forms, as the representatives of Tokyo's Yotsuya district parish, headed by the dominant Fr. Samuel Uzawa, solidified

[73]Council (1950), 54, 58.

[74]Council (1951), 49.

[75]Thus, he successfully subjected to the American Metropolia the previously Moscow-aligned parishes in Seoul and Kobe. In both cases the matter seems to have enjoyed the backing of many believers involved as well as considerable support of occupation authorities. RAOM (1947.05 - № 5), 77; Pozdniaev (1999c), 360-362.

[76]Benjamin (1947).

[77]See for instance Pash's letter of appeal to Bishop John (Shakhovskoi) from December 2 1949—Pash (1949).

control over the Consistory at the 1948 Council. In October 1948 a sizeable group of Japanese believers filed a complaint with occupation authorities about Benjamin's behavior "not as a Japanese bishop, but as an American subject," whose unfair preference for the Yotsuya group caused the breakup of the Church into three factions.[78] As attempted parley with the bishop failed, one of the Japanese Church's leading activists, layman Alexander Manabe, spearheaded a movement to have the bishop replaced. This, however, quickly led to Manabe's arrest by the American military police, as US occupation authorities forcefully intervened into the conflict. Amid disturbances and a widely publicized hunger strike by the leader of the Tokyo Orthodox youth in support of Manabe (the so-called "Christmas barricaded belfry incident"), occupation troops descended upon the Tokyo cathedral compound and bullied the unruly element, reportedly promising arrest to any who would resist the bishop. The showdown forced Manabe's retreat in a legally formulated truce with Benjamin at the start of 1949.[79]

The Americans' overreaction was due to the fear, shared by the bishop and occupation authorities, that Manabe's movement was a front for an attempted Soviet takeover of the Orthodox Church—at a time when what was later to become the Cold War was on the verge of going "hot" in the neighboring divided Korea. In fact, this show of force stimulated what it was supposed to squash. While displeasure with the American bishop assumed subdued forms among the cowed majority, an unlikely alliance of opposition factions united in a new campaign—this time with active Soviet diplomatic support, in the name of the Moscow Patriarchate, with the Japanese Bishop Nicholas as their banner and weapon.

[78]ГАРФ, ф. 6991, оп. 1, д. 588, л. 59-64.

[79]For Manabe's own biased, but invaluable summary of these events, see Manabe (1996), 15-16. For the official American presentation see Woodard (1972), 214. The "truce" was made public at the time in Orthodox Messenger (1949.03.15 - № 717), 1.

The episcopal rank of the hapless Bishop Nicholas prevented him from finding peace in provincial retirement,
at the side of his wife-turned-nun in Kannari. Already
at the end of 1947 he had been persuaded by another
marginalized cleric—the far more charismatic Fr. Anthony
Takai who had accepted the post of priest for the handful of
Moscow-aligned Russian émigrés in Tokyo—to return to the
capital and reassert his episcopal authority. Given Nicholas'
stigma of "militarism," very few were prepared to heed his
voice, but the Japanese bishop received unexpected initial
encouragement from none other than Benjamin himself, who
affirmed that, as an American hierarch, "he only came for a
time, to ordain priests, and does not wish to interfere in the
administrative affairs of the Japanese Orthodox Church." In
the autumn of 1948 the reassured Nicholas addressed a letter
to Metropolitan Theophilus in New York with a request to
remove the American emissary-bishop, whose services were
no longer required.[80]

Having thus been sucked into a struggle to reassert his
authority, Nicholas found himself labeled a "Bolshevik," since
his post-war allegiance to the Moscow Patriarchate—still
matter-of-fact in 1946—had become politically volatile by
1948. Manabe's highly publicized struggle with the Americans,
his resultant ouster and his decision to join the Moscow-
aligned ecclesiastical opposition finally attracted official Soviet attention to this ready-made vehicle for intervention.
In late spring of 1949 Soviet planners deemed it possible
to sponsor the restoration of Moscow Patriarchate's Russian
Orthodox Mission in Japan under Bishop Nicholas, for which
local Soviet diplomatic attaches pledged to "provide aid
and influence."[81] A court-case was masterminded, whereby
Nicholas as the valid head of the valid Japanese Orthodox
Church stood a good chance to acquire legal title to its
symbolic heart, the Tokyo cathedral compound.

[80]ГАРФ, ф. 6991, оп. 1, д. 588, л. 67-68.
[81]ГАРФ, ф. 6991, оп. 1, д. 588, л. 102.

Nicholas found himself playing his wartime role of an assertive minority bishop yet again, proclaiming his legitimacy through court and luring away or else ordaining new clergy. Soon after the filing of the court-case, in October 1949, Nicholas was formally expelled by the majority, but by 1951, their situation in court and among local churches aggravated, Benjamin's side initiated arbitration talks to bring Nicholas back into its fold.[82] Talks stalled, and the frustrated delegates of the majority at their 1952 Council resolved in principle against reinstating the Japanese hierarch on account of his odious character.[83] Yet, they were hardly pleased with their own "do nothing" bishop, although the fact that "Archbishop Benjamin had been chosen by UN troops"[84] made open resistance to him unthinkable for most. When the American had finally been relieved from his Japanese post in mid-1953, the barely-concealed sarcasm of the public parting address by Fr. Ōta distilled the frustration of the Japanese flock by underlining the fact that, during his six-year stay, the hierarch had managed to do little other than ordain preselected clergy.[85] Just as during the war, the majority of Japanese Orthodox had found themselves devoid of effective episcopal leadership in the face of the deft bishop-wielding minority.

With the withdrawn Benjamin unable to pose as a unifying leader, the American-aligned majority turned to the towering figure of their founding father to support their claim to legitimate episcopal succession and rally the believers. Although Archbishop Nicholas' name had never ceased being a watchword for the Japanese Orthodox, nearly ten years have elapsed, filled with unprecedented destruction and turmoil, since he had been extensively treated in ecclesiastical press or otherwise celebrated.

[82]Council (1950), 12; (1952), 31-33, 40-41.
[83]Council (1952), 42-52, 62-64.
[84]Council (1951), 39.
[85]Orthodox Messenger (1953.07.25 - № 768), 1.

Commemorations of the 90 year anniversary of Nicholas's arrival to Japan commenced with a celebration in Hakodate on June 12 1950, a local initiative eagerly supported by the Consistory.[86] Thereafter, a nationwide campaign was organized for the recollection of Japanese Orthodoxy's Meiji-period halcyon days, culminating with the festivities on July 12 1951, timed to coincide with the annual Council. The church services and the following program of speeches and concerts were attended by thousands, with many high SCAP officials and Japanese Christian leaders in attendance, not to mention most Japanese Orthodox clergy. Addresses by William Bunce, Chief of the Religious Division of the GHQ, and the Greek Major General Anastasios Paskarolis, as well as the prominent presence of the wounded soldiers from the fields of the Korean War, linked Nicholas' religious legacy to the ongoing conflict with the atheistic world, while a concert of Russian folk songs reaffirmed the continuity of genuine Russian tradition in the camp of "free nations."[87] The outpouring of articles in the *Orthodox Messenger* throughout 1951 and well into 1952 celebrated not only Nicholas' person, but also his closest aides, like the translator Paul Nakai, as well as historic churches built under Nicholas' supervision, exemplified by the Kyoto church.[88]

On this occasion the Church likewise resumed its publication activity, with its first brochure being a brief *Life* of Archbishop Nicholas by one of his few still living disciples, followed by three works of Russian hierarchs—the *Catechism* of St. Philaret of Moscow and two pamphlets by the contemporary Bishop John (Shakhovskoi) of the American Metropolia.[89] In context of this praise for hierarchs, disciples,

[86]Council (1950), 12-13.

[87]Karp (1951).

[88]Beginning with Orthodox Messenger (1951.02.25 - № 739), 1, articles recalling St. Nicholas and his time appeared in almost every issue of the *Orthodox Messenger*, down to Orthodox Messenger (1952.04.25 - № 755), 1.

[89]The *Catechism* has been treated extensively in chapter 3, while the other works in question were Mochizuki (1951); John (1953a, 1953b).

the Meiji period and non-communist Russians, Fr. Uzawa's stray invocation of Archbishop Nicholas and the ecclesiastical *Constitution* as the twin foundations of the Japanese Church's "independence" proved him a man of the previous age.[90] For all the talk of democracy and independence, current in the wake of the 1952 termination of US occupation, it was internationalist dependence which beaconed in the future for the Japanese, rendering the long-awaited new hierarch from America an object of great expectations among Orthodox believers.

The leaders of the American Metropolia, aware of complications in Japan, had long been searching for a suitable candidate who might fill the vacuum of episcopal authority among the Japanese flock.[91] Such a leader was found, upon the death of his spouse, in the person of the experienced and dynamic administrator-priest John Bekish, who had fled his native Poland in the face of Soviet advance and made his way to the US in 1952. Prepared and ordained specifically as Bishop of Japan and Tokyo,[92] under the name of Irenaeus, he arrived in mid-1953 with a motivation and an agenda to master the situation. As he carried out his obligatory first tour of the country's parishes, he asserted himself as a moral authority over the Japanese Church by openly challenging the believers to lay aside endemic petty hatreds and unite for the sake of constructive work.[93] His terse rhetoric consistently zeroed in on three crucial themes—responsibility before the holy founder, promise of help from America, and need for relentless activity: "No one helps lazy people. If we are active God will help, and Archbishop Nicholas and American Orthodox with their prayers and joy will also help."[94]

[90] Uzawa (1953).

[91] ROJ (1952.11 - № 26-7), 12.

[92] For the programmatic speech of Metropolitan Leontius (Turkevich) upon Irenaus' episcopal ordination see Leontius (1969b).

[93] Orthodox Messenger (1953.11.25 - № 771), 1.

[94] Council (1955), 7.

Backing up his appeal with tireless action, he hurriedly launched a restoration campaign which rivaled Meiji-period efforts in its scope and the extent of episcopal leadership—in less than two years Irenaeus' concrete pleas for help inundated the Russian-American press and garnered good returns, his daring plan to immediately reopen the inactive seminary succeeded, at his initiative theological students and prospective nuns had been summarily sent to study abroad for the first time since 1910's. The hierarch's prodding and eagerness to tap the post-war "Christian boom" spurred local reconstruction efforts in many directions, including the reconstruction of church-buildings, invigorated mission, and reintegration of each parish into the framework of the national ecclesiastical body under the provisions of the liberalized post-war Religious Organizations Law.

However, the most decisive success of this *blitzkrieg* had been a series of stealthy meetings with Bishop Nicholas and his leading aides, initiated and conducted personally by Irenaeus, which produced a reconciliation of all but one Moscow-aligned cleric—the diehard Fr. Anthony Takai—with the majority group on Easter 1954. All saved face, litigation ceased, Irenaeus retained the reins of leadership and trumpeted his triumph over Soviet machinations.[95] On November 8 1955, Irenaeus became the first Japanese Orthodox hierarch since Archbishop Nicholas to participate in a promenade at the Imperial Court.[96] The new bishop was judged by some insiders as too worldly and preoccupied with external effects, at times resorting to questionable cutting of corners.[97] However, his authoritative voice, his avalanche of activity and his bountiful fundraising united, mobilized, and inspired the Japanese Orthodox, who had long hungered for effective leadership and external support. The July

[95]The event was summarily publicized by secular mass media, which stressed the reconciliation to be a "break" with Moscow and Irenaeus' achievement. See for instance Nippon Times, № 19,825 (1954.04.25).

[96]Orthodox Messenger (1955.11.25 - № 792), 1.

[97]Manabe (1996), 19-21.

1955 Council of the reunited Church resolved to petition for Irenaeus to be promoted to the rank of archbishop, admitting that:

> At present our Church is run almost entirely by his effort, he even created a seminary. Although Bishop Ono had become a bishop as much as ten years before him, since Bishop Irenaeus now stands above him and governs the Church, it would be much more desirable for him to be made archbishop.[98]

While Irenaeus had thus confirmed his hold and begun to set the pattern for dependence upon and integration into the American Metropolia, the present discussion of apostolicity in the era of the Japanese Orthodox Church's relative independence concludes with the demise of Bishop Nicholas (Ono), the first Japanese national to have been ordained as Orthodox bishop. Since his quiet progress along the path of a parish priest had been interrupted by unsought-for ordination, he had come to personify the contradictions of the emergent Japanese Orthodox notion of episcopacy. Striving to embody both a venerable "Portable Shrine" supposed to unite autonomous sub-leaders under the broad shadow of its "democratic" passivity, as well as a strong charismatic leader in the vein of his predecessor and namesake, Bishop Nicholas displayed contradictory modes of behavior when the question of episcopacy was at stake. For instance, at the April 1946 Council, he had first boldly declared episcopal power to trump that of the Council and offered the delegates to "tie my hands and feet and cast me into the sea" if they would compel him to retire, but then meekly accepted withdrawal to Kannari "for recuperation."[99] He had shown himself unable to decline whenever appeals to common good

[98]Council (1955), 11-12.
[99]Council Provisional (1946), 40, 51.

Figure 7.3: Tokyo Resurrection cathedral, April 24 1954. Triumphant Bishop Irenaeus looks on as Bishop Nicholas signs the reconciliation document. From John Shōji Masatoshi.

had required a drastic, even sacrificial step on his part. Yet, once the step was taken, he found himself compelled to play the painful part of a peremptory ruler, openly challenging the will of the majority in the name of principles. Nicholas' private admissions and daily prayers for the forgiveness of his "unworthiness" of episcopal office reveal not only contrition, but also a struggle to comprehend what it is he, as bishop, was supposed to be.[100]

When Irenaeus suddenly approached Nicholas with an offer to arrange a general reconciliation, guarantee their parity as fellow bishops, and preserve the dignity of his followers—on condition of severing ties with Moscow—the

[100] Manabe (1996), 20.

189

81-year-old hierarch once more gave in. Although the text of the agreement presented by Irenaeus' side for signing at the reconciliation ceremony on April 24 1954 had been severely altered from what had been agreed upon earlier, the Japanese bishop signed it all the same, accepting the status of a subordinate and retired hierarch in order to "jointly continue God's work initiated by the great hierarch of the Japanese Church Archbishop Nicholas."[101] His last years passed in obscurity, but he attended his last two Councils— in 1954 and 1956—as both legitimate and tolerated, receiving an honorable burial at the Yanaka cemetery at the side of his predecessor-hierarchs.[102] His death on November 19 1956 robbed the American-aligned Japanese Orthodox Church of the last Meiji-period cleric trained by the Church's legendary founder.

Yet, one more such cleric, Fr. Anthony Takai, lived on in righteous defiance, as the sole representative of the Moscow Patriarchate in Japan, ensuring that the symbolic finale sounded by Bishop Nicholas' death could be interpreted equally well as a comma in the ongoing narration. Far from morphing into a frozen form, the Japanese Orthodox conception of apostolicity remained fluid.

However, the first trial of reconciling charisma and bureaucracy, democracy and autocracy, the political and the familial, canons and desires, the Japanese and the Russian, had run its logical course, encoding an important lesson into the corporate memory of the community.

---

[101] The preparatory talks, the text of the original draft of the agreement, and the consummation of the reconciliation are detailed in Manabe (1996), 18-19. The text of the agreement actually signed on April 24 1954 has been printed in Orthodox Messenger (1954.08.25 - № 778), 2.

[102] On Bishop Nicholas' funeral see Manabe (1996), 20; Orthodox Messenger (1956.12.05 - № 805), 3.

Chapter 8

Conclusion

There is a cyclical quality to the foregoing account, whereby post-war America displaced pre-revolutionary Russia. These countries figure as the source of orthodoxy, bishops and funds for the Japanese Orthodox Church, with foreign hierarchs attracting and managing money from abroad, and a domestic advisory organ assisting bishops in routine Church governance. Yet, a crucial difference in the vector of change vis-à-vis episcopal government is obvious. In the 1910's the newly established Conference was the first manifestation of the mounting anti-episcopal tide which had taken shape in opposition to the Church's founding father. In the 1950's the Consistory was an obedient tool of the newly-arrived foreign bishop, prodding believers to do their part in Church restoration efforts because, "as the bishop said," they "bear responsibility before Archbishop Nicholas."[1] The Japanese Orthodox Church has gone from a struggle for independence from the bishop to treasuring the connections a bishop brought, from confrontation with their ruling hierarch to veneration of him as their founding father. This turnaround had been worked by some four decades of de

---

[1]Council (1955), 8.

facto independence, which had provided the community with experience of manipulating and discovering the meaning of apostolicity.

The Russian Revolution left the unfunded bishop at the mercy of his flock, which, armed with Japanese cultural, Russian bureaucratic, and modern political models, proceeded to erect a partially encoded legal regimen to restrain the bishop, empower a largely self-selecting elite, and proclaim a democratic and constitutional "Council-centrism." The prevailing notion of the bishop split into three—the idealized founder in heaven, his despotic alter-ego in opprobrium, and the "ruling" bishop in the margins. The latter, himself a devotee of democracy, did not attempt to counteract this structure, instead seeking fulfillment on its periphery—in emergencies and external relations. Yet, the direction of his quest rendered the peripheral bishop increasingly inconvenient, and the onset of wartime "national mobilization" pushed the Japanese community to finally assume total self-control by removing its nominal head. Only then did it appear, that, as guarantor of unity and legitimacy, the bishop had been the linchpin of the ecclesiastical edifice. With factionalism rampant, it was a matter of very brief time before one of the competing groups would seize upon the universal canonical foundations of episcopal power and shatter the parochial democratic presentism of its opponents. For all its unpopularity, a small minority which effectively wielded a legitimate bishop turned the tide of competition in its favor—and did so twice, despite the weak character of its compromised hierarch. Having thus catalyzed and witnessed the unexpected power of apostolic authority, the Japanese also found themselves in utter destitution, with an influential foreigner from a winning superpower as their best bet for speedy recovery. Yet, as if in a twist of poetic justice, at the time when they were most eager to procure an activist bishop from abroad, they received a most passive one, who surpassed the erstwhile constitutionalists' dreams by his staid inactivity.

Only after enduring six years of such stop-gap episcopacy were the Japanese provided with a possessive and energetic hierarch they, despite themselves, had come to desire.

Destructive and transformative cataclysms of the Russian Revolution and World War II, marked by dramatic interventions of various state agents, were for the Japanese Orthodox community not so much meaning-making events, as stimulators in its process of self-discovery. Having enacted episcopal primacy in himself, Archbishop Nicholas confirmed the validity of the canonical tradition of the Orthodox Church for the body of believers which depended on his person and the corpus of Orthodox teachings for its self-definition. Yet, this dependence did not presuppose active reliance or even cognizance—it took nearly forty years of harsh calamities for canons to become actively quoted and the memories of both the "great" and the "despotic" Nicholas to once again merge into a more realistic image of the "apostle."

Part III

Circumscribing catholic selfhood

Chapter 9

Catholicity and its agents

Part III queries the practice and perception of Japanese Orthodox Church's external relations. Defining and dealing with the "external" involves resolving the basic "internal" question of the boundaries of the self. For an Orthodox Christian community the prescribed answer is furnished by the notion of *catholicity*—the most elusive of the creedal self-definitions of the Church. Derived from the Greek *cath ola* – "throughout the whole"—this word can only be approximated by a translation like "all-pertinence." Operating in the milieu where *cosmos* ("the world") and *oikoumene* ("the inhabited earth") were common terms, the creators of original Christian terminology consistently denoted the Church's vast reach as neither "cosmic" nor "ecumenical" but "catholic"[1]—a usage which remained an untranslated loanword throughout the languages of Western Christendom. Eastern Christendom was bolder in its attempts to clarify the term, thus producing the Slavonic *sobornost'* and the Japanese *ōyake*, rich with resonant

[1]Pomazansky (2005), 245.

197

but divergent associations within each linguistic system. As a result, in its engagement with the notion of catholicity, the Japanese Orthodox Church was equipped with as much as three explanatory avenues for this confusing word—from Orthodox catechisms, from Russian philosophy, and from Japanese language. This introduction aims to present the basic notion of catholicity and characterize the agents involved in its practical elaboration.

The catechetical literature, generally available to Japanese Orthodox believers, presented catholicity as "universality." This was the most readily apparent upshot of the exposition on the subject in St. Philaret's *Catechism*, detailed in chapter 3. Further simplified in Fr. Symeon Mii's explanation, "catholicity" became global openness. Because all men are able and are meant to belong to it, the Church "is indeed a common society for the whole world which accepts all people, for which reason the Church is called 'catholic.'"[2] Key to this definition is the overcoming of the boundaries of space, time and ethnicity. To be catholic in this sense meant to be in connection—or, as the ecclesiastical usage goes, in communion—with fellow Orthodox of all places, epochs and peoples, as well as being ready to include seekers from every direction. This chapter is centrally concerned with the application of this primary sense of catholicity.

Another current interpretation, purveyed by some Russians and by their Japanese initiates, saw catholicity as "conciliarity." This term, subsequently exported worldwide as a qualitatively new loanword, is in fact a literal rendition of the preferred Slavonic translation for catholicity—*sobornost'*—whose root is the word *sobor* ("gathering," "assembly," "council"). The powerful intellectual current of anti-Western Slavophilism, which sought universal verities in the distinctive life and spirituality of the Russian people, reinvented this ecclesiological term into an ideological banner. Alexis

[2]Mii (1934), 27.

Khomiakov, the most influential exponent and most profound theologian among the Slavophiles, set the stage by his writings since the 1840's. His fresh perspective centered on the catholicity of the Church as the Divinely maintained unity of all right believers joined by love and truth. The corollary to this view was the relative marginalization of apostolicity, and thus of hierarchy. Once they became fodder for broader public, Khomiakov's notions were soon vulgarized into a teaching akin to popular sovereignty within the Church, with the "conciliarity" of the believers' masses juxtaposed against the authority of the hierarchy.[3] Hereafter, to be catholic in this sense would require conciliar popular consensus to all significant decisions in Church life—the very "democracy" as contrasted with the bishop's "autocracy," treated in Part II.

There was also a third explanation, available to the Japanese believers through the testimony of the Japanese language, which rendered catholicity as "publicness". Well before the rise of the 19th century missionary movement in East Asia the character 公 (ōyake or kō in Japanese) had become identified with catholicity in Chinese Roman Catholic terminology, a crucial theological decision appropriated into modern Japanese Christian parlance during its formative 1870's.[4] In Japan the term ōyake had a millennial pedigree, with the basic sense of "public" and primary connotations of "governmental," "official," "unselfish," "open." Although the Western notions of a "public" made up of individuals standing apart, even against the state—i.e. the "society"—had penetrated Japanese discourse in the latter 19th century, the strong tie of "publicness" to both the state-centered nation and selfless service thereto remained a hallmark of

[3] For Khomiakov's ecclesiological teachings see an overview in Florovsky ([1937] 1983), 270-285. Fr. Florovsky is at pains to defend Khomiakov's Orthodoxy against the influential attack of Fr. Paul Florenskii, precisely on the question of catholicity-as-conciliarity. For an appraisal of what Khomiakov's views often meant in the practice of 20th century Russian émigré communities see Protopopov (2005), 73-75.

[4] Japan Christian dictionary (1988), 378.

the Japanese public man until after World War II. To be catholic in this sense was to participate in the cause of the nation's enlightenment, to embrace a statist nationalism, which, although globally-aware, was hardly universalist.[5]

The foregoing triple definition made for a confusing idea of catholicity at best. Universalism, popular sovereignty and unselfish nationalism were easy enough to commingle, but not to integrate. Attempts to stay true to multiple definitions yielded uncanny chains of reasoning, such as:

> *Universality* ("catholicity"/公) is... the preservation by the Church of the core of Christianity [...] through two millennia in all countries of the world [...] through the united cooperation of clergy, teachers and believers... in a *Council* ("catholic gathering"/公会).[6]

In addition to this, it might further follow that since

> a *Council* ("catholic gathering"/公会) is a public deliberation... private feelings must be cast aside for the sake of *publicness* ("catholicity"/公).[7]

Alternatively, those writers who wished to escape the maze of meanings and delineate "catholicity" more precisely, were reduced to sacrificing the overloaded *ōyake* for a more cumbersome but clear compound, like *fuse*—(普世)—"throughout the world".[8] Balking at the conundrum, Japanese Orthodox discourse explicitly evoked and interrogated catholicity less often than the other creedal traits of the Church.

---

[5]The question of "publicness" in the thought and practice of Japan's pre-war intellectuals received an admirable treatment by Barshay (1988). For the discussion of term see especially pp. 5-19.

[6]Saikaishi (1931a).

[7]Council (1923), 44.

[8]Sergius (1933), 7.

This did not imply that the riddle of catholic selfhood—of identifying with the expansive "self" from the catechetical definition of catholicity-as-universality—was less significant than other definitional dilemmas of the community. The initial working model, established by Nicholas, built the Japanese Church into local, regional, global and universal contexts of Orthodoxy. This framework structured the Japanese community's socialization with a variety of mutually external agents who were supposed to be internalized by Orthodox believers into the all-embracing catholic self. Given the coexistence within the Japanese Orthodox "catholic field" of diverse Orthodox contingents, of the globally dispersed ecclesiastical administrative headquarters, of the non-Orthodox religious communions, and of the governments of secular world powers, just how were Japanese believers to digest this kaleidoscopic mix into a coherent identity? In the era of the World Wars this question was settled for them no less then by them, given the magnitude, multitude and mutability of actors on the catholic field of Japanese Orthodoxy.

Foremost actors in their own story were of course native believers of East Asia. The central presence were the Japanese, with maximal claims around 40,000 and realistic ones below 15,000 members.[9] There were also Koreans hovering around 500,[10] as well as at least a few hundred Chinese who became involved in the life of the Japanese Church. They imbibed the prevailing tenor of East Asia's age of nationalism, all the more so since Orthodoxy, while outlining wider conceptual spheres of existence, decisively confirmed the validity of the national one. Heightened esteem for the native customs, history and sovereign was more encouraged by the Orthodox Church than by other Christian missionary groups. Consequently, national liberation and introversion

[9]For details refer to the statistical table in fig. 2.4.
[10]In 1900-1925 the Korean Orthodox Mission recorded 675 baptisms, mostly of Koreans. There are reports of 700 native believers in 1934, and about 400 in 1957. See consecutively Theodosius ([1926] 1999), 306; Bolshakoff (1943), 74-75, citing *Irénikon*, January-April 1934, 100; Rutt (1957), 489.

became pronounced trends among native Orthodox believers. Occasionally detectible idealistic universalism of devoted missionaries, provincial ecumenists and leftist literati might easily blend into messianic readings of expansive nationalism. Given the strength of the divisive forces of political hostility, cultural alienation, and sheer ignorance, Russian attachments could rarely achieve popularity. "Independence," not catholicity, was the watchword of native Orthodox discourse in East Asia with regard to external relations.

The chief human fabric which prevented independence movements from completely fragmenting the East Asian Orthodox scene were the expatriates from the Russian Empire, the most numerous and complex Orthodox presence in early 20th century East Asia. Both Russian missionaries and migrants were often rather unwilling residents of the region, only few remaining for long—for instance, only five of over forty Russian clergy to serve in the Japanese Church until 1950's stayed on until death.[11] However, the post-revolutionary émigré wave was so great that its long-term "sediment" amounted to over 100,000 former Russian subjects.[12] Centered on Harbin, this large community was in close touch with other hubs of Russian dispersion throughout the world, its national links thus becoming global bridges.

The conclusion of World War II flooded the former Japanese Empire with foreign troops and new refugees, whose Orthodox representatives for a few years became guests,

[11] Aside from St. Nicholas (+ 1912) they were Metropolitan Sergius (Tikhomirov, + 1945), Archimandrite Theodosius (Perevalov, + 1933), Proto-priest Gregory Khodakovskii (+ 1950) and Protodeacon Demetrius L'vovskii (+ 1921).

[12] For a useful summation of statistical assessments see Markovchin (2003), 203-204. For a modern-day researcher's appraisal of the statistics of Russians in Manchuria alone—some 110,000 in 1931; some 61,000 in 1940—see Aurilene & Potapova (2004), 8, 57. The initial tide was much higher—a conservative estimate puts the number of Russians in January 1921 at 165,857 in Harbin, 288,225 in the Chinese Eastern Railroad zone, according to Melikhov (1997), 57-58.

members and masters of the local Church. The scope of this presence briefly rivaled that of native believers—in addition to the sizeable groups of American Orthodox and Russian refugees in occupied Japan, the combined Ethiopian and Greek expeditionary forces in the Korean War numbered over 5,000 servicemen.[13] These newcomers, most importantly officers and chaplains, brought previously unrepresented backgrounds, networks and preoccupations to the ecclesiastical life of East Asia, enabling and imposing scenarios of radical realignment in a global context.

All Orthodox believers depend for administrative legitimacy and global orientation on recognized ecclesiastical ruling organs of what are known as "autocephalous" (self-headed) Churches—in effect sovereign members of a commonwealth which forms the one global Orthodox Church. Distant headquarters might provide their authority, clergy, education, supplies and funds, exacting obedience and legitimization in return. It was within the purview of these centers to review the boundaries or status of local establishments, to promote senior clergy, and to alter canonical and statutory fixtures. Having been founded by the Russian Church, Orthodox bodies of East Asia were inscribed into its institutional edifice, so that an extension into this region of a non-Russian ecclesiastical jurisdiction in principle figured as an invasion. Yet, soon after the succession of the Moscow Patriarchate to the authority of Russia's pre-revolutionary Most Holy Synod, the persecuted Russian Church's central governance fell into disarray, fragmenting and drawing competitors into the whirlpool. The Synod of the Russian Orthodox Church Abroad posed as the alternative pan-Russian center, striving to unite all shards of the Russian Church around Sremski Karlovci or Munich instead of Moscow. A number of ecclesiastical headquarters sprung up on the periphery of the former Russian Empire, each asserting some form of local independence from

[13] The total of Ethiopians who fought in Korea is given as 3,518, while Greeks peaked with 1,263 soldiers according to Sandler (1995), 110, 126.

203

the Russian Church—saliently for East Asia, these included Orthodox establishments in Tokyo, Harbin and New York. Finally, the venerable Church of Constantinople operating from Istanbul, in a bid to recoup the loss of most of its flock in the 1922 Turko-Greek population exchange, made itself into a global competitor with the Russians by seeking to subordinate to itself all Orthodox outside of their traditional habitat. Bracketed between the struggle for total hegemony and the resignation to administrative pluralism, the jostling of jurisdictions was emerging as a tolerated norm in the post-revolutionary Orthodox ecclesiastical life of East Asia.

As intra-ecclesiastical jurisdictional disunity deepened, the interwar period saw the peak of Orthodox involvement with Protestants—first of all Anglicans—over the issues of inter-ecclesiastical unity. Encounters steering the ecumenical movement occurred primarily in Europe, but the phenomenon penetrated globally through self-selected channels. Meanwhile, the regional leadership of Protestantism in defining a generic conception of Christianity in East Asia, as well as the post-war relationship with the somewhat Protestantized Russian-Americans, catalyzed the otherwise subtle global dynamic into a Protestant-oriented drift in the life of Japan's Orthodox.

The most important non-religious entity to sway the region's ecclesiastical life was the Japanese imperial state. As the chief arbiter of the region's ethno-political boundaries, both territorial and conceptual, it played the role of an architect of those ecclesiastical establishments ideologically tied to these boundaries. The state's conceptions of civic orthodoxy manifested themselves most palpably in the evolution of the formal ritual structure of state Shintoism, the legal regimen for religious organizations, and the demands for the severance of extra-Japanese ties by religious bodies. Particular salience of Orthodoxy to burdened relations with Russia ensured for the Church "special treatment" from Japanese officials, while dozens of notable Japanese Orthodox Russia-hands employed by the state served as important conduits in this uneasy international relationship. As a result of clashing religious policies by competing agencies—one developed for religion in general, another tailored to Russian Orthodoxy in particular—Japanese official figures eventually involved themselves both in Japanizing and Russifying, isolating and linking, fostering and combating the Orthodox Church throughout East Asia.

The approach of the USSR and the USA was simpler, dovetailing with the confrontational policies of the Cold War. While the former succeeded the Russian imperial government, which had once supported Orthodoxy throughout the world with its supplies and prestige, this heritage was initially employed by the Soviets only to wrestle for control of East Asian missions' properties. Significant involvement of Soviet authorities with the region's believers came only in the latter phase of World War II, in line with Stalin's project to employ the world's Orthodox Churches as information gathering, social engineering and public relations networks. This, in turn, drew the Americans into a reactive effort, which included exclusions, purges, counterespionage and counterpropaganda in the name of anti-communism. As a prolongation of the Russian Civil War in a new guise, the Cold War manifested itself in the ecclesiastical sphere both swiftly and decisively.

The shape and success of the balancing acts, new en-counters and partings, which formed the current of the Japanese Church's catholic life in the post-Nicholaevan period, was predicated on the acts, relationships and perceptions held by the above constituent and associated communities, organizations and institutions. The notion of catholicity insured than none of them could be excluded from compre-hensive ecclesiastical self-definition. However, each brought distinctive views and commitments to the configuration of the local, regional, global and universal in the life of the Orthodox Church. The groping engagement of these mutually "external" agents became an "internal" clarification of the

205

boundaries of the Japanese Orthodox Church's corporate self—an experiential realization of catholicity.

Chapter 10

The fourfold identity and its fissures

Nicholas' foundation of the Orthodox Church in Japan became a globally noted event because he had been engaged in a universalist venture. Building up a new community within a delineated space, time and population, he had been simultaneously fusing it into a tiered global society. By drawing people into that global society, he had been introducing a new universalist presence into his limited field of activity. As a result, the emerging community was not only inscribed, but also involved in the life of a worldwide matrix. This involvement might be usefully delineated into four concentric spheres—local, regional, global and universal. The Japanese Orthodox Church under Nicholas exhibited meaningful engagement at all of these levels of its fourfold self, coming close to actuating claimed catholicity.

In line with Nicholas' initial resolution, the documents which chartered the Orthodox Mission in Japan—its June 3 1871 *Statute* and *Instruction*—provided for its operation in "Japan" and among the "Japanese."[1]   This postulated the ethno-political integrity of Japan, already established in Western discourse, confirming the nation-building effort of the modern Japanese state. Although the earliest Orthodox publications in Japan were marked as issuing from the "Orthodox Church," by the start of 1880's they were increasingly invoking the "Japanese Orthodox Church,"[2] just as Nicholas' diaries showed him beginning to write of the "Japanese Church."[3]

The totality of Japan was the principal locus for Nicholas' efforts at creating a self-sufficient local Orthodox Church—of, by and for the Japanese people. His abiding efforts to train a full array of Japanese ecclesiastical servitors—clergy, catechists, teachers, translators, iconographers, choirmasters, monastics, even an architect—made for an exceptionally high percentage of diversified native cadres compared to other Christian missionary organizations in contemporary Japan. Special attention to women's education helped anchor this elite into self-propagating ecclesiastically-devoted households, following the familial pattern of the Japanese religious economy.

Nicholas' welcoming attitude allowed for the "churching" of complex terminology from Sino-Japanese literary culture, as well as of distinctive practices which seasoned the Japanese Orthodox Church with a domestic savor absent from most Western-originated religious bodies. For instance, the ecclesiastically sanctioned routine included removing shoes in church,[4] using rice for ritual memorial meals,[5]

---

[1] Sablina (2006), 307-315.

[2] For example Council (1881).

[3] For one of the earliest uses of the "Japanese Church" in Nicholas' diaries see Nicholas (2004), vol. 1 (1879.11.27), 119. By the end of his life this usage almost wholly supplanted the original "Japanese Mission" in his diaries.

[4] In line with the removal of shoes in Japanese homes, Shintoist shrines and Buddhist temples. Ubiquitous Orthodox Christian practice in other countries presumes shoes.

[5] Rice being the principal crop of Japan. Orthodox Christians in their historic habitat use wheat.

refurbishing household Buddhist and Shintoist altars for Christian use, practicing martial arts as means of hygiene,[6] reverencing the sites and objects of state Shintoism.[7] The latter, having been declared by the Japanese state a matter of every loyal subject's duty, illustrated another avenue whereby Nicholas endeavored to ensure the nativization of Orthodoxy—patriotism. Conscientious support for Japan's wars with China and Russia, the veneration of imperial and ancestral monuments, and above all a deferent and transparent attitude toward the government, earned the Japanese Orthodox a reputation for loyalty. The well-publicized Japanese Orthodox blueprint of the ideal Church-state symbiosis embraced the constitutional description of the Japanese emperor as "sacred and inviolable," drawing on the Orthodox rendition of the theory of the Divine right of kings.[8] The three "nationalist virtues" of raising native personnel, recycling customary practices, and reaffirming ascendant patriotism, while to a degree common among missionary Christian groups in Japan, were uncommonly pronounced in Nicholas' Japanese Orthodox Church.

The principal counterpart to the Japanese Church at the national level had been the state—Japan's main arbiter of the national definition and religious economy. The first response of the Japanese official elite to the appearance of Orthodox Christianity in Japan was predictably hostile. For example, Kuroda Kiyotaka combated the spread of Orthodoxy in 1870's Hakodate with specially dispatched counter-propagandists,[9] and Sugi Kōji opined that, since "Russia regards the Greek Church as a tool for expansion... the danger arising from its long-term penetration cannot be expressed in words."[10]

---

[6]Judō was taught at the Orthodox Tokyo Theological Seminary. For Nicholas' high opinion of this martial art see Nicholas (2004), vol. 5 (1909.04.24), 517.

[7]For instance see Nicholas (2004), vol. 5 (1911.11.01), 807.

[8]Ishikawa (1892), 66-83.

[9]Sasaki (2004), 363.

[10]Braisted (1976), 37.

By 1885 Inoue Kakugorō of the Japanese Foreign Ministry, claiming to represent such leading Japanese political luminaries as Fukuzawa, Gotō, Ōkuma and Ichigaki, had come to trust the Japanese Orthodox establishment sufficiently to ask from it Russia's aid in the dissidents' plans to topple the ruling Meiji regime. To his surprise, Inoue learned in a confidential talk with Nicholas that the mission was in fact a religious institution with little capacity and no desire to involve itself in subversive politics.[11]

However, despite a clear preference for the position of premier cultural intermediaries rather than secondary political agents, Nicholas and his adepts were drawn as brokers into a variety of vital Russo-Japanese official encounters. These included serving as principal interpreters each time a member of the Russian imperial family visited Japan during the Meiji period,[12] and playing the role of Japan's spokesmen after the assault on the Russian crown prince in the Ōtsu incident of 1891. By the time of the 1895 Tripartite intervention, as Russia hampered the Japanese takeover of China's strategic Liaodong Peninsula, the Japanese state had learned to value the Japanese Orthodox community sufficiently to become its protector against possible anti-Russian mob violence.[13] Since the close of 1890's a group of Japanese Orthodox seminary-graduates—soon known as the Army's "Nicholas-band"—quickly established themselves as notable Russia-hands in Japanese military schools.[14] Ranking together with the Tokyo Foreign Language School and the military schools as one of three major centers of Russian-language learning, the Japanese Orthodox Church would

[11] Nicholas (2004), vol. 2 (1885.09.07), 279.

[12] The Japanese Orthodox interpreters in question were Nicholas himself and a Japanese Orthodox convert from the ranks of imperial courtier nobility, Sergius Made-no-Kōji. Orthodox Messenger (1914.06.20 - №3-12), 42.

[13] Nicholas (2004), vol. 3 (1895.05.26), 88.

[14] Daniel Konishi began teaching Russian at military schools in late 1890's; Emelian Higuchi—in 1900; Arsenius Iwasawa—in 1902. Many more joined during the Russo-Japanese War, including Basil Nobori, Panteleimon Satō and Sergius Shōji. See their profiles in Naganawa (2007), 213-219, 223-224.

thereafter serve as a notable source of Russia-hands for official
professorial and translation jobs.[15] During the Russo-Japanese
War the Japanese secular authorities not only guarded the
Orthodox Church, but employed it overtly as a facet of Japan's
humanitarian public relations campaign and covertly as a
network for espionage in Russia.[16] Representation at the
state-convoked Pan-religious Conferences in 1906 and 1913,
at which the government mustered mainstream Shintoist,
Buddhist and Christian groups behind its moral suasion
initiatives, proved the Orthodox to have gained a reputable
spot in Japan's state-sanctioned religioscape.[17]

Although the Japanese statesmen have thus gradually
developed a comparatively favorable attitude to the Japanese
Orthodox community, the trajectory of broader Japanese
public discourse was more complex. Until the Russo-Japanese
War decisively "purified the atmosphere around the Mission"
by convincing public opinion of the Church's patriotic loyalty,
the Orthodox community struggled to disprove popular
Japanese suspicions "of political connections: that it is
preparing the conquest of Japan by Russia and the like."[18]
Just as in the case of other missionary groups, self-sufficiency
of the nascent Japanese Orthodox community was partial,
its local reality being rooted in a larger regional—in this
case Russian—presence. In the recurrent organic metaphor
of Orthodox parlance, the Russian Orthodox Church was
the "Mother" of the Japanese "Daughter," with the Russian
Spiritual Mission in Japan as an umbilical cord.

[15]For an overview of Japanese Russian-language education see Nobori &
Akamatsu (1981), 11-33.

[16]While the humanitarian campaign to aid Russian POWs is well known, an
example of Japanese espionage via ecclesiastical channels is one Basil Ozeki.
He assumed a role of a fervent convert, deceived Bishop Nicholas and other
clergy, and surveyed the military installations of Siberia enjoying the trust of
Russian elites. See Nicholas (2004), vol. 5 (1906.01.10), 305-307.

[17]The Orthodox were represented at these conferences by their leading
layman, Peter Ishikawa. See Ishikawa's *curriculum vitae* in the Foreign Ministry
file on the Siberian dispatch (1918), 410114.

[18]Nicholas (2004), vol. 5 (1909.02.19), 496.

Figure 10.1: Tokyo Orthodox Seminary, ca. 1910. Archbishop Nicholas and Bishop Sergius surrounded by instructors, Japanese seminarians, and Russian pupils in jūdō uniforms. From Nagoya Orthodox church collection.

The only perennial member of this Mission was Nicholas himself, Japan's premier teacher of things Russian and Russia's pioneer Japanologist. However, a few of his Russian aides did make valuable contributions especially in the field of education, while the supplies conveyed from official and private Russian sources were indispensable to the emergence of the Japanese Church. The principal prop was grant-money, consistently providing for over 90% of the Japanese Orthodox community's material needs. Material support also included such requisites as candles, personal devotional items, icons, vestments, bells, church-furnishings, and a broad selection of books—in sum, not only munitions, but a thick deposit of Russian material and spiritual culture which shaped the environment of Japanese believers and spilled into the popular perception of Russia in contemporary Japan.

A vital aspect of intangible aid was education. During Nicholas' days, well over a thousand Japanese received a hybrid Russo-Japanese ecclesiastical training in Japan's Orthodox schools,[19] while Russia's theological and artistic higher educational establishments hosted some twenty promising Japanese high-achievers.[20] Finally valuable assistance was rendered by Russia's diplomats, who eased the complex matter of initial acquisition and registration of property.[21] Without strong and steady Russian support the Japanese Orthodox community would not have materialized.

However, once extant, the Japanese believers entered into a mutually transforming relationship with their neighboring coreligionists. Nicholas explicitly charged his Japanese study abroad students to work for the "rapprochement of their

[19]Naganawa (2007), 210, estimates there to have been about 1000 students during the 50-year operation of the Tokyo Theological Seminary alone. In addition, one must consider the students of the Tokyo Catechist School, Tokyo and Kyoto Women's Seminaries.

[20]For the most up-to-date summary on Nicholas-era Japanese students sent to Russia by the Orthodox Church see Naganawa (2007), 208-227. He accounts for the following 18 persons: Irene Yamashita Rin (sent in 1880 to study iconography at the St. Petersburg Novodevichii Resurrection monastery), Alexander Matsui Jurō (1882, St. Petersburg Theological Academy), Symeon Mii Michirō (1883, Kiev Theological Academy), Arsenius Iwasawa Heikichi (1883, Moscow Theological Seminary, St. Petersburg Theological Academy), Gregory Nagazaka (1884, died en route), Panteleimon Satō Yoshiharu (1884, Kazan Theological Academy), Andrew Minamoto Keizō (1887, St. Petersburg Theological Academy), Peter Ishigame (1887, Moscow Theological Academy), Daniel Konishi Masutarō (1887, Kiev Theological Academy), Clement Nameta Yoshio (1888, Kiev Theological Academy), Sergius Shōji Shōgorō (1888, St. Petersburg Theological Academy), John Senuma Kakusaburō (1890, St. Petersburg Theological Seminary, Kiev Theological Academy), Mark Saikaishi Shizuka (1890, Kiev Theological Academy), Emelian Higuchi Tsuyanosuke (1890, St. Petersburg Theological Academy), Innocent Kisu Yoshinoshin (1981, St. Petersburg Imperial Conservatory), Gordius Shiina Kotei (1892, Irkutsk Theological Seminary, Kazan Theological Academy, St. Petersburg Theological Academy), Theodore Yansen/Yanase Heinoshin (1899, St. Petersburg Theological Academy), Mary Shibayama Hideko (1909, St. Petersburg Imperial Fine Arts School)—the latter two were not sent directly through ecclesiastical channels, but performed a similar liaison function. Naganawa fails to account for one Nakakōji, mentioned—perhaps mistakenly—as a theological academy student in Nishimura (1972), 57.

[21]For an overview of the complex tangle of the property rights to the Tokyo Orthodox headquarters compound which resulted from the Meiji-period arrangements see Orthodox Messenger (1954.10.25 - № 780), 5.

motherland with Russia,"[22] and they joined the veteran missionary and his Russian aides as early popularizers of Japan in Russia. As "the glory and strength" of Russian missions,[23] the Japanese venture—well-known among non-Orthodox Christians and appreciated even by Russia's liberals, otherwise critical of the oppressive religio-political condominium inside the empire[24]—was becoming a public relations boon for the Mother-Church. As such, it enjoyed stable, interested and non-interventionist support of the one figure which dominated the Russian Orthodox Church at the close of the 19th century—Constantine Pobedonostsev, Over-Procurator of the Most Holy Synod (Russia's *de facto* Minister of Religion).[25]

The Russo-Japanese War furnished many Russians with large-scale first-hand experience of Japan and its Church, as tens of thousands of POWs found themselves the temporary flock of Japanese clerics. Thereafter Russian scholars, students and travelers increasingly trickled into the country of their victors, many making the Tokyo Orthodox compound their frequent haunt and temporary home.[26] By the end of Nicholas' tenure the initial mission-centered one-way traffic from Russia to Japan was becoming a ramified two-

[22]Nicholas (2004), vol.3 (1895.11.24), 210.

[23]The expression from the October 22 1917 epistle from the Council of the Russian Orthodox Church to the Japanese Church, cited in Mii (1982), 143.

[24]For a sample of the sentiment see Seryshev (1952-1968), 51.

[25]In addition to frequent mentions in Nicholas' diaries, see the overview of Pobedonostsev's attitude toward the Japanese Church in Byrnes (1968), 217, 449.

[26]The most notable of the scholars was the prominent Russian Japanologist, Professor Demetrius Matveevich Pozdneev, who spent five years at the side of Archbishop Nicholas. Frequently mentioned in Nicholas' diaries, "his name known in the Japanese Orthodox Church," his writings were occasionally published in the Japanese *Orthodox Messenger*. See Orthodox Messenger (1914.05.20 - № 3-10), 54; Ihaho (1915), 22-25. The enrollment of Russian students at the Tokyo Orthodox Theological Seminary was probably near its peak in 1908, when there were 16 (of them 13 sent to Japan by the Khabarovsk and Harbin Russian military administrations)—see Michaelson (1999), 350-351, citing Orthodox Evangelist (1909.09 - № 17), 50-56.

way network, whose illustrious byproducts included the popularization of Russian 19th century literature and four-part singing in Japan,[27] and of the Chinese Classics and Judō in Russia.[28] The regional missionary presence of the Russian Orthodox Church had also provided the medium for Pan-Asian ventures, with the Chinese Orthodox Mission supplying its bicentennial expertise in Classical Chinese theological terminology, and the Japanese Mission becoming the hub for ordaining both Chinese and Korean Orthodox clergy. With the improvement of Russo-Japanese political clime, the Japanese community's place in the life of the wider Russian Church was shifting into a more profound participation with a prospect of partnership.

If the international existence of the Japanese Orthodox Church had been grounded solely in Russia, the community is unlikely to have withstood Japan's popular anti-Russianism, especially its intense wave during the decade preceding the Russo-Japanese War. Nicholas made a point of publicizing the global presence of Orthodoxy whenever he had positive first-hand illustrations. After his 1879-1880 circumnavigation of the globe, in a November 1880 sermon to the Japanese believers Nicholas highlighted his encounter with the most eminent Orthodox prelate in the world, Patriarch Joachim III of Constantinople, emphasizing that

> there was no place in the world that did not know about the Orthodox Church in Japan, [...] However

[27]For the best summary of the Russian cultural imports into Japan under the auspices of Nicholas' Orthodox mission see Potapov (2004), who treats art, architecture, music, education, literature, philosophy, translations and political relations.

[28]Compared to Japanese imports from Russia via the Orthodox mission, Russian imports from Japan along the same route are understudied. The translations of the Chinese Classics into Russian were done by the Japanese Orthodox disciple of Tolstoy, Daniel Konishi Masutarō; Judō was redacted into the Russian Sambo by Basil Sergeevich Oshchepkov, a one-time student at the Tokyo Orthodox Seminary. On Konishi see especially Ōta (2007), with a Tolstoyan emphasis, and Sugii (1984), 413-424, which inscribes him into the broad Japanese Christian context. On Oshchepkov see Lukashev (1982, 2003).

small our Japanese Church may be, we should know that it has already joined the One Holy Apostolic Church, become one of its members.[29]

Among these "members" of world Orthodoxy, Nicholas stressed Greek Churches—the most ancient and prominent non-Slavic Orthodox communities. The Japanese Church often evoked their existence to deflect anti-Russianism in the later 1890's and early 1900's. Thus, in early 1894 an unexpected visit to the Tokyo Orthodox cathedral by a Greek Metropolitan, Dionysius (Latas) of Zante, was transformed into a vindication of Orthodoxy's global character. To com-memorate this event, Dionysius' sermon, spoken in Tokyo, was translated and widely distributed as a booklet throughout Japanese Orthodox parishes.[30] Through connections with the Jerusalem Orthodox Church, in 1895-1897 Nicholas received and publicized a number of letters and hallowed objects from the Holy Land, making as many as 500 copies of the portrait of Patriarch Gerasimus II of Jerusalem for distribution.[31]

As anti-Russianism mounted, the standard Orthodox re-sponse was to retrace the historical track of Christianity—through Russia to Greece and thence Judea—pointing out the age-old Orthodox presence in each of these lands.[32] Compared to the otherwise common usage of Russian vignettes, the lavishly decorated 1905 album celebrating Japanese Orthodox soldiers of the Russo-Japanese War was striking by the abundance of Greek inscriptions.[33] In sum, even if the Russian Church was the proximate "Mother" of the Japanese Church, it was vital for the young community to assert familial links

[29] Nicholas (1933), 18.

[30] For a testimony of the significance of the event see Mii (1982), 78-80. See Dionysius' sermon printed in Orthodox Messenger (1950.07.15 - № 732), 1.

[31] For an overview of the links between the Japanese and Jerusalem Orthodox Churches see Besstremiannaia (2007), for the events of the 1890's see pp. 331-334.

[32] Nicholas (2004), vol. 4 (1903.10.17), 878.

[33] Mizushima (1905).

worldwide, averring that even the "Jerusalem Church, the Mother of Christian Churches... accepts our Church into the number of its Daughters."[34]

Last but not least, the existence of an Orthodox community was impossible without a universal dimension, which posited and engaged the entire world—from the microcosm of personal conscience through the macrocosm of the spiritual realm to the supracosmic presence of God. It is in this space, as envisioned by Orthodox theology, that each believer was brought into mystical communion with all other members of the Church, received aid and harm from fellow men and spiritual beings, and ultimate salvation from God—the ruling Head of the Church in the person of Jesus Christ. For believers, arguably the most important fruit of the mission was the formation of "a small colony of Japanese in the Kingdom of Heaven."[35]

If ecclesiastical boundaries at the local, regional and global levels of the Church were ethno-territorial, the boundary at the universal level was doctrinal. Indeed, only those who first accepted its existence could be equipped to engage this universe. In Nicholas' words,

> the Church, as a Divinely-established Community, solemnly repeats its Rules, placed at the community's foundation—its Creed—and solemnly declares, that all, who do not wish to adhere to these rules, are rejected by her as non-members, as aliens.[36]

Coupled with an imperative to preach the purport of their creed, this lucid yet easy-to-cross demarcation between "us" and "them" provided for the most readily apparent testimony

[34]Nicholas (2004), vol. 3 (1896.01.12), 237.
[35]Nicholas (2004), vol. 2 (1885.01.23), 267.
[36]Nicholas (2004), vol. 1 (1870.03.13), 72.

to universality—missionary openness. Abiding concern for the propagation of Orthodoxy rendered Nicholas an avid inquirer into mission as practiced the world over by various Christian denominations, drew him into lively discussions with a diverse cross-section of the religiously-concerned public, and finally earned him a seal of "apostleship" from his own Orthodox Church.[37]   Indeed, it appears that the sole cause for which Nicholas seriously considered leaving Japan in his mature years was his plan to mastermind a global Orthodox outreach program for the "unification of all."[38]   The nascent Japanese Orthodox community brought new prominence to the office of the catechist—full-time lay preacher.   An ancient office long lapsed in the Orthodox Church, it had been revived in Russian Orthodox missionary establishments in the 19th century, and flourished in Japan, becoming the motor of on-the-ground missionary work.[39] Even regular Japanese parishioners were encouraged to engage in public sermonizing and expected to introduce new inquirers to local catechists. Viewing missionary orientation as a barometer of universalist practice, one must place the Japanese Orthodox community at the vanguard of their contemporary coreligionists.

Although individual outreach efforts of the Japanese Orthodox extended in any promising direction, Nicholas generally saw better prospects in dealing with Buddhists in the non-Christian milieu and with Protestants in the Christian one. Among the latter the main interlocutor of the contemporary worldwide Orthodox Church had been the Anglican

[37]While Nicholas' diaries abound with accounts about his missionary encounters and considerations, one of the more intriguing documents to have emerged from the camp of Nicholas' opponents is the transcript of what purportedly was a formal religious dispute between the Archbishop and a famous Shintoist preacher Sano Tsunehiko, presented in Inoue (1991), 191-209.

[38]See Nicholas (2004), vol.   2 (1889.04.18), 318-320; (1889.04.19), 320; (1889.05.02), 321.

[39]A brief introduction to the Japanese Orthodox catechist system is available in Oda (1996).

Communion. Since mid-1800's individual Englishmen—and by the end of the century periodical Lambeth Conferences—made efforts to draw the Orthodox into union talks, spurring Russians and Greeks to undertake considerable research into the nature of Anglicanism.[40] Just as mission became the "mother of ecumenism" among various Protestant groups, the same occurred between the Anglicans and the Orthodox, as they encountered each other face-to-face outside of their habitual settings. In America the prominent Orthodox missionary St. Tikhon (Bellavin) went as far as to approve for Orthodox usage a modified Anglican liturgy,[41] in Korea the Orthodox left Anglicans in charge of their mission for the duration of the Russo-Japanese War,[42] and in Persia Anglicans in effect handed over their vast mission-field among Urmia's Assyrians to the Orthodox.[43]

The Japanese dimension of the encounter was no less significant. Nicholas was a regular host and occasional guest of many Anglican clergy, and repeated Anglican-Orthodox reunion conferences after the Russo-Japanese War were attended by both Western and Japanese ecclesiastical notables.[44] To be sure, Nicholas's view of the "unification of the Churches" demanded of his Anglican visitors to "discard everything contrary to the dogmas of the Orthodox Church,"[45] a subject on which he was ready to defend his unyielding position, even if it meant "greater disunity."[46]

Yet, his approachable earnestness, his ready allowance for variation in "everything non-dogmatic," and the general progress of pan-Christian and Anglican-Orthodox cooperation created many scenes of apparent unity. For instance, in the distant town of Abashiri on Hokkaido the freshly-arrived

[40]Geffert (2010), 9-29.
[41]The so-called "Liturgy of St. Tikhon."
[42]Rutt, 484.
[43]Coakley (1992), 216-234.
[44]For a brief summary see Nakamura (2003), 98-101.
[45]Nicholas (2004), vol. 3 (1895.06.07), 96.
[46]Nicholas (2004), vol. 5 (1909.10.25), 588.

Bishop Sergius was greeted jointly by the local Orthodox and Anglicans, who then processed through the town, drawing in some other Protestants along the way.[47] Under Nicholas' leadership, nascent Orthodox inter-Christian ecumenism in Japan exhibited both a pointed missionary purpose and a certain pull on Protestants.

As follows from the above, the Orthodox body in Japan was a distinct local Japanese collective, a filial of a regional Russian organization, a branch of a global communion, and an agent of a universal conceptual community. Being catholic, then, meant maintaining this fourfold identity through coordinated operation of the local, regional, global and universal spheres. This required considerable familiarity with and adherence to each sphere, but above all a masterful balance of them all—qualities authoritatively wielded by Nicholas to allow the Japanese Orthodox Church to develop its expansive matrix of relationships.

His statements on the subject of catholic links manifested a simplicity both disarming and deceptive. Witness his 1909 response to the query from the Department of Religions of the Japanese Ministry of Internal Affairs about the relationship between the Japanese and Russian Churches: "By the decree of the Russian Most Holy Synod in 1870 the Japanese Mission was established... in fulfillment of the Savior's commandment to preach the Gospel to all peoples." Here was a local entity created by a regional agent to carry out the global will of a universal actor. Nicholas then went on to make assertions of Japanese Church's independence in two different spheres—as a diocese with its own hierarch *among* those of the Russian Church, and as a local Church with its nascent internal rules *apart* from those of the Russian Church. Simultaneously, he confirmed the Japanese Church's dependence within the same spheres—financially on organizations operating from *within*

[47] Sergius ([1941] 1971), 1-2.

Russia, and legislatively on the ecclesiastical canons mandated from *without* Russia.[48]

These statements were equally as transparent and yet puzzling as his momentous general epistles upon the outbreak of the Russo-Japanese War. In the first such epistle he called his flock to "fulfill everything, which love for the fatherland requires," and to remember that "in addition to the earthly fatherland, we also have a Heavenly Fatherland [which is] the Church."[49] Thus, the war proved sufficiently manageable for Nicholas to publicly declare it "useful, inasmuch as it will rectify incorrect notions about the relationship of Japanese Orthodox Christians to Russia," in particular debunking the notion that "the Orthodox depend on the Russian emperor, who is supposedly the head of the Orthodox Church."[50] The resultant manifestation of the Japanese Church's catholicity, as native clergy and their bishop prayed separately for the victory of their respective empires, but worked together to pastor Japanese believers and Russian POWs, illustrated the import of drawing superable boundaries through foundational Christian formulae.

Nicholas' centrality to the life of the Japanese Church and his strong purpose-driven will had allowed him to assign most events with their "proper place" within a universal ecclesiastical relational scheme. However, given the towering presence of the state in structuring the religious life of contemporary Japan and Russia, Nicholas' had well realized that the mission's decisive success hinged on a "political combination, whereby the Japanese government would find it expedient to adhere to Russia—just as now it adheres to Germany and England."[51]

---

[48]Nicholas (2004), vol. 5 (1909.04.23), 516-517.

[49]"General Epistle №1" was issued on February 14 1904. Russian original transcribed in Nicholas (2004), vol. 5 (1904.02.12), 16-17; Japanese translation reprinted in Kushiro church (1992), 245.

[50]From the wartime "General Epistle №2," issued on March 13 1904. Nicholas (2004), vol. 5 (1904.03.13), 38-40.

[51]Nicholas (2004), vol. 2 (1889.08.16), 324.

By the time of Nicholas' death in 1912, this hoped-for combination appeared to be materializing at last, paving the way for the Russo-Japanese alliance of 1916. The resultant pro-Russian current in Japan's public life buoyed the Orthodox mission precisely at the time of its precarious regime change, as Japan's new Orthodox hierarch, Bishop Sergius, groped for a new balance of power with the influential Japanese ecclesiastical elite. With the coordination of catholicity increasingly diffused among Nicholas' disciples, the socio-political "trends of the times" came to play a prominent role in the broadening of Russo-Japanese ecclesiastical links in the 1910's.

About a year into his tenure at the helm of the Japanese Church, in 1913, Bishop Sergius received an order of St. Anna 1st class from the Russian emperor.[52] This early show of favor and stimulus toward further achievement was likely connected with Sergius' pronounced Russian orientation, which distinguished him from the more balanced approach of his predecessor. Making use of the favorable political conditions, Sergius summarily carried out a number of initiatives aimed at strengthening Russo-Japanese ecclesiastical links. The moratorium on sending Japanese seminarians to Russian schools—in place since 1893 on account of Nicholas' dissatisfaction with the returnees' lack of piety[53] and high desertion rate to secular jobs—was immediately lifted by the new bishop.[54]

If Nicholas had made two unaccompanied trips to Russia in as much as fifty-two years, Sergius made as many in only two years, both times engineering previously unprecedented group-visitations in concert with the neighboring Vladivostok diocese. Namely, in 1915 Sergius lead a team of Japanese

[52]Consistory (1933), 10.

[53]Nicholas (2004), vol. 2 (1893.02.25), 737-738.

[54]The first 1912 study-abroad student was Matthew Kageta, sent to the Bethany Theological Seminary, according to Orthodox Messenger (1913.10.05 - № 2-19), 40.

Orthodox youth for a tour of the Shmakovka Holy Trinity monastery as part of a project to plant in Hokkaido a similar "factory-like monastery."[55] Then, in 1916 Sergius participated in the episcopal ordination of Nestor (Anisimov) as Bishop of Kamchatka, after which the two prelates went to Japan to consecrate the rebuilt Orthodox church in Hakodate—the symbolic fountainhead of Japanese Orthodoxy.[56]

In Sergius' favored field of periodical publication, he inaugurated the magazine *Trends of Orthodox Thought* to propagate contemporary Russian theological and philosophical thinkers in Japanese translation. He also ensured that almost each issue of the Church's official *Orthodox Messenger* delivered diverse reportage of Russian ecclesiastical news and supplied Russian-themed or even Russian-penned articles. Although domestic Japanese reports dwarfed foreign ones, the coverage of Russia in the *Orthodox Messenger* exceeded the combined volume of news about non-Russian Orthodox Churches and the non-Orthodox Christian circles. A topical article on a contemporary subject framed neither as universally Orthodox nor as Russo-Japanese was exceptional, like a solitary piece on Serbia which celebrated the arrival to Japan of a Serbian Orthodox missionary, Archimandrite George (Kojic).[57] In fact, Serbia appears to have been the only land outside the Russian and Japanese Empires with which Bishop Sergius developed ties—through Serbian seminarians in St. Petersburg.[58] A relationship with Serbia, the most Russophile sovereign country of the age, contrasted starkly with Nicholaevan-era connections with the Greek world, which had been called upon to balance Russian links. As a result, the focus on Russia as the sole window of the Japanese community onto the global Orthodox scene was significantly sharpened by Sergius.

[55] Remortel & Chang (2003), 153; Council (1917), 70.

[56] Nestor (2002), 403; Pozdniaev (1999c), 357.

[57] Sukitaretsu (1914).

[58] Sergius' solicitude to Serbian seminarians earned him an order of St. Savvas 1st class from the Serbian king Peter I in 1908. Consistory (1933), 10.

However, the campaign to emphasize Russian ties was hardly Sergius' single-handed feat. It enjoyed wide support by such key Japanese churchmen as senior priests Symeon Mii, Paul Morita, Peter Shibayama and Romanus Chiba, who had individually visited Russia at this time and joined the cheer-leading for Russia in general and the Shmakovka monastery in particular.[59] Russo-Japanese ties were likewise backed by the numerous young leaders who headed to post-graduate theological studies in Russia in this pre-revolutionary period, including Matthew Kageta, John Usui, Peter Uchiyama, Micah Nakamura, Sergius Watanabe, Matthew Suzuki and Ambrose Hibi.[60] In the political clime when being pro-Russian aligned well with being patriotic, the Japanese Orthodox Church seized its chance to celebrate its once-maligned function of being "the pioneer in introducing Russia's conditions" to Japan by expanding its program of Russian-language courses and compiling an exhaustive Russo-Japanese dictionary.[61]

[59]Fr. Symeon Mii had spent part of the December of 1914 in Vladivostok and its environs, thereafter penning many glowing reports about the Shmakovka monastery for the *Orthodox Messenger* throughout 1915. See especially Orthodox Messenger (1915.01.20 - № 4-2), 31; (1915.02.05 - № 4-3), 7-11. Materials on Fr. Peter Shibayama's 1917 visit to Shmakovka and other parts of Russia's Maritime province are found in the family collection of Andrew Shibayama in Koganei. Fr. Romanus Chiba spent a few months at the Shmakovka monastery in 1917 observing the monastic life and even received an award from the abbot, see Orthodox Messenger (1933.01.20 - № 22-01), 21. On the activities of Fr. Paul Morita see below.

[60]Kageta studied at the Bethany Theological Seminary near Moscow and published many reports about his experiences in the *Orthodox Messenger* before he died abroad in 1913, as reported in Orthodox Messenger (1913.10.05 - № 2-19), 36-40. Usui was the next in line to be sent after Kageta, but his eagerly awaited turn never came, according to Yoshimura (1968), 23-24. Uchiyama and Nakamura had both been enrolled at the Kazan Theological Academy until their studies were interrupted in 1917, see Naganawa (2007), 225-226. Watanabe had completed the course at the Irkutsk Theological Seminary, but had not left Russia in time to avoid the chaos of the Russian Revolution, according to the recollections in Korshunov ([1998] 2004). Suzuki and Hibi left for Russia in 1915, to the Irkutsk Theological Seminary and to the Shmakovka monastery respectively, as reported in Orthodox Messenger (1915.07.20 - № 4-14), 34.

[61]Orthodox Messenger (1915.02.05 - № 4-3), 23-24.

As World War I enlivened military and humanitarian exchanges between the two countries, the Orthodox received further opportunities for prominence. One of the most important Orthodox employees of the Japanese Army, Professor Emelian Higuchi Tsuyanosuke, used his connections to procure a central spot for Fr. Paul Morita on the Japanese Red Cross team being sent to St. Petersburg in 1914. This extended tour, lasting well over a year, provided Fr. Morita with a multitude of important connections, gained for him broad publicity in Russia as Japan's Orthodox representative, and favorably introduced his experiences to the Japanese audience.[62] His work earned for the Japanese Orthodox priest as many as two Russian imperial decorations in 1916.[63] Purveying images of an exotic, embattled and holy Russia, the Japanese *Orthodox Messenger* repeatedly took up collections in support of the Russian and Serbian war-effort.[64] Finally, Russo-Japanese ecclesiastical integration peaked in 1917, when Fr. Symeon Mii headed to Moscow as the Japanese representative at the long-awaited Council of the Russian Orthodox Church.[65] The embrace of Russian connections by the Japanese Orthodox Church in mid-1910's drew on a broad base of supporters and dynamics, reflecting what has been called the "golden age" of Russo-Japanese relations.[66]

However, Japanese Orthodox enthusiasm over warming Russo-Japanese relations was circumscribed by the contest over the ecclesiastical boundaries of Japan—a juncture between the local and regional dimensions of catholicity. By the

[62]Orthodox Messenger (1914.10.20 - № 3-20), 44-45. Morita's lengthy reports from Russia abound throughout the 1915 and early 1916 issues of the *Orthodox Messenger*.

[63]The orders of St. Stanislaus 3-rd class and St. Anna 3-rd class. See Siberian dispatch (1918), 410117.

[64]On collections for Russia see Orthodox Messenger (1914.12.05 - №3-23), appendix; (1915.01.20 - №4-2), appendix; (1915.02.05 - №4-3), appendix; (1915.02.20 - №4-4), 29. On a collection for Serbia see Orthodox Messenger (1915.08.20 - №4-16), insert.

[65]Fr. Mii detailed his experiences in Mii (1982), 97-143.

[66]Expression from Molodiakov (2010).

1910's, the facile and foundational notion of Japanese identity encoded into the ecclesiastical context, which held that the "Japanese Church" is the "Church of Japan" and the "Church of the Japanese," had came into conflict with multiple remappings of "Japan." Tension between the Russian hierarchy and the Japanese Church over the contours of Japan's ecclesiastical "proper place" starkly revealed the dilemmas of catholic self-definition, as the Japanese Church manifested unilateralism, rhetorical amnesia and even disobedience in its attempts to retain congruence with its increasingly incongruous "local" construct.

A few illustrative incidents involved Russian hierarchs' unsuccessful attempts to broaden the Japanese Church's boundaries beyond the borders of the Japanese state. Two cases occurred in 1915, when Russian ecclesiastics strove to link the Japanese Church with the Anglo-Saxon world and met with indifference and insubordination. First, an invitation by Bishop Eudocimus (Meshcherskii) of North America for the Japanese Church to send a priest to pastor the Japanese emigrants on the West Coast of the United States remained at the level of personal discussion.[67] More significantly, the official directive from the Russian Most Holy Synod to the Japanese hierarch, charging him to extend his care to the Russian Orthodox flock in Australia, appears to have been sabotaged through inaction.[68] While the mundane shortage of personnel and funds might explain these incidents, one must also allow for a possible statement of identity. If it was the latter, it would appear that even ethnic Japanese outside the political bounds of Japan were beyond the "local" pale of the Japanese Orthodox Church.

---

[67]Morita (1915), 21. It is not clear from Morita's article whether the Japanese emigrants in question were Orthodox Christians or only a potential field of mission. Research of the Japanese Orthodox materials brought to light only isolated instances of lone Japanese Orthodox believers in the US. However, one dubious article by Bazhenova (1937), from Harbin's Russian magazine *Frontier* (*Rubezh*), claims that the Japanese were the largest contingent of Hawaii's Orthodox parish at the time of the writing.

[68]RAOM (1916.08 - № 8-20), 697.

A far more significant set of mild contests occurred within the continually expanding sphere of Japanese political domination, where the Japanese Church, conversely, forestalled the directives of Russian ecclesiastical superiors in extending its jurisdiction. The first instance occurred in connection with the 1875 Japanese acquisition of the Kurile islands, which were a part of the Kamchatka diocese of the Russian Orthodox Church. Although the Russian missionaries stopped visiting the islands, "having no right to fare into Japanese territory,"[69] the ecclesiastical title to the Kuriles was still formally maintained by the bishop of Kamchatka as late as 1890.[70] Yet, by that date the Japanese Orthodox Church had already extended its sway over the few remaining local believers and showed itself a decisive force for assimilating Russified Ainu into their new Japanese context. According to Lawrence, the Shikotan Ainu chieftain's adopted son, his 1885 encounter with bearded Russian-speaking Orthodox Christian agents of Japan had been the moment when he "for the first time resolved to enter under the protection of the Japanese state, to become one of its subjects."[71] As a result, although Russians still imagined in 1911 that the Kurile Ainu had retained their Russian language along with their Orthodox faith, the two had long become decoupled, with the Orthodox parish on Shikotan made up entirely of Japanese-speakers.[72]

The second territorial expansion of the Japanese Church followed Japan's annexation of Taiwan from China in 1895. Once again, it is uncertain whether the Most Holy Synod ever formally sanctioned the extension of the Japanese Church's jurisdiction onto this island, but at least this move had been

[69]Sergius ([1909] 1998), 35.

[70]An incongruence noted at the time by Chekhov (2007), 265, 416.

[71]The Japanese Orthodox delegation was made up of Fr. Titus Komatsu, who sported an impressive beard, and of the catechist Alexis Sawabe, with a particularly good command of Russian. Sapporo church (1987), 136.

[72]Nicholas (2004), vol. 5, (1911.02.15), 734-735.

legitimized by the simple fact that the only Orthodox believers on the ground appear to have been Japanese settlers.[73]

Next came the 1905 acquisitions of the Russo-Japanese War, of which the greatly depopulated South Sakhalin largely followed the precedent set by the Kuriles. Japanese ecclesiastical agents once again outran feet-dragging Russian Synodal authorities in assuming *de facto* jurisdiction over local Orthodox Russians, who were soon augmented by Japanese Orthodox settlers. The main distinctive feature of this case had been the attempt by the Most Holy Synod to ward off expected assimilation of the local population. Specifically, when the Synod finally approved the transfer of South Sakhalin from the Vladivostok diocese to the Japanese Church in 1911, it stipulated that the local Orthodox priest be necessarily a Russian.[74]

However, when it came to the new Japanese conquests on the Asian continent—in Korea and Southern Manchuria—the pattern of Japanese advance and Russian acquiescence broke down. To be sure, the Japanese Orthodox clergy began to visit the continent, but, unlike in prior cases, non-Japanese Orthodox clergy and institutions also remained in place. This generated a new kind of friction, as the Japanese ecclesiastical emissaries sensed their advance to be transgressive— "impolite toward the Russian Orthodox Church"[75]—yet necessitated by ongoing ethno-political boundary shifts. Although the Russo-Japanese War had assured official Russian acquiescence to Japanese dominance in Korea and Southern Manchuria, the Russian Orthodox Church failed to readjust the region's ecclesiastical boundaries accordingly, leaving Japan's continental "New Possessions" in the jurisdiction of the administratively separate Korean and Chinese Orthodox

---

[73] On the history of Japanese Orthodox Church's activity on Taiwan see Tsukamoto (2005), 157-169.

[74] Nicholas (2004), vol. 5 (1911.06.04), 767.

[75] The words of Fr. Peter Shibayama about his activity as a visiting Japanese pastor of Japanese Orthodox scattered in Korea. Council (1910), 79.

Missions. The former in fact scored missionary successes in the agitated annexation-era Korea,[76] but the latter lost most of its South-Manchurian flock as Russian settlers deserted the region. This evacuation invited the Japanese state to reorder the local Orthodox presence by redistributing vacated ecclesiastical property. The solution of Japanese secular authorities was to either put the abandoned churches to new uses or offer them to "their own"—Japanese—Orthodox Church.[77]

At first Archbishop Nicholas declined to overstep ecclesi-astical boundaries at the state's behest and the Chinese Mis-sion successfully repossessed some of its South-Manchurian properties.[78] However, by 1910's the increase of Japanese Orthodox settlers on the continent drew the Japanese Church into the contested space. Exchanges between Russian heads of East Asian missionary establishments eventually effected an informal jurisdictional settlement, partially substituting the territorial principle with the ethnic one.[79] Acting upon this accord, the Japanese Church took charge of ecclesiastical

[76] See the overview in Theodosius ([1926] 1999), 220-251.

[77] Initially the Orthodox churches in Tieling, Liaoyang, Wafangdian, Yingkou and Gongzhuling were reported closed by the terms of the 1905 Portsmouth Peace Treaty. Subsequently the latter two, as well as the one in Dalian and church furnishings from Lushun, had been repeatedly offered by the Japanese authorities to the Japanese Church. See Pozdniaev (1998), 41; Kaneishi (1993), 207; Nicholas (2004), vol. 5 (1908.02.25), 361; Council (1913), 44.

[78] In 1906 Nicholas had still been worried that the Japanese state would not return any buildings to the Church at all. By 1909 the churches in Dalian and Lushun had been repossessed by the Chinese Mission. Nicholas (2004), vol. 5 (1906.02.10 - 13), 315; Pozdniaev (1998), 39.

[79] The language barrier figured as a major factor in the requests for a Japanese priest emanating from both Japanese Orthodox expatriates and Russian missionaries. The sending of Japanese priests to Korea began no later than 1907 and was settled in principle during the 1911 Council of the Japanese Church, attended by Archimandrite Paul (Ivanovskii) of the Korean Mission. At the 1915 Council Bishop Sergius reported on his settlement with Archbishop Innocent (Figurovskii) of the Chinese Mission. See Council (1910), 78-82; (1911), 90-98; (1915), 36, 40-43.

properties on the Liaodong peninsula[80] and in 1915 posted Fr. Sergius Suzuki to pastor Japanese Orthodox continental expatriates—over 60 persons in Dalian and Lushun, as well as others scattered across Manchuria and Korea.[81] Fr. Suzuki did receive Bishop Sergius' injunction to also shepherd the remaining Russians,[82] but the kind of jurisdiction the Japanese Church gained on the continent was a hybrid between territorial and ethnic, tipped decisively in favor of the latter. Reports of contemporary continental pastoral peregrinations of Japanese Orthodox clerics focused narrowly on Japanese expatriates, with no mention of native Chinese and Korean believers, and only Russians—mostly clergy—occasionally figuring as intermediaries among sundered groups of East Asia's Orthodox.[83]

As colonial expansion broke down the congruence between ethnic and political boundaries of Japan, the Japanese Orthodox Church lost its one-to-one Church-state correspondence. It still enjoyed jurisdiction over *all* Orthodox believers on the "Home Islands," but only over *some* in the "New Possessions." By offending both Orthodox canonical order and Japanese nationalist sensibility this limitation produced rhetorical amnesia of the non-Japanese Orthodox on the continent. Thus, even as the *Orthodox Messenger* printed informed articles on the Orthodox mission among the Koreans and the Chinese,[84] when speaking about the Japanese Church's

[80]In 1913 Fr. Symeon Mii accepted from the Japanese officials the churches in Gongzhuling and Yingkou; in 1915 Bishop Sergius procured from the Chinese Mission permission to use the church in Dalian. See Mii (1913), 43; Council (1913), 44; (1915), 36.

[81]The geography of Fr. Suzuki's first pastoral excursion from his home-base in Dalian included Harbin, Changchun, Kuanchengzi, Lushun, Mukden, Fushun. Japanese Orthodox in Korea, who in 1910 numbered some 37 persons most represented in Pusan, were eventually also subordinated to him. Kaneishi (1993), 205; Council (1910), 80-81.

[82]Council (1915), 36, 43.

[83]Witness accounts in Takai (1913a), 45-50; (1913b), 54-58; Mii (1913), 43-49.

[84]Orthodox Messenger (1914.05.20 - № 3-10), 53-54; (1915.03.20 - № 4-6), 40-41; Iwasawa (1915), 6-11.

continental activity it chronically neglected to mention parallel Orthodox bodies.[85] The characteristic initial Japanese response to the dilemma of fusing national and imperial identities into a single consciousness—potentially both local and regional—was an isolationist attempt at effacing the "other," the very opposite of a catholic embrace of a tiered world.

Nativist currents, bolstered by Japanese imperialism, manifested themselves throughout the Japanese society in the early 1900's. The meshing of a strong nationalism with weaker regionalist, globalist and universalist identities in the form secessionist trends, commonplace in contemporary Japanese Christian circles, was also at work in the Orthodox context. Vocal demands for variously understood "independence" had entered the mainstream of Japanese Orthodox rhetoric during the episcopal transition from Nicholas to Sergius.[86] Much of Japanese ecclesiastical public rhetoric, including Russophile and formal statements, paired the Russian and Japanese Churches as comparable, if not quite equal, entities.[87] Rashly phrased calls to abolish such foreign customs as kissing in church in order to "shed Russian color" for the sake of the "uniquely Japanese warrior spirit" were limited to marginal activists,[88] but the difference between these shrill appeals and calmer expositions by key churchmen often appeared to be merely one of tone and emphasis. Thus, the leading

[85] See for example Orthodox Messenger (1915.09.05 - № 4-17), 1.

[86] The most concerted compendium of contemporary rhetoric and demands of this independence movement was the 1909 All-Japan Laity Conference, presented in Yahagi (1909). On the need for elaborating distinctive Japanese ecclesiastical regulations see especially Ihaho (1912). For calls to translate Christian names into Japanese see Sukitaretsu (1914), 16; Iwasawa (1916). For the adoption of the Japanese custom of mass commemoration of the family's ancestors and for participating in Buddhist and Shintoist funerals see Ishikawa (1915b).

[87] For instance see Orthodox Messenger (1914.10.20 - № 3-20), 44-45; (1914.08.05 - № 3-15), 35.

[88] Like Aquila Kajima Akira in his *New Orthodoxy*. See the summary in Kaneishi (1993), 194-197.

Japanese lay voice—the main editor of the *Orthodox Messenger* and professor of the Tokyo Theological Seminary Peter Ishikawa—waxed about the Japanese "special life of the heart, almost unimaginable to other peoples."[89] Ishikawa's prolific 1910's output celebrated the "great debt of Christianity to Confucian literature" in Japan, expressed a "hope for a similar assimilation of Buddhist civilization," and generally enjoined that "the historical customs of religious faith of our Japanese nationals, being united and harmonized with the conservative might of Christianity, should be perpetuated eternally."[90] The independence movement adumbrated not only a distinctive Orthodox organization for Japan, but one-of-a-kind Japanese Orthodoxy.

Archbishop Nicholas possessed the authority to put down unwelcome talk of independence in no uncertain terms. During the unruly 1909 All-Japan Laity Conference he reminded the delegates of their financial dependence on Russia and warned them "henceforth not to raise such irreverent issues with fantasy-talk about how the Church of Russia is supposedly oppressing the Japanese Church."[91] Yet, after his death, the Most Holy Synod and Bishop Sergius were so unsure of making informed and effective decisions in the Japanese community as to offer little opposition. Instead, they were largely content to pump funds, to hush-up offenses, and to sponsor some of the milder schemes for the nativization of Japan's in-house ecclesiastical life, as long as the mission's

---

[89]Ishikawa (1915b), 12. In addition to a multitude of articles, Ishikawa had translated theological works from Russian and authored such monographs as the fundamental *History of Orthodox evangelism in Japan* in 1901 and the programmatic *Orthodoxy and State* in 1892. Despite his prominence, research about him is lagging. See on him Remortel (2003), 162 culled from Naganawa; Seraphim (2007b).

[90]Consecutively Ishikawa (1914e), 4, 5; Ishikawa (1914b), 12. Ishikawa even began to research Buddhist philosophy in search of points of contact. See Ishikawa (1916).

[91]Yahagi (1909), 37 (2nd pagination).

apparent successes continued.[92] Scant and yielding foreign missionary presence, complete with overwhelming dependence on foreign subsidies, introduced an exceptional amount of self-searching into what would otherwise appear as an externalized international confrontation. Even at the pre-revolutionary peak of cooperation with Russia it was largely up to the Japanese Orthodox themselves to settle what they meant by ecclesiastical independence,[93] what reforms they wished to see effected in the Church,[94] and what stance they would assume in the all-important encounter with the Japanese religioscape.

The relationship of the Orthodox Church with Japan's dominant religious practices made Japanese believers into frontiersmen of their universal thought-world, tasked with charting a novel religious encounter. However, since it was the Japanese government which arbitrated the country's religious scene, this encounter figured primarily as a vital facet of Church-state relations. A substantial doze of loyalist conformism in the religious metaphor was a predictable consequence of the nationalist climate. However, the simultaneous wielding of Christianity's countercultural edge against some emerging fixtures of the Japanese religioscape was a more intriguing side of the Japanese Orthodox discourse in 1910's, revealing a measure of independence from the state's preferred views.

Presented in Peter Ishikawa's writings, Orthodox criticism of the officially sanctioned religious regime focused on the contradictions of state Shintoism. For instance, in the case of the establishment of the Meiji Shrine to celebrate the

[92]For instance, Bishop Sergius himself proposed to formally institute ecclesiastical celebration of the Japanese agricultural (*Niiname-sai*) and memorial (Spring and Autumn *Kōrei-sai*) holidays. See Council (1914), 79-81.

[93]See a debate on this already in Yahagi (1909), 66-70.

[94]These discussions extended not only to the Japanese Church, but also to the Russian, with Peter Ishikawa opining that it would be desirable for the Japanese to have the Synod abolished and the Patriarchate restored. Ishikawa (1913),18.

deceased Meiji Emperor, Ishikawa proclaimed that the government's intention to apotheosize the monarch as a Shintoist deity would "unavoidably lead to disrespectful interpretations which would soil the brilliant glory of the Meiji Emperor the world over."[95] While upholding the sacredness of properly dereligionized commemorative shrines, Ishikawa time and again blasted the extension of the protective umbrella of ostensibly non-religious state Shintoism to institutions that offered unabashedly religious fortune prayers.[96] On the occasion of the Japanese state's plan to pass the first general law on the subject of religion, the July 1914 *Orthodox Messenger* featured a bold indictment of Japan's "utterly coarse religions which remain from the unenlightened age before [Japan's - INK] opening."[97] However, rather than attacking Buddhist or Shintoist "superstitions," the article once more emphasized state Shintoism as the main culprit. The new religious law, Ishikawa demanded, must restrain state Shintoist functionaries from extorting money by "force-feeding to the people the line that they are shrine parishioners... under the pretext that shrines are non-religious."[98] The stand against religious compulsion under the mask of patriotism thus remained as an enduring theme of Japanese Orthodox discourse throughout the 1910's.

Most importantly, the same stand is detectable on the most sensitive religio-political topic of the time—the emperor. The Orthodox were eager to showcase their loyalty by diverse prayers for the members of the Japanese imperial family. Yet, these ostensible testaments of Japaneseness were in fact adopted wholesale from Russian Orthodox usage, augmented with only a handful of new Japanese composi-

---

[95] Ishikawa (1914c), 7.
[96] For some of the bolder pieces see Ishikawa (1914a, 1915a).
[97] Ishikawa (1914d), 2.
[98] Ishikawa (1914d), 2, 4.

Figure 10.2: Their Majesties the Emperors (*kōtei*) of Russia, Japan and England—sacred monarchy as common norm. From Orthodox Messenger (1915.01.20 - № 4-2), insert.

tions.[99] Correspondingly, Japanese Orthodox liturgical texts employed the generic term for "emperor," *kōtei*, instead of the uniquely Japanese and officially preferred *tennō*. Such usage placed a pagan ruler unto the same discursive plane as an Orthodox emperor and denied qualitative distinctiveness to the Japanese sovereign. Indeed, as Peter Ishikawa defended the notion of a special religious bond between the sovereign and his subjects, he vocally affirmed equal sacredness of all the world's monarchs.[100]

In line with this belief, some Japanese Orthodox firebrands among older contemporaries, like the catechist Gabriel Ichikawa, had even refused to utter the word *tennō*, considering *kōtei* solely normative.[101] Consequently, when the

[99]For one possibly original composition see the prayers in connection with the accession of the Taishō Emperor, printed in Orthodox Messenger (1915.11.05 - № 4-21), front matter.
[100]Ishikawa (1915c), 4-5.
[101]Higuchi (1996), 13.

title page of the January 1915 *Orthodox Messenger* displayed a line-up of parade-dress photographs of the Russian tsar, the Japanese mikado and the English king, all three captioned with the identical "His Majesty the Emperor (*kōtei*)," the patriotic statement bore a hint of theological subversion. This view of the monarch was neither an unreflective Russian import, nor a surrender to the prevailing Japanese context. Even as they called for more independence from Russia in the name of their nation, the Japanese Orthodox were able to assume an independent posture vis-à-vis some of their state's religious policies in the name of their universal creed.

Strained by ascendant nationalism, declining global engagement, and imperial diversity, the fourfold framework of the Japanese Orthodox Church's catholic relations survived the death of its visionary arbiter, Archbishop Nicholas. The self-assured Japanese Orthodox stirrings of independence from both Russian ecclesiastics and Japanese officials remained tempered by manifestations of loyalty and rested upon the assumption of continued disengaged benevolence from both quarters. The propitious climate of Russo-Japanese relations in mid-1910's allowed the Japanese Orthodox community to assume a bolder stance in its already established web of relationships without sacrificing any of the possessed patronage. It was amidst this tide of confidence, when outside observers judged the Church's "conditions favorable" and predicted "smooth sailing and a calm wind,"[102] that the explosion of the 1917 Russian Revolution delivered a shattering blow to the existential framework of the Japanese Church.

---

[102] Inglehart (1959), 163.

Chapter 11

Independence from catholicity

The 1917 Russian Revolution and its decades-long after-shocks wrought a globally-felt tectonic shift, leaving nothing hitherto connected with the fabric of the Russian Empire unaltered. The revolution's primary meaning for the Japanese Orthodox Church had been to thrust Japanese believers with so much more independence than they had bargained for as to place the very survival of their community in jeopardy. Gone were the grants and the educational facilities, the missionaries and the sponsors, the theological and the administrative authorities, the model of Church-state relationships and the apparent might of the Church-state complex, the Russian-centered network of global connections and animosities, the "old" Russian Orthodox Church and the "old" Russian imperial state.

The trauma of this collapse was masked by the resultant triumph of Japanese Orthodox "independence," a facile victory and an unavoidable condition, which helped present loss as gain, bereavement as secession, and isolation as goal. As shards of the pre-revolutionary Russian Orthodox world began to adjust amid new conditions, the Japanese Church charted its course away from Russia and away from catholicity.

The aspect most painfully and immediately apparent was the onset of financial independence due to the cessation of Russian funding. This kind of independence had been the least popular with Japanese believers and the one Russian missionaries were keenest to foster. In fact, the notion was so basic to Nicholas' thinking that in his diaries he would occasionally denote ecclesiastical "financial independence" with the untranslated Japanese word for "independence"— *dokuritsu*.[1] Upon the foundation of the Japanese Mission Nicholas had rashly promised the Most Holy Synod that the Japanese Church would achieve financial independence in seven years,[2] but he soon despaired of extracting sufficient funds from his flock and privately bemoaned his resigned receivership. Things were similar with Nicholas' would-be helper, Andronicus (Nikol'skii), who had concluded in 1898 that little could be done about self-financing "until the affair should settle itself."[3] The dependence was no less overwhelming in 1917, when even among clergy there were "those who do not send contributions toward the Japanese Orthodox Church's independence fund," to speak nothing of the rank-and-file believers.[4] Unwilling to constrain their unmotivated flock into material self-support, Russian clerics in Japan revealed themselves "missionaries come from an Orthodox state" with its government-subsidized Church.[5]

This blind spot brought panic to the Tokyo Orthodox headquarters in 1917, as financial managers—chief among them Bishop Sergius himself—found nothing better than

[1] For instance see Nicholas (2004), vol. 3 (1895.08.13), 145.
[2] Council (1914), 40.
[3] Andronicus (2007), 36.
[4] Council (1917), 74.
[5] Seraphim (2008-2010 - №1415), 19.

to borrow some ¥25,000 for the rest of that year, and a stupendous ¥80,000 for the next.[6]   The February 1918 circular brought the struggle home to each engaged believer by tasking parishes to hold talks on immediate financial "independence."[7] However, the one "parish" slated to suffer most were the headquarters themselves. Within two years the central Orthodox establishment in Japan has had to slash almost everything not directly involved in the daily life of a parish—the seminaries and the schools, the periodicals, the occasional publications, the charity and construction projects, the iconographic and translation workshops, and the majority of the Church's students and salaried staff. "Financial independence" spelt first of all independence from missionary cares, as the Church shriveled in the image of its new financial pillar—the provincial parish.

Assumption of financial independence caused a momentary nationwide grassroots mobilization which made the 1919 "Constitutional" Council into the most representative and the most vocal of Japanese Orthodox gatherings to date, a "great renewal unseen since the propagation of the Orthodox Church in our country."[8]   For most Japanese believers financial self-support appeared the most daunting—and therefore the most "real"—kind of ecclesiastical independence.   Therefore, rising to the challenge of feeding priests and paying taxes was already seen as a triumph, while the successful 1923-1929 Church-wide campaign to restore the Tokyo Resurrection cathedral, severely damaged in the Great Kantō Earthquake, became a symbol of self-sufficiency *par excellence*. If the cathedral's original construction was financed by Russian money and masterminded by the Russian and English architects, Shchurupov and Condor,

[6]Naganawa (1989), 209.

[7]Kushiro church (1992), 117.

[8]Morita (1919b), 3. The 1919 Council brought together 141 delegates and may have been the first where laymen appeared to be more vocal than the clergy.

Figure 11.1: Icon of the Mother of God "Joy of all who sorrow," by Japan's resident Russian artist, Barbara Bubnova. Painted and donated to the Tokyo St. Nicholas church in 1925.

the restoration relied primarily on the contributions of the Japanese believers themselves, who also provided a team of in-house architects for the job—Elijah Okada Shin'ichi and his pupil, Fr. Symeon Mii's son, Michio.[9] This feat received wide and comparatively favorable publicity even in the secular press. It was a wonder to the broader Japanese public, how a community so small as the Orthodox, managed to accomplish so much, while the well-established Honganji sect of True Pure Land Buddhism had yet to rebuild its edifices in Tsukiji and Asakusa.[10]

Buoyed by this achievement, in 1930's Japanese Orthodox believers went on to erect a few new churches of some architectural worth, relying on their own funds and home-grown church architects—the most notable cases being the Transfiguration church in Sapporo, built according to the plans of Protodeacon Moses Kawamura in 1935-1936, and St. John the Theologian's church in Kannari, built by Kawa-mura's son Sergius in 1934.[11] The material standing of the

[9]On the architects see Mii (1982), 144-145.

[10]Kajima (1931a), 10.

[11]Sapporo church (1987), 121-124; Ruisu (2008), 70-72. A useful overview on the Kawamura-Uchii clan of Orthodox architects—Fr. Moses Kawamura Izō, Sergius Uchii Susumu and Gabriel Uchii Shōzō—is found in the treatments focusing on its notable third-generation representative, like Uchii (1981), 175-

Church rose sufficiently to attract and even publicize an occasional international seeker, like a traveling hieromonk who came to Tokyo in 1931 to gather funds for the monasteries of Mount Athos.[12]   At the price of its severe contraction, Japanese believers learned to fund their own collective venture.

Precipitated by the dramatic termination of central Russian sponsorship in 1917, this achievement was facilitated by a trickle of informal Russian material support which continued for well over a decade after the revolution. During the fluid civil-war era Bishop Sergius engaged in agitated activity to procure stop-gap funds. The network of Russian sponsors revealed by these efforts included most notably the political leaders of the Whites in East Asia General Horvath and Chieftain Semenov, the Orthodox dioceses of Vladivostok and America, the population of the Maritime region and the Chinese Eastern Railway zone in Northern Manchuria, and a host of diplomatic agents in Japan—particularly the keeper of Russian diplomatic funds, agent of trade and manufacture Miller; the last "master" of the Russian embassy, 1st secretary D. I. Abrikosov; and the Russian consul in Tsuruga, agent of the volunteer fleet N. D. Fedorov.[13]   There were also occasional gifts from Anglicans, as well as a unique case of a Russian Jewish merchant, Judaist by faith, one M. A. Ginsburg from Yokohama, who contributed 10,000 rubles for the Korean Orthodox Mission.[14] In sum, these sources provided perhaps two years' worth of funding for the attenuated Orthodox

192; Visual Architecture (2006), 123-129.

[12]Orthodox Messenger (1931.03.20 - № 20-3), 20-21.

[13]The most extensive funding came in a one-time fundraising effort in the Maritime Province and Northern Manchuria in March 1919, with Horvath making especially lavish promises, see Senuma (1919); Sergius (1919a). Semenov's help is mentioned in Kandidov (1937), 25. On sponsorship from Miller and Abrikosov see Theodosius ([1926] 1999), 280-282. On Fedorov, the sponsor of the Kansai women's school, see Nakamura & Nakamura (2003), 418-429.

[14]Theodosius ([1926] 1999), 277-278. On Anglican support see chapter 13.

establishments in the Japanese Empire[15] and kept its last educational institution—Kansai Orthodox women's school—in operation until 1921.

However, in the face of Soviet victory in the civil war, most of these sponsors vanished, Abrikosov's final contribution being the furnishings of the defunct embassy chapel in 1925.[16] Meanwhile, the destruction of the Tokyo cathedral compound in 1923 gave new urgency to Sergius' fundraising efforts and helped convince the Russian Orthodox that need was still acute in Japan, uncannily making refugees into donors. The principal origin of Russian contributions for the Tokyo cathedral was the newly instituted diocese of Harbin in Northern Manchuria—Sergius went there at least three times in the 1920's,[17] and his local friend, Bishop Nestor, spearheaded a fund-raising campaign for Japan among Manchuria's Russians in 1924-1925.[18] Compatriots from Hankou,[19] Copenhagen,[20] Danzig,[21] and even Vladivostok,[22] not to mention émigrés in Japan, also took part. While a

[15]The worth of rubles is difficult to calculate due to skyrocketing inflation at the time. The largest one-time donation, 151,060 rubles raised in March 1919, was probably worth at that moment only about one fifth of that amount in yen, as reported in Theodosius ([1926] 1999), 277-278.

[16]Lensen (1964), 318; Council (1930), 22.

[17]For the late 1923-early 1924 visit see Theodosius ([1926] 1999), 303-304; for the 1925 or 1926 visit see Hauth (1996), 72; for the April-May 1928 trip see Orthodox Messenger (1928.05.10 - № 17-05), 16; (1928.06.10 - № 17-06), 25; Yeast (1928.06 - № 7-6), 25-26.

[18]Seryshev (1952-1968), 581.

[19]Sergius was close with one Unzhenin in Hankou, who paid for the decoration of one of the new cathedral's side-temples. Council (1929), 62.

[20]Sergius drew on his good relationship with the Grand Duchess Olga Alexandrovna, resident in Copenhagen, whom he asked to paint an icon for the cathedral as a symbolic replacement for many treasures previously donated to the cathedral by the Russian imperial family. In 1933 the icon of St. Olga was finally received. Orthodox Messenger (1933.09.20 - № 22-9), 37; Vorres (1964), 201.

[21]Five new bells for the cathedral were crafted in Danzig with half of the price borne by the Polish Orthodox Church. See, Sergius (1930), 15.

[22]A certain Helen (last name is rendered in Japanese as "Stsuretsukii") in Vladivostok, who lost her daughters in the Great Kantō Earthquake, managed to circumvent Soviet rules against the export of precious metals and

claim that Russians in sum donated as much as 25% of the restoration funds appears grossly exaggerated,[23] their most significant contribution was not money but necessary custom-made church-supplies, requiring an expertise both expensive and rare in Japan. Thus, the cathedral's new iconostasis and individual icons, various sacred vessels and accoutrements, liturgical vestments, and even candles were mostly provided by Russians.[24] A prominent delegation from the Harbin diocese—the only representation from beyond the borders of Japan at the 1929 consecration of the Tokyo cathedral—testified to continued significance of Russians in the life of the Japanese Church.[25] It was only after Sergius' break with most émigré ecclesiastical circles in 1931 that the trickle of foreign donations for the Japanese Church dried up.

While Russian contributions gradually dwindled to in-significance, the overall transformation of the Russian pres-ence in Japan after the Russian Revolution changed the course of the Japanese Orthodox Church and gave new meaning to the domestic ecclesiastical independence movement. By 1917 Russians have become a familiar set of resident aliens for the Japanese Church, inscribed into local ecclesiastical scene in a variety of ways. In the pre-revolutionary period most Russian church-servitors belonged to the Russian Spiritual Mission in Japan, Russian laymen in Tokyo entered the purview of the Russian embassy chaplaincy,[26] the Russian consulate personnel in Nagasaki had been merged into one flock with

contributed, via a Japanese intermediary, a large selection of church utensils. See Council (1926), 24-25; Council (1930), 22.

[23] Seryshev (1952-1968), 580. The actual sums were much smaller—for instance, at the 1925 Council an annual contribution from Harbin was reported as ¥ 3469.58, at the 1928 Council—¥ 1710.56. In addition, Naganawa's estimate places the donations of Japan's Russians at some ¥ 2000. See Council (1925), 114; (1928), 20; Naganawa (2001), 198.

[24] Yeast (1928.06 - № 7-6), 25; Council (1926), 24; (1929), 61-62; Sergius (1930), 15, 17-18.

[25] Sergius (1930), 15, 18.

[26] Nicholas (2004), vol. 5 (1911.06.18), 771.

the local Japanese Orthodox,[27] and the Russian-dominated parish in South Sakhalin was ambiguously subordinated to the Japanese hierarch but omitted from Japanese Church statistics.[28]

However, neither Japan's secular authorities nor its Orthodox Church envisioned dealing with the flood of émigrés and refugees which came in the wake of the revolution. As a Japanese Foreign police survey showed, 7251 Russians entered the country in 1918 alone.[29] As the Japanese official and public attitude toward Russians as possible "Reds" once more turned defensive, the state endeavored to minimize this refugee population by instituting a steep property requirement to enter the country.[30] Those who did make it in faced excessive police attention, which included encouragement and even help with leaving Japan.[31] Combined with the Russians' poor preparedness for Japanese conditions and their drive to reach more welcoming shores in America or Europe, this policy made the refugee tide a transitory one, with only 1714 Russians registered in Japan's 1920 census.[32] Yet, even this number was significant for the diminutive Japanese Orthodox Church.

Not only were most newcomers members of the Orthodox Church, but they included an illustrious host of fleeing

[27]Council (1910), 81.

[28]The parish, headed by the Russian priest Nicholas Kuz'min, existed since 1911, and was individually financed by Russia's Most Holy Synod. See Nicholas (2004), vol. 5 (1911.06.04), 767.

[29]Sawada (2002).

[30]The "cash presentation system" introduced in February 1920 required any unsponsored foreigner—including all refugees—to present at the border ¥ 1500 to be allowed entry into Japan. For a useful overview on the methods and characteristics of Russian entry into Japan in the first half of the 20th century see Podalko (2003).

[31]Among stories of police attention to the Russian diaspora, Fr. Innocent Seryshev notes that his overseeing police agent had offered him ¥100 for a ticket out of Japan. Seryshev (1952-1968), 24-25.

[32]With concentrations of 145 on Hokkaido, 229 in Tokyo, 739 in the Kanagawa Prefecture, 212 in Hyōgo Prefecture, 256 in Nagasaki Prefecture. Census (1920), 102.

clerics. Among the latter were bishops from the neighboring Russian dioceses primed by prior contacts with Japanese Orthodox intermediaries,[33] returning Russian-American clergy befriended by Fr. Symeon Mii at the 1917 Council of the Russian Orthodox Church,[34] refugee priests from the Altai, the Maritime Province and Mongolia.[35] The self-selected Russian diaspora included the most implacable, fearful or uprooted non-Bolsheviks who were uncommonly Orthodox—both in the number of ecclesiastical servitors and in the significance consensually accorded to religion—but also uncommonly poor, radicalized and nationalistic. In other words, in addition to its universal spiritual function, they approached the Church with an expectation of entitlement, as a humanitarian agency and a bulwark of Russianness.   At the time when the impoverished Japanese Orthodox establishment was in the throes of assuming its independence from things Russian, such a Russian infusion preordained a collision over the course of what both parties viewed as "their own" community.

As groups of Russian émigré believers in Japan began to congeal around Russian clerics, these new congregations exhibited a variety of organizational shapes and relationships with local coreligionists.   Fr. Innocent Seryshev does not seem to have ever assumed the part of a parish priest, and was content to attend the Easter 1920 celebrations at the Tokyo Resurrection cathedral as part of an unstructured

---

[33]The hierarchs who stayed in Japan were Bishops Michael (Bogdanov) of Vladivostok and Nestor (Anisimov) of Kamchatka. Research has found no support for a claim, made in Rutt (1957), 486, that Bishop Paul (Ivanovskii) supposedly died in Japan in 1920.

[34]On the stay of Protopriests Leonidas Turkevich and Alexander Kukulevskii in Japan see Benzin (1944), 285-286; Seryshev (1952-1968), 10, 21. On the Japanese links developed by Fr. Turkevich, who went on to become the ruling hierarch of the American Orthodox Metropolia and thus indirectly govern the entire Japanese Church in 1950's and 1960's, see more below.

[35]Exemplified by the eccentric esperantist Fr. Innocent Seryshev and the two unnamed "businessmen"-priests he had denounced for their worldliness during their stay in Japan. Seryshev (1952-1968), 55-56.

Russian émigré contingent of some 360 or 370.[36]   Bishop Nestor of Kamchatka set up in 1920 a church in Tsuruga, where he attempted to pastor both Russians and Japanese.[37] Fr. Leontius Protopopov in Kobe headed a new Russian parish which procured in 1921 a two-story building separate from the local Japanese congregation.[38] Finally, Fr. Peter Bulgakov organized a new exclusively Russian parish in Yokohama under the auspices of the Russian embassy chaplaincy.

While the refugees generally looked to Bishop Sergius for support, he often turned seekers away with a terse statement about the "lack of food... and housing."[39] Instead, the refugees themselves were being asked to help the Japanese Church in distress. As dissatisfaction with the Japanese Church's apparent aloofness grew among new arrivals, the Tokyo Russian embassy chaplain Bulgakov made a bid for the mantle of Japan's premier Russian ecclesiastic and champion of the refugees.[40] Administratively independent from the Japanese Church and financed from diplomatic funds, Bulgakov was well-placed to foster an alternative Russian Orthodox presence in Japan and soon attracted to his side the disgruntled refugee Fr. Innocent Seryshev. These vocal clerics turned the Japanese rhetoric of ecclesiastical "independence" around, by insisting that, if "the Russian Church is also for Russians only," then the collections among the refugees for the needs of the Japanese mission must stop.[41] Bulgakov went as far as to denounce Bishop Sergius as a money-grubbing, devious, and possibly adulterous "fox," and the Japanese Church—as an ingeniously masked anti-Russian "school of spies."[42]

[36] Orthodox Messenger (1920.05.15 - № 9-5), 5.

[37] Fomin (2002), 53.

[38] Kobe church (1983), 24, 34.

[39] Seryshev (1952-1968), 49.

[40] He emphasized as his sworn duty the "faithful service to the Russian state" in Bulgakov (1920), 11.18-36.

[41] Much of the material targeted against Bishop Sergius in Seryshev's archive, penned chiefly by Frs. Peter Bulgakov and Innocent Seryshev, circles around this topic. See especially Seryshev (1952-1968), 49-52.

[42] Seryshev (1952-1968), 574-579.

With their open dislike for the rightists, the rich, and the monastics, the embassy chaplain and his allies could not hope to rally the leading figures of the Russian émigré community, but contributed greatly toward fragmentation and alienation in the tangle of Russo-Japanese ecclesiastical relationships. The intensity of the contest lessened quickly, as the destructive 1923 Great Kantō Earthquake, the rise of Harbin as the Russian Orthodox hub of East Asia, and the impending Japanese diplomatic recognition of the USSR combined to push most refugee clerics out of Japan. However, for decades afterwards, the much diminished community of Russian émigrés in Japan would remain a source and barometer of ecclesiastical strife in the local Orthodox scene.

The dynamic of double exclusion of the Russian émigrés—from both the Japanese state and the Japanese Orthodox Church—meant that Japan's Orthodox community retained its overwhelmingly native composition, even as China's was radically transformed. Russians reconceived Harbin, to the exclusion of Tokyo, as the center of East Asia's "sole diocese free of Bolshevik tyranny,"[43] and quickly reshaped China's Orthodox landscape. Soon native Chinese believers found themselves sidelined by the huge new Russian presence, and the Japanese Church became the lone island of native "independence" in the Russian-dominated sea of East Asian Orthodoxy.

Although few in the Japanese Orthodox Church engaged deeply with the émigré ecclesiastical challenge,[44] the perplexed relationship with post-revolutionary Russian Church was a matter of broader concern for Japanese believers. The Japanese Church could not help joining a new kind of war unleashed by Bolshevik revolutionaries against the "capitalist" rest of the world. Fr. Mii, his community's

---

[43] Popov (2004) citing ГАРФ, ф. 6343, оп. 1, д. 235, л. 1-10.
[44] Bishop Sergius bore the brunt of that challenge, but his closest aide, Fr. Symeon Mii, was also deeply involved. See Council (1920), 62-63; Seryshev (1952-1968), 9-11.

representative at the 1917-1918 Council of the Russian Church, became the first Japanese Orthodox to experience this new war firsthand—before returning to Japan in January 1918 he witnessed fighting in Moscow and bloody chaos along the Trans-Siberian Railway.[45]

Soon, Japan's entire Orthodox community was drawn in—as a religious institution against the revolutionaries' atheism, as a "Daughter" of the Russian Orthodox Church against her "Mother's" persecutors, but above all as the principal human fabric connecting Russia and Japan at the time when anti-Bolshevik White Russians and expansionist Japanese found themselves allied against the Red rebels. However, even as the civil-war era Japanese *Orthodox Messenger* extolled the "heroic" White fighters,[46] it likewise aired classic across-the-board critiques of Russia. The Russian Church was being faulted for its "extreme bureaucratization;"[47] the Russian intellectual world, for its penchant "to run from one extreme to another;"[48] the Russian spirituality, for its fear of "human freedom, human responsibility, human activity;"[49] and the Russian people, for their cruelty.[50]

The rhetoric of Russo-Japanese alliance swiftly lost ground to that of Japanese supremacy. In January 1919 a strongly worded article in the *Orthodox Messenger* called for the Japanese Church to advance along its own path instead of cultivating a "transplant from an old Russian-grown stump."[51] In May of that year the crucial *Constitution of the Japanese Christian Orthodox Church* sealed the isolationist trend by omitting any mention of extra-Japanese links. Unsurprisingly, even as Russian refugee clergy and believers began to figure in local ecclesiastical reportage, they almost never entered

[45]Mii (1982), 97-143.
[46]See for example Morita (1919a).
[47]Mokushi-sei (1919), 13.
[48]Mokushi-sei (1919), 15.
[49]Naganawa (1989), 206, citing Orthodox Messenger (1917.12.20 - № 6-24).
[50]Ōba (1920), 3.
[51]Mokushi-sei (1919), 14.

the organizational structures and statistics of the Japanese Orthodox Church. It was not the inclusion of Russian newcomers, but the extrication from Russian entanglements that came to dominate the Japanese Orthodox engagement— or rather disengagement—with catholicity.

While financial self-reliance, native make-up and a self-referential Constitution became potent proofs of Japanese Church's post-revolutionary "independence" from Russia, it was an open secret that this independence was somehow imperfect, with Councils, conferences, lectures and articles repeatedly attempting to "clarify" its nature. In view of Soviet Russia's metamorphosis into the epicenter of an alternative communist world—an alien and hostile one in Japan's public consensus—even Japan's Russian bishop resorted to an open defense of Russian links only at the most critical junctures, like the Councils of 1919 and 1940.[52] Instead, Sergius battled isolationism by raising awareness of the global Orthodox communion in which, alongside and through their "Mother-Church," the Japanese believers were inscribed. The hierarch would explain the need to seek recognition for ecclesiastical independence from the world's peer local Churches,[53] fault the Japanese Orthodox establishment for being a "Greek Church that doesn't know Greek,"[54] and expound on the contemporary Church-state relationships in the Orthodox world.[55]

Sergius' efforts against introversion enjoyed support from a handful of clerics—those most globally exposed, like Frs. Mii and Morita,[56] or those most canonically faithful, like

[52]Council (1919), 12-14; (1940), 86-88.
[53]Council (1923), 10-11.
[54]Council (1926), 118.
[55]Council (1931), 48-50
[56]Frs. Mii and Morita are profiled in chapter 3. The former was exceptional among the Japanese in his currency with the Russian ecclesiastical world. After 1927, he too preferred to sever ties with Moscow's ecclesiastical headquarters, but was keen to avoid schism. See Orthodox Messenger (1928.08.10 - № 17-8), 19; (1928.10.10 - № 17-10), 18; (1933.05.20 - № 22-5),

Fr. Moses Kasai.[57]   In the decade after mid-1920's the editors of the *Orthodox Messenger* also provided a trickle of international news and Russian-themed articles, usually lifted from Russian émigré or Polish Orthodox press.   Finally, a few Japanese laymen who combined involvement in the Church with secular posts in the scholarly, diplomatic and journalistic spheres—like Basil Nobori, John Senuma and Nahum Yamauchi—brought occasional first-hand impressions and analyses of Orthodox life from abroad.[58]

Ironically, since the global Orthodox scene into which the Japanese believers were being integrated was one of disintegration and disorder, anti-isolationist efforts rubbed off on the ecclesiastical independence movement in the form of convenient precedents and rhetorical megalomania. Thus, in 1931 Professor Arsenius Iwasawa mustered the Finnish model of viable semi-independence for a small Orthodox Church as an example for Japan to follow.[59]   In 1933 an unnamed editor cited the large and fully independent Romanian Church as an example of his desired unilateral change of the liturgical calendar.[60]   Finally, in 1939 an obscure Nicholas Yamamoto went as far as to expound utterly unrealistic plans for Japanese leadership in the Balkan-centered Orthodox world.[61] However, the one contemporary Orthodox case study which provided the champions of ecclesiastical separation from Russia their best ammunition was the Russian Orthodox

25. Fr. Morita was distinctly less involved in defending foreign links, but his interventions in their favor were sometimes crucial, as in Council (1920), 60, 95-96, and Council (1930), 110-111.

[57]Council (1925), 70-71.

[58]Nobori, who had penned dozens of Russia-related articles in Japanese Orthodox press, is profiled in chapter 3. Senuma, until his brief arrest by Japanese authorities for suspected espionage in 1936, served as a Japanese language instructor at the Soviet embassy in Tokyo, and had occasion to travel to the USSR, as reported in Senuma (1928). Yamauchi, a journalist with Russian expertise, contributed a series of frank articles on the state of the Russian Church in Yamauchi (1938).

[59]Iwasawa (1931), 3.

[60]Orthodox Messenger (1933.12.01 - № 22-12), 40.

[61]Yamamoto (1939), 26.

Church itself, rent by the destructive dynamic of persecution and schism.

"Blessed is the one who can stand on his own feet" amid the chaos of contemporary Russian ecclesiastical life—thus wrote the former Japanese missionary and future Russian Patriarch Sergius (Stragorodskii) in his letter to Japan's hierarch in the wake of the 1917 Revolution.[62] As civil war engulfed Russia, already in 1918 communication with the Russian Church's headquarters in Moscow had become nearly impossible for those outside the sphere of Bolshevik control. This generated Provisional Supreme Church Administrations—temporarily self-governing regional assemblies of Russian Church's bishops in Bolshevik-free zones. It is unclear whether Bishop Sergius of Japan became involved with the Siberian PSCA which was based successively in Tomsk, Omsk and Irkutsk in 1918-1920, but he did personally participate in its last abortive incarnation—the September 1922 Hierarchal Conference in Nikol'sk-Ussuriiskii.[63] Meanwhile, the South-Russian PSCA had emigrated via Constantinople to Serbia's Sremski Karlovci and, since 1920, began to claim jurisdiction over all Russian Orthodox believers outside Soviet control. Soon this body gained enough reach in East Asia to institute by its authority a new diocese of Harbin on March 29 1922.[64] As for the oppressed Patriarch of Moscow St. Tikhon (Bellavin), who realized his inability to govern the war-torn Church effectively, on 20 November 1920 he issued a decree allowing provisional self-rule by dioceses and groups of dioceses isolated from ecclesiastical headquarters. However, such autonomy did not rule out direct obedience, when possible, to the patriarch.

In the case of Japan, Tikhon commanded sufficient international connections to inform the Japanese hierarch of a

[62]Council (1918), 9.
[63]Khvalin (1999), 62.
[64]Gerasimov (1931), 6.

promotion to the rank of archbishop on May 1 1921,[65] and sufficient international esteem to have special prayers for himself said throughout the Japanese Church in 1922.[66] Thus, when Sergius of Japan assumed charge of the Korean Orthodox Mission in 1923, he did so via as many as three systems of ecclesiastical governance. Namely, the transfer of Korea to the Japanese bishop had been first settled locally between ecclesiastics in Vladivostok and Tokyo in 1917, then mandated by the Patriarchal Synod in Moscow on November 17 1921, and finally confirmed by the Synod in Sremski Karlovci on December 16 1922.[67] Such coordination was not only cumbersome, but extremely fragile, a momentary balance fostered by solidarity with the persecuted Patriarch Tikhon and by opposition to the Soviet-backed "Renovationist" schism in the Russian Church. Death of the patriarch in 1925, decline of the "Renovationists," and fragmentation among the persecuted bishops in the USSR plunged the pulverized Russian Church into jurisdictional chaos.

In 1923-1927 as many as five divergent fractions came into focus in the globally dispersed Russian Orthodox Church, with each camp eager to claim the Japanese community. Unilateral independence appealed to many on nationalistic, political, or practical grounds, and has been instituted in Poland through state pressure and in America through in-house populism. In this camp Japanese figured as pioneers of ecclesiastical independence, with American secessionists calling upon the delegates at the decisive 1924 Detroit Council to "take example from the Japanese Church."[68] Opposing this centrifugal trend were global integrative efforts of the former South-Russian PSCA, since 1922 styled Hierarchal Synod of the Russian Orthodox Church Abroad in Sremski

[65] This news reached Japan indirectly, via Metropolitan Eusebius (Nikol'skii), by November of 1921, according to Orthodox Messenger (1921.11.15 - № 10-11), 7.

[66] Orthodox Messenger (1922.09.15 - № 11-09), 7.

[67] Council (1917), 76-77; Theodosius ([1926] 1999), 182, 263, 290-291.

[68] Sobor (1924), 15.

Karlovci, which likewise had ways to list the Japanese Church among its allies. Indeed, the 1923 Council of the Japanese Church appraised the Karlovci Synod as a bulwark of "pure Orthodoxy."[69]   More consequentially, in a July 1926 letter Sergius of Japan had asked the Synod's chairman, Metropolitan Anthony (Khrapovitskii), for permission to alter the organizational nomenclature and liturgical calendar of the Japanese Church.[70] Meanwhile, a much more pedigreed claimant to unify the global Orthodox "diaspora" arose in the Istanbul-based Church of Constantinople. At the May-June 1923 Pan-Orthodox Congress the activist Patriarch Meletius (Metaxakis) of Constantinople hinted that he was ready to accept the Japanese community as a bona-fide autonomous local church.[71] Russian nationalism inclined Sergius of Japan to eventually dismiss the Constantinopolitan option as one for "hotheads,"[72] but he was in no hurry to take sides. In this he followed the withdrawn position of Metropolitan Eulogius (Georgievskii) of Western Europe, who in turn appraised the Japanese hierarch's policy as "keeping silent."[73] Only in 1927, when Soviet authorities at long last permitted the battered Moscow Patriarchate to mend its international contacts, did Sergius finally cast his die. Forgoing suspense, independence, Karlovci and Constantinople, the Japanese hierarch opted for a direct relationship with Moscow.

Sergius' decade-long balancing act amid post-revolutionary jurisdictional disorder fostered among Japanese believers a convenient notion that external administrative alignments could be dismissed as their

[69] Council (1923), 7, 22.

[70] Although Sergius would later claim that the 1926 letter was merely "private" and consultative, it was manifestly read as "official" by the Karlovci Synod. See Anthony (1988), 186-187, 191; Council (1930), 64-65.

[71] Congress (1923), 162.

[72] Sergius (1930), 26. Compare Sergius' assertions that "as a Russian" he would follow the Russian hierarchy in Sergius (1935b), Iwasawa (1941).

[73] Anthony (1988), 186. Compare Sergius' own claim to have "kept silent" at this time, recorded in Council (1930), 64.

hierarch's "private" links.[74]   Russian detractors likewise accused Sergius of "chang[ing] jurisdictions like gloves."[75] However, his 1927 stand with the Moscow Patriarchate proved decisive. This choice had its attractions—while displaying commendably strict obedience to the "Mother-Church," it guaranteed *de facto* independence, since the USSR-entrapped Deputy Patriarchal *locum tenens* Metropolitan Sergius (Stragorodskii) would limit his actions vis-à-vis the Japanese Church to infrequent greetings and awards. However, since the Patriarchate's accommodation with Soviet authorities had compromised it among most Russians abroad, siding with Moscow meant breaking with Karlovci—the leading diasporic Russian ecclesiastical center, which chose the path of restorationist monarchism.

Initially, an informal "non-aggression pact," arranged in autumn 1927 between Karlovci's Metropolitan Anthony and Japan's Archbishop Sergius, postponed the confrontation.[76] This allowed the tacitly Moscow-aligned Japanese and vocally anti-Moscow émigré Russians to concelebrate at the consecration of the Tokyo cathedral as late as December 1929.[77] But with the cathedral safely completed the Japanese hierarch began to air his pro-Moscow views in brochures, mass mailings and at public assemblies, stirring uproar against his "Bolshevism" in Russian émigré circles. The formal termination of communion with Japan's hierarch, announced by the Karlovci Synod in autumn 1931,[78] put an end to ambiguity and launched a struggle for the Orthodox flock of East Asia. In an uncanny meshing of oppositions, the Japanese Church and the Korean Mission represented "communist"

[74]In 1930 Sergius would claim that the relationship with Karlovci was merely his "private" correspondence, while in 1940 the Japanese Consistory would say the same about links with Moscow. See Council (1930), 64; (1940), 88.

[75]Expression from Seryshev (1952-1968), 42.   See similar sentiments expressed in Council (1930), 62-63.

[76]Sergius (1931b), 26.

[77]Sergius (1930), 19.

[78]Naitō (1943), 7.

Moscow, "imperial" Japan and "native" separatism, while the dioceses of Harbin and Beijing stood for "monarchist" Karlovci, "republican" China and "Russian" integralism.

In 1931-1933 jurisdiction contestation flared up in Japan, Korea and China.[79] Although from 1934 Karlovci and Tokyo began taking steps to freeze the unsightly conflict,[80] cooperative exchanges were out of the question—the best they could do was "maintain silence to avoid upsetting the peace."[81] This ceasefire hid a continuing shift in the ecclesiastical economy, as the Karlovci Synod greatly advanced its global cause at the 1935 Hierarchal Conference,[82] while the Moscow Patriarchate lost almost all adherents outside of the USSR and Japan.[83] As the Soviet government shut off the Patriarchate's foreign communication, the 1936 Paschal telegram became the last notable pre-war ecclesiastical missive from Moscow to Tokyo.[84] Henceforth, when Sergius of Japan would be asked to contact Moscow, he could only advise seekers "to wait for favorable times."[85] The jurisdictional alignment of the

[79]In addition to the diminutive schism in Japan, treated in chapter 6, see Pozdniaev (1999c), 358 and Fomin (2004), 203, citing ГАРФ, ф. 6343, оп. 1, д. 204, л. 87-87 об. (the protocol of the November 7 1933 sitting of the Hierarchal Synod of the Russian Orthodox Church Abroad) on Korea; Du (1999) and Council (1933), 24-26, 35-37, 39-44 on China.

[80]On April 13 1934 the Karlovci Synod relieved Archbishop Nestor of the title to the Korean Mission, while at the 1934 Council of the Japanese Church Sergius spoke against attempting radical administrative rearrangements in Manchuria. See Fomin (2004), 203; Council (1934), 83-84.

[81]Orthodox Messenger (1941.03.01 - № 31-3), 2.

[82]Published by Soldatov (2004).

[83]According to early 1945 statistics, when the number of Moscow-aligned parishes has once again increased, the Moscow Patriarchate still numbered only 12 churches in America and 5 in Western Europe (France). See Karpov (2009), 103-105.

[84]See the contents of the telegram discussed in Council (1936), 5-6. Sergius of Japan lost communication with his family in the USSR already in 1932, according to Polycarp (1946), 175. As for ecclesiastical correspondence from Japan to Moscow, the 1935 congratulation must have been one of the last, since it almost lead to the arrest of the Deputy Patriarchal *locum tenens* on charges of "spying for Japan," according to Tsypin (1999), 288.

[85]Victor (2003b), 325.

Japanese Church, chosen by its key champion of catholicity, had thus become yet another element in its isolation.

The 1940 Council of the Japanese Orthodox Church proved to be the climax of isolationist "independence" trends, as Japan's national mobilization placed the delegates under pressure to take decisive steps towards Japanization. In the course of this decisive Council a multitude of proposals envisioned Shintoizing Church ritual, the lingering formal connections with the Moscow Patriarchate were declared severed, and Metropolitan Sergius, as a "foreigner," was given to understand his need to retire.[86] This juncture appeared to afford a unique moment for a self-conscious departure from the world's Orthodox Church as such. However, while old isolationist dynamics completed their course, there surfaced a new network of connections and a new extraverted program. The delegates repeatedly voiced the need to mend ties with the neighboring Orthodox dioceses on the continent, and the Council resolved to arrange for the ordination of the new Japanese bishop at the hands of Russian hierarchs in Harbin.[87]

The 1940 turn away from the fundamentally reactive anti-Russian cluster of secessionist trends meant that the connections and complexes inherited from the once mighty Russian Orthodox Church withered to such an extent that alternative currents of Japano-centric expansionism were coming to the fore in structuring the catholic life of the Japanese Orthodox community. This shift redefined Russians—the principal "other" of the Japanese Orthodox—from an alien presence in the narrow circle of the Japanese community into peers and allies in a wider "Pan-Asian" world. Most fatefully, the 1940 reorientation signaled the activist entry of the Japanese state into the reordering of ecclesiastical life in East Asia. Catholic connectedness, encoded into the Church's nature, had ceased to be an eroding liability, and reemerged as an active asset. It

[86]Council (1941), 27-35, 50-52, 71-72, 77-78, 84-96.
[87]Council (1941), 35-36, 69, 75, 91-94.

is to the background and consequences of this shift that the narration turns next.

Chapter 12

East Asian Orthodox Church

At the 1931 Church Council Sergius extolled the "pure freedom" given by the secular authorities to the Orthodox Church in Japan, stating that "in other countries all manner of problems occur between the government and the Church and there is no place like Japan." To illustrate his case, he prefaced this surprisingly mild hyperbole with a compelling overview of contemporary Orthodox Churches in distress. As Sergius detailed, in Finland the state forced the Church to reform its calendar, in Poland the state forbade the convocation of the Council, in Romania the state imprisoned priests daring to serve on the Julian calendar, in Turkey the state openly oppressed the Church, in Egypt the state chose which candidate to appoint as patriarch, and even in China (in this case Manchuria) the state outlawed ecclesiastical convocations lasting longer than three days.[1]

Although Sergius' adherence to the Moscow Patriarchate prevented him from naming the main culprit—the Soviet

[1] Council (1931), 48-50.

state—the global picture of official intrusion into the life of the Church was vivid enough. On the other hand, in contemporary Japan secular authorities hardly intervened into questions of internal ecclesiastical significance. Here, the Orthodox community was neither deep-rooted nor foreign-dominated, both insufficiently deviant to draw persecution by its heterodoxy and overly alien to draw intervention by its familiarity, and above all minute and introverted. To be sure, the Russian links of the Church were of singular significance to the Japanese state, but favorable experience since Nicholas' days had shown these connections to be relatively harmless, even useful as far as the officials were concerned. It was therefore less as an object of investigation and intervention, but rather as a Russian policy tool, that the Japanese Orthodox Church would periodically attract the attention of Japanese officials.

The most important of such periods was no doubt Japan's 1918-1922 Siberian Intervention in the Russian Civil War. This was a period of Japan's deepest involvement with Russia, and—by consequence—of the Japanese state's deepest involvement with the Japanese Orthodox to date. The scant public relations coups of the enfeebled Japanese Church at this time were intimately connected with the Russian public relations campaigns of the Japanese government. The most notable example of such a public event was the grand Orthodox memorial service in Tokyo for Admiral Alexander Kolchak, the one-time leader of the White movement in Siberia. Attended by a multitude of high representatives of Allied powers, it acted as a symbolic reaffirmation of the Allied nations' resolve to continue the anti-communist fight.[2] At the time when the Japanese Orthodox believers struggled to feed their priests and sped to confirm their independence from Russia, the publication by the Church of the long-awaited Russo-Japanese

---

[2] Orthodox Messenger (1920.03.15 - № 9-3), 6.

dictionary and phrase-book appeared transparently as state-sponsored labor.[3]

However, since the Japanese Church was in poor shape to tackle the unfolding events as an organization, its most notable engagement with the intervention came in the guise of informal cadre transfer. Even as Japan scrambled to mass-produce more Russian specialists, the dearth of immediately available bilinguals made the Japanese Orthodox seminary-trained elite into valuable Russia-hands. During the intervention years at least 11 Japanese Orthodox graduates of Russia's theological schools had served in key Russo-Japanese liaison posts—either as full-time employees, usually with the Japanese Army or the South Manchurian Railway, or as members of specially dispatched official missions.[4] As for the trainees of Japanese Orthodox theological institutions, they served as intervention-era intermediaries in their tens. The bitter hyperbole of Bishop Sergius at the time held that "all catechists have gone... into expeditionary forces."[5] A preliminary survey has yielded the names of 66 Japanese Orthodox seminary-trained specialists involved as Russia-hands in various facets of Japan's Siberian Intervention,[6] in

---

[3] Orthodox Messenger (1919.11.15 - № 8-13), 1; (1920.01.15 - № 9-1), 10.
[4] See profiles of most in Naganawa (2007).
[5] Seryshev (1952-1968), 34.
[6] Fr. Symeon Mii Michirō, Fr. Paul Morita Ryō, ex-Priest John Suzuki Shin'ichi, ex-Priest Ignatius Matsumoto Takatarō, Peter Ishikawa Kisaburō, John Senuma Kakusaburō, Matthew Suzuki Yōjirō, Arsenius Iwasawa Heikichi, Mark Saikaishi Shizuka, Emelian Higuchi Tsuyanosuke, Innocent Kisu Yoshinoshin, Peter Uchiyama Petoru, Micah Nakamura Kōsuke, Sergius Shōji Shōgorō, Basil Nobori Naotaka, Arsenius Ishida Toramatsu, Andrew Fukihara Kihei, Timothy Seki Takesaburō, James Igari Shinzō, Ignatius Takaku Yoshio, Sergius Shionoya Sadakichi, Gabriel Toda Jinzō, Timothy Takahashi Yoshio, Peter Kaminaga Sampei, Gregory Morita Keio, Basil Nagai Masunobu, Aquila Ōzawa Akira, Justin Mii Yoshio, Nicetas Kondō Shōtarō, Nahum Yamauchi Fusuke, Peter Nakayama Sadao, Tikhon Oota Koshirō, Samuel Uzawa Tokujū, Basil Takeoka Takeo, John Endō Ibō, Peter Takeuchi Kenzaburō, Daniel Hirooka Tadachi, Bessarion Takahashi Chōshichirō, Nicholas Takahashi Kenji, Basil Okuyama Wahei, Barnabas Osozawa Eiji, Sergius Watanabe, James Matsubara, James Kawamura, Katō Hidemi, Yuhasi Shigetō, Fujima Morinobu,

addition to two Japanese monks resident at the Shmakovka monastery near Vladivostok.[7]

Mobilization of Japanese Orthodox liaison figures for the expeditionary effort started at an early date. Before Japanese troops made landfall in Russia, Foreign Minister Gotō Shimpei had already began planning the dispatch to the continent of a Japanese Orthodox delegation to "prevent any misunderstandings of the true intention of the Japanese intervention as well as to further the trend of amity between Japan and Russia."[8] As a result, the four best qualified churchmen were sent in August 1918 on a state-sponsored mission to preach Japan's goodwill, distribute humanitarian aid, as well as "observe" and "report" the goings on along two trails of Russian ecclesiastical institutions—Fr. Paul Morita and John Senuma to the Maritime Province, Fr. Symeon Mii and Peter Ishikawa via Manchuria to Transbaikalia. The delegation presented itself as an ecclesiastical rescue team and made a favorable public-relations impact before reporting back to Japan's Prime Minister Hara Takashi in January 1919.[9]

Gunshi Yoshio, Satō Yasuo, Kageta Shimon, Yamaguchi Jumpei, Andō Seiichi, Asano Kazuo, Suzuki Akira, Igari Yukisaburō, Suzuki Sadajirō, Asano Jūrō, Ono Kiyoji, Miyake Akio, Aizawa Akira, Zealot Mogi, Paul Makishima, Peter Terazawa, Ogawa, Oka, Satō. In a few cases pronunciation of names is conjectural. For contemporaneous lists of some Orthodox serving in various capacities in Harbin and across Russia see Orthodox Messenger (1919.02.20 - № 8-4), front matter; (1920.01.15 - № 9-1), 11. In addition to the materials indicated in the following two paragraphs see also Orthodox Messenger (1919.06.15 - № 8-8), 15; (1919.09.15 - № 8-11), 16-17; (1919.10.15 - № 8-12), 23; (1920.01.15 - № 9-1), 9-10; (1920.08.15 - № 9-8), 6; (1981.06.20 - № 1089), 9; Council (1923), 41-43; (1926), 70; Korshunov ([1998] 2004); Odawara church (2002), 208; Osozawa (1976), 72.

[7] Monk Ambrose (Hibi) and Hierodeacon Seraphim (Minato). See Council (1919), 3; Orthodox Messenger (1919.08.15 - № 8-10), appendix 4.

[8] Siberian dispatch (1918), 410107.

[9] The Japanese Orthodox mission to Siberia is best covered in Naganawa (1989), 208-222. Some details from the mission's reports, as published in the contemporary Orthodox Messenger, are collected in Oguri (2009). The collection of Japanese Foreign Ministry files on the mission has been released on internet by the Japan Center for Asian Historical Records—see particularly the materials of Siberian dispatch (1918).

Starting with this prominent "greeting card," a number of individual Orthodox believers—though no longer as formal representatives of their Church—performed missions of special import to the intervention effort. Fr. Symeon Mii merits repeated mention, since, in the 1919 estimation of one Russian spy in Japan, "one could not do without his help in resolving any question with the Japanese."[10] This distinguished cleric served as an interpreter at "all Russian representations in Tokyo" and figured as an informal diplomat in appraising the validity of dubious Russian "emissaries" who poured into Japan in search of sponsors. The vital intervention-era roles of other well-known leaders of the Japanese Church, Professor Arsenius Iwasawa and Basil Nobori, have been already noted.[11]

The next most notable personage was probably the graduate of the St. Petersburg Theological Academy and veteran professor of Russian at military schools, Emelian Higuchi Tsuyanosuke. He spent as much as 39 months with the Japanese Army in Russia, acting as its intermediary with the Merkulov regime in Vladivostok and participating as the only non-military Japanese delegate in the Sakhalin Treaty talks of 1920.[12]

The most widely publicized Japanese Orthodox believer swept into the intervention was the ex-seminarian Arsenius Ishida Toramatsu, Japan's consul in Nikolaevsk-on-the-Amur. Massacred by Russian anarchists in the Nikolaevsk incident of 1920 together with his family and other Japanese residents, Ishida headed the list of Japan's symbolic victims not only

---

[10]Markovchin (2003), 250.
[11]See profiles in chapter 3.
[12]Higuchi's biography is yet to be written, but a variety of summaries combine to provide an outline. See his obituary in Orthodox Messenger (1931.10.20 - № 20-10), 21; (1931.11.20 - № 20-11), 20-21; profiles in Japan Christian dictionary (1988), 1156, and Naganawa (2007), 223-224; mentions in Kandidov (1932), 58-59; Hara (1989), 529; Goodman & Miyazawa, 80; Seryshev (1952-1968), 577.

in the *Orthodox Messenger*, but in much of the contemporary Japanese secular press.[13]

Turning from individuals to systemic groups, the most common function of Japanese Orthodox Russia-hands was that of military interpreters, a role in which they received praise from Japanese and Russian generals alike.[14] While most army translators' jobs were occupied exclusively with written texts, those better versed in the living language received regimental and Red Cross posts, while the best interpreters sported officers' uniforms and functioned as adjutants and representatives of senior commanders in dealings with the Russians. It appears that graduates of Russia's seminaries, like Matthew Suzuki serving at the military mission in Chita, occupied the latter exalted category.[15] Former Japanese Orthodox catechists and lower clergy appear to have entered the intermediary positions, like James Igari, who saw service in Nikol'sk, Khabarovsk and Harbin.[16] A few key posts were available for the producers of propagandist Russo-Japanese press, like the Orthodox ex-seminarians Nahum Yamauchi and Peter Nakayama, who served as leading journalists of the Vladivostok Japanese newspaper *Urajio-Nippo*.[17] Finally, another expanding niche was that of Russian relations specialists in Japan's mushrooming continental economic network, extending from the colossal semi-official South Manchurian Railway to minute trading firms in remote Russian towns, like the Shimada Trading Company's branch in Nikolaevsk-on-the-Amur, which employed the stellar Orthodox theological writer Timothy Seki.[18] Taken together, Orthodox were

[13]Theological writer Timothy Seki and former catechist Andrew Fukihara were other notable Japanese Orthodox figures who also perished in the massacre. For reportage in the Japanese Orthodox press see Orthodox Messenger (1920.07.15 - № 9-7), 7; Orthodox Messenger (1920.08.15 - № 9-8), 4-7. For the summary of Japan's general reaction to the incident see Izao (2009).

[14]Kandidov (1937), 25.

[15]Markovchin (2003), 236.

[16]Sapporo church (1987), 119-120.

[17]See a study of the newspaper by Morgun (2006).

[18]On Seki see Naganawa (1989), 139-149.

disproportionately represented as Japan's intervention-era "face" vis-à-vis the Russians, just as Orthodox Christianity itself was increasingly evoked by Russians as a banner of the anti-Bolshevik camp.

This intervention-era integrative dynamic pulled the Japanese into Russian ideological discourses, pulled Russian religionists into closer contact with the Japanese, and pulled the shards of the disintegrating Orthodox empire into a new East Asian whole. On the Japanese side one saw solid backing for Orthodox instruction in Russian schools—witness the survival of catechism classes on North Sakhalin until the very end of the Japanese occupation in 1925.[19] In the realm of propaganda, Orthodox-tinged Judophobia crept into the Japanese thought-world, most notably through the *Protocols of the Elders of Zion*.[20] Another revolution-era apologetic—a book by Bishop Nestor of Kamchatka on *The Shooting of the Moscow Kremlin*—was published by the author in both Russian and Japanese, and in 1921 presented to the imperial family and the Japanese Emperor himself.[21] The Russian Far East, in turn, developed a network of ecclesiastical ties with Japan, as coreligionists befriended, supported and guided Russians in their encounters with interventionists. Thus, Emelian Higuchi gifted his own money to struggling Russian clerics, Peter Ishikawa distributed the largess of the Japanese Foreign Ministry to the Transbaikal diocese, and John Senuma directed a Russian priest to appeal to the Japanese consul in Vladivostok.[22] As late as the 1930's, when the involvement of the Japanese Orthodox in the

---

[19]Kostanov (1992), 49, quoting *Социальное строительство на Сахалине (1925-1945 гг.): Сборник документов*, Южно-Сахалинск, 1967, 24.

[20]They were being printed by Russians in Japan, translated and popularized by Orthodox and non-Orthodox Japanese alike, and distributed to Japanese soldiers. Goodman and Miyazawa (1995), 78-87; Cohn (1981), 118.

[21]Orthodox Messenger (1921.03.15 - № 10-3), 9; Fomin (2002), 53.

[22]See consecutively Orthodox Messenger (1931.11.20 - № 20-11), 21; Ishikawa (1919), 8; Hara (1989), 417, quoting a telegram from the chief of the political section Matsudaira to Foreign Minister Uchida, December 19 1918, in 外務省記録 1/6/3/24/13/34, (1).

intervention was being re-remembered in the USSR as a facet of anti-Japanese propaganda,[23] there were still clergy in Soviet Russia who could be executed for erstwhile association with Japanese counterparts, especially "the resident of the Japanese intelligence Mii [i.e. Fr. Symeon Mii]."[24]

For many other Russian ecclesiastics who chose flight, Tokyo figured as a possible rallying point. At the time the Japanese capital was not only the base of regional anti-Bolshevik resistance, but the site of East Asia's largest Orthodox cathedral in addition to ten other Orthodox temples and prayer-houses.[25] After the fall of Vladivostok to the Reds in 1922, Russian hierarchs chose Tokyo as the best location for a major ecclesiastical gathering. The December 4 1922 ordination of Paul (Vvedenskii) as Bishop of Nikol'sk-Ussuriiskii became an unprecedented ceremony in the history of the Japanese Church, assembling at the Tokyo Resurrection cathedral four bishops, 14 priests, five deacons and over a thousand believers from Russia, Japan and Manchuria.[26] This juncture showed what Tokyo might become in the life of the Russian Church "after Russia"—the Orthodox capital of East Asia.

As the previous chapter has shown, the agents who could have undergirded such central status for Tokyo proved disinterested in creating a regional, post-Russian, East Asian Orthodox Church. The Japanese Orthodox Church recoiled into isolationism, the region's Russian ecclesiastical emigration strove to recreate pre-revolutionary ways in China, and the dispersed claimants to the Russian Orthodox diaspora

[23]Notably in the works of Kandidov (1932, 1937).

[24]This was one of the charges against Archbishop Cyprian (Komarovskii). See his profile in the New-martyrs database.

[25]Tokyo cathedral (1998), 75.

[26]Orthodox Messenger (1923.01.15 - № 12-1), 5-6. A major ecclesiastical event like an episcopal ordination was at the time usually reserved for regional metropolitan centers. By comparison, the first episcopal ordination to be conducted in the capital of the Russian Far East, Vladivostok, occurred as recently as 1916. Nestor (2002), 401.

endeavored to draw the region into their global ecclesiastical economy. The Japanese state likewise disengaged from the Church, cut Russia-oriented jobs, and impelled many Japanese Orthodox liaison figures to resume ecclesiastical service, making this a period when "for the sake of bread clergy became interpreters and interpreters became priests."[27]   Amid the gradual disintegration of pre-revolutionary ties, centripetal forces withdrew onto the periphery of Japanese projects, shifting the locus of visions of a united regional Orthodox Church to the continental crossroads of East Asia.

One set of such visions clustered around the neighborly relations between the Orthodox dioceses of Harbin and Japan, which revolved around Sergius' repeated visits to solicit donations from Manchuria's Russians since mid-1920's. As material aid from the émigrés flowed to Japan, Sergius held up the self-sacrificial piety of Russian Harbinites as an example to the Orthodox Japanese.[28] Conversely, the Tokyo cathedral restoration campaign introduced the Japanese Orthodox Church as a topic into Harbin-based émigré press.[29] Orthodox ecclesiastics other than Sergius began to exchange visits between Japan and Manchuria,[30] and even pupils of Harbin's schools, where Sergius enjoyed giving talks, carried out lasting impressions of his visits.[31] Until its derailment in 1931, this

[27]Suzuki (1931), 10.

[28]For such exhortations see Consistory (1933), 154; Koike (n/d), 144-145.

[29]All five pre-1931 pieces on the Japanese Church in Harbin's leading Russian cultural magazine, *Frontier (Rubezh)*, had to do with the restoration of the Tokyo cathedral according to Sawada (2005), 98.

[30]For visitors from Harbin to Japan see Bishop Nestor of Kamchatka visiting Tokyo and Hakodate in 1926, reported in Consistory (1933), 181; Orthodox Messenger (1926.11.20 - № 15-11), 19; and Protodeacon Procopius Makoveev serving at the Tokyo cathedral for about a year and a half according to Heavenly Bread (1940 - № 7), 58. For visits of Tokyo's Church-servitors to Harbin see the travels of Deacon Basil Chuvashov and Regent Victor Pokrovskii in Orthodox Messenger (1926.09.20 - № 15-9), 21; (1928.02.10 - № 17-2), 28.

[31]For an example of Sergius' lecture tour in Harbin's middle schools see Yeast (1928.06 - № 7-6), 25-26. According to his own testimony, the well-known Russian émigré poet Valerius Pereleshin became a monk due to one

Tokyo-Harbin rapprochement set an important precedent of regional ecclesiastical cooperation.

Continuing Japanese settlement in Korea and Manchuria was disproportionately significant to the Japanese Orthodox Church, inasmuch as many of the intervention-era Japanese Orthodox Russia-hands who retained their positions in the secular world did so in the service of Japan's Manchurian establishments, primarily the South Manchurian Railway. Also, in addition to the small trickle of Orthodox Japanese moving to the continent, the 1920's saw the beginning of isolated Japanese conversions to Orthodoxy in Manchuria, primarily through marriage to Russian women. The most famous such case is the "Japanese Schindler" who went on to save Lithuanian Jews in 1938, Sugihara Chiune. In 1924 he married one Claudia Apollonova and was baptized in Harbin under the name of Sergius.[32]

Yet another aspect of the expansion of the Japanese Orthodox sphere was the cognitive shift toward a broader mixed-nation consciousness, which conditioned the "discovery" of the previously "invisible" native continental believers in the *Orthodox Messenger* around the close of 1920's. For instance, in December 1929 an article reported "Japanese, Russian and Korean" clergy and believers welcoming Archbishop Sergius in Seoul,[33] and the Easter service of 1931 was described as marked by a "curious" event of reading the Gospel in Korean at the Tokyo cathedral.[34] Once the Japanese Army occupied all of Manchuria in 1931, turning the region into Japan's arena of grand exploitative and developmental projects, the flow of Japanese and Korean colonists into the region—as well as the rate of its conceptual appropriation by the metropole—increased exponentially. Intensified Japanese interaction with Manchuria's Russians once more created the demand for

such childhood encounter with the Japanese hierarch. Hauth (1996), 72.

[32]Levine (1996), 69.

[33]Orthodox Messenger (1929.12.15 - №18-12), 29.

[34]Orthodox Messenger (1931.05.20 - №20-5), 15.

Japanese Orthodox Russia-hands. As the July 1 1936 statistics of Tokyo Orthodox Seminary graduates show, one-forth of them resided in Manchuria, and Harbin was second only to Tokyo in their concentration.[35]

The number of Japanese migrants converting to Ortho-doxy among the Russians in Manchuria likewise grew, as Japanese and Russians—usually Japanese men and Russian women—formed mixed families whose offspring frequently grew up with an identity that was both Russo-Japanese and Orthodox.[36] Caught on the fork of ethno-linguistic and geo-jurisdictional divides, these believers often became "unincluded and unregistered wanderers who belong neither to the Japanese nor to the Russian Church,"[37] or else attempted to belong to both at once. In this striving to straddle the fence they formed an increasingly potent force for integrating the Orthodox Church of East Asia, none of them so strategically placed to "wag the dog" as Fr. Sergius Suzuki—the lone Japanese Orthodox priest on the continent.

The Dalian-based Fr. Suzuki began his post-revolutionary career with a loss of his entrusted ecclesiastical property to a swindler in 1918—a misadventure which cost the hapless cleric his salary and status. Yet, since he consented to serve without pay, already the next year Fr. Suzuki was reinstated as Manchuria's Japanese Orthodox pastor. At the same time, he also enrolled himself as a priest of Mukden's cemetery church, which functioned under the aegis of the Russian-dominated

[35]The list includes 45 seminary graduates in Manchuria with 27 in Harbin. Altogether the list includes 174 persons with 44 of them in Tokyo. See Orthodox Messenger (1936.09.01 - №25-9), 34-37; (1936.10.01 - №25-10), 35.

[36]The process of such cultural merging in the settler villages in the Three Rivers region along the Soviet-Manchurian border was reported to the author in an interview by the son of a Japanese soldier-settler and Russian émigré woman, George Shima Toshihiko, at the Nagoya Orthodox church in the spring of 2004. For an urban perspective see the famous case of another Russian-Japanese of similar background, the Harbin-born singer Nicetas Yamashita, in Osanai (2005).

[37]Suzuki (1933), 8.

269

Orthodox diocese of Beijing. The unique stance of serving in two jurisdictions made him the herald of Japanese Church's involvement on the continent,[38] the one Japanese priest most involved with Manchuria's Russians,[39] and—although never a missionary to the Chinese[40]—the champion of regional ecclesiastical unification. Even the Japanese Guandong Army, in its own way, reportedly took note of his Russo-Japanese bridging function by requesting his assistance in drafting Russian "comfort women" for Japanese soldiers in Mukden.[41] Fr. Suzuki's copious contributions to the Japanese Orthodox press pioneered the integration of what he portrayed as the continental past and future of the Japanese Church into an imperial purpose beyond independence. In one vivid 1933 exemplar of such rhetoric, he affirmed:

> I believe that it is the Heavenly mission for our independent Japanese Orthodox Church to turn around and exert ourselves in planting in Siberia and Manchuria that seed of Orthodoxy, which was brought some 70 years ago from European Russia, across Siberia, and implanted in the fertile vineyard of our Japan. It is the same with the Heavenly mission of the Japanese people—to lead Manchukuo in building the Eden of the Kingly Way.[42]

Fr. Suzuki's actions spoke no less loudly, as he successfully disregarded the Moscow-Karlovci split by continuing to serve

[38] Thus, already in 1919 he called the Japanese Church to assume charge over the Orthodox flock of Mukden in Orthodox Messenger (1919.01.05 - №8-1), 19.

[39] He appears to be the sole Japanese priest to have a special article dedicated to him in the official organ of the Harbin diocese in Heavenly Bread (1941 - №11), 7-8.

[40] Although he is said to have liked China, Fr. Suzuki demonstrated the characteristic obliviousness of a colonizer in his unconcern for the Chinese people and language according to Kaneishi (1993), 248-249.

[41] Hauth (1996), 76.

[42] Suzuki (1933), 31.

both Japanese and Russian coreligionists. In 1929 he moved back to Dalian, where he began to gather funds for a new prayer-house and simultaneously conduct services at a Russian cemetery church. While his principal local flock was Japanese,[43] he continued services for local Russians, who in turn made contributions toward his construction project.[44] The consecration of the Japanese Church's Dalian prayer-house on April 3 1937 testified to the unity underneath jurisdictional division—Fr. Suzuki concelebrated with the Russian Hieromonk Gabriel from the Beijing diocese, the assembled believers included 50 Japanese and 70 Russians, and the article in the Japanese *Orthodox Messenger* justifiably spoke of "diligent cooperation of Japanese and Russian believers."[45]

Even more impressive than this local overcoming of the global jurisdictional split was the emergence of the long-peripheral Fr. Suzuki as a powerful voice at the Tokyo ecclesiastical headquarters in 1940. At the 1940 Council he effectively challenged Metropolitan Sergius' alignment with Moscow in the name of "peace in the Orthodox Church of Japan, Manchuria and China."[46] Fr. Suzuki's position as champion of imperial integration changed little, but if his 1920's appeals were musings of a marginal activist, in 1940 he spoke for what had become Japan's mainstream ideology and practice of expansionist Pan-Asianism.[47]

While the dilemma of choice between a narrowly national and a broader imperial identity had emerged since the close of Nicholas' period, the expansionist drift which eventually brought Fr. Suzuki into limelight had become noticeable in

[43] According to the 1935-1940 annual Council minutes, the number of active Japanese Orthodox here averaged 195.

[44] The report on the consecration of the Dalian church lists 89 Russian contributors. See Orthodox Messenger (1937.06.01 - №26-6), 38-39.

[45] Orthodox Messenger (1937.06.01 - №26-6), 30-31.

[46] Council (1941), 93.

[47] Fr. Sergius Suzuki's biography has been thoroughly researched and admirably presented in Kaneishi (1993). For data pertinent to this paragraph see especially pp. 209, 211, 214-215, 236.

Japanese Orthodox ecclesiastical discourse since early 1930's, a time when Manchuria's conquest unleashed a supportive "war fever" in Japanese mass-media. Japanese conciliar delegates began raising the question of forming a single "independent episcopal jurisdiction for the Far East" since at least 1934.[48] By the latter part of the 1930's, as the need to mobilize people for war introduced into the Japanese Orthodox press an unprecedented outpouring of modern-day miracle-accounts—a genre virtually non-existent in prior years—stories of non-burning churches from Japan and of self-renewing icons from Harbin aligned next to each other in a show of spiritual unity.[49] In a bid to mend fences with estranged neighbors the most esteemed Japanese cleric, Fr. Symeon Mii, in August of 1937 paid an unofficial visit to Archbishop Meletius and other senior clergy of the Harbin diocese.[50] At that time, a few Japanese Orthodox believers in Manchuria, like Peter Takeuchi Kenzaburō with Harbin's security authorities, had already become a vital presence in the life of the local Church.[51] Thus Japan's imperial expansion conditioned an increasingly insistent Japanese Orthodox outreach effort.

Behind the urgency of calls to overcome divisions with neighboring Russo-Chinese dioceses also stood the increased dependence of the Japanese Orthodox community on domestic "trends of the time." The pull of Japanese statism, with its increasingly enforced and sharply-defined civic religion of state Shintoism, had manifested itself early in the most important sphere of emperor veneration. Around mid-1920's Japanese Orthodox discourse began to retreat from the rhetorical equation of the world's monarchs and instead fell in line with Japan's prevailing exceptionalism. Thus, in 1927 the Orthodox formally mourned Japan's Taishō "Emperor" already as a uniquely native *tennō*, even as the Russian

[48]Council (1934), 83-84.
[49]See for instance Nakai (1938b); Satō (1939); Ōzawa (1939).
[50]Mii (1937), 14; (1940), 10.
[51]Beacon of Love (1939.08.06), 27; Endō (1942), 28.

"emperor" and Serbian "king" both retained the title of *kōtei*.[52] Orthodox criticism of enduring polytheistic implications behind state-mandated Shintoist rites lasted a little longer,[53] but soon gave way to an increasingly impressive array of ultrapatriotic style and ritual assimilated into Japanese Orthodox practice. By 1938 Church Councils began with a bow in the direction of the imperial palace followed by the singing of the national anthem and a triple "Long live His Majesty!"[54] The contemporary *Orthodox Messenger* explained and enjoined pilgrimage to the Grand Shrine of Ise, the principal sanctuary of state Shintoism.[55] Japanese Orthodox clergy have undergone a nearly total sartorial conversion from the once-ubiquitous "Russian" clerical cassocks to the "native" *haori*-and-*hakama* formal wear.

The driving force behind adopting more and more self-consciously Japanese trappings included an increasing dose of fear to diverge from the escalating and vague demands of patriotism. As Fr. Kodera took part in the Ministry of Education's Conference of Religious Organizations in 1938, he was eager to learn what new "suggestion" the Church might need to fulfill next.[56] Calls for total mobilization, wartime prayers, extensive coverage of war-heroes' funerals, special appeals for the front, thrift and health tips, injunctions to venerate imperial photographs—all of these new fixtures of the *Orthodox Messenger* were centrally handed down and broadcast throughout wartime Japanese press. In this context of "working towards the state" the Japanese Orthodox elite was increasingly given to understand that, in addition to the demands made upon all of Japan's religious bodies, their

---

[52]See special prayer texts for the Taishō emperor printed in Orthodox Messenger (1915.11.05 - № 4-21), front matter; (1927.01.20 - № 16-01), 1-2. For a late reference to Russian and Serbian rulers see Consistory (1933), 10.

[53]As in Nakajima (1927), 8.

[54]Council (1938), 3.

[55]Endō (1938).

[56]Kodera (1938).

Figure 12.1: Japanese Orthodox Churchmen, 1914.

Figure 12.2: Church Council, 1940.

Figure 12.3: Consistory, ca. 1947. From ROJ (1948.11 - No 22-7), 8.

Self-presentation and socio-political clime through the sartorial prism. In 1914 the majority of Church-servitors display Russian-style cassocks, a few, Japanese-style haori-and-hakama wear. By 1940 only the Metropolitan and four other figures retain cassocks, the rest of the Council delegates are split between Japanese-style (clergy) and Western-style (laymen) formal dress. In the post-war scene cassocks reemerge into the mainstream, while Japanese-style wear disappears altogether.

community was also asked to play a special part in Japan's Russian policy.

In later 1930's regular reportage about the global situation of the Orthodox Church disappeared from the pages of the *Orthodox Messenger*, but more and more articles on the religious and socio-political trends in the Soviet Union took its place. In June 1938 Basil Nobori explained just why the Japanese Orthodox needed to be up to speed with Soviet developments:

> Since we, as Orthodox, are coreligionists of the people of former Russia, even in the most unlikely circumstances we must have resolve to throw ourselves at the forefront of propagandist efforts—in the sense of saving coreligionists from communist oppression.[57]

These "most unlikely circumstances" referred obliquely to the escalation of Soviet-Japanese border violence which augured no less than the annexation of all or part of the Soviet Far East to Manchukuo. Just as Japanese planners were readying an émigré-staffed government for Soviet territories to be potentially annexed,[58] they appear to have been likewise preparing the Japanese Orthodox to reenact their Siberian Intervention-era liaison role. Interestingly, there is a hint that this time the role would include a formulation of philo-Semitism, in line with the Japanese plans to entice Jews to Manchuria. Thus, the August 1938 issue of the *Orthodox Messenger* came out with a lead piece devoted to debunking Judophobia and proving the falsity of the *Protocols of the Elders of Zion*.[59] However, whatever the mobilization plans,

---

[57] Orthodox Messenger (1938.06.01 - №27-6), 4.

[58] A rare insider's perspective on the personnel involved in the Japanese annexation designs of the time is provided by Chieftain Semenov in Markovchin (2003), 166-172.

[59] Nobori (1938b).

they remained but obscure hints to the Orthodox believers themselves, since a dramatic revelation of Soviet strength soon compelled Japanese military planners to rethink their Soviet strategy.

After Japan's military failure in the Nomonhan Incident of 1939, the Imperial Army became more concerned with non-military methods of anti-Soviet struggle, applying itself to devising what appears as the first proactive policy for mobilizing the region's entire Orthodox Church. However, precisely because this plan was comprehensive, it assigned only a small role to Japanese believers, who were but a marginal presence in what remained a decidedly "Russian religion" as far as Japanese anti-Soviet planners were concerned. As a result, the "Orthodox plan" was reportedly developed at the General Staff of the Japanese Imperial Army, in the Russian commission under the direction of Lieutenant Colonel Yabe Chūta.[60] Yabe, a key staff officer rated among the most sober-minded and informed Japanese specialists in "informational warfare" against the USSR, had already directed Japanese Army's policy vis-à-vis Muslims, since August 1 1939 headed a committee of the Strategic Planning Department of the General Staff, and on August 25 1941 was appointed to the Intelligence Department of the Guandong Army.[61]

With Yabe centrally involved, in 1939-1942 the Imperial General Staff and Guandong Army's Harbin Military Mission engaged in rationalizing the Orthodox of East Asia into a single externally-unconnected Russian-dominated and Soviet-targeted organization with a center in Harbin. Unlike Nazi Germany, whose basic policy toward the Orthodox Church in the historical sphere of Russian influence had been atomization,[62] Japan thus embarked upon consolidation.

[60] Manabe (1996), 6.

[61] Iwanaga (1982), 11; Toyama (1981), 458; Coox (1985), 263, 852.

[62] For a terse overview of Nazi policy and the conditions of the Russian Orthodox Church under German control in wartime see Shkarovskii (2005), 137-183; for a monograph treatment see Shkarovskii (2007).

While the intervention of a high military officer might have conceivably swayed such policy, akin to the appeal of Admiral Yamamoto Shinjirō in the case of Japanese Roman Catholicism,[63] the ranking Japanese Orthodox personage— Vice Admiral John Takahashi Ibō—does not appear to have spoken on behalf of his communion.[64] Ironically, the Japan-centered Great East Asian Co-Prosperity Sphere was to have an Orthodox Church in which Japan and its believers were a mere appendage of the Russian majority.

The focus of Japanese Army's Church-construction efforts was Harbin, the center of Russian diaspora in East Asia, where extensive shows of patronage and anti-Soviet solidarity were designed to ally the Orthodox Church with the Japanese regime. One of the first Japanese military trials at orchestrating major socio-ecclesiastical events in Harbin had been the solemn funeral of a Manchukuoan Russian junior officer Michael Natarov, who fell in the fight against the Soviets at Nomonhan. Following the practices of special veneration for the war-dead in contemporary state Shintoism, Japanese masterminds turned the August 27 1939 obsequies of this no-name émigré youth into a grand spectacle of civil religion unprecedented in Harbin's history. Natarov received the unique—and, according to many Russians, unbecoming— honor of burial on cathedral grounds, by hierarchs, in the presence senior Japanese and Chinese officials from Harbin and Xinjing, not to mention a multitude of humbler spectators. The Japanese military administration, which lavishly funded and broadcast the affair, also sponsored the erection in Harbin and Hailar of memorial Orthodox chapels to honor Natarov and all "fighters against the Comintern."[65]

[63] Yamamoto's appeal helped Roman Catholics preserve their vital tie with the Vatican. Drummond (1971), 322.

[64] See about him Orthodox Messenger (1942.11.01 - №32-10), 30.

[65] Kyō-wa-kai (1942), 321-324; Koval'chuk-Koval' (1996), 234-237, 242-243. On the less than favorable reaction in some Russian quarters to such an extravagant and artificial show of veneration see Karaulov & Korostelev (2001), 39.

Next, Japanese heads of the Harbin Military Mission began to display well-publicized attention to Orthodox religious festivals and offer generous contributions toward the construction of new Orthodox churches.[66]   In 1941 signs of favor redoubled, as Metropolitan Meletius of Harbin began to be greeted with Japanese honorguards, invited and visited by Manchukuo's politicians.[67]   At the same time the Orthodox Church received recognition as a national state-subsidized organization. This meant that, unlike all "Russian" organizations in Manchukuo, which were registered with the Bureau of Russian Émigrés, the Orthodox Church enjoyed "Manchukuoan" status and was registered with Manchukuo's Ministry of Welfare. Each of its clerics was supposed to be provided with a state-issued license and each ecclesiastical establishment—freed from all taxes and fees.[68]   Even as the Japanese authorities strangled the once thriving scene of Russian higher education in Harbin, the city's Orthodox ecclesiastical schools were allowed to expand, with a new theological institute and seminary inaugurated in 1938.[69] The Japanese rulers thus endeavored to turn the diocese of Harbin into a showcase of Church-state harmony, with "the government of the empire and local authorities invariably displaying attention to the needs of the Orthodox Church."[70]

While the earmarked Pan-Asian Orthodox metropolis in Harbin received special treatment, the remaining Orthodox institutions of the region were consigned to the periphery and bore the brunt of military intrusion without compensating perquisites. The diocese of Beijing in China required the least

[66]On official attention to Harbin's sensationalized Theophany festivities of 1940 see Heavenly Bread (1940 - № 2), 57-58; (1940 - № 4), 56; on the 1941 contribution of General Yanagita toward Harbin's new Annunciation church see Viktorov (1942), 328.

[67]Bolshakoff (1943), 115-116.

[68]Heavenly Bread (1941 - № 7), 47; Viktorov (1942), 326.

[69]For a detailed article on higher Orthodox theological schools of Harbin see Pozdniaev (1999a).

[70]Viktorov (1942), 330.

intervention, being already Russian-dominated, Karlovci-aligned, and thus organically tied to the diocese of Harbin. The sole jurisdictional matter which Japanese authorities chose to "rectify" with respect to the Chinese diocese involved the churches, cemeteries and a monastery which, while located in Manchuria, were in the purview of the Beijing hierarch. Whether as yet another "favor" for East Asia's Orthodox metropolis, or as part of administrative rationalization, these establishments were to be resubordinated to Metropolitan Meletius of Harbin. For this purpose, in 1942 Harbin's Japanese military authorities summoned Archbishop Victor of Beijing and compelled him, under threat of being declared a war criminal, to sign the necessary "lease."[71]

Next in the order of magnitude of official intervention came the minute Korean Orthodox Mission. Its alignment with the Japanese Orthodox Church and its attempts at missionary outreach to the Koreans, however slight, proved undesirable to the Army planners. Therefore, at the military authorities' behest, by the October 8 1941 decree of the Japanese Metropolitan Sergius the Korean Mission was decoupled from Tokyo's ecclesiastical authority and confirmed as a non-missionary "Russian" body. Its pastoral care was deliberately limited to émigrés in what appeared as a prime example of Japanese-sanctioned Russification—the preferred Army method of forging a Russian-dominated East Asian Orthodox Church.[72]

In the light of the Chinese and Korean cases, it is clear that the Japanese Orthodox Church required the deepest intervention to fit into the projected Pan-Asian ecclesiastical unity. The nativist and isolated profile of the Japanese

[71]Compare the descriptions by the participant in Victor (2003a), 316; contemporary ecclesiastic in Hauth (1996), 75; and modern-day investigator in Pozdniaev (1998), 81.

[72]A few Korean Orthodox believers who lived in Seoul did continue to participate in worship, but services in Korean appear to have halted. Pozdniaev (1999c), 359; Anisimov (1991), 58-59.

Orthodox community may have been a nationalist virtue from the viewpoint of the Japanese Ministry of Education, while its stable hierarchical structure and conservative theological stance attracted almost no attention of the mushrooming religious Special Higher Police of the Ministry of the Interior.[73] However, the Japanese Army's strategists required an extroverted, regionally-connected Japanese Orthodoxy. Wading into Tokyo's Orthodox scene, the Army undertook to be the Church's imperious guide toward reintegration with the surrounding Russian milieu. The military could draw on such potent levers as the diverse grassroots currents of catholic integration in East Asia's Orthodoxy, the deferential stance of Japanese believers toward the state, the carefully cultivated Karlovci-aligned Russian hierarchs in Harbin, and sheer force. The still-significant "Nicholas-band" of Japanese Orthodox Russian-language teachers at military schools offered a ready-made contingent of intermediaries.[74] Even a formal justification of secular dictate in ecclesiastical matters was attempted by comparing the Japanese Army to imperial Russia's "Minister of Religion"—the over-procurator of the Most Holy Synod.[75] Yet, despite all this, the imposition of "new order" upon Japanese Orthodoxy proved partial and traumatic, as pressure fragmented the community and drew competing government agencies into the vortex.

At first, the military planners appear to have counted on attracting the entire Orthodox contingent in Japan through elevating its Russian leader to the post of a *de facto* independent (but nominally Karlovci-aligned) Harbin-based "Metropolitan of East Asia." This ideal scenario removed the foreigner from a leadership post in Japan, inscribed the Japanese body into the

[73]The only systemic approach to the Orthodox Church in the pre-1940 publications of the Special Higher Police, as compiled in Dōshisha (1981), vol. 1, appears to be the vague localiztion of Orthodoxy in the Roman Catholic-defined category of Christian "Old Teaching"—as opposed to the Protestant "New Teaching."

[74]Manabe lists 8 such professors in 1930's in Manabe (1996), 6.

[75]See this parallel drawn in Yoshimura (1941b), 9.

Pan-Asian whole, and placed a Japan-attuned Russian at the helm of East Asia's Orthodoxy. Offers to that effect, citing the "assent of Harbin's military authorities," arrived at Sergius' door in the first half of 1940, first from Archbishop Nestor (Anisimov), and then from as many as five Orthodox hierarchs gathered in Harbin.[76] However, Sergius' adamant refusal to break with Moscow at the July 1940 Council consigned him to forced retirement and spurred Japan's Russian émigrés to rally around a mistreated hierarch.[77] This put the first dent in the Army's plan by compounding the difficulties of jurisdictional realignment with leaderlessness.

To be sure, the Army had the man for the top post— the senior member of the military's "Nicholas-band" Professor Arsenius Iwasawa. Upon accession as the "general administrator" of the Japanese Church, he began to preach the requisite "strengthening of the Orthodox block in East Asia" via merging with the "White Russian Church."[78] However, Iwasawa's aberrant position of a dubiously empowered layman acting like a ruling bishop made him odious to a mushrooming majority of believers, although the Army stood with him in the hope of settling the quarrel by means of a legitimate Japanese bishop. The military ensured smooth communications between ecclesiastical centers in Karlovci, Harbin and Tokyo, pressuring Manchukuo's Orthodox hierarchs to speed the episcopal ordination of Iwasawa's nominee, Nicholas (Ono).[79] However, at the start of April 1941, with Nicholas finally a bishop and Iwasawans openly boasting of the Army's support, the alienated majority retorted by claiming as their official sponsor the Ministry of the Interior,

[76]Council (1941), 91-92. The reference to five bishops suggests that, in addition to Harbin's regularly resident hierarchs—Meletius (Zaborovskii), Juvenal (Kilin), Demetrius (Voznesenskii) and Nestor (Anisimov)—one other bishop was involved.

[77]While the mobilization of Japan's Russians in support of Sergius would advance with time, see its first stirrings reported in Lensen (1966), 271-272.

[78]Iwasawa (1940), 3; (1941).

[79]Special Higher Monthly (1941 - № 6), 37; Council Provisional (1946), 38.

which had in the meantime legalized anti-Iwasawans as an association.[80] The Ministry of Education also favored the anti-Iwasawan majority, until the Army compelled the Ministry's officials to withdraw into "silent observation."[81] By May the escalating violence of the Japanese Orthodox factional struggle attracted also the attention of the Metropolitan Police, worried about the quarrel's "extremely bad influence upon the White Russians" and the "risk of it being used in the schemes of the USSR or another third country."[82] The Army's Church-building venture in Japan backfired badly, crumbling the would-be propaganda tool, fragmenting the façade of government unity, inundating the media with unwanted publicity, and generating a powerful current of opposition among the one Orthodox contingent most loyal to Japan.

Unable to steer the Japanese Orthodox effectively, by the close of 1941 the Army began losing interest in this foray. The military allowed competing state agencies to join in formulating the terms of a "ceasefire" to be forced upon the Japanese Orthodox factions, and abandoned—upon the outbreak of the Pacific War—the projected ordination of a second Japanese Orthodox bishop. However, by 1942 the painfully and partially accomplished "new order" of the Japanese Orthodox Church was beginning to settle into the mold of the wartime empire. Isolationism at the national level had been decisively supplanted. With Bishop Nicholas (Ono) ordained by the decree of the Karlovci Synod at the hands of Russian hierarchs from Harbin and Beijing, the *Orthodox Messenger* proclaimed that "the Orthodox Churches of Japan, Manchuria and China have become completely reconciled" into "one great mutual protection camp" against

---

[80] See particularly Kitamura (1941), 16-17, 24-26.

[81] Special Higher Monthly (1941 - № 6), 37. The Ministry of Education's condition for recognizing the Orthodox was their merger with Roman Catholics—a proposition which the Orthodox rejected out of hand, according to Sergius (1944), 3.

[82] Special Higher Monthly (1941 - № 6), 37-38.

communism and atheism.[83] In fact, for the Japanese Church this "reconciliation" meant resubordination to an effective jurisdiction—one of Metropolitan Meletius (Zaborovskii) of Harbin, Karlovci's "Synodal representative in the Far East" and head of the Far-Eastern Metropolitan District of the Russian Orthodox Church Abroad.[84] In the interwar decades of *de facto* self-rule, the Japanese Church had existed without "a single 'administrative' paper" coming their way from Moscow.[85] Henceforth, the new order, grounded in the "legitimacy" and "purity" of the anti-Moscow "Russian Mother-Church," obliged its Japanese followers to promote decrees from Karlovci and Harbin.[86]

The early 1940's brought prominence for those Japanese who linked up with Russians in Manchukuo—Bishop Nicholas (Ono) himself; his much-praised wife-turned-nun Helen (Ono);[87] Japanese representatives at Bishop Nicholas' ordination, Fr. Sergius Suzuki and Deacon Nicon Endō;[88] the Onos' Manchurian host, timber trader Peter Kaminaga; the Church-Army middleman, Peter Takeuchi with Harbin's security authorities.[89] More importantly, the Japanese

[83] Endō (1941), 24.
[84] The Far-Eastern Metropolitan district had been mandated by the Karlovci Conference in 1935, and the appointment of Metropolitan Meletius as its head came by the decree of the Karlovci Synod on September 17 1939, according to Heavenly Bread (1939 - № 11), front matter.
[85] In the expression of Metropolitan Sergius in Sergius (1935b).
[86] See Bishop Nicholas's assertion of the exclusive legitimacy of Karlovci and Harbin in Protopriests' Conference (1943), 24-25; the prominent printing of the Harbin Hierarchal Conference resolutions in Meletius et al. (1942).
[87] Her story—of having to part with her husband and accept monasticism in Harbin, struggling with the difficulties of monastic life in her infirm old age, and coming home to Japan to found a monastery in her homeland—became a heroic saga covered in well over a dozen entries in the wartime *Orthodox Messenger*. See particularly Orthodox Messenger (1941.03.01 - № 31-3), 4; (1941.07.01 - № 31-6), 25-27; Endō (1941), 16-19; Satō (1941); Murata (1942).
[88] Deacon Endō became a priest and the chief reporter on Harbin in the Japanese Orthodox press. Fr. Suzuki emerged as an esteemed elder and received an episcopal miter as a token of special recognition. On Fr. Suzuki at this time see especially Kaneishi (1993), 254-258.
[89] See Endō (1941); Kaminaga (2000).

Figure 12.4: Manchukuo's Russo-Japanese Orthodox, ca. 1941. Left to right – Russian orphans and nuns of the Harbin Vladimir Mother of God monastery, Protopriest Andrew Goloskevich, a Russian cleric, Peter Kaminaga Sampei, nun Helen (Ono, formerly Bishop Nicholas' wife), Japanese believers. From Nagoya Orthodox church collection, original preserved by Eugenia Kaminaga Mitsue.

Church's press of the time lavished affectionate attention upon Manchukuo's Russians themselves. Starting from "His Eminence our Metropolitan" Meletius himself, the Russians were represented as evoking "surprise, praise, admiration," "unprecedented shame" for the sad state of the Japanese Orthodox community, and "gratitude" for saving the Japanese Church from "shipwreck and sinking."[90] Amid wartime Japanese triumphalism, masters of the empire were relearning the ways of followers.

This humbling reconnection occurred under the watchful eyes of Japanese officials of many stripes. Toward the end of the war the daily routine of the Tokyo Orthodox head-quarters involved consecutive visits by as many as five police

[90] See consecutively Endō (1941), 15-16; Murata (1942), 21; Suzuki (1941), 6.

overseers—one agent from the Military Police, two from the Metropolitan Police Department, and two more from the local Western Kanda district police station.[91] The intimidation could be worse in the provinces, like in Shirakawa, where the fear of a background check by the Military Police was sufficient to have some nominal believers formally renounce their Church-membership.[92] Although no loud Japanese Orthodox "cases" emerged at this time, frequent arrests of the more radical Protestants for suspected thought-crimes and of resident foreigners for suspected espionage were a perennial cautionary spectacle to the believers.[93] Russian émigrés offered a vivid case—they were expelled from cities, forbidden to congregate on high ground, and arrested with such frequency that many chose to acquire Soviet citizenship in the hope of the modicum of official patronage which came with it.[94] Such stifling context ensured that the full array of contradictions which characterized the official external self-presentation of the Japanese wartime empire duly manifested itself through the "official" Japanese Orthodox prism.

First of all, bombast of regional leadership produced vain calls to expand the sphere of the Japanese Church's action beyond Manchuria to "Aleutian New Possessions" and Southeast Asia—because, "together with the boundlessness of the Japanese people," "the stage for the activity of Japanese-quality Orthodoxy is boundlessly broad."[95] Like stakes marking this ever-expanding field of possible appropriation, Japanese military triumphs were met with thanksgiving prayers at the Tokyo cathedral.[96] Wartime alliances energized long-standing projects to form closer ties with coreligionists

[91] Satō (1955), 4.

[92] Shirakawa church (2006), 170.

[93] For a useful overview of the wartime context of fear in a provincial Orthodox church see Kushiro church (1992), 159-163.

[94] Written testimony of Victor Pokrovskii, author's collection; Yoshimura (1968), 25.

[95] Mieda (1942), 4.

[96] See the report of thanksgiving prayers after the fall of Singapore on February 18 1942 in Orthodox Messenger (1942.03.01- № 32-3), 29.

in Eastern Europe, as the Japanese Orthodox press recounted fables about Hitler's supposed favor for Orthodoxy, cheered the establishment of the official Japanese-Bulgarian society, and publicized a visit by the Romanian ambassador to the Tokyo cathedral.[97] Yet, evidently the state continued to mandate that the most important external link of the Japanese Orthodox community remain Russian. The Church's Tokyo Russian language school revived in late 1941,[98] and occasional Sovietological articles continued to appear in the *Orthodox Messenger* all the way until the paper's suspension, due to paper shortages, in 1944.[99] In this extraverted context an abrupt decline in reportage from the neighboring Harbin in 1943 contrasted sharply with the frequent evocations of Manchukuo's Russian Orthodox in 1941-1942. Censors allowed only a few mysterious notes—like one from Peter Takeuchi in early 1944, about "extraordinary activity" in Harbin[100]— to penetrate this new information blockade. Indeed, there was ample reason for secrecy, because the events unfolding in Manchukuo spelled the terminal crash of the Harbin-centered "East Asian Orthodox Church."

The high-point in the Japanese military project to integrate, isolate and control the Orthodox Church of the region came on November 13 1942, when a hierarchal conference in Harbin resolved, in light of the cessation of all communication with the Karlovci Synod, to organize a "Provisional Supreme Church Administration in East Asian lands."[101] This was to be a "temporarily" self-governing entity embracing all Orthodox establishments of Manchuria, China, Japan, Korea,

[97]See consecutively Neduzetskii (1941); Murata (1943); Orthodox Messenger (1942.04.01 - № 32-4), 23.

[98]The Church's wartime "Russian language college" was in the works (initially as a "Russo-Japanese language school") since the summer of 1941, and finally opened in December. See on this Orthodox Messenger (1941.09.01 - № 31-8), 29; (1942.01.01 - № 32-1), 32.

[99]See particularly Yamauchi (1942) and Nakayama (1944).

[100]Orthodox Messenger (1944.04.01 - № 34-3), 11.

[101]Meletius et. al. (1942).

Philippines, and the Dutch East Indies—an apparent fulfillment of the Japanese Army's plan.[102] However, in less than a month's time, Manchukuo's Japanese rulers ensured that this ecclesiastical block which they had done so much to build up would become the motivating and coordinating center for Russian émigré anti-Japanese resistance.

The crisis surrounded state Shintoism, which had long been incrementally imported into Manchukuo. By the end of 1942 extensive construction of state Shintoist shrines and "faithful-spirit" steles, the formal conversion of the Manchukuoan Emperor Puyi to Shintoism, and obligatory bows in the symbolic direction of the Japanese and Manchukuoan Emperors, have conditioned the decisive step in the official religious policy. This came on December 8 1942 with the promulgation of the *Rules of the People* which required all Manchukuoans to "venerate Amaterasu-ōmikami"—the mythical progenitrix of the Japanese imperial house and chief deity of the state Shintoist pantheon.[103] Japanese Guandong Army planners appear to have aimed at extending established Japanese practice to Manchuria, presuming that, just as Japanese Christians, their coreligionists will accept the new religious economy as a "debt of courtesy and etiquette."[104] However, the transparently religious terminology of the official Russian-language translation of the *Rules*,[105] as well as the rumor that Japanese are installing statues of Amaterasu

[102]The Philippines and the Dutch East Indies had only one parish each, subordinate to the Beijing and Harbin dioceses respectively, see Victor (2003a), 316; Heavenly Bread (1939 - № 10), 111.

[103]Tsukase (1998), 73-74; Yamamuro (2006), 163-165, 212.

[104]In the terms of one Colonel Maeda, who explained state Shintoism to Manchukuo's Russians in Maeda (n/d), 103.

[105]The original Classical Chinese and Japanese 「致崇敬於天照大神／崇敬ヲ天照大神ニ致シ」 (literally "venerate Amaterasu-ōmikami") was strengthened in the Russian version as "благоговейно почитать богиню Аматерасу Оомиками" (literally: "piously venerate the goddess Amaterasu-ōmikami"), as cited in Diakov (1998), 180.

in churches,[106] left most Orthodox Russians little room to conscientiously consider "state" Shintoism as anything other than "religious" dogma. If previous incremental impositions of civic ritual proved compatible with the Russians' Orthodoxy, the new requirement was widely read as a demand to renounce the Christian faith.

The proclamation of the "Rules" stirred the Russian community and cornered Harbin's high clergy between protesters and collaborators. As their first official response the hierarchs forwarded to the Japanese authorities a treatise on Christian monotheism in early 1943.[107] This was followed by an appeal to free one of the first imprisoned religious resisters— inspector of the Russians schools of the Three Rivers region, John Diakov. The rumored involvement of Professor Arsenius Iwasawa in parleying on this question with the Japanese Army marked, if true, a unique case of Japanese Orthodox influence in the increasingly cordoned-off diocese of Harbin.[108] As a result, already in the spring of 1943 the chief of the Harbin Military Mission General Yanagita arranged for Diakov's liberation and for an amendment of the Russian text of the *Rules* to more acceptable phrasing.[109] However, since this altered neither the overall Japanese policy of enacting state Shintoism, nor the prevailing Russian interpretation thereof, the struggle continued, with Russian public offices, schools

[106]The veracity of this rumor remains to be confirmed in Japanese sources, but the wide spread of this notion among the Russians is attested to in Karaulov & Korostelev (2001), 40; Koval'chuk-Koval' (1996), 176.

[107]Khailarov (2000), 23.

[108]The report about rumors on Iwasawa comes from Koval'chuk-Koval' (1996), 176. Iwasawa's death on October 23 1943 was marked in Harbin by a solemn memorial service arranged by the leading Japanese Orthodox residents and celebrated by a key opponent of Amaterasu-veneration, Protopresbyter Michael Filologov, as reported in Orthodox Messenger (1944.02.01 - № 34-2), 14.

[109]Diakov detailed his saga in a 1949 autobiographical account. According to him, the order for his liberation came on April 4 1943, while the decision to amend the Russian text of the "Rules" was taken shortly before. Diakov (1999), 238.

and churches across Manchukuo becoming focal points of conflict.

By the start of 1944, when intimidation, incarceration and banishment of ecclesiastical opponents of Shintoist "bows" were becoming widespread, the Orthodox hierarchs resolved to speak more decisively. First Archbishop Demetrius (Voznesenskii) of Hailar mass-distributed an underground appeal against "idol-worship,"[110] and then, on February 12 1944, Metropolitan Meletius of Harbin signed the general epistle calling believers to reject paganism and accept martyrdom.[111] With the confrontation defined sharply and officially, the best compromise the Japanese authorities were able to wring out of the hierarchs, was a promise—at the "insistence" of Harbin's chief of police Kobayashi—to refrain from further public condemnations of Shintoist ritual for the duration of the war, as long as no Orthodox believers were "compelled" to participate.[112] The stand of Harbin's hierarchs has been read as a half-way compromise which prevented mass apostasy among nominal Christians, or, alternatively, as a show of strength which staved off a "bloody resolution" by "compelling pagan forces to retreat."[113] While both verdicts reflect a measure of truth, it is beyond question that the conflict over state Shintoism struck at the core of the would-be "East Asian Orthodox Church" and obliterated the semblance of Church-state harmony and Pan-Asian integration which Japanese authorities had sought to foster amidst the region's Orthodox.

[110]Koval'chuk-Koval' (1996), 175-176.
[111]The epistle, however, was not printed in an official publication, according to Fomin (2002), 137. See its full text in Sannikov (1990), 105-107.
[112]Khailarov (2000), 26.
[113]The first appraisal of the conflict is from a modern investigative biographer in Fomin (2002), 138. The latter opinion was voiced by many contemporaries, the quotes drawn from Nathaniel (1995), 133 and Razumovskii (1946) respectively. The best modern-day research piece on the 1943-1945 Manchukuoan showdown between the Orthodox community and the Japanese authorities issues a reserved verdict in favor of the Church's relative strength in Khailarov (2000), 27. The richest treatment of the matter remains the account by Diakov (1998).

With the Japanese wartime empire on its last legs, the breakdown of communication and unity of its incongruent components showed itself starkly in the unprecedented fragmentation of the Japanese Orthodox Church's network of relationships. Obliged to mouth as its aim "a leadership position" in "the Greek Orthodox Church of the Great East Asian Co-Prosperity Sphere,"[114] the Japanese Orthodox community remained suspended in forcibly imposed subordination to Harbin, amidst a stiffening information blockade both from the world and from other parts of the crumbling empire. Every ecclesiastical center in Japan, China and Korea, as well as the newest Orthodox community in the Japanese sphere—the Native American Aleutian islanders—each underwent its privations in increasing isolation, compartmentalized by the exigencies of war and the efforts of the war's architects. However, although the half-baked scheme for imperial integration of the "East Asian Orthodox Church" was in shambles well before the final collapse of the imperial state, the Japanese Army's ecclesiastical policies did contribute to a certain unity. Namely, they mobilized believers of every jurisdiction into a polycentric protest movement, of which the "rebellion" of the Russian Orthodox in Manchukuo was only the most glaring manifestation. In uncoordinated unanimity diverse Orthodox agents throughout the "Great East Asian Co-Prosperity Sphere" were reaching out to their yesterday's nemesis—the Moscow Patriarchate, which figured as the region's lone credible Church center with catholic reach. It had been up to the Japanese Empire to dismantle local isolationism of the Japanese Orthodox by constructing a regional "new order," but it appeared the task of the Soviet Union to bring this regional Church into a global internationalist future in the wake of Japan's defeat.

[114]Nakayama (1944), 7.

Chapter 13

The world comes home

The metamorphosis of the prevailing Soviet image from that of an ideological enemy to that of an endearing compatriot began among émigré Russians in East Asia at the close of 1930's. The Soviet-Japanese conflicts of the time precipitated a combination of Russian patriotism and alienation from Japanese rulers which began to outweigh Russian Civil War-era "irreconcilability" with the Reds. Powerfully catalyzed by the German invasion of the USSR in 1941, this trend was thereafter cultivated by Soviet propaganda, which underlined the turnaround in Stalin's politics vis-à-vis traditional national values and, specifically, the Orthodox Church. Indeed, since 1943, as Stalin set about envisioning the post-war world order, ecclesiastical policy became one of his chosen vectors of activity, with the long-persecuted Russian Orthodox Church surfacing as a valuable channel of external relations, to be paraded, supported—and employed—by the Soviet state.

Stalin's ostensible "rebirth" converted Soviet diplomatic representations into two-way ecclesiastical portals which drew East Asia's embattled and isolated ecclesiastics into reunion-talks with the Moscow Patriarchate. Already in late 1943 Archbishop Nestor of Kamchatka, who illegally tuned in to Soviet radio broadcasts, began corresponding with the USSR via the Soviet consulate in Harbin.[1] At the close of 1944 Archbishop Victor of Beijing made his first attempt to join the Patriarchate via the Soviet embassy in Beijing.[2] Finally, in early July 1945 all of Harbin's four resident hierarchs formally requested acceptance under Moscow's ecclesiastical authority.[3]

These maneuvers occurred during Japanese occupation, under an imminent threat of arrest,[4] but by July 1945 Harbin's hierarchs possessed sufficient confidence of mass support among Russian believers to proclaim the restoration of communion with Moscow openly.[5] With the final collapse of the Japanese regime in August, the pro-Moscow enthusiasm in Orthodox ecclesiastical life on the East Asian continent reigned supreme, with Soviet troops feted in churches and ecclesiastical leaders eager to confirm their inclusion into the Patriarchate.

Amid bustling worldwide activity aimed at eliminating ecclesiastical opponents in the Russian diaspora and reestablishing church-diplomatic ties, the Moscow Patriarchate and its curators in Kremlin saw little need to rush in East Asia, where things were manifestly going their way. The Soviet delegation to "reunite" the region's believers with the Patriarchate arrived in Harbin only in October of 1945, and its results were ratified by the Moscow Synod on December 27 1945, when an East Asian Metropolitan District was created for all Orthodox churches in China and Korea.[6]

[1] Karaulov & Korostelev (2001), 44.

[2] Kepping (2003b), 249.

[3] The July 8 1945 petition of the four hierarchs was promptly published in JMP (1945 - № 9), 5-6.

[4] There are reports that Archbishop Nestor, as a pioneer of reconciliation with Moscow, was briefly arrested by the Japanese already in 1944. See Dzemeshkevich (1998), 78-79; Karaulov & Korostelev (2001), 46-47.

[5] Koval'chuk-Koval' (1996), 256.

[6] The shift of the East Asian émigré Orthodox Church to a pro-Moscow position is best treated in Karaulov & Korostelev (2001).

The Japanese Orthodox Church, in which the dominant but diminutive Iwasawan faction, the diffuse majority of Japanese anti-Iwasawans, and a handful of Russians retained only a very tenuous unity amid the extremities of war, was in much worse shape in terms of logistics, cohesion and morale than the diocese of Harbin. However, although disconcerted and delayed, its turn toward the Soviet Church appeared inevitable—independence could be neither sustained nor legitimized, the Karlovci Synod was widely rumored extinct,[7] and no other ecclesiastical center appeared accessible. Therefore, especially since mid-1944, the retired Metropolitan Sergius, Japan's representative of the Moscow Patriarchate, began to attract the attention of both the Soviet embassy and an increasing number of anti-Iwasawan Japanese Orthodox. Sergius' tragic death on the eve of Japan's surrender slowed reintegration with the Patriarchate, but the Church's Consistory was keen to reestablish much-needed global ties—the badge of newly-prestigious "internationalism" and the sole hope of external support for a war-ravaged Church. The Japanese began by purging some superficial signs of ritual and theological nativization, especially those which entered the ecclesiastical routine since the later 1930's. Thus, the Meiji-period custom of taking off shoes in church remained inviolate, but the substitution of priestly cassocks with Japanese-style apparel and the "absurd" innovations intended "to curry favor with the militarists"—epitomized by Iwasawa's attempt at a patriotic creed—were consigned to oblivion.[8]

On March 10 1946 a leaflet by a key activist Linus Satō indicated Harbin, Beijing or San-Francisco—each spot a home to a Moscow-aligned Orthodox bishop—as possible locations

---

[7]Sollogub (1968), 181, 202-203. After years of isolation, the first communication from Metropolitan Anastasius, the chief of what had been the Karlovci Synod, was received in East Asia by Bishop John (Maximovich) of Shanghai in September 1945.

[8]The expression from a lay delegate in Council Provisional (1947), 24. The creed in question is the one treated in chapter 3.

for procuring a new hierarch.[9]   Shortly afterwards, on
March 27, the Consistory dispatched a formal request to
join the Moscow Patriarchate. The anti-Iwasawan Consistory
apparently counted on linking reunion with the Patriarchate
to the purge of the Iwasawan "militarist" Bishop Nicholas,
but the latter managed to get his signature on the petition
to Moscow.   As a result, on April 6 1946, when the
specially convoked Council forced Nicholas into retirement,
a response from the USSR accepted him—and the entire
Japanese Church—into the Patriarchate.[10] This acceptance did
not prevent Nicholas' ouster, but did stimulate the delegates'
new-found eagerness to maximize foreign links. For their
part, they determined to recognize the Moscow Patriarchate,
collaborate with the Supreme Commander of Allied Powers
(SCAP) in Japan, introduce a Russian representative into the
Consistory, send theology students to the USSR or the US, and
procure "one Russian bishop from America."[11]

In a bid to speed the arrival of the ecclesiastical "rescue
mission," the Japanese appealed in every direction of the dominant Soviet-American continuum—to the Soviet consular
representative in Japan Volgin,[12] to an émigré businessman-
turned Soviet activist in Tokyo, Philip Shvets,[13] directly to
the representative of the Moscow Patriarchate in New York
Metropolitan Benjamin (Fedchenkov),[14] and, of course, to the
SCAP administration—Japan's potent American arbiter in the
sphere of religion.

[9] Satō (1946), 44.

[10] Dating according to Takai (1956), ii. Ushimaru indicates that the response
telegram was dated April 3, in Ushimaru (1985), 60.

[11] Council Provisional (1946), 47-49.

[12] Consistory News (1946.05.25 - № 1).

[13] Pash (1958), 42. Shvets briefly served as a Russian representative in the
Japanese Church's Consistory in 1946. For research on the Shvets family see
Shimizu (2001, 2003).

[14] This missive was transmitted by a repatriating American Orthodox officer
Robert Royster, who would personally present the case of the Japanese Church
to Metropolitan Benjamin in June. See Council (1946), 30.

As Metropolitan Benjamin (Fedchenkov)'s wartime activity in America has shown, there was nothing impossible about the Moscow Patriarchate functioning in US-controlled territory in 1940's. As late as mid-1947, when parishioners of the Moscow-aligned Archimandrite Polycarp (Priimak) in Seoul rebelled against their pastor—providing Americans a perfect pretext to eliminate this "Red" ecclesiastical enclave— Korea's occupation authorities under Lieutenant General John Hodge in fact helped Fr. Polycarp retain hold of the Korean Orthodox Mission.[15]

However, Japan's military ruler, General Douglas MacArthur, was both more messianic and more anti-communist, famously summoning Protestants to fill Japan's "spiritual vacuum" with Christianity lest it be filled with communism.[16] Even more consequentially, MacArthur had as chief of his staff's Foreign Liaison Section the fiercely anti-communist Russian-American Colonel Boris Pash who was intimately involved in Orthodox Church's high politics via his father, Metropolitan Theophilus (Pashkovskii) of San Francisco, the ruling hierarch of the "Greek-Catholic Russian Orthodox North American Metropolia." The latter religious body—itself in the process of assuming independence from the Russian Church—united the majority of Russian émigrés in America under the nominal authority of what had been the Karlovci Synod. The latter body under Metropolitan Anastasius had by than relocated into the US-occupied Munich and continued its anti-Moscow ecclesiastical line under the protection of American forces. It was as a partisan of this anti-Soviet Russian-American Orthodoxy that Pash reconfigured the Japanese Church's relationship with SCAP from an obscure one, focused on the purge of "militarists" conducted by the Religious Division,[17] to an internationally

[15] Pozdniaev (1999c), 360-361.
[16] Cited in Woodard (1972), 243.
[17] For an example of this relationship witness Linus Satō's description of his February 21 1946 interview with a certain Johnson of the Religious Division in Satō (1946), 43-44.

significant facet of the inchoate Cold War.

First, Pash held talks with Japanese believers, presenting to them his vision of a global battle for the Orthodox Church, and convincing them to reject Soviet "control" under the Patriarchate in favor of "independence" under the American Metropolia.　Next came Pash's appeal to his father, who already in August requested Metropolitan Anastasius' blessing to dispatch a bishop to Japan.[18]　Finally, through the Diplomatic Section and the chief of staff, Pash brought the matter before MacArthur himself and received the Supreme Commander's complete support.[19] By November, when Soviet agents began to pull their diplomatic, ecclesiastical and media levers to avert the debacle,[20] it was too late—SCAP had denied entry visas to the Soviet ecclesiastical delegation[21] and on October 7 1946 ceremoniously informed the Japanese Consistory that the procedures for bringing a bishop from the US were underway.[22]

Impending inscription into the orbit of American Christianity lent new significance to the baggage of Japanese Orthodox relations with the non-Orthodox Christian world around them.　Japanese Orthodox have long perceived themselves amidst advancing "Americanization" of Japan's— predominantly Protestant—Christian scene, a mainstream process which edged its liberal discontents into Uchimura Kanzō's "No-Church" and its conservative detractors into the Roman Catholic "Super-Church."[23]

[18] See Metropolitan Theophilus' letter from August 17 1946, in Sollogub (1968), 153-154.

[19] Pash (1958), 42-43.

[20] The November-December 1946 Soviet effort involved parleying with the Japanese Consistory by the Soviet general consul Volgin, attempts to change SCAP's position by Lieutenant General Derevianko of the Allied Council of Japan, broadcasts decrying American's intervention into religious life by TASS press, and telegrams to the Japanese Church from the Patriarch of Moscow. See Manabe (1996), 11-13.

[21] In addition to two bishops, Boris (Vik) and Sergius (Larin), the delegation to Japan also included a secretary, according to Pash (1958), 15.

[22] Manabe (1996), 13.

[23] Kajima (1931b), 13.

This, at least, was how the Orthodox tried to map the situation, positioning themselves as the centrist or transcendent solution to the Protestant-Catholic tug-of-war.[24] Such aplomb could not mask the loss of missionary self-confidence in Japan's globally isolated, financially struggling, and therefore more compromise-prone Orthodox camp. To be sure, the community's identity remained robust enough to rebut frontal attacks. Thus, when Roman Catholics challenged Metropolitan Sergius to a decisive debate on papal primacy in 1933, they provoked the penning of the anti-papalist treatise *The Apostolic Twelvesome*, the only major apologetic work issued by the interwar Japanese Orthodox Church.[25]

However, the Orthodox relationship with Japan's Protestant presence was a very different matter. Not only did Protestants appear as the magnetizing prototypical "Christians" in Japan's popular culture, but they were uniquely connected to the Orthodox via traditionalist Anglicans, possible union with whom became the focus of Orthodox involvement in the Protestant-led ecumenical movement. In the interwar era Anglicans played the part of "good Samaritans" to the Orthodox the world over, sponsoring Greek-dominated ancient Orthodox Churches in the Levant, financing the foundation of the Parisian Orthodox Theological Institute of St. Sergius, and engaging in a grand attempt to aid and "domesticate" the Russian ecclesiastical diaspora in America.[26] Sympathizing Anglicans and Protestant ecumenists performed a similar function in the Japanese Empire. Thus,

[24]The Orthodox Church was held up a locus of harmony between Protestant "freedom" and Roman Catholic "authority" or as uniquely free of the "dictatorship" of either the ecclesiastical elites (in Roman Catholicism) or the ecclesiastical masses (in Protestantism). See Kajima (1931b); Sergius (1933), 9.

[25]See the description of this incident in Senuma (1938), 5-6.

[26]The best treatment of interwar Anglican-Orthodox rapprochement is Geffert (2010). For a revealing insider view of the American Orthodox scene at the time, including its connection with the Anglicans, see Vitalius (1955). The title of "good Samaritan" comes from a characteristic Russian-American encomium to Paul B. Anderson, one of the influential Anglican actors of this rapprochement, celebrated in Milkovich (1969).

the Anglican Bishop Mark Trollope subsidized the Korean Orthodox Mission for nearly a year and a half in the wake of the Russian Revolution,[27] YMCA's general secretary J. R. Mott offered occasional funding to the Japanese Church,[28] the Anglican *Rikkyō* University tutored Japanese Orthodox seminarians,[29] and the leading Protestant newspapers like Kagawa Toyohiko's *Kingdom of God newspaper* (*Kami no kuni shimbun*) favorably publicizing the Orthodox as pioneers in the general effort by Japanese Christians to break free of foreign dependence.[30] The consequence of such fellowship was the easing of the Orthodox into a Protestant-dominated context of "generic" Christianity.

Conscious of the promise of Protestant networking, a few of Japan's Orthodox leaders strove to show their appreciation and amity. Throughout the 1920's—the peak of pre-war global Orthodox ecumenical involvement—Japan's *Orthodox Messenger* reported on Anglican-Orthodox rapprochement in the upbeat tone of impending union.[31] Simultaneously, Sergius cultivated his ties with J. R. Mott,[32] exerted himself to befriend Japan's Anglican hierarchs,[33] and defended them against charges of un-Orthodoxy.[34] However, more consequential

[27] Between June 1918 and December 1919 he provided monthly subsidies of ¥250-300, a total of ¥5,100, according to Theodosius ([1926] 1999), 277-278; Rutt (1957), 486.

[28] Mott had provided Sergius with ¥ 5,000 in 1922-1923 for educational and publication projects, later he promised a more substantial sum for the cathedral restoration effort, and, by 1930, had contributed at least another ¥ 5,000. See Council (1923), 111-112; (1926), 45-46; (1930), 26.

[29] In 1925 three Japanese Orthodox seminarians were sent to this school. See Council (1926), 12.

[30] For an example of such praise in 1933 see Endō (1933), 23.

[31] See Bohan (1928); Saikaishi (1929).

[32] The two were in contact since Sergius' first years in Japan, according to Council (1926), 45.

[33] He was a frequent visitor of Bishop Mark Trollope in Korea, made sure to attend the 1928 ordination of Bishop Matsui Yonetarō, and welcomed Bishop John McKim to the consecration of the restored Tokyo Resurrection cathedral the following year. See consecutively Rutt (1957), 486; Ion (1993), xi; Sergius (1930), 19.

[34] As in Council (1926), 117-118.

shifts occurred through Orthodox immersion into Protestant-dictated discourse, most apparent in the linguistic sphere. Since mid-1920's the *Orthodox Messenger* increasingly quoted the Bible in simpler Protestant renditions.[35] By the mid-1930's a terminological conversion among the Orthodox was well under way from meaning-based Nicholas-era translations to sound-based English loanwords—including *insupirēshon* ("inspiration"), *ribaibaru* ("revival"), *Kurisumasu* ("Christmas"), and even an occasional *Orusodokishii* ("Orthodoxy," used in a sense of identity, akin to "Orthodoxism").[36]

A fervent believer of the Tokushima Orthodox parish, one John Miyai, left a characteristic monument to the piety emerging behind new terminology. Citing as his inspiration Lincoln's mother, Miyai hand-copied the New Testament as a spiritual inheritance for his children and adorned his work with autographs of the luminaries of his religious world—a mix of Orthodox clerics and Protestant preachers.[37] As for the leading cadre of the Orthodox Church, one must single out Basil Nobori as the most outspoken and influential advocate of a Protestant-style humanistic "reformation," complete with the deritualization of the liturgy, the elimination of the hierarchy, and even the institution of female clergy.[38] This interwar undercurrent of "Americanization" and "Protestantization" was the ground on which the Japanese Orthodox community could stand to embrace their SCAP-mandated American future.

In their apology to the incensed Soviet consular representative Volgin, the Japanese Consistory members repeatedly

---

[35]Orthodox Messenger (1928.08.10 - № 17-8), 20. Metropolitan Sergius voiced his appraisal of Nicholas' Bible translations as redundant already in 1922, according to Seryshev (1952-1968), 33.

[36]See examples of these usages consecutively in Council (1941), 49; Orthodox Messenger (1933.05.20 - № 22-05), 23; (1938.01.01 - № 27-01), 8; (1939.02.01 - № 28-02), 15.

[37]Tokushima church (1980), 17-18.

[38]His 1940 programmatic text, treated in chapter 3, did not include a call for female clergy, which was voiced earlier in Nobori (1939).

cited the *force majeure* argument for their acceptance of American jurisdiction, averring that "we, the Japanese Church... have no power to refuse SCAP's arrangements, and have no choice but to gladly accept them."[39] Indeed, the fundamental attitude of the Japanese Church leaders to the jurisdictional transfer appears to have been resigned—the bishop could come "from wherever," as long as he speedily ordained clergy and surveyed the situation to help launch the restoration effort.[40] However, unlike the totalizing tutelage which the Japanese Army once sought to exercise over the region's Orthodox affairs, "SCAP's arrangements" for the Church were episodic, called into being by the perceived need to scuttle a specific Soviet scheme, and did not include a road-map for the religious body being reorganized.

Once an American bishop, Benjamin (Basalyga) of Pittsburgh, made his way to Japan in early 1947, occupation authorities initially provided him with special amenities and stood ready to "rescue" their protégé from any hint of a violent "communist takeover" at the hands of "Japanese ruffians," but would not involve themselves in the Church's "internal matters."[41] In practice this meant that the American administration would occasionally use military and police intimidation against suspected communist activists, but provided no official guidance as to how the Japanese Church was to arrange its new relationship with the American Metropolia and the global Orthodox scene. Colonel Pash, who at first endeavored to conceal his family ties and the scope of his involvement, was left largely to his own devices in guiding the "eternal friendship between the Japanese Church and the American Church."[42] With the initial vector and outer

[39] Words of Alexander Manabe. See the various expressions of the same sentiment in Consistory News (1946.11.29 - № 6), 3, 5, 7.

[40] The frank formulation of the treasurer Mori in Consistory News (1946.11.29 - № 6), 6.

[41] Formulations of SCAP's position from Woodard (1972), 214-215.

[42] Pash's quote from his address to the Japanese Church in Orthodox Messenger (1950.08.15 - № 733), 2. In addition to Pash's published piece

bounds of the Japano-American ecclesiastical relationship imperiously set by the occupation authorities, the interplay of in-house factionalism, disorder, nationalism and misunderstanding was allowed to reemerge with new force in the diversified religious economy of Orthodox Christianity in the former Japanese Empire.

Already the first appeal from Japanese believers for an American hierarch, mediated by occupation authorities, resulted in characteristic miscommunication, in which, true to stereotypes, Japanese only hinted at the full extent of their hopes, while the Americans responded to a literal reading of the text. Instead of *admission*, as in the case of the Moscow Patriarchate, the Japanese requested a *visit* of one bishop for the limited purpose of "ordaining clerics and observing the situation."[43] In line with the request, Bishop Benjamin (Basalyga) was dispatched by the Metropolia—and issued an initial military permit by the Office of the Joints Chiefs of Staff—for a mere six-month tour, "retaining the title and all rights of bishop of Pittsburgh and West Virginia."[44] It was only in the course of 1947 that the emissary-bishop gradually realized, to his unpleasant surprise, that the leading figures of the Japanese Church expected a lasting dependence on American coreligionists, that occupation authorities would rely on the American bishop as a permanent anti-Soviet mechanism, and that there already was in Japan a competitor

—Pash (1958)—valuable glimpses of his prominent involvement in Japan's ecclesiastical situation are furnished by his private letters to his father, Metropolitan Theophilus, reproduced in Shōji (2007), 62-69. Manabe reports Pash's initial cover-up of his family ties in Manabe (1996), 13, but by 1950 the Japanese Orthodox Messenger prominently revealed the identity of its patron in *Orthodox Messenger* (1950.08.15 - № 733), 2.

[43]Communication between the Japanese Church and the American Metropolia appears to have been initiated through the transmission of the resolutions of the Japanese 1946 Council by the American occupation authorities. See the pertinent resolutions in Council (1946), 65-68.

[44]Formulation of Benjamin's status from the November 1 decision of the Hierarchal Council in New York, according to RAOM (1946.11 - № 11), 163. See also RAOM (1947.02 - № 2), 18; (1947.03 - № 3), 43.

for episcopal authority in the person of Bishop Nicholas (Ono).[45]

The Japanese Council in January 1947 hurriedly "erased" previous acceptance of Moscow's jurisdiction and resolved to enter the American Metropolia as a diocese.[46] However, Japanese eagerness to partake of the benefits of such incorporation went largely unrequited. Russian-Americans formally accepted the Japanese Church into their jurisdiction only in November 1947,[47] the Metropolia's "Committee for support of the Japanese Orthodox Church" had yet to send a noticeable contribution to Japan as of mid-1950,[48] and Benjamin appears to have never reconciled himself with the need to pastor the Japanese. Leaders of the underfunded and fractious North American Russian Orthodox Metropolia, drawn into becoming donors and missionaries to Japan and South America in the wake of World War II, were manifestly unprepared for that role. Their pre-war history, not unlike that of the Japanese Orthodox elite, involved an effort at securing introverted "independence" through indigenization and withdrawal from the global Russian Orthodox circles. Therefore, a sudden expansion onto new shores was predictably hard to swallow. As late as December 1950 the rising leader of the Metropolia, Archbishop Leontius (Turkevich), still spoke of Benjamin having been "borrowed" for the "autonomous" Japanese Church.[49]

[45]See Bishop Benjamin's surprise at being asked by the Japanese Council in January 1947 to be "considered their bishop" in RAOM (1947.03 - № 3), 43. Witness also his astonishment at confronting Bishop Nicholas (Ono) in October 1947, reported by Takai (1956), ii.

[46]Council Provisional (1947), 17-20, 23-29.

[47]Council (1948), 10-11.

[48]The committee, extant since at least early 1949, was prodded into action by Pash, but the results of its collections were still unknown to the Japanese delegates at the 1950 Council. See Pash (1949); Orthodox Messenger (1950.05.15 - № 730), 2; Council (1950), 53.

[49]Leontius (1969a), 37. Compare this statement with the 1950 *Yearbook* of the Metropolia, which listed Archbishop Benjamin as a "diocesan bishop," but the Japanese Orthodox community as the "Orthodox Church in Japan," separate from the Metropolia's dioceses. Yearbook (1949), 46, 79.

The situation shifted only after Leontius—the sole American hierarch possessed of significant prior contact with the Japanese Church[50]—acceded to the post of Metropolitan and appointed to Japan an energetic Bishop Irenaeus (Bekish) in 1953. The cooperation of these two influential leaders finally provided for Japan significant and systemic support in the form of regular subsidies from the Metropolia's central administration and study-abroad grants from the Federated Russian Orthodox Clubs and the All-American Russian Orthodox Sisterhood.[51]

As foreign Christian missionaries poured back into occupied Japan, their number soon surpassed the 1940 level, but the total of Orthodox among them remained stable at one, in the person of the ruling bishop. However, this lone "official" Orthodox missionary was complemented in the post-war years by a multitude of "unofficial" agents. These included thousands of refugees and occupation personnel—mostly hyphenated Americans of Eastern European extraction, new Russian émigré refugees from China, and members of the international UN forces from the Korean front. Leading contingents of new parishioners at the Tokyo cathedral were

[50]Metropolitan Leontius befriended the Japanese Fr. Symeon Mii at the 1917 Council of the Russian Church in Moscow and afterwards spent some time in Tokyo. He subsequently maintained occasional correspondence with Japan's Metropolitan Sergius. On the warm ties between Fr. Mii and Metropolitan Leontius see especially Mii (1965). On the relationship and correspondence between Sergius and Leontius see the latter's own presentation in Leontius (1946a, 1946b); a confidential appeal in which Leontius sought Sergius' cooperation in linking the American Metropolia with the Moscow Patriarchate in Leontius (n/d); and notes in Leontius' diary from early February 1933.

[51]The funding for the first two Japanese seminarians at St. Vladimir's Orthodox Seminary near New York, future Japanese bishops Nicholas (Sayama) and Peter (Arihara) who went abroad in 1954, came from the Federated Russian Orthodox Clubs, according to ROJ (1971.01 - № 44-8), 6; Orthodox Messenger (1954.09.25 - № 779), 1. The funding for the two Japanese would-be nuns, Elizabeth (Hirayama) and Catherine (Tsunoda) who left in 1955 for the monastery in Calistoga, was provided by the All-American Russian Orthodox Sisterhood, according to Council (1955), 6; Orthodox Messenger (1955.10.25 - № 791), 9.

listed in 1951 as "Greeks, Greek-Americans, White Russians, Serbs, Armenians."[52]

Soon after Japan's surrender, persons designated as a "certain officer of the occupation troops" entered the Japanese Orthodox discourse as globally-oriented informers, well-supplied sponsors, and foreign-language teachers.[53] For young women—especially Russo-Japanese repatriants from Manchukuo, who appear to have thus capitalized on the "Russian" side of their identity *en masse*—American Orthodox servicemen were also prime marriage partners.[54] Thus, the most spectacular manifestations of the new foreign presence in Japanese Orthodox churches were weddings—a characteristic 1949 report spoke of the Tokyo cathedral "swamped mostly with GHQ officers and their wives" for the wedding of a certain Greek-American and his Japanese fiancée.[55]

As Bishop Benjamin, Orthodox military chaplains and new Russian refugee priests entered the life of the Japanese Church,[56] lay Orthodox foreigners likewise began to assume a measure of responsibility for sustaining the local Church. By October 1949, a group of activists led by a civilian occupation official Alexander Grey undertook to mobilize the principal foreign Orthodox contingents—American and non-American "Greeks" and "Russians." The resulting "Three

[52] Orthodox Messenger (1951.06.20 - № 743), 1

[53] See one such reference already in April 1946 in Council Provisional (1946), 49.

[54] Osanai (2005), 12. This appears to have also held true for the diminutive group of Russian émigré youth born in Japan—one such case was Lydia Kosar (nee Pokrovskaia), introduced at the beginning of Part I.

[55] Orthodox Messenger (1949.10.15 - № 723), 2.

[56] Of the American chaplains, Fr. Nicholas Kiryluk appears to have become most deeply involved in the life of the Japanese Church for many years—see on him Chucovich (1963). Of the Russian refugee clergy who served in Japan in this period the best-known in Archimandrite Benjamin (Garshin), treated in Protopopov (2005), 204-279, 382. As for Greek military priests from the Korean theater, by mid-1953 three of them had served at the Tokyo Orthodox cathedral according to Orthodox Messenger (1953.09.25 - № 769), 1.

Figure 13.1: A mid-to-late 1950's snapshot of Tokyo's "Orthodox Church leaders" includes only two or three Japanese. Among the rest, Slavic names have a slight edge over the Greek. From ROJ (1959.02 - №32-10), 7.

nations committee," which included a coordinating Japanese presence, embarked on a successful campaign to repair, beautify and maintain the Tokyo Orthodox compound. Only around 1955, due to the advance of post-war recovery and the shrinking of Japan's foreign Orthodox presence, did the principal burden of care for their headquarters revert to Japanese believers.[57] Last but not least, the foreign Orthodox community served for the Japanese coreligionists as a living testament to the global diversity of the Orthodox Church, as illustrated starkly by the case of a Japanese Christian who could not believe that an exotic "Ethiopian Orthodox" turned out to look just like an "American Negro."[58] In sum, for the duration of the Japanese Church's groping acquaintance with

[57]See an overview of the committee's history in Orthodox Messenger (1955.10.25 - № 791), 2; a presentation of all the committee's projects up to the end of 1955 in Orthodox Messenger (1955.12.25 - №793), 7-8, 11; and an early signal of the committee's decline in Orthodox Messenger (1955.11.25 - № 792), 2.

[58]Nayko (1953), 15.

the American Metropolia, Japan's transitory mass of Orthodox foreigners assumed some aspects of a "Mother-Church," revitalizing the catholic dimension of local ecclesiastical life.

Yet, the disorganized diversity of the foreign Orthodox presence challenged the coherence of the Japanese Orthodox Church by helping legitimize the simultaneous and competing presence of multiple jurisdictions in the same territory. As before, Japan's Russians were central to furthering such divisiveness. In the post-war decade they formed three distinct groups—established émigrés, Russian-American occupation personnel, and new refugees from the continent—with corresponding diversity of ecclesiastical views. Since all Russians partook of the prestige and material advantages extended by occupation authorities to UN nationals, their status rose to new heights in Japan's post-war Orthodox community. In 1946, for the first time in the history of Japanese Orthodoxy, Russian believers were allowed to elect a representative to the Church's Consistory.[59] The first school set up by the post-war Japanese Church was an "Institute of Russian" in Tokyo, with over 700 students by the end of 1946.[60] According to a bitter commentary by a Japanese believer, many émigrés "who had been very small until now, all of a sudden turned Soviet and went about boasting that the [Tokyo] headquarters church is a Russian church."[61]

While Sovietophilia did not characterize all émigrés,[62] let alone other Russian groups in Japan, their collective

[59] At first the Russians' representative was the Moscow-aligned Tokyo émigré Philip Shvets, who participated at the July 1946 Council and in subsequent Consistory meetings. In 1947 he was followed by Russian-Americans—first Savitskii, then 1st Lieutenant Iankov, according to Orthodox Messenger (1947.08.15 - № "765"), 1.

[60] On the early condition of the institute, since 1947 known as the more neutral-sounding "Nicholas Institute," see Consistory News (1946.10.25 - № 5), 8.

[61] Consistory News (1946.09 - № 4), 9.

[62] The leaders of the Kobe Russian émigré parish in particular appear to have been eager to avoid Soviet connections. See Shōji (2007), 65; RAOM (1947.05 - № 5), 77.

prominence in the post-war life of the Japanese Church cast jurisdictional arguments chiefly in intra-Russian ecclesiastical terms. The post-1947 Japanese *Orthodox Messenger* relied heavily on the legitimizing rhetoric of the American Metropolia, which invoked the authority of the Russian Patriarch Tikhon, the persecution of the Church in the USSR, and the legacy of the Russian mission in Alaska.[63] Ironically, the deployment of these Russo-centric arguments only underscored the rival claims of the two principal Russian Orthodox bodies—the Moscow Patriarchate and the Russian Church Abroad.[64] Japan's proponents of the Church Abroad were never numerous enough to form a separate organization, although the chief East Asian representative of this orientation—Archbishop of Shanghai St. John (Maximovich)—did visit Japan in 1949.[65] However, the Moscow Patriarchate did manage to become a serious competitor to the American Metropolia. The initial pro-Moscow core consisted of a group of Soviet-aligned émigrés in Tokyo. In 1947 it attracted to itself the Japanese clergy expelled by the majority, in 1948—the Japanese activists dissatisfied with the American Metropolia's inaction, and in 1949—the attention and backing of Soviet diplomatic and ecclesiastical authorities, who helped orchestrate a legal battle for the Tokyo cathedral. With the US occupation contracting after 1949, American authorities would no longer forcefully "discourage" of Moscow's increasing adherents. Only the deft diplomacy of the new American Bishop of Tokyo, Irenaeus (Bekish), brought about in 1954 the diffusion of the conflict in what was hailed as an end to "some 14-year-long... period of chaos" in the Japanese Orthodox community.[66]

[63]For examples see, consecutively, Orthodox Messenger (1950.10.15 - № 735), 1; (1949.11.15 - № 724), 1; (1955.01.25—№ 783), 3.
[64]When contact between the Japanese Church and the American Metropolia was broached, the latter still maintained ties with the Russian Orthodox Church Abroad, but cut them at the November 26-29 1946 Council in Cleveland.
[65]Orthodox Messenger (1949.08.15 - № 721), 1.
[66]Quote from the Orthodox Messenger (1954.06.25 - № 777), 2.

Indeed, by unifying the vast majority of the Japanese Orthodox flock under the American Metropolia, Irenaeus' 1954 coup not only reversed Moscow's gains, but forestalled an imminent challenge from another direction—the Greeks. Greek-dominated Orthodox Churches of the Levant, led by the Patriarchate of Constantinople, were mustered as a Western counterweight to Soviet leadership in the Cold War polarization of Orthodoxy.[67] The notion of Constantinople's global ("Ecumenical") primacy in the Orthodox world made Greeks both experienced and theoretically equipped in rejecting Russian Orthodox jurisdictional claims. Thus, since at least 1908, the Patriarchate of Constantinople disposed of Greek émigré ecclesiastical affairs without regard to the parallel diasporic presence of the Russian Church,[68] and in the early 1950's Patriarch of Constantinople Athenagoras claimed to be "the patriarch of all the Russians, since they too depend on me."[69] Greek religious activity in US-dominated Asia was, therefore, both unproblematic as far as Americans' Cold War fears were concerned, and potentially threatening to all Russian Orthodox jurisdictions.

While Greek-American occupation personnel figured in Japanese Orthodox life since early post-war years, the Greeks' profile rose markedly with the arrival of Greek UN troops to the Korean War front in 1950. The Japanese *Orthodox Messenger* welcomed the new arrivals with an encomium to

---

[67]Summary treatments of the Orthodox Church's Cold War experience are taking shape with collections like Leustean (2010). The pivotal event which sealed the Soviet vs. Greek polarization of the Cold War Orthodox world appears to have been the forced retirement in 1948 of the vacillating Patriarch of Constantinople Maximus V (Vaportses) and his replacement with the adamantly anti-Soviet Greek-American Athenagoras (Spirou) under the pressure of US, Greek and Turkish secular agents. See on this Kitromilides (2010), 222-224.

[68]On the 1908 "Greek diaspora" decree of the Patriarchate of Constantinople see Trempelas (1974), 25-26.

[69]Cited in Savchenko (2009), 1009.

the global significance of the Greek nation.[70] The Greeks soon outnumbered Russians in the Tokyo Orthodox "Three nations committee," whose new projects included creating in Japan a cemetery for fallen Greek soldiers.[71] Throughout 1951 news of deepening sympathetic Greek involvement in the life of the local Orthodox community were regularly featured in Japanese Orthodox reportage.[72] Emerging grass-roots collaboration adumbrated jurisdictional contestation, as a Greek chaplain promised: "because the Japanese Orthodox Church is weak, I will transmit this to the Greek authorities to help you thrive."[73] Soon afterwards Archbishop of Athens Spyridon (Vlachos) began gathering data on the Japanese Church and established indirect contact with the Kyoto University classics professor, Tanaka Hideo.[74] By 1953 a message from no less than the "20,000 Sunday schools of Greece," ostensibly primed by a presentation on the Japanese Orthodox Sunday schools in a Greek children's magazine, sought communication with Japanese peers.[75] Given the Japanese believers' willingness to publicize such exchanges and air calls for a more consequential association with the Hellenic "homeland" of Orthodoxy to finally build "close ties

[70]This was a reprint of the sermon delivered by Metropolitan Dionysius of Zante during his visit to Japan in 1894. See Orthodox Messenger (1950.07.15 - № 732), 1.

[71]The family names of the committee members in early 1951 included five Greek, three Japanese, two Russian and one Anglo-Saxon name, as reported in Orthodox Messenger (1951.02.25 - № 739), 1.

[72]The topics included the mobilization of Greeks to aid the Japanese Church, service of Greek military chaplains at the Japanese Church's headquarters, ecclesiastical celebrations in Tokyo of the Greek Independence Day, speeches and church attendance by Greek troops, in Orthodox Messenger (1951.01.25 - № 738), 1; (1951.04.20 - № 741), 2; (1951.05.20 - № 742), 4; (1951.08.25 - № 745), 2.

[73]Orthodox Messenger (1951.05.20 - № 742), 4.

[74]Orthodox Messenger (1952.09.25 - № 758), 1.

[75]The message was communicated by chaplain Archimandrite Andrew (Chalkiopoulos) serving at the Tokyo cathedral in August 1953, according to Orthodox Messenger (1953.09.25 - № 769), 1.

with an overseas Church and advance evangelism,"[76] the Greek option was becoming increasingly attractive. Decisive integration with the American Metropolia in 1954-1955 came just in time to avert what occurred in the neighboring Korea.

To appraise the Korean situation, one must step back into the wider regional context. Instead of the initially expected unity under Moscow, the decade of post-war decolonization brought decentralization and disintegration for the Orthodox Church in East Asia. The Japanese Church made no attempt to retain its imperial periphery. Already at the July 1946 Council Japanese parishioners in Korea, Taiwan, South Sakhalin and the Kuriles were stricken from the Church's registers.[77] Manchuria went unmentioned because the dying Fr. Sergius Suzuki still remained in Dalian, but his funeral on August 18 1946, although attended by well over a hundred Russians, showed that there were nearly no Japanese believers left to bid him farewell. Thanks to their connections with the military and the South Manchurian Railway, most of Manchuria's Japanese Orthodox managed to escape to Japan before the Soviet takeover.[78]

Amid snapping living links, each fragment of the Japanese wartime empire and its would-be East Asian Orthodox Church faced a distinct future. The Aleutian Islands reverted back to the US and to the Alaskan diocese of the American Metropolia, with the Japanese Church sending a memorial candle-stand to the Orthodox church on the Attu Island as a sign of atonement.[79] The Kurile Islands Orthodox community which dated to the 18th century Ainu conversions and was once proudly claimed by the Japanese Orthodox believers as "Japan's oldest," fell under Soviet control and soon disappeared. The only Orthodox sanctuary on the

---

[76]In the expression of an article from the August 26 1952 edition of *Chūgai Nippō* reproduced in Orthodox Messenger (1952.09.25 - № 758), 1.

[77]Council (1946), 6.

[78]Kaneishi (1993), 275.

[79]Orthodox Messenger (1953.07.25 - № 768), 2.

Kuriles, the Shikotan Holy Trinity church, perished already in the process of the 1945 Soviet takeover.[80] In the vastness of continental China ascendant Sino-Soviet communists at first allowed a brief efflorescence of ecclesiastical activity to reassure resident Russians and defeat the opponents of the Moscow Patriarchate. However, from the end of the 1940's communist authorities waged a campaign to squeeze out Russian émigrés into "re-emigration" and strangle the native remnant of the hastily organized autonomous Chinese Orthodox Church.[81]

Predictably, the one part of China excepted from this rule was the nationalist-occupied Taiwan, whose new Sino-Russian Orthodox flock—which completely displaced pre-war Japanese believers—was integrated via US military clergy and Tokyo's Bishop Irenaeus into the American Metropolia.[82] As for the Orthodox flock of Korea, caught between the US and the USSR, its post-1945 regime changes uniquely reflected the full spectrum of political challenges and jurisdictional options facing the Orthodox Church in contemporary East Asia.

As Korea's North and South parted ways under their respective Soviet and US administrations, the initially un-problematic post-war adherence of Seoul's presiding Archi-mandrite Polycarp (Priimak) to the Moscow Patriarchate became untenable. In 1948 he confronted a triple attack—jurisdictional challenge of the American Metropolia, nation-alist discontent of the Korean flock, and politicized suspicion

[80]On the history of the Ainu Orthodox within the Japanese Church see especially Sapporo church (1987), 133-139; Kushiro church (1992), 3-13, 116-117, 136-137. On the demise of the Shikotan church in 1945 see Kostanov (1992), 46-47.

[81]The post-war history of what became the Chinese Orthodox Church is best covered in Pozdniaev, (1998), 109-163. Among articles devoted to narrower subjects special notice must be made of key biographies in Karaulov & Korostelev (2003a, 2003b) and Kepping (2003a, 2003b).

[82]The notable, though belated reports on the post-war Taiwan Orthodox come from Russian-American sources, like Chucovich (1963) and Sacharov (1971).

311

of the secular authorities. This produced the first post-war "takeover" of the Korean Mission, effected by a Korean priest who had been ordained by Bishop Benjamin in Tokyo and installed with the aid of the Korean police. In the course of the following year the hapless Fr. Polycarp was branded a Soviet spy, imprisoned, and then expelled to the North. The victorious Korean, Fr. Alexis Kim, in his report to the Japanese hierarch assured that the Korean Orthodox Mission was "on the way to a bright future." [83] However, upon the outbreak of the Korean War, as the dispersed Korean Orthodox believers lost their sole pastor and much of their property, theirs became in fact a very dim prospect, if not for the unexpected lifeline. From around the start of 1953 the Korean coreligionists gained the steady and generous patronage of the Greek Expeditionary Force. By the end of the war, the Greeks helped set up an Orthodox school and sponsored two Korean believers to receive theological education in Corinth. With none of the Cold War stigma of things Russian, and none of the colonial-era Japanese links, the vibrant Greek option appeared far superior to the Russian-American hierarch in Tokyo. Although Japan's new dynamic Bishop Irenaeus did speedily ordain a new native priest for the Koreans at the start of 1954, it was too late to stem the tide. The assembly of Korean Orthodox believers resolved to join the Patriarchate of Constantinople on December 24 1955, and were promptly received into the jurisdiction of the Greek Orthodox Archdiocese of America.[84]

Already in 1956 both Japanese and Korean Orthodox believers eagerly denied having ever been in the same ecclesiastical body.[85] This summary rewriting of history

[83] Orthodox Messenger (1949.10.15 - № 723), 2.

[84] For the post-war history of the Korean Orthodox Mission to 1956 see the best treatment in the contemporary article by Rutt (1957), 486-490. For an informed perspective from the Soviet side see Pozdniaev (1999c), 359-362. Much less dependable with regard to detail, but very useful as testimonies of the current sentiments, are the overviews by two key Korean Orthodox leaders of those years in Chang (1964), 325-327, and Moon (1964).

[85] Rutt (1957), 486.

aptly illustrated the onset of a new era, in which the boundaries, connections and memories inherited from the Japanese Empire have been decisively supplanted by a new set of Cold War fixtures. The transitional decade was at an end, as US and UN troops departed. As far as the Orthodox presence was concerned, by the end of 1955 there were less than 200 Greek members of the expeditionary force left in Korea, while the religiously active group of American Orthodox in all of East Asia shrank to only some 740 individuals by 1954.[86] Japan's post-war wave of Russian refugees was likewise ebbing, and even the strongest émigré parish in Kobe proved unable to procure a new permanent Russian priest after 1960.[87] Yet, the retreating tide left behind not only permanent footholds in the form of military bases, but a decisively altered and recontextualized landscape which would endure for decades.

With the Koreans' ecclesiastical independence from Japan finalized, the Japanese Orthodox Church's withdrawal from former imperial dominions was essentially complete—only the Sino-Russian Taiwanese parish remained tenuously affiliated to the American bishop in Tokyo. However, contraction to the Japanese "Home Islands" and the obligatory drive to regain a measure material self-sufficiency did not spell a new round of isolationism. Rather, the new situation of Japanese Orthodoxy was one of deliberate dependence on and expanding contact with the increasingly accessible ecclesiastical centers of the "far abroad." An unprecedentedly deregulated religious market allowed as many as three Orthodox jurisdictions to ensconce themselves in immediate proximity, each of the three claiming to be the rightful Orthodox Church for Japan. With the Patriarchate of Constantinople in charge in South Korea and the Patriarchate of Moscow confirming its hold over a small band of devotees in Japan, the leaders of the New York-aligned Japanese Orthodox majority were continuously reminded and engaged

[86] Chucovich (1963), 4.
[87] Kobe church (1983), 37.

in the global and regional complications besetting their communion. The Japanese Church would forge ahead in its Americanization, in step with the mainstream culture of contemporary Japan, but mavericks occasionally broke ranks to embrace an alternative jurisdiction, testifying to the scandalizing and liberating diversity which distinguished the post-war resurgence of the global dimension of catholicity. It was only in this climate, when isolationist nationalism and regional imperialism gave way to globalist reconstructionism as the driving sentiment of ecclesiastical activity, that the first signs of renewed universalist confidence began to appear in the form of missionary outreach.

Chapter 14

Conclusion

Overlapping phases in the history of Japanese Orthodox Church's external relations in the first half of the 20th century were intimately conditioned by the geopolitical shifts in the history of East Asia—the rise and fall of the Russian and Japanese Empires, and the ascent of the USSR and the USA to take their place. In its final burst of vitality, the Russian Empire sponsored and socialized the Japanese community into a universal relational matrix to which the Russo-Japanese link was central. At the expense of some measure of globalism, the Russo-Japanese political rapprochement helped further strengthen this bond in the 1910's. By consequence, the abrupt implosion of Russia after 1917 not only wrecked the web of ecclesiastical connections, but brought on a state of the Japanese community's near-isolation. This condition was continually deepened by the ongoing disintegration of such a crucial Russian imperial remnant as the global unity of the dispersed and persecuted Russian Orthodox Church. However, the parallel rise of the Japanese Empire drew the enfeebled Japanese Church into a new circle of external connections, at first subtly—through expanding the notion of "Japan"—but with increasing imperiousness, inviting and impressing this strategically placed religious body into Japan's Russian-targeted geopolitical battles.

The Japanese militarist scheme of regional ecclesiastical integration in early 1940's nearly succeeded in engineering an "East Asian Orthodox Church," but the Imperial Army's inexperience with manipulating the target group allowed divergent and unsustainable wartime imperial strivings to explode the would-be Pan-Asian ecclesiastical unity. As the USSR and the USA sifted the religious legacies of the Japanese Empire, the former approached the region with an established practice and a clear purpose for "taming," mobilizing and neutralizing Orthodox bodies, a methodical globalist approach which relied effectively on Soviet triumphalism, formal legitimacy of the Moscow Patriarchate, and coordinated action by local agents of the Soviet state. Americans had little in the way of a counter-plan, but benefited from a commanding position in occupation-era Japan and, most importantly, from diversity—in this case crucially enacted by a prominent Russian-American ecclesiastical agent of what for him figured as a continuing global Russian Civil War. This combination ensured American victory in this early bout of the Cold War and anchored the Japanese community into a loosely-policed ecclesiastical context of the Western world.

Given such unambiguous dependence on geopolitical shifts, it is perhaps unsurprising that the central nerve of the parallel history of what might be termed the "foreign policy" of the Japanese Orthodox Church was "independence," its realization, reinterpretation and resolution into catholicity. Since inception, the Japanese Orthodox community grew as an integrated and self-consciously "Japanese" organism, an ethno-political counterpart to the modern Japanese state. The fourfold catholic identity of the Orthodox Church configured this "local" level with corresponding regional, global and universal involvements, but the prevailing Japanese nationalist sentiment demanded "independence" from these entanglements. The Russian Revolution and consequent decay of

Russian legacies permitted and provided such independence, goading the Japanese community to ever greater isolation.

However, as the relevance of de-Russification receded, deepening dependence on the nation's socio-political climate shifted the problematic of "independence" to reflect imperialist outreach. Local ecclesiastical self-rule was becoming a given, but the boundaries of the "local" blurred with the "regional." The inclusion of East Asia's Orthodox—Koreans, Chinese, and above all Russians—required an expansion of corporate selfhood, a vision of a supranational "East Asian Orthodox Church." The trumpeted acquiescence of non-Japanese Pan-Asian Russian ecclesiastical superiors in Harbin emerged as a crucial aspect of the wartime struggle for legitimacy inside the Japanese Orthodox community and decisively rehabilitated foreign links. In their post-war reconstructionist drive to net external aid, leading Japanese ecclesiastics reinterpreted prior isolationism as outright baneful, making the post-war decade into an effort by the Japanese Church to surrender itself to the most promising sponsor, be it Soviet, American, or Greek. In the end, Japanese Orthodox believers found themselves unable to shrug off much of the burden of autonomy, but the trajectory of the "independence" problematic showed up the unmistakable broadening of the believers' horizons. Their desire for local independence from external controls sated, they began to broaden the bounds of their newly-independent unit into a regional presence, and ended up by attempting to surrender their independence in a global context.

This process of expanding self-consciousness represented a gradual realization of catholicity. Barely acknowledged and elusive, catholicity emerged as that structural fixture of the Orthodox community which injected integrative force into what often were disintegrative and disintegrating contexts. No matter the strength of isolationism, this quality ensured the impossibility of a complete corporate self-definition in purely local terms, apart from the regional, global and universal aspects of ecclesiastical life. Catholicity was the handle which both Japanese believers and interested third parties seized in order to engage an integrating relationship which emerged almost effortlessly, but which often proved difficult to break off. This was true above all with respect to the intimate and central connection of the Japanese Church with Russia and Russians, so fraught with danger and conflict, and yet so inextricable—in the apt 1956 summation of Fr. Anthony Takai, "a family relationship which cannot be severed even when one severs it."[1]

[1] Takai (1956), i.

Chapter 15

Epilogue: wholeness, integration, maturation

The self-realization of the Japanese Orthodox Church, uncovered in the present study, offers a platform for some concluding considerations and prospects for further inquiry. The notions of apostolicity and catholicity have been chosen as the primary vectors of investigation because both possessed a pronounced linkage with the Church's administrative structure and both were effectively challenged by secular statist fixtures in the seminal 1919 *Constitution of the Japanese Christian Orthodox Church*, thus showing up a considerable gap between conscious practice and formally maintained prescription.

A study of the changing contours of that gap revealed starkly the dynamic whereby largely undesirable and unacknowledged foundational corporate self-definitions eventually achieved conscious appropriation into the Japanese Orthodox identity and practice. As a result, the Japanese Orthodox case emerges as a prominent instance of the direction and limits of a characteristic modern Japanese "syncretism" between ecclesiastical and political models; an incarnation of a convulsed and yet coherent irreducibly Russo-Japanese community; and above all as a model of an emergent new Orthodox Church. It is perhaps now possible to extend this axis of meaning into a few related narratives and outline the immediate perspectives for research which this thesis was unable to tackle.

First of all, the process of Japanese Orthodox self-realization appears to illustrate both how and why the Japanese Orthodox community did not become, in Archbishop Nicholas' terms, "something like a Protestant sect," did not enter the ranks of Mullins' "Christianity made in Japan." Inasmuch as the Orthodox—either since their community's inception or else since 1917—have been largely free of the strong foreign ties characteristic of mainline Western Christians, many preconditions for such a rearticulation were in place long before the decisive crisis of 1940-1941, which did bring to light projects of a "New Orthodoxy" for Japan. However, at this decisive juncture, the imperial Japanese state showed itself less an ideological agent than a disjointed power-machine: instead of backing comprehensive Shintoization of spiritual life, various government agencies clashed and ultimately retreated from a transformative engagement in the face of schism in the Japanese Orthodox community.

Yet, amid the wartime agitation, fragmentation and isolation, compounded by the immediate post-war deregulation of the religious market, when a considerable selection of Japanese Christian "new religions" made their appearance, there were no comparable breakaway post-Orthodox bodies. The Church's fundamental integrity—signified by the creedal definitions of "holiness" and "unity," but perhaps best rendered in the present discussion as "wholeness"—played a major part in forestalling such a dramatic reconfiguration. In contrast to the contested apostolicity and catholicity, the wholeness of the "Japanese Orthodox Church" enjoyed the decisive support of Japan's prevailing socio-political currents.

The powerful influence of national and statist categories upon the life of the Japanese Orthodox Church, observed throughout the study, consolidated this community as the "one and only" counterpart to the Japanese nation-state. The pull of Protestant circles, while real enough, did not compare with the strength of nation-state categories and proved insufficient to break down the Orthodox community's aloofness from Japan's fragmented generic "Christianity."

The cataclysms which unleashed the quest for Japanese Orthodox self-realization—St. Nicholas' death and the Russian Revolution—showed the tenuousness of the believers' adherence to apostolicity and catholicity, but only confirmed the discursive integrity of the Japanese Orthodox Church. Therefore, the surfacing of factional strife in the wake of the 1940 crisis appeared to most Japanese believers as a much more bewildering testimony to the breakdown of internal— "Japanese"—coherence than either the externalized ousting of the "Russian" bishop or the severance of "Soviet" ties. It was this breakdown of Japanese wholeness which loomed as the most damaging and definitive dimension of the wartime and post-war "period of chaos." A detailed study of the discourse and practice of "holiness" and "unity" of the Japanese Orthodox Church remains an outstanding task, but it appears transparent that the efforts at wartime and post-war healing were directed towards a speedy restoration of authenticity and legitimacy through the "recovery" of an already conceived integral Japanese Orthodoxy, not through its elaboration or "renovation."

A vital locus of authenticity—and a major area requiring further research—was of course the grass-roots experience of Japanese Orthodox believers. It was first of all at the parish and family levels, where Japanese Orthodoxy became a lived routine phenomenon, that its inscription into the fabric of the daily life of modern Japan took place. It is too early to make a generalization with regard to the pattern of this inscription, although a variety of surface phenomena attest both to advancing indigenization as well as hybridity.

For example, pervasive Japanese ancestor veneration at times morphed into a heightened emphasis on memorial services, frequent and often better-attended than the ostensibly central rite of the Divine Liturgy. The consolidating hegemony of cremation in Japanese burial practice eventually drove the Japanese Orthodox community to break with the long-standing Christian taboo on burning their dead and conditioned the emergence of special mausolea for the preservation of the remains. The shifting pattern of the Christmas party—from a Russian-style "Yoruka" (from *iolka*—"fir-tree" in Russian) to a US-style "Kurisumasu"—illustrated the malleability of such newly-derived communal celebrations.

However, the central fact of the parish life which bears the most pertinence to the Church-wide experience of self-realization appears to be the vital link between the church-as-congregation and church-as-sanctuary, manifested in all parochially-produced micro-histories of Japanese Orthodox congregations. Illustrated starkly on the Church-wide scene in the form of the Tokyo cathedral restoration campaign, the construction and reconstruction of church buildings was seminal to consolidating and enacting any given community of believers. The frequent fires of the still largely wood-built Japanese cities and villages, Japan's high seismic activity, and the unprecedented wave of urban destruction in the last phase of World War II, by repeatedly levelling ecclesiastical edifices across the country, appear to have been the unlikely stimulants for the parochial communities' vitality in the long run. Thus, the notion that "churches build churches"—that is, spaces construct communities and vice versa—appears to be a promising premise for a study of the grass-roots experience of Japanese Orthodox.

Next, one must stress that Japanese Orthodox self-realization occurred amid—and helped ensure—continuing and deepening Russo-Japanese engagement in the first half of the 20th century. If a transformation of Japanese Orthodoxy into a "new religion" augured the community's withdrawal from fraught international context, its adherence to fundamental self-definitions necessitated a sustained presence at the forefront of this encounter. The forces of alienation between Japan and Russia were not a mere figment of historiography, ensuring that "escape" from Russia and the Russians was manifestly desired and periodically attempted on the Japanese Orthodox stage. At the same time, such an escape would prove a difficult task indeed, inasmuch as the Russian counterpart transparently appears both as the principal "other," and the extension of the "self" in the experience of the Japanese Orthodox community. In this instance the Russian function in Japanese self-definition appears considerably greater than Bukh's category of secondary alterity, because not only conceptual, but perennial personal and institutional contacts with Russians ensured the need for constructive interaction and integration.

For its part, the pragmatic Japanese imperial state also showed itself a proponent and even sponsor of expanding Russo-Japanese links, inasmuch as the Japanese Orthodox Church continued to be a valuable Russian policy tool only as long as it retained a measure of Russian linkage. However, starting from the prominent participation of Japanese Orthodox as Japan's liaison network in the Siberian Intervention, their ongoing involvement with the Russian alter ego occurred primarily with those Russian agents who were outside and in opposition to the new Soviet state. To be sure, even "Red" Soviet links were retained almost uninterruptedly, although they remained mostly rhetorical and potential. In contrast, "White" Russian links were abundantly and intimately enacted by the successive clashes, coexistence and integration with the émigrés in Japan and Manchuria; by formal submission to the Russian Orthodox Church Abroad;

and by the eventual ascent of Russian-Americans to the position of post-war arbiters of Orthodoxy. Here, the Russians figured in a bewildering variety of national, regional and global stages, appearing as both refugees and donors in the immediate post-revolutionary years; as neighbors, spouses and authorities at the time of Japan's final imperialist surge; and finally as guides and masters in the bipolar Cold War world.

This history raises the issue of the Japanese involvement with the global Russian diaspora in general. The study of Russo-Japanese relations in the period of the World Wars has heavily prioritized the Soviet Union at the expense of the diasporic stateless "Russia Abroad." Through reintegrating these two Russias into a single complex counterpart, as in the context of the Orthodox Church, the new conception of Russo-Japanese relations in the 20th century would go beyond the borderland-studies approach, exemplified by Stephan, to show up that the two nations were in fact much less "distant"—and in a few instances much less "distinct"—than commonly portrayed. While in the sphere of cultural interaction between Russia and Japan such integration has already begun in contemporary scholarship, the inscription of the centrally placed experience of East Asia's Orthodox Church promises to considerably advance the understanding of Russo-Japanese links as involving entire bridging communities, loci of binational and bicultural synthesis.

Yet, through the medium of their core self-definition as an Orthodox Church the Japanese community was organically connected not only to Russians but also to many other coreligionists. This connection, usually latent and peripheral, was on the verge of going very active and central with regard to the Greeks in the first half of the 1950's. This potential for a radical international reconfiguration within the boundaries of an unchanging Orthodoxy serves as a reminder of the global implications of the Japanese Orthodox experience of self-realization.

In Japan, Orthodox believers appeared only tangentially conscious of the structural role which episcopal authority and global connectedness played in the ordering of their community as an Orthodox Church. Instead, they were under the strong influence of the political ideologies of sovereign nationhood and constitutional democracy—the "modern myths" with which Orthodoxy has had to enter into a "syncretic" relationship. Given considerable freedom to reinvent their corporate life, the Japanese believers proceeded to dismantle its fundamental fixtures and install models derived from political ideologies—all the while vocally asserting the supposedly unchanging "Orthodoxy." It was only when the most obvious fixture of their communal ecclesiastical life—its collective unity—gave way to faction-alism amid leaderlessness and isolation, that the gravity of the structural breakdown became apparent. At this point, activists sped to repair the broken whole through reaching for an authentic legitimate "Orthodoxy" incarnated precisely in those practices which had been the least popular in the prior decades—strong episcopal authority and effective subordination to external agents.

The reimposition of effective central leadership and the luring of external agents also proved to be a long and tortuous process—almost as long as the previous run of self-assured self-destruction. In the end, with the hard-won integrity of their Orthodoxy repaired, the community of believers reemerged into a new kind of collective consciousness, marked by an active adherence to mandatory institutional fixtures. This process—which I have designated as self-realization—would appear to be the practical elaboration of Stamoolis' idea of "mission," and might well be a collective "maturing," a discovery and embrace of some inherent and irreducible traits of one's own identity. One might look well beyond the minute Japanese Orthodox case—first of all to newly-engendered or newly-organized Orthodox Christian groups, but also to other communities with similar corporate constitutions, either nascent or possessed of short communal "memory spans," to find similar dynamics at play.

Bibliography

Primary Sources

Abramius ([1956] 1998)　　　Авраамий,　　архим.　　«Первый благовестник Православия в Японии Архиепископ Николай (Касаткин)». *Вечное* (Париж) № 7-8 (1956). Реприн в Сергий (Страгородский), архим. *По Японии: Записки Миссионера*, 191-228. М.: Крутицкое Патриаршее подворье. Общество любителей церковной истории, 1998 [1909].

Aizawa & Kumagai (1983)　　相沢英資アンドレイ・輔祭、熊谷信男ペトル編『中新田ハリストス正教会沿革史　開教100周年記念』中新田：中新田ハリストス正教会、1983。

Andronicus (2007)　　　Андроник　　(Никольский),　　архиеп. Пермский. *Пишу от избытка скорбящего сердца: Сб. писем*, сост. Г. Г. Гуличкина. М.: Изд-во Сретенского монастыря, 2007.

Anthony (1988)　　　　Антоний　　(Храповицкий),　　митр. Киевский. *Письма Блаженнейшего митрополита Антония Храповицкого*. Джорданвилль, Нью-Йорк: 1988.

Anthony et al. (1927)　　アントニイ（日比）・修道司祭他編『豊橋ハリストス正教昇天教会五十年史表』豊橋：豊橋ハリストス正教会、1927。

Ashikaga church (1983)　　『足利昇天教会起源』足利：足利ハリストス正教会、1983。

Baba (1996)　　　馬場登イオフ・司祭編『120周年記念誌』上磯ハリストス正教会、1996。

Babkin (2006)　　　Бабкин, М. А., сост. *Духовенство и свержение монархии в 1917 году. Материалы и архивные документы по истории Русской Православной Церкви.* М.: Изд-во «Индрик», 2006.

327

Barsov (1885)   Барсов, Т. В., сост. *Сборник действующих и руководственных церковных и церковно-гражданских постановлений по ведомству православного исповедания.* СПб.: Синодальная типография, 1885.

Basil (1952)   ワシリイ（プレオブラジェンスキイ）・モジャイスクの主教著、武岡武夫ワシリイ・輔祭編『正教要理』東京：日本ハリストス正教会宗務局、1952。

Bazhenova (1937)   Баженова, Таисия. «С острова на остров со словом Божиим на устах: как живёт и работает единственный православный священник на островах». *Рубеж* (20 февр. 1937).

Benjamin (1935)   Вениамин   (Басалыга),   еп. Питтсбургский.   «Речь сказанная Преосвященным Вениамином, Епископом Питсбургским, на сорании Питсбургского Благочиния 18 июля, 1935 г.». Hoover Institution Archives, *Vladimir A. Maevskii papers*, Box 32, Folder 13.

_____ (1947)   ヴェニアミン（バサルィガ）・ピッツバーグの大主教「日本の兄弟姉妹達に」『正教時報』"765"号（1947・08・15）1。

_____ (2000)   Вениамин (Федченков), еп. Письмо митр.   Нижегородскому Сергию (Страгородскому) от 1931.03.07. *Церковь и Время* № 1 (10) (2000): 307-313.

Benzin (1944)   Бензин,   Василий   М.   «Важнейшие моменты в истории Русской Православной Церкви в Америке». *Юбилейный сборник в память 150-летия Русской Православной Церкви в Северной Америке.* ч. 1, 284-286. New York, 1944.

Bogdanovich (1990)   Богданович,   А.   В.   *Три последних самодержца.* М.: Новости, 1990.

Bohan (1928)   ボハン・デ著、武岡武夫ワシリイ抄訳「過去及び現在に於ける英国教会と正教会」『正教時報』17巻9号（1928・09・10）4-7；17巻10号（1928・10・10）9-12；17巻11号（1928・11・10）5-9。

Braisted (1976)   Braisted, William Reynolds, trans. *Meiroku zasshi: journal of the Japanese enlightenment.* Tokyo: University of Tokyo Press, 1976.

Brumbaugh (1947)   Brumbaugh, Thoburn T. "The Protestant Handicap in Japan." *Christian Century* 64, № 23 (4 June 1947): 708-709.

Bulgakov (1920)   Булгаков, Петр Иванович, прот. Письмо еп. Японскому Сергию (Тихомирову) от 1920.12.16. Hoover Institution Archives, *Innokentii Nikolaevich Seryshev papers*, Box 11, Folder 19, 11.18-36 - 11.18-38.

Cabinet (1999)　　　　　　　内閣印刷局編『昭和年間法令全書　昭和十四年 2』13 巻・2、東京：1999。

Census (1920)　　　　　　　　『大正九年国勢調査報告　全国の部』1 巻、東京：内閣統計局、1920。

＿＿＿ (1930)　　　　　　　　『昭和五年国勢調査報告』1 巻、東京：内閣統計局、1930。

Chang (1964)　　　　　　　　Chang, Alexander. "Land of the Morning Calm." In *A Sign of God. Orthodoxy 1964. A Pan-Orthodox Symposium*, ed. "Zoe," the Brotherhood of Theologians, 320-327. Athens, Greece, 1964.

Chekhov (2007)　　　　　　　Chekhov, Anton, *Sakhalin Island* (rev. ed.), trans. Brian Reeve. Richmond, Surrey: Oneworld Classics, 2007.

Chertkov (1977)　　　　　　　Чертков, Г. И. «Православное Христианство в Японии». *Новое русское слово – Russian Daily* (11 сент. 1977): 2, 7.

Chucovich (1963)　　　　　　Chucovich, Cyril. "How a chaplain spends his time." *The Russian Orthodox Journal* 36, № 10 (Feb. 1963): 4-6.

Congress (1923)　　　　　　　Viscuso, Patrick, Priest. *A quest for reform of the Orthodox Church: the 1923 Pan-Orthodox Congress: an analysis and translation of its acts and decisions.* Berkeley: InterOrthodox Press, 2006.

Consistory (1920a)　　　　　『日本正教会財政総監』東京：日本ハリストス正教会総務局、1920。

＿＿＿ (1920b)　　　　　　　『日本正教会独立基本金現在高』東京：日本ハリストス正教会総務局、1920。

＿＿＿ (1933)　　　　　　　　日本ハリストス正教会総務局編『府主教渡来廿五年記念誌』東京：日本ハリストス正教会総務局、1933。

＿＿＿ (1936)　　　　　　　　＿＿＿『大主教ニコライ師事蹟』東京：日本ハリストス正教会総務局、1936。

＿＿＿ (1942)　　　　　　　　日本総務局編『長司祭藤平新太郎主教叙聖交渉顛末報告書』東京：日本総務局、1942。

Constitution (1919)　　　　　『日本ハリストス正教会憲法及附帯諸規則』日本ハリストス正教会、1919・06・08 公布。

Council (1881)　　　　　　　『大日本正教会公会議事録』東京：正教会、1881。

＿＿＿ (1910-1911)　　　　　『大日本正教会公会議事録』東京：日本正教会、1910-1911。

_____ (1912-1919) 『大日本正教会神品公会議事録』東京：日本正教会、1912-1919。

_____ (1920-1925) 日本正教会総務局編『日本正教会公会議事録』東京：正教本会事務所、1920-1925。

_____ (1926) _____『公会議事録』東京：正教本会事務所、1926。

_____ (1929-1939) _____『公会議事録』東京：正教本会、1929-1939。

_____ (1941) _____『公会議事録　附：宗教団体法・主教選立特別委員会決議録』東京：正教本会発行、1941。

_____ (1946) _____『正教会公会議事録』東京：正教本会、1946。

_____ (1947) 『公会議事録』東京：日本ハリストス正教会宗務局、1947。

_____ (1948) 『公会議事録』東京：正教本会、1948。

_____ (1949) 『公会議事録』東京、1949。

_____ (1950-1951) 『公会議事録』東京：正教本会、1950-1951。

_____ (1952-1956) 『公会議事録』東京：日本ハリストス正教会、1952-1956。

Council Provisional (1923) 日本正教会総務局編『日本正教会臨時公会議事録』東京：正教本会事務所、1923。

_____ (1941a) 『日本正教会全国教役者信徒大会・臨時公会議事録　附経過報告』1941、大阪ハリストス正教会蔵書。

_____ (1941b) 日本正教会総務局編『公会議事録　全国教役者信徒大会・臨時公会議事録』東京：宗教結社日本正教会本部 1941。

_____ (1941c) _____『臨時公会議事録』東京：正教本会、1941。

_____ (1946) _____『臨時公会議事録』東京：正教本会、1946。

_____ (1947) _____『正教会臨時公会議事録』東京：正教本会、1947。

Diakov (1998) Дьяков, И. А. Аматерасу. Правда о пережитом в Трехречье за веру и отчизну. Дионисий Поздняев, свящ. Православие в Китае (1900-1997 гг.), 164-243. М.: Изд-во Свято-Владимирского братства, 1998.

330

Dōshisha (1981)　　　　　　　　同志社大学人文科学研究所・キリスト教社会
問題研究会編／和田洋一研修、杉井六郎、太田雅夫編『戦時下のキリスト教
運動─特高資料による』（第一版第三刷）東京：新教出版社、1981。

Du (1999)　　　　　　　　　　　Ду　　　　Ликунь　　Иоанн,　　прот.
«Распространение Русской Православной Церкви в Тяньцзине и его
окресностях», пер. Д. И. Петровский. *Китайский благовестник* № 2
(1999): 24-39.

Dubrovin (1906)　　　　　　　　Дубровин, А. И. «Открытое письмо
Председателя Главного Совета Союза Русского Народа А.
И. Дубровина от 2 декабря 1906 года митрополиту Санкт-
Петербургскому Антонию, Первенствующему члену Священного
Синода». *Вече* № 97 (7 дек. 1906): 1-3.

Dzemeshkevich (1998)　　　　　Дземешкевич, Л. К. *Харбинцы.*　Омск:
Изд. автора, 1998.

Endō (1933)　　　　　　　　　　遠藤富男ニコン「外人帰化問題を繞って」『正
教時報』22 巻 9 号（1933・09・20）19-23。

_____ (1938)　　　　　　　　　_____「伊勢大廟の道徳的意義」『正教時報』
27 巻 3 号（1938・03・01）22-23。

_____ (1940)　　　　　　　　　_____「新体制と大主教ニコライ」『正教時報』
30 巻 10 号（1940・10・01）11-16。

_____ (1941)　　　　　　　　　_____・輔祭「アクシオス」『正教時報』31 巻
5 号（1941・06・01）12-24。

_____ (1942)　　　　　　　　　_____・司祭（尼港）「哈爾濱点画」『正教時
報』32 巻 1 号（1942・01・01）23-28。

Fukuzawa (2003)　　　　　　　　福沢諭吉『福翁自伝』東京：慶應義塾大学出
版会、2003。

Gerasimov (1931)　　　　　　　Герасимов,　В.,　свящ.　«Русская
Православная церковь на Д. Востоке». *Православные храмы в Северной
Маньчжурии*, 3-6. Харбин, 1931.

_____ (1939)　　　　　　　　　_____.　«Обзор состояния Харбинской
Епархии на 1 Октября 1939 г.». *Хлеб небесный* № 10 (1939), 82-113.

Golden Jubilee Committee (1961)
　　　　　　　　　　Golden Jubilee Committee. *Golden Anniver-
sary Banquet. 50 years of priesthood of His Eminence, Archbishop Benjamin of
Pittsburgh and West Virginia. 1911-1961.* Pittsburgh, PA, 1961.

Guzanov (2002)　　　　　　　　Гузанов,　В.　Г.　Иеромонах:
документальное повествование.　Жизнь и подвиги Святителя
Николая Японского. М.: Об-во «Россия – Япония», 2002.

_____ (2003a) _____. Архиепископ: *Документальное повествование. Жизнь и подвиги Святителя Николая Японского*. М.: Юго-Восток-сервис, 2003.

_____ (2003b) _____. «Ваш слуга и богомолец». *Переписка контр-адмирала С.О. Макарова с Николаем, епископом Ревельским начальником Русской Духовной Миссии 1888-1890 гг.* М.: Юго-Восток-сервис, 2003.

Hauth (1996) Hauth, Thomas, ed. *Russian Literary and Ecclesiastical Life in Manchuria and China from 1920 to 1952. Unpublished Memoirs of Valerij Perelešin*. The Hague: Leuxenhoff Publishing, 1996.

Hibi (1948) 日比義夫イアコフ・輔祭『正教会の表象』豊橋：豊橋ハリストス正教会、1948。

Hilarion (1997) Ilarion (Troitsky), Abp. of Vereia. *Christianity or the Church?* trans. Jordanville, NY: Printshop of St. Job of Pochaev, Holy Trinity Monastery, 1997.

Huntington (1933) Huntington, W. Chapin. *The Homesick Million: Russia-out-of-Russia*. Boston, MA: The Stratford Company Publishers, 1933.

Ihaho (1912) いはほ「教会法の研究を促す」『正教時報』1巻1号（1912・11・10）12-21。

_____ (1915) _____「日露の親交」『正教時報』4巻6号(1915・03・20) 22-25。

Ishikawa (1892) 石川喜三郎ペトル『正教と国家』東京：愛々者、1892。

_____ (1901) _____『日本正教伝道史』東京：日本正教会編輯局、1901。

_____ (1913) _____「露国正教会の公会問題」『正教時報』2巻7号（1913・04・05）12-18。

_____ (1914a) _____「神社と宗教」『正教時報』3巻3号(1914・02・05) 2-6。

_____ (1914b) _____「基督教に対する政策に就きて」『正教時報』3巻11号（1914・06・05）5-12。

_____ (1914c) _____「明治神宮奉祀と吾人正教徒の希望（上）」『正教時報』3巻12号（1914・06・20）2-7。

_____ (1914d) _____「宗教法制定と希望」『正教時報』3巻13号（1914・07・05）2-6。

_____ (1914e)　　　　　　_____「基督教と儒教の文明」『正教時報』3巻 22 号（1914・11・20）2-5。

_____ (1915a)　　　　　　_____「我が国の神社に就きて」『正教時報』4巻 9 号（1915・05・05）2-6。

_____ (1915b)　　　　　　_____「基督教と神仏の祭祀〔一〕」『正教時報』4巻 18 号（1915・09・20）11-16。

_____ (1915c)　　　　　　_____「大典奉祝（皇位神聖の教意）」『正教時報』4巻 21 号（1915・11・05）1-5。

_____ (1916)　　　　　　_____「我が日本の人格崇敬主義に就きて」『正教時報』5巻 2 号（1916・01・20）10-14。

_____ (1919)　　　　　　_____「経済員会贈物（第 1 信）」『正教時報』8巻 4 号（1919・02・20）7-9。

Iwama (1937)　　　　　　岩間与一イグナティイ・司祭『ハリストス正教会に就て』仙台：仙台ハリストス正教会、1937。

_____ (1955)　　　　　　岩間正光シメオン『日本正教史概略』東京：日本正教会宗務局、1955。

_____ (1959)　　　　　　_____編『仙台ハリストス正教会福音聖堂復興再建成聖式記念』仙台：仙台ハリストス正教会、1959。

Iwanaga (1982)　　　　　　岩永博「小林元教授の生涯」『日本とアラブ―思い出の記―（その 3）』日本アラブ関係国際共同研究国内委員会事務局、1982、1-25。

Iwasawa (1912)　　　　　　岩沢丙吉アルセニイ「ニコライ大主教の三誘惑」『正教時報』1巻 2 号（1912・11・20）16-20。

_____ (1915)　　　　　　_____（三里野人）「支那に於ける露国宣教会」『正教時報』4巻 2 号（1915・01・20）6-11。

_____ (1916)　　　　　　_____（三里野人）「再録聖名考」『正教時報』5巻 2 号（1916・01・20）14-16。

_____ (1925)　　　　　　_____「全露総主教チーホン師を悼む」『正教時報』14巻 9 号（1925・09・15）11-12。

_____ (1931)　　　　　　_____「最も緊要な教勢振興策」『日本正教』1巻 4 号（1931・06・01）2-3。

_____ (1933)　　　　　　_____「主教の詮衡問題に就て」『正教時報』22巻 10 号（1933・10・20）12-14。

_____ (1938)　　　　　　_____「ニコライ大主教追想の断片」『正教時報』27巻 2 号（1938・02・01）9-11。

_____ (1940)　　　　　　　_____「日本正教代表者トシテ就任ニ際シテノ挨拶」『正教時報』30 巻 10 号（1940・10・01）1-3。

_____ (1941)　　　　　　　_____『諭告第一号　教会紛擾の根源』仙台ハリストス正教会蔵書。

Izawa (1955)　　　　　　　井沢庄一郎テリホン編『横浜ハリストス正教会史』横浜：横浜ハリストス正教会、1955。

John (1953a)　　　　　　　イオアン（シャホフスコイ）・サンフランシスコの主教『信仰についての教話』東京：日本ハリストス正教会宗務局、1953。

_____ (1953b)　　　　　　　_____『復活を讃美する』東京：日本ハリストス正教会宗務局、1953。

Kajima (1931a)　　　　　　加島生「精神復興」『日本正教』1 巻 1 号（1931・03・01）9-11。

_____ (1931b)　　　　　　　加島倫「教会か無教会」『日本正教』1 巻 2 号（1931・04・01）13-14。

Kamada (1941)　　　　　　鎌田悦朗イオアン編『日本正教と主権問題』東京：皇国正教青年聯盟、1941。

Kaminaga (2000)　　　　　加美長美津枝エヴゲニヤ「エレナ修道女の想い出」『こひつじ』横浜：横浜ハリストス正教会・婦人会会報、40 号（2000・07・16）。

Kandidov (1932)　　　　　Кандидов, Б. П. _Японская интервенция в Сибири и Церковь_. М., 1932.

_____ (1937)　　　　　　　_____. «Церковные шпионы японского империализма». _Спутник агитатора_ № 14 (1937): 24-27.

Kannari church (1924)　　『金成正教会沿革』金成：金成ハリストス正教会、1924。

Karp (1951)　　　　　　　Karp, George G. "90th Anniversary of the Orthodox Church in Japan." _The Russian Orthodox Journal_ 25, № 6 (Oct. 1951): 5-6.

Karpov (2009)　　　　　　«№ 28. Докладая записка Г. Г. Карпова И. В. Сталину о предложениях Совета по делам РПЦ по ликвидации греко-католической церкви в СССР, укреплению влияния Русской православной церкви за рубежом и организации Всемирной конференции христианских церквей в Москве» от 1945.03.15. ГАРФ, ф. 6991, оп. 1, д. 29, л. 101-109. _Власть и церковь в Восточной Европе. 1944-1953 гг. Документы российских архивов: в 2 т._, ред. Т. В. Волокитина, Г. П. Мурашко, А. Ф. Носкова и Д. Н. Нохотович, т. 1, 99-108. М.: Российская политическая энциклопедия, 2009.

Katō (1947)　　　　　　　加藤繁雄「ありし日のセルギー師」『正教時報』"765"号（1947・08・15）2。

_____ (1985)　　　　　　　加藤直四郎ティト『セルギイ府主教の思い出 (1985 年 5 月記)』未刊稿本、大阪ハリストス正教会蔵書。

Kepping (2003a)　　　　　　Кепинг, Ксения. «Последний начальник Российской духовной миссии в Китае – архиепископ Виктор». Ксения Кепинг. _Последние статьи и документы._ т. 2, 264-272. СПб.: Изд-во «Омега», 2003.

_____ (2003b)　　　　　　_____. «Судьба Российской духовной миссии в Китае». Ксения Кепинг. _Последние статьи и документы._ т. 2, 236-263. СПб.: Изд-во «Омега».

Kitamura (1941)　　　　　　北村秀次郎マヌイル『教会事態の説明』東京：宗教結社・日本正教会総務局、1941。

Kodera (1938)　　　　　　　小寺德イオアン・長司祭「宗教団体代表者協議会に就て」『正教時報』27 巻 5 号（1938・05・01）9-11。

Korshunov ([1998] 2004)　　Коршунов, Гавриил. «Святитель Иона и чудесноявленный портрет императора Николая II». _На сопках Манчжурии_ (Новосибирск) № 55 (1998). Репринт в «Новый святой эмиграции: свт. Иона Ханькоуский. Материалы к жизнеописанию». _Русский Инок_ № 20 (183) (апр. 2004, http://www.russian-inok.org /page.php?page=way1&dir=way&month=0404#local5).

Koval'chuk-Koval' (1996)　　Ковальчук-Коваль, Игорь Константинович. _Свидание с памятью (Воспоминания). Документы по истории движения инакомыслящих,_ вып. № 5. М.: Информационно-экспертная группа «Панорама», 1996.

Kyō-wa-kai (1942)　　　　　_Великая Маньчжурская Империя. К десятилетнему юбилею._ Харбин: Изд. Государственной организации Кио-ва-кай и Главного Бюро по делам российских эмигрантов в Маньчжурской Империи, 1942.

Lattimore (1932)　　　　　Lattimore, Owen. _Manchuria: Cradle of conflict._ New York: MacMillan Company, 1932.

Lensen (1952)　　　　　　Lensen, George Alexander. "The Orthodox Church in Occupied Japan." _Florida State University Studies_ (Tallahassee) № 8 (1952): 93-95.

Leontius (1946a)　　　　　Леонтий (Туркевич), архиеп. Чикагский. «Памяти Японского митрополита Сергия Тихомирова». _Русско-Американский Православный вестник_ № 2 (1946): 23-25.

_____ (1946b)　　　　　　_____. «Русские иерархи в Японии Николай и Сергий (Очерк 2-й на тему о памяти М. Сергия

Тихомирова)». *Русско-Американский Православный вестник* № 4 (1946): 59-60.

Leontius (1969a) _____. «Речь при открытии 8-го Всеамериканского Церковного Собора Русской Православной Северо-Американской Митрополии 5-го декабря 1950-го года в Св. Покровском Кафедральном Митрополичьем Соборе в гор. Нью Иорк». *Жизнь и труды Высокопреосвященнейшего Митрополита Леонтия*, 35-43. Нью-Йорк, 1969.

_____ (1969b) _____, митр. Нью-Йоркский. «Слово при вручении архиерейского жезла Преосвященнейшему Иринею, Епископу Японскому и Токийскому». *Жизнь и труды Высокопреосвященнейшего Митрополита Леонтия*, 49-52. Нью-Йорк, 1969.

_____ (n/d) Туркевич, Леонид, прот. Письмо митр. Японскому Сергию (Тихомирову) с докладом митр. Нижегородскому Сергию (Страгородскому) от нач. 1930-х гг. Hoover Institution Archives, *Vladimir A. Maevskii papers*, Box 32, Folder 13 (Arsenii (Chagovtsov)).

Maeda (n/d) Маэда, полк. «Разъяснения полк. Маэда». ГАХК, ф. 830, оп. 1, д. 189, сс. 102-104.

Manabe (1941) 真鍋理従アレキサンドル（真鍋盡洲）「主権問題と紛争の真相」鎌田悦朗イオアン編『日本正教と主権問題』東京：皇国正教青年聯盟、1941、9-27。

_____ (1996) _____（真鍋歴山）著、真鍋理一郎筆耕・発行『ニコライ師の永眠以降現代まで（一九一二年～一九六八年）―日本正教会五十年史』私家版、1996。

Markovchin (2003) Марковчин, В. В. *Три атамана*. М.: Изд. дом «Звонница – МГ», 2003.

Maruyama (1930) 丸山鶴吉・警視総監「10. ニコライ正教」『本邦ニ於ケル宗教及布教関係雑件』1巻、1930・08・30、外務省記録1門2類（国立公文書館アジア歴史資料センター、http://www.jacar.go.jp）。

Meletius et al. (1942) メレティイ（ザボロフスキイ）・ハルビンの府主教他「東亜の地域に臨時最高教会本部設置」『正教時報』32巻11号（1942・12・01）2-4。

Mieda (1942) 三枝義夫「正教会の南方圏進行」『正教時報』32巻9号（1942・09・01）2-4。

Mii (1913) 三井道朗シメオン・長司祭「三井神父満鮮巡教紀行」『正教時報』2巻19号（1913・10・05）43-49。

_____ (1925) _____「府主教ヒラレト師教訓」『正教時報』14巻9号（1925・09・15）7-8；14巻10号（1925・10・15）2-5（未完）。

_____ ([1928] 1935)　　　　　_____『正教要理』東京：日本ハリストス正教会、1935 [1928]。

_____ (1931)　　　　　_____「永眠前の総主教チーホン師」『正教時報』20 巻 4 号（1931・04・20）3-6；20 巻 5 号（1931・05・20）5-8；20 巻 7 号（1931・07・20）6-9。

_____ (1934)　　　　　_____『ハリストス正教会及其の教義大要』東京：東方書院、日本宗教講座―第八回配本、1934。

_____ (1937)　　　　　_____「満鮮旅行記」『正教時報』26 巻 10 号（1937・10・01）13-14。

_____ (1940)　　　　　三井義人イウスティン「亡父三井道朗を語る」『正教時報』29 巻 4 号（1940・04・01）8-11。

_____ (1965)　　　　　_____「レオンティー府主教永眠の悲報に接して」『正教時報』905 号（1965・05・20）1。

_____ (1982)　　　　　三井道朗シメオン・長司祭著、三井義人イウスティン編『三井道朗回顧録』群馬県藤岡市：私家版、1982。

Milkovich (1969)　　　　　Milkovich, Annette. "Dr. Paul B. Anderson – Good Samaritan to Russian Orthodox." *The Russian Orthodox Journal* 43, № 4 (Sept. 1969): 9-11, 20.

Missionary Committee (2004)
全国宣教委員会編『正教会の手引』日本ハリストス正教会教団・全国宣教委員会、2004。

Mitani (1960)　　　　　三谷武雄編『エホバ与へエホバ取るエホバの御名はほむべき哉』川西：私家版、1960。

Mizushima (1905)　　　　　水島行楊イサイヤ『軍国正教徒献身実記』東京：大日本正教会編輯所、1905。

Mizutani (1912)　　　　　水谷鍉『大主教尼闊頼師紀念写真帖』東京：水谷写真場、1912。

Mochizuki (1930)　　　　　望月富之助ペトル（望月鼓堂）『ニコライ大主教追懐録』半田：覚醒社、1930。

_____ (1951)　　　　　_____『ニコライ師渡来九十年追憶』東京：日本ハリストス正教会宗務局、1951。

Mokushi-sei (1919)　　　　　黙思生「日本正教会の自覚（二）」『正教時報』8 巻 2 号（1919・01・20）、12-17。

Moon (1964)　　　　　Moon, Boris, Priest. "The Greek Orthodox Church in Korea today." In *A Sign of God. Orthodoxy 1964. A Pan-Orthodox*

Symposium, ed. "Zoe," the Brotherhood of Theologians, 327-330. Athens, Greece, 1964.

Mori (1941)　　　　　　　　森謙キリル「日本正教会最近の事象」鎌田悦朗イオアン編『日本正教と主権問題』東京：皇国正教青年聯盟、1941、1-8。

Morita (1891)　　　　　　　森田亮パヴェル「不敬事件を論じて吾正教会の主義を明にす」『正教新報』245 号（1891・02・15）。

_____ (1915)　　　　　　　_____・司祭「露都通信（第一報）」『正教時報』4 巻 2 号（1915・01・20）17-23。

_____ (1919a)　　　　　　_____「西伯利紀行」『正教時報』8 巻 1 号（1919・01・15）10-14。

_____ (1919b)　　　　　　_____「敢て我が会の諸父兄姉に告ぐ」『正教時報』8 巻 9 号（1919・07・15）2-5。

_____ (1931)　　　　　　_____・長司祭校閲『正教の道しるべ』（訂正）東京：日本クリストス正教会、総務局、1931。

Murata (1942)　　　　　　　村田完造「エレナ修道女と修道院」『正教時報』32 巻 2 号（1942・02・01）19-22。

_____ (1943)　　　　　　_____「日本ブルガリア協会発会に寄せて」『正教時報』33 巻 2 号（1943・02・01）15。

Naitō (1943)　　　　　　　内藤節爾「モスクワ教権と日本正教会と地歩」『正教時報』33 巻 10 号（1943・11・01）3-8。

Nakai (1913)　　　　　　　中井木菟麿パヴェル（中井天生）「尼師翻経室談片」『正教時報（大主教ニコライ師永眠一周年記念号）』2 巻 4 号（1913・02・10）56-59。

_____ (1938a)　　　　　　_____（中井天生）「戦歿者救霊祈願及歌詞の私案」『正教時報』27 巻 9 号（1938・09・01）11-15。

_____ (1938b)　　　　　　_____（中井天生）「皇太子殿下御降誕の祈願」『正教時報』27 巻 10 号（1938・10・01）18-19。

_____ (1940)　　　　　　_____（中井天生）「四十五年前のニコライ大主教の遺訓を顧みて」『正教時報』30 巻 9 号（1940・09・01）8-10。

Nakajima (1927)　　　　　中島市造「御大喪儀を拝し奉りて神社問題の考察に及ぶ」『正教時報』16 巻 2 号（1927・02・20）6-8。

Nakayama (1944)　　　　　中山疎林「正教随感」『正教時報』34 巻 3 号（1944・04・01）5-7。

Nathaniel (1995)　　　　　Нафанаил (Львов), архиеп. Венский. *Беседы о Священном Писании и о вере и Церкви*, т. 3. Нью-Йорк: Изд. Комитета Русской Православной молодежи заграницей, 1995.

Nayko (1953)　　　　　　　　Nayko, Nicholas, M/Sgt. "Orthodox Christmas Festivities in the Far East." *The Russian Orthodox Journal* 26, № 11 (March 1953): 15, 19.

Neduzetskii (1941)　　　　　　ネドウゼツキイ・ミハイル「独逸に於けるギリシャ正教の運動」『正教時報』31巻9号（1941・10・01）1-3。

Nestor (2002)　　　　　　Нестор　　　　　（Анисимов),　　　　митр. Кировоградский. *Моя Камчатка. С. В. Фомин. Божией милостию архиерей Русской Церкви. Три жизни митрополита Нестора Камчатского*, 189-408. М.: Изд-во «Правило веры», 2002.

Nicholas (1910)　　　　　　　Николай (Касаткин), архиеп. Японский. «Приветствие Архиепископа Японского Николая Миссионерскому съезду в Иркутске». *Православный благовестник* 2, № 16 (авг. 1910): 146-149.

_____ (1913)　　　　　　　　ニコライ（カサトキン）・日本の大主教「故大主教ニコライ師が主教セルギイ師に与へられたる書翰」『正教時報（大主教ニコライ師永眠一周年記念号）』2巻4号（1913・02・10）1-4。

_____ (1933)　　　　　　　　_____「兄弟に告ぐ」『正教時報』22巻8号（1933・08・20）17-18。

_____ ([1934] 1976)　　　　　小野帰一イオアン・長司祭『イオアン川股篤礼小伝』金成町：私家版、1976 [1934]。

_____ (1941)　　　　　　　　_____「信徒大会に対する疑義」『正教時報』31巻3号（1941・03・01）5-10, 22。

_____ (1943)　　　　　　　　ニコライ（小野）・東京の主教「巡回日記（上）」『正教時報』33巻1号（1943・01・01）24-26。

_____ (1944a)　　　　　　　_____『金成正教会成聖式拾週年を迎へて』金成：金成ハリストス正教会、1944。

_____ (1944b)　　　　　　　_____「示達」『正教時報』34巻3号（1944・04・01）2。

_____ (1994)　　　　　　　　Николай (Касаткин), архиеп. Японский. *Дневники святого Николая Японского*, сост. К. Накамура, Ё. Накамура, Р. Ясуи и М. Наганава. Саппоро: Изд-во Хоккайдского Университета, 1994.

_____ (2004)　　　　　　　　_____. *Дневники святого Николая Японского*, ред. К. Накамура. СПб.: Гиперион, 2004.

_____ (2007)　　　　　　　　ニコライ（カサトキン）・日本の大主教著、中村健之介監修『宣教師ニコライの全日記』東京：教文館、2007。

Nobata (1997)　　　　　　　野畑太郎イオアン『半田ハリストス正教会小史』半田：私家版、1997。

Nobori (1931)　　　　　　　昇直隆ワシリイ「地上教会の建設」『日本正教』1巻2号（1931・04・01）2-3、5。

＿＿＿ (1933)　　　　　　　＿＿＿「渡来二十五年」『正教時報（府主教座下本邦渡来廿五周年記念号）』22巻7号（1933・07・20）1-3。

＿＿＿ (1938a)　　　　　　　＿＿＿「故森田長老と四谷教会」『正教時報』27巻3号（1938・03・01）3-5。

＿＿＿ (1938b)　　　　　　　＿＿＿「所謂猶太人の陰謀に就て」『正教時報』27巻8号（1938・08・01）3-8。

＿＿＿ (1939)　　　　　　　＿＿＿「婦人教役者の出現を望む」『正教時報』28巻6号（1939・06・01）2-4。

＿＿＿ (1940)　　　　　　　＿＿＿「日本正教会の再出発」『正教時報』30巻8号（1940・08・01）1-6。

Ōba (1920)　　　　　　　　大庭柯公「露西人の残虐性」『正教時報』9巻8号（1920・08・15）3。

Oka (1931)　　　　　　　　岡正雄・兵庫県知事「8. 露国人経営ノ教会」『本邦ニ於ケル教会関係雑件』1931・05・06、外務省記録1門2類（国立公文書館アジア歴史資料センター、http://www.jacar.go.jp）。

Okuntsov (1967)　　　　　　Окунцов, И. К. *Русская эмиграция в Северной и Южной Америке.* Буэнос Айрес: Изд-во «Сеятель», 1967.

Osozawa (1976)　　　　　　遅沢栄二ワルナワ『私の思出』泉佐野市：私家版、1976。

Ōzawa (1939)　　　　　　　大沢正「三度復興せる聖像の話」『正教時報』28巻4号（1939・04・01）16-17。

Pash (1949)　　　　　　　　Pash, Boris, Col. Letter to Bishop John (Shakhovskoi) from December 2 1949. Archive of the Orthodox Church in America, Syosset, NY, Folder *Japan, Diocese of - Correspondence and Reports: Committee for Aid to Orthodox Church in Japan.* 1949-56, 1960-63.

＿＿＿ (1958)　　　　　　　＿＿＿. "Checkmate!" *The American Legion magazine* 64, № 4 (Apr. 1958): 14-15, 42-43.

Philaret (1907)　　　　　　フィラレト（ドロズドフ）・モスクワの府主教著、三井道朗シメオン・長司祭訳『正教訓蒙』（第三・改訂版）東京：日本正教会事務所、1907。

＿＿＿ (1971)　　　　　　　Philaret (Drozdov), Met. of Moscow. *The Catechism of the Orthodox Church.* Willits, CA: Eastern Orthodox Books, 1971.

Polycarp (1946)   Поликарп (Приймак), архим. Письмо
архиеп. Харбинскому Нестору (Анисимову) от 1946.06.21. ГАРФ, ф.
6991, оп. 1, д. 75, лл. 174-176.

Protopriests' Conference (1943)
                    『長司祭会議議事録』東京：日本ハリストス
正教本会、1943。

Razumovskii (1946)   Разумовский, Григорий, прот.«Памяти
Высокопреосвященнейшего Мелетия, митрополита Харбинского и
Маньчжурского». *Журнал Московской Патриархии* № 5 (1946): 11-12.

Responses (2004)   *Отзывы епархиальных архиереев по вопросу о*
церковной реформе. 2 чч. М.: Изд-во Крутицкого подворья. Общество
любителей церковной истории, 2004.

Rutt (1957)   Rutt, Richard. "The Orthodox Church in
Korea." *Sobornost* 3, № 21 (Summer 1957): 480-490.

Sacharov (1971)   Sacharov, Olga T. "A new destiny." *The*
Russian Orthodox Journal 44, № 8 (Jan. 1971): 6-7.

Saikaishi (1929)   西海枝静マルコ「英露両教会聖職の会合」『正
教時報』18 巻 10 号 (1929 ・ 10 ・ 15) 7-9。

_____ (1931a)   _____「公会の意義」『正教時報』20 巻 8 号
(1931 ・ 08 ・ 20) 1。

_____ (1931b)   _____「府主教セルギイ師の閲歴」『正教時報』
20 巻 5 号 (1931 ・ 05 ・ 20) 10-11。

Saitō (1941)   齊藤東吉「世の終りまで存續する使徒權」『正
教時報』31 巻 6 号 (1941 ・ 07 ・ 01) 6-9。

Satō (1939)   佐藤武雄「火より救はれた諸教会」『正教時
報』28 巻 9 号 (1939 ・ 09 ・ 01) 16-19。

_____ (1941)   _____「エレナ修道女と語る」『正教時報』31
巻 9 号 (1941 ・ 10 ・ 01) 19-28。

_____ (1946)   Сато, Шинэй. «Обращение ко всем
христианам, братьям и сестрам, руководителям Церкви Японии» от
1946.03.10. ГАРФ, ф. 6991, оп. 1, д. 142, л. 39-45.

_____ (1955)   佐藤武雄「府主教セルギイ永眠十周年を迎え
て」『正教時報』789 号 (1955 ・ 08 ・ 25) 4-5。

Savchenko (2009)   «№ 281. Сопроводительное письмо С.
Р. Савченко Г. Г. Карпову с приложением обзора материалов об
отношениях власти и православной церкви в странах народной
демократии» от 1952.10.10. ГАРФ, ф. 6991, оп. 1, д. 981, л. 228-256.

Власть и церковь в Восточной Европе. 1944-1953 гг. Документы российских архивов: в 2 т., ред. Т. В. Волокитина, Г. П. Мурашко, А. Ф. Носкова и Д. Н. Нохотович, т. 2, 989-1012. М.: Российская политическая энциклопедия, 2009.

Senuma (1919)　　　　　　　瀬沼恪三郎イオアン「浦潮に於けるセルギイ主教」『正教時報』8 巻 6 号（1919・04・15）5-10。

_____ (1928)　　　_____「サウェト治下の主教達」『正教時報』17 巻 6 号（1928・06・10）17-20。

_____ (1938)　　　_____「府主教セリギイ師の新著「十二位一体の聖使徒」に就いて」『正教時報』27 巻 6 号（1938・06・01）5-9。

Sergius (1905a)　　　　　　Сергий (Тихомиров), архим.　*Карты Водской пятины и ее погостов в 1500 году.* СПб., 1905.

_____ (1905b)　　　　_____.　*Черты церковно-приходского и монастырского быта в писцовой книге Водской пятины 1500 г. (в связи с общими условиями жизни).* СПб., 1905.

_____ (1907)　　　_____, еп. Ямбургский. «Новгородские погосты, волости и села к XV ст.». *Христианское чтение* № 12 (1907): 689-709.

_____ (1908-1909)　　　_____, еп. Японский. «Месяц по Японии: Путевые заметки и впечатления». *Христианское чтение* № 11 (1908), 1470-1486; № 12 (1908), 1573-1586; № 1 (1909), 22-36; № 2 (1909), 238-251; № 3 (1909), 390-402; № 4 (1909), 574-587; № 5 (1909), 725-736; № 6-7 (1909), 965-981.

_____ ([1909] 1998)　　　Сергий (Страгородский), архим.　*По Японии (записки миссионера).* М.: Крутицкое Патриаршее Подворье. Общество любителей церковной истории, 1998 [1909].

_____ (1913)　　　Сергий (Тихомиров), еп.　Японский. *Памяти Высокопреосвященного Николая, Архиепископа Японского (С портретом его).* СПб.: Типография М. Меркушева, 1913.

_____ (1914)　　　_____.　*На Южном Сахалине (Из путевых заметок).* М.: Русская Печать, 1914.

_____ (1915)　　　セルギイ（ティホミロフ）・日本の主教『信仰と宗教』東京：大主教館、1915。

_____ (1919a)　　　_____「セルギイ主教の西伯利旅行談」『正教時報』8 巻 7 号（1919・05・15）4-9。

_____ (1919b)　　　_____「日本正教会総公会概報・公会議場に於ける主教閣下の御訓辞」『正教時報』8 巻 8 号（1919・06・15）15-21。

_____ (1924) _____ 大主教『親愛なる日本正教会信徒に告ぐ』東京：日本正教本会、1924。

_____ (1930) Сергий (Тихомиров), архиеп. Японский. *Освящение Воскресенскаго Кафедральнаго Собора в Тоокёо. С историческим предисловием*. Токио, 1930.

_____ (1931a) _____. «Краткая конспективная запись слова Высокопреосвященнаго Сергия, Архиепископа Японского, произнесенного с амвона церкви Православной Миссии в Токио в воскресенье 29-го марта 1931 года» от 1931.07.02. Archive of the Orthodox Church in America, Syosset, NY.

Sergius (1931b) _____, митр. Японский, Письмо еп. Шанхайскому Симону (Виноградову) от 1931.07.14. Archive of the Orthodox Church in America, Syosset, NY.

_____ (1933) セルギイ（ティホミロフ）・日本の府主教「教会はハリストスの体なり（教会の理想とする生活)」『正教時報』22 巻 11 号 (1933・11・01) 3-12。

_____ (1935a) Сергий (Тихомиров), митр. Японский, *Двоенадесятница Святых Апостолов*, Париж: YMCA-Press, 1935.

_____ (1935b) _____, Письмо И. В. Шевченко от 1935.09.01, Архив Отдела внешних церковных связей Московского Патриархата.

_____ (1939) _____, Письмо о. Иннокентию Серышеву от 1939.01.11. Hoover Institution Archives, *Innokentii Nikolaevich Seryshev papers*, Box 1, Folder 5, 151.

_____ ([1941] 1971) セルギイ（ティホミロフ）・日本の府主教著、瀬沼恪三郎イオアン訳、ニコライ（佐山）・ラメンスコエの主教及び高藤九朗ワシリイ・長司祭監修『十二位一体の聖使徒』(改訂版) 東京：警醒社書店、1971 [1941]。

_____ (1944) Сергий (Тихомиров), митр. Японский. Письмо митр. Ленинградскому Алексию (Симанскому) ок. середины 1944. ГАРФ, ф. 6991, оп. 1, д. 23, лл. 2-5.

_____ (2000) _____. Письмо митр. Нижегородскому Сергию (Страгородскому) от 1931.08.10. *Церковь и Время* № 1 (10) (2000): 321-325.

_____ (2007) _____. Письмо Кириллу Мори Кэн от 1943.07.17. John Shōji Masatoshi. *The Orthodox Church of Japan, 1912-1954: A time of troubles* (M. Div. thesis), 50-53. St. Vladimir's Orthodox Theological Seminary, Crestwood, NY, 2007.

Seryshev (1952-1968)   Серышев, Иннокентий, свящ. *В земном плане моего вечного бытия*, т. 2 (1952-1968). Hoover Institution Archives, *Innokentii Nikolaevich Seryshev papers*, Box 9, Folder 2.

Shibayama (1928)   柴山準行ペトル・長司祭『正教の栞』名古屋：ぱんだね社、1928。

Shirakawa church (2006)   教会史編集委員会『白河ハリストス正教会史』白河：白河ハリストス正教会、2006.

Siberian dispatch (1918)   『希臘正教会員教師ヲ西比利亜ニ派遣ノ件1』1918・08・08～09・02、外務省記録1門6類3項、露国革命一件／出兵関係／出兵及撤兵8巻 (国立公文書館アジア歴史資料センター、http://www.jacar.go.jp)。

Sobor (1924)   *Постановления Освященного Собора Русской Православной Греко-Кафолической Церкви в Соединенных Штатах Северной Америки, состоявшегося в городе Детройте, шт. Мичиган в 1924 году 20-23 марта, 2-4 апреля*. Нью-Йорк: Издательский отдел епархиального совета, 1924.

Soldatov (2004)   Солдатов, Г. М., ред. *Совещание глав Русской Зарубежной Церкви под председательством Святейшего Патриарха Варнавы. Сремские Карловцы 1935*. Minneapolis, MN: AARDM Press, 2004.

Sukitaretsu (1914)   犁垂津「塞耳比風俗の一斑 (附新来朝ゲオルギイ師の伝)」『正教時報』3巻3号 (1914・02・05) 11-19.

Suzuki (1925)   鈴木透「大主教の帰化問題」『正教時報』14巻12号 (1925・12・15) 14-15。

_____ (1931)   鈴木重夫「漫語一束」『日本正教』1巻1号 (1931・03・01) 10-11。

_____ (1933)   鈴木九八セルギイ・長司祭「満洲国巡廻の感想」『正教時報』22巻8号 (1933・08・20) 8-10、31。

_____ (1941)   _____「主教叙聖祝賀会に於ける挨拶」『正教時報』31巻5号 (1941・06・01) 5-6。

Takai (1913a)   高井万亀尾アントニイ・司祭「高井神父満鮮巡廻日誌」『正教時報』2巻15号 (1913・08・05) 45-50。

_____ (1913b)   _____「高井司祭満鮮巡回日誌」『正教時報』2巻16号 (1913・08・20) 54-58。

_____ (1919)   _____「朝鮮満洲巡廻略報」『正教時報』8巻12号 (1919・10・15) 11-17。

_____ (1956)   _____・長司祭『全国日本正教会教役者並に信徒諸兄姉に告ぐ』東京、1956。

Takeoka (1932)　　　　　　　　武岡武夫ワシリイ編『七十徒小伝』名古屋：
ぱんだね社、1932。

_____ (1989)　　　　　　　　_____・首司祭『竹陵生　随想集　"徑"』春
日部：私家版、1989。

Theodosius ([1926] 1999)　　　Феодосий　　　(Перевалов),　　архим.
Российская Духовная Миссия в Корее (1900-1925 гг.). Харбин, 1926. Репринт
в *История Российской Духовной Миссии в Корее. Сборник статей*, сост.
Дионисий Поздняев, прот., 171-317. М.: Изд-во Свято-Владимирского
Братства, 1999.

Thought Section (1945)　　　　大審院刑事局思想課『昭和二十年五月・連絡
会議々事録』1945・05、国立公文書館、返還文書（旧内務省等関係）（国立
公文書館アジア歴史資料センター、http://www.jacar.go.jp)。

Tōhei (1976)　　　　　　　　　藤平和雄ワシリイ『大正から昭和初期の大阪
正教会の追憶』私家版、1976。

Tokutomi (1936)　　　　　　　徳富蘇峰『近世日本国民史、徳川幕府上記』
下巻、東京：民友社、1936。

Uchii (1981)　　　　　　　　　内井昭蔵ガヴリイル『内井昭蔵・日本現代建
築家シリーズ 2』東京：新建築社、1981。

Uzawa (1953)　　　　　　　　　鵜沢徳寿サムイル・長司祭「日本正教会独立
の基礎・佐藤新衛氏を悼む」『正教時報』762 号（1953・01・25）2。

Victor (2003a)　　　　　　　　Виктор (Святин), архиеп. Пекинский.
Выписка из рапорта № 266 патр. Московскому и всея Руси Алексию
(Симанскому) от 1949.12.03. Ксения Кепинг. *Последние статьи и
документы*, т. 3, 314-317. СПб.: Изд-во «Омега», 2003.

_____ (2003b)　　　　　　　_____, митр. Краснодарский. Письмо
митр. Минскому Никодиму (Ротову) от 1963.09.17. Ксения Кепинг,
Последние статьи и документы, т. 3, 325-327. СПб.: Изд-во «Омега»,
2003.

Viktorov (1942)　　　　　　　　Викторов, Леонид Николаевич, прот.
«Русская Православная Церковь в Маньчжурской Империи». *Великая
Маньчжурская Империя. К десятилетнему юбилею*, 325-330.　Харбин:
Изд. Государственной организации Кио-ва-кай и Главного Бюро по
делам российских эмигрантов в Маньчжурской Империи, 1942.

Vitalius (1955)　　　　　　　　Виталий (Максименко), архиеп.
Восточно-Американский. *Мотивы моей жизни* (2 изд., дополненное).
Jordanville, NY: Holy Trinity Monastery, 1955.

Volokitina et al. (2009)　　　Волокитина, Т. В., Г. П. Мурашко, А.
Ф. Носкова и Д. Н. Нохотович, ред. *Власть и церковь в Восточной*

Европе. 1944-1953 гг. Документы российских архивов: в 2 т. М.: Российская политическая энциклопедия, 2009.

Vorres (1964)　　　　　　　　Vorres, Ian. *The Last Grand-Duchess.* London: Hutchinson & Co., Ltd., 1964.

Yahagi (1909)　　　　　　　　矢萩源次郎イオフ編『日本ハリストス正教会全国信徒大会議事録』東京：全国信徒大会事務所、1909。

Yamamoto (1939)　　　　　　　山本和夫ニコライ「一、我等為すべき事（日本正教会発展策に就て）」『正教時報』28 巻 10 号（1939・10・01）25-26。

Yamauchi (1938)　　　　　　　山内封介ナウム（山内那宇夢）「母教会の現状」『正教時報』27 巻 8 号（1938・08・01）9-11；27 巻 9 号（1938・09・01）16-17、20；27 巻 10 号（1938・10・01）12-14。

＿＿＿＿ (1941)　　　　　　　山内通靖「教会紛擾の禍根を衝く」『正教時報』31 巻 3 号（1941・03・01）17-22。

＿＿＿＿ (1942)　　　　　　　＿＿＿＿「共産主義者の宗教心」『正教時報』32 巻 7 号（1942・08・01）2-6。

Yearbook (1949)　　　　　　　*1950 Year book and church directory of the Russian Orthodox Greek Catholic Church in North America.* New York: Metropolitan Council, 1949.

Yoshikawa (1977)　　　　　　吉川多馬フォマ編『名古屋正教会小史』名古屋：名古屋ハリストス正教会、1977。

Yoshimura (1929)　　　　　　吉村忠三イオアン・司祭『基督教講和』名古屋：ぱんだね社、1929。

＿＿＿＿ (1938)　　　　　　　吉村柳里「二、三の希望」『正教時報』27 巻 2 号（1938・02・01）19-20。

＿＿＿＿ (1941a)　　　　　　吉村忠三イオアン・司祭「セルギイ府主教と藤平長司祭」『正教時報』31 巻 3 号（1941.03.01）11-16。

＿＿＿＿ (1941b)　　　　　　＿＿＿＿「誰が主教を選んだか」『正教時報』31 巻 5 号（1941・06・01）7-11、24。

＿＿＿＿ (1954)　　　　　　　＿＿＿＿・長司祭「海外正教会消息」『正教時報』780 号（1954・10・25）4。

＿＿＿＿ (1968)　　　　　　　Иосимура Иоанн, прот. «60 лет в духовной миссии». *Журнал Московской Патриархии* № 12 (1968): 21-26.

Periodicals

Asahi	『朝日新聞』(Tokyo)
Beacon of Love	*Светоч любви* (Harbin)
Christian Reading	*Христианское чтение* (St. Petersburg)
Church Messenger	*Церковный вестник* (St. Petersburg)
Consistory News	『総務局報』(Tokyo)
Heavenly Bread	*Хлеб небесный* (Harbin)
Japanese Orthodoxy	『日本正教』(Tokyo)
JMP	*Журнал Московской Патриархии* (Moscow)
Nippon Times	*Nippon Times* (Tokyo)
Orthodox Discourses	『正教要話』(Tokyo)
Orthodox Evangelist	*Православный благовестник* (Moscow)
Orthodox Messenger	『正教時報』(Tokyo)
Orthodox Review	*Православное обозрение* (Moscow)
Orthodox Thought	『正教思潮』(Tokyo)
PTsV	*Прибавление к Церковным ведомостям* (St. Petersburg)
RAOM	*The Russian American Orthodox Messenger*/*Русско-Американский Православный Вестник* (New York)
ROJ	*The Russian Orthodox Journal* (Wilkes-Barre, PA)
Special Higher Monthly	『特高月報』(Tokyo)
Tokyo Daily	『東京日日新聞』(Tokyo)
Yeast	『ぱんだね』(Nagoya)

Secondary sources

Akizuki (1983)   Akizuki, Takako. "Major Russian/Slavonic Collections in Japan." *Acta Slavica Japonica* № 1 (1983): 153-164.

Angold (2006)   Angold, Michael, ed. *Eastern Christianity*, vol. 5 of *The Cambridge history of Christianity*. Cambridge and New York: Cambridge University Press, 2006.

Anisimov (1991)   Анисимов, Л. «Православная миссия в Корее. К 90-летию основания». *Журнал Московской Патриархии* № 5 (1991): 56-60.

Anthony (1974)   Антоний   (Мельников),   архиеп. Минский.   «Святой   равноапостольный   архиепископ   Японский Николай». *Богословские труды* № 14 (1975): 5-61.

Aurilene & Potapova (2004)   Аурилене, Е. Е. и И. В. Потапова. *Русские в Маньчжоу-Ди-Го: «Эмигрантское правительство»*.   Хабаровск: Хабаровский пограничный институт ФСБ РФ, 2004.

Baker (2006)   Baker, Kevin. *A History of the Orthodox Church in China, Korea and Japan*. Lewiston, NY: Edwin Mellen Press, 2006.

Barshay (1988)   Barshay, Andrew Evan. *State and intellectual in imperial Japan: the public man in crisis*. Berkeley, Los Angeles and London: University of California Press, 1988.

Baryshev (2007)   バールィシェフ・エドワルド『日露同盟の時代 1914 〜 1917 年—「例外的な友好」の真相』福岡：花書院、2007。

Bellah (2003)   Bellah, Robert N. *Imagining Japan. The Japanese tradition and its modern interpretation*. Berkley and Los Angeles: University of California Press, 2003.

Berton (1956)   Berton, Peter Alexander. *The Secret Russo-Japanese Alliance of 1916* (Ph. D. thesis). Columbia University, New York, 1956.

Besstremiannaia (2006)   Бесстремянная, Г. Е. *Христианство и Библия в Японии. Часть 1. Исторический очерк и лингвистический анализ*. М.: Отдел внешних церковных связей Московского Патриархата, 2006.

_____ (2007)   _____. «Из Японии в Иерусалим». *Альфа и Омега* № 1 (48) (2007): 319-340.

Binns (2002)   Binns, John. *An introduction to the Christian Orthodox churches*. Cambridge, UK and New York: Cambridge University Press, 2002.

Black et al. (1975) Black, Cyril E., Marius B. Jansen, Herbert S. Levine, Marion J. Levy Jr., Henry Rosovsky, Gilbert Rozman, Henry D. Smith II and S. Frederick Starr. *The Modernization of Japan and Russia. A Comparative Study*. New York and London: The Free Press, Collier Macmillan Publishers, 1975.

Bogoliubov & Augustine (1993-2004) Боголюбов, М. Н. и Августин (Никитин), архим., ред. *Православие на Дальнем Востоке: Сборник статей*. вып. 1 («275-летие Российской духовной миссии в Китае»). СПб.: Изд-во «Андреев и сыновья», 1993; вып. 2 («Памяти святителя Николая, апостола Японии, 1836-1912»). СПб.: Изд-во Санкт-Петербургского государственного университета, 1996; вып. 3, СПб.: Изд-во Санкт-Петербургского государственного университета, 2001; вып. 4, Изд-во Санкт-Петербургского государственного университета и Санкт-Петербургской духовной академии, 2004.

Bolshakoff (1943) Bolshakoff, Serge. *The Foreign Missions of the Russian Orthodox Church*. London and New York: McMillan Co., 1943.

Boxer (1951) Boxer, Charles Ralph. *The Christian century in Japan, 1549-1650*. Berkeley: University of California Press, 1951.

Breen & Williams (1996) Breen, John and Mark Williams. *Japan and Christianity: impacts and responses*. New York: St. Martin's Press, 1996.

Brower & Lazzerini (1997) Brower, Daniel R. and Edward J. Lazzerini, eds., *Russia's Orient: imperial borderlands and peoples, 1700-1917*. Bloomington: Indiana University Press, 1997.

Bukh (2010) Bukh, Alexander. *Japan's national identity and foreign policy: Russia as Japan's 'other'*. London and New York: Routledge, 2010.

Bulgakov (1926) Булгаков, Сергий Николаевич, прот. *Святые Петр и Иоанн. Два первоапостола*. Париж, 1926.

Byrnes (1968) Byrnes, Robert F. *Pobedonostsev: His life and thought*. Bloomington and London: Indiana University Press, 1968.

Caldarola (1979) Caldarola, Carlo. *Christianity, the Japanese way*. Leiden: Brill, 1979.

Cary (1909) Cary, Otis. *A History of Christianity in Japan*. 2 vols. New York: Fleming H. Revell, 1909.

Chaillot (2009) Chaillot, Christine, ed. *L'Eglise orthodoxe en Europe occidentale au XXe siecle*. Paris: Cerf, 2009.

Cherevko (1999) Черевко, Кирилл Евгеньевич. *Зарождение русско-японских отношений XVII-XIX века*. М.: «Наука», 1999.

BIBLIOGRAPHY

Coakley (1992)   Coakley, J. F. *The Church of the East and the Church of England: a history of the Archbishop of Canterbury's Assyrian Mission.* Oxford: Clarendon Press, 1992.

Cohn (1981)   Cohn, Norman. *Warrant for Genocide. The myth of the Jewish world-conspiracy and the Protocols of the Elders of Zion.* Chico, CA: Scholars Press, 1981.

Coox (1977)   Coox, Alvin D. *The anatomy of a small war: the Soviet-Japanese struggle for Changkufeng-Khasan, 1938.* Westport, CT: Greenwood Press, 1977.

_____ (1985)   _____. *Nomonhan: Japan against Russia, 1939.* 2 vols. Stanford, CA: Stanford University Press, 1985.

Cracraft (1971)   Cracraft, James. *The Church Reform of Peter the Great.* Stanford, CA: Stanford University Press, 1971.

Craig (1970)   Craig, Albert M. "Introduction: Perspectives on Personality in Japanese History." In *Personality in Japanese History*, eds. Albert M. Craig and Donald H. Shively, 1-28. Berkley, Los Angeles and London: University of California Press, 1970.

Cunningham (1981)   Cunningham, James W. *A Vanquished Hope. The Movement for Church Renewal in Russia, 1905-1906.* Crestwood, NY: St. Vladimir's Seminary Press, 1981.

Davis (1995)   Davis, Nathaniel. *A long walk to church: a contemporary history of Russian Orthodoxy.* Boulder, San Francisco and Oxford: Westview Press, 1995.

Doi (1980)   土肥昭夫『日本プロテスタント・キリスト教史』東京：新教出版社、1980。

Dōshisha (1996)   同志社大学人文科学研究所編・土肥昭夫、田中真人編『近代天皇制とキリスト教』京都市：人文書院、1996。

Drummond (1971)   Drummond, R. H. *A History of Christianity in Japan.* Grand Rapids, MI: William B. Eerdmans Publ. Co., 1971.

Duara (2003)   Duara, Prasenjit. *Sovereignty and authenticity: Manchukuo and the East Asian Modern.* Lanham: Rowman & Littlefield Publishers, Inc., 2003.

Dummelow (1926)   Dummelow, J. R., ed. *A Commentary on the Holy Bible by various writers.* 1926.

Dunscomb (2011)   Dunscomb, Paul E. *Japan's Siberian intervention, 1918-1922: "a great disobedience against the people".* Lanham, MD: Lexington Books, 2011.

Ebisawa (1989)　　　　　　　海老澤有道『日本の聖書』東京：講談社、1989。

Ebisawa & Ōuchi (1971)　　　海老澤有道、大内三郎『日本キリスト教史』東京：日本基督教団出版局、1971。

Eingorn (1987)　　　　　　　Эйнгорн, И. Д. «Союз незбывшихся надежд: Церковь и контрреволюция в Сибири (1918-1922)». *Наука и религия*, № 2 (1987): 23-24.

Eiselen et al. (1929)　　　　　Eiselen, Frederick Carl, Edwin Lewis and David G. Downey, eds. *The Abingdon Bible commentary*. New York: The Abingdon-Cokesbury Press, 1929.

Elison (1973)　　　　　　　　Elison, George. *Deus destroyed; the image of Christianity in early modern Japan*. Cambridge, MA: Harvard University Press, 1973.

Ermakova (2005)　　　　　　エルマコーワ・リョドミーラ「江戸絵画における『モスクワ大公』と『ネヴァ川に臨む河岸通り』」中村喜和、安井亮平、長繩光男、長與進編『遥かなり、わが故郷―異郷に生きる III』横浜：成分社、2005、225-238。

Florenskii (1929)　　　　　　Флоренский, Павел Александрович, свящ. *Столп и утверждение Истины*. Берлин, 1929.

Florovsky ([1937] 1983)　　　Флоровский, Георгий Васильевич, прот. *Пути русского богословия* (3-е изд.). Париж: YMCA-Press, 1983 [1937].

Fomin (2002)　　　　　　　　Фомин, С. В. *Божией милостию архиерей Русской Церкви. Три жизни митрополита Нестора Камчатского*. М.: «Правило веры», 2002.

_____ (2004)　　　　　　　_____. *Апостол Камчатки. Митрополит Нестор (Анисимов)*. М.: Форум, 2004.

Fujitani (1996)　　　　　　　Fujitani, Takashi. *Splendid monarchy: power and pageantry in modern Japan*. Berkeley: University of California Press, 1996.

Fukuda et al. (1976)　　　　　福田光治、剣持武彦、小玉晃一編『ロシア・北欧・南欧篇』、『欧米作家と日本近代文学』3 巻、東京：教育出版センター、1976。

Garon (1997)　　　　　　　　Garon, Sheldon. *Molding Japanese minds. The state in everyday life*. Princeton: Princeton University Press, 1997.

Garrett ([1979] 2006)　　　　Garrett, Paul D. *Saint Innocent, apostle to America*. Crestwood, NY: St. Vladimir's Seminary Press, 2006 [1979].

Geffert (2010)　　　　　　　Geffert, Bryn. *Eastern Orthodox and Anglicans: diplomacy, theology, and the politics of interwar ecumenism*. Notre Dame, IN: University of Notre Dame Press, 2010.

Geraci & Khodarkovsky (2001)
Geraci, Robert P. and Michael Khodark-ovsky, eds. *Of religion and empire: missions, conversion, and tolerance in Tsarist Russia.* Ithaca: Cornell University Press, 2001.

Gluck (1985)　　　　　　　　　Gluck, Carol. *Japan's Modern Myths.* Princeton: Princeton University Press, 1985.

Goodman & Miyazawa (1995)
Goodman, David G. and Miyazawa, Masanori. *Jews in the Japanese mind: the history and uses of a cultural stereotype.* New York: Free Press, 1995.

Gordon (1991)　　　　　　　　Gordon, Andrew. *Labor and Imperial Democracy in Prewar Japan.* Berkley, Los Angeles and Oxford: University of California Press, 1991.

Hara (1989)　　　　　　　原暉之『シベリア出兵—革命と干渉　1917 〜 1922』東京：筑摩書房、1989。

Hardacre (1989)　　　　　　　Hardacre, Helen. *Shintō and the State, 1868-1988.* Princeton: Princeton University Press, 1989.

Hasegawa (1998)　　　　　　Hasegawa, Tsuyoshi. *The Northern Territories dispute and Russo-Japanese relations.* 2 vols. Berkeley, CA: University of California, International and Area Studies, 1998.

＿＿＿ (2005)　　　　　　　　＿＿＿. *Racing the enemy: Stalin, Truman, and the surrender of Japan.* Cambridge, MA and London, England: the Belknap Press of Harvard University Press, 2005.

Higashibaba (2001)　　　　　　Higashibaba, Ikuo. *Christianity in early modern Japan: Kirishitan belief and practice.* Leiden and Boston: Brill, 2001.

Higuchi (1996)　　　　　　　樋口雄彦「明治期ロシア正教の伊豆伝道」『沼津市博物館紀要 20』沼津：沼津市歴史民俗資料館・沼津市明治史料館、1996、2 部、1-31。

Hoston (1986)　　　　　　　Hoston, Germaine A. *Marxism and the crisis of development in prewar Japan.* Princeton: Princeton University Press, 1986.

Hussey (1986)　　　　　　　Hussey, Joan Mervyn. *The Orthodox Church in the Byzantine Empire.* Oxford: Clarendon Press, 1986.

Iglehart (1959)　　　　　　　Iglehart, Charles W. *A Century of Protestant Christianity in Japan.* Rutland and Tokyo: Charles E. Tuttle Co., 1959.

Ikuta (2008)　　　　　　　生田美智子『外交儀礼から見た幕末日露文化交流史—描かれた相互イメージ・表象』東京：ミネルヴァ書房、2008。

Inoue（1991）　　　　　　　　　井上順孝『教派神道の形成』東京：弘文堂、1991。

Ion（1990）　　　　　　　　　　Ion, A. Hamish. *The cross and the rising sun. Vol. 1: The Canadian Protestant missionary movement in the Japanese empire, 1872-1931.* Waterloo, Ontario, Canada: Wilfrid Laurier University Press, 1990.

＿＿＿（1993）　　　　　　　　　＿＿＿. *The cross and the rising sun. Vol. 2: The British Protestant missionary movement in Japan, Korea and Taiwan, 1865-1945.* Waterloo, Ontario, Canada: Wilfrid Laurier University Press, 1993.

＿＿＿（2003）　　　　　　　　　＿＿＿. "The cross under an imperial sun." *Handbook of Christianity in Japan*, ed. Mark R. Mullins, 69-100. Leiden and Boston: Brill, 2003.

Iorga（2000）　　　　　　　　　Iorga, Nicolae. *Byzantium after Byzantium*, trans. Laura Treptow. Iaşi, Romania, and Portland: The Center for Romanian Studies: Romanian Institute of International Studies, 2000.

Ise（1984）　　　　　　　　　　伊勢東太郎ニコライ編『盛昇天教会開教百年史』大船渡：盛ハリストス正教会、1984。

Ishigaki（2001）　　　　　　　　石垣香津「セルゲイ・キターエフと第二の故郷日本」長縄光男、沢田和彦編『異郷に生きる一来日ロシア人の足跡』横浜：成分社、2001、105-120。

Itō（2008a）　　　　　　　　　　伊藤慶郎グリゴリイ「セルギイ府主教の引退と日本正教会の内紛」『HUMANITAS』（奈良県立医科大学）33 号（2008・03）15-31。

＿＿＿（2008b）　　　　　　　　＿＿＿「日本の府主教セルギイとソビエト下のロシア正教会」『基督教研究』70 巻 2 号（2008・12）111-128。

＿＿＿（2010）　　　　　　　　　＿＿＿『神現聖堂成聖記念名古屋教会史』名古屋：名古屋ハリストス正教会、2010。

Iwama（1975）　　　　　　　　　岩間正光シメオン『ヨーロッパ世界の形成』東京：ミネルヴァ書房、1975。

＿＿＿（1979）　　　　　　　　　＿＿＿『イギリス議会改革と民衆』東京：風間書房、1979。

Izao（2003）　　　　　　　　　　井竿富雄『初期シベリア出兵の研究ー「新しき救世軍」構想の登場と展開』福岡：九州大学出版会、2003。

＿＿＿（2009）　　　　　　　　　＿＿＿「尼港事件と日本社会、一九二〇年」『山口県立大学学術情報一国際文化文部紀要』2 号（2009）1-13。

Japan Christian dictionary（1988）　　　日本キリスト教歴史大事典編集委員会『日本キリスト教歴史大事典』東京：教文館、1988。

Johnson (1929)   Johnson, Vernon.   *One Lord – One Faith*. London: Sheed and Ward, 1929.

Kallistos (1997)   Kallistos (Ware), Bp.   of Diokleia.   *The Orthodox Church* (rev. ed.). London: Penguin Books, 1997.

Kan (1999a)   Kan, Sergei. *Memory eternal: Tlingit culture and Russian Orthodox Christianity through two centuries*. Seattle and London: University of Washington Press, 1999.

_____ (1999b)   韓晳曦『日本の満州支配と満州伝道会』東京：日本基督教団出版局、1999。

Kaneishi (1993)   金石仲華『ニコライ大主教の弟子　鈴木九八伝』名古屋：私家版、1993。

Karaulov & Korostelev (2001)
                                   Караулов, А. К. и В. В. Коростелев. «Поборник церковного единения (к 40-летию со дня блаженной кончины митрополита Нестора)». *Русская Атлантида* № 8 (2001): 36-50.

_____ (2003a)   _____.   «Экзарх   Восточной   Азии». *Русская Атлантида* № 9 (2003): 17-24.

_____ (2003b)   _____.   «Арест   Экзарха».   *Русская Атлантида* № 10 (2003): 11-26.

Katayama (2009)   片山慶隆『日露戦争と新聞：「世界の中の日本」をどう論じたか』東京：講談社、2009。

Keene (2002)   Keene, Donald. *Emperor of Japan: Meiji and his world, 1852-1912*. New York: Columbia University Press, 2002.

Ketelaar (1990)   Ketelaar, James Edward.   *Of heretics and martyrs in Meiji, Japan: Buddhism and its persecution*. Princeton: Princeton University Press, 1990.

Khailarov (2000)   Хайларов, Иоанн, диакон. «Харбинские архиереи и поклонение Аматерасу в Маньчжурской империи». *Китайский благовестник* № 2 (2000): 18-27.

Kharlampovich (2001)   Kharlampovich,   Konstantin   Vasil'evich. *Archimandrite Makarii Glukharev: founder of the Altai Mission*, trans. James Lawton Haney. Lewiston, NY: Edwin Mellen Press, 2001.

Khvalin (1999)   Хвалин, А. Ю. *Государь и Дальняя Россия: Уроки церковно-самодержавной политики.   Восстановление монархии в России. Приамурский Земский Собор 1922 года во Владивостоке.*   М. и Владивосток: Купина, 1999.

Kikuchi (1986)　　　　　　菊池道夫イオアン編『上武佐ハリストス正教会　開教70周年史』中標津：上武佐ハリストス正教会、1986。

Kim (1987)　　　　　　Ким, Рехо. *Русская классика и японская литература.* М.: Художественная литература, 1987.

Kimura (2005)　　　　　木村汎『新版日露国境交渉史：北方領土返還への道』東京：角川学芸出版、発売元角川書店、2005。

Kitromilides (2010)　　　　Kitromilides, Paschalis M. "The Ecumenical Patriarchate." In *Eastern Christianity and the Cold War, 1945-91,* ed. Lucian N. Leustean, 221-239. London; New York: Routledge, 2010.

Kobayashi (1985)　　　　小林幸男『日ソ政治外交史：ロシア革命と治安維持法』東京：有斐閣、1985。

Kobe church (1983)　　　　『"神戸聖母就寝聖堂" 聖堂成聖30周年記念誌』神戸：神戸ハリストス正教会、1983。

Koike (n/d)　　　　　小池祐幸マルコ『マルコ小池祐幸卒業論文』(卒業論文) 東京正教神学校、大阪ハリストス正教会蔵書。

Kostanov (1992)　　　　Костанов, А. И. *Русская Православная Церковь на Сахалине и Курильских островах. Исторический очерк.* Южно-Сахалинск: Общество изучения Сахалина и Курильских островов, 1992.

Kowner (2006)　　　　Kowner, Rotem. *Historical dictionary of the Russo-Japanese War.* Lanham, MD: Scarecrow Press, 2006.

_____ (2007)　　　　_____, ed. *Rethinking the Russo-Japanese War, 1904-05.* 2 vols. Folkestone: Global Oriental, 2007.

Kurata (1991)　　　　蔵田雅彦『天皇制と韓国キリスト教』東京：新教出版社、1991。

Kuriyagawa (1994)　　　　厨川勇イオアン・司祭『ガンガン寺物語』札幌：北海道新聞社、1994。

Kushiro church (1992)　　　釧路正教会百年史委員会編『釧路正教会百年の歩み』釧路：釧路ハリストス正教会、1992。

Kuznetsov (1994)　　　　Кузнецов, С. И. *Проблема военнопленных в российско-японских отношениях после второй мировой войны.* Иркутск: Издательство Иркутского университета, 1994.

_____ (1997)　　　　_____ *Японцы в сибирском плену (1945-1956 гг.).* Иркутск: Центр международных исследований ИГУ, 1997.

Kyoto church (1978)　　　京都ハリストス正教会開教100周年記念誌編集委員会『京都ハリストス正教会　開教100周年記念誌』京都：京都ハリストス正教会、1978。

355

Larionov (2006)   Ларионов, А. А. «Особенности восприятия буддизма святителем Николаем (Касаткиным), просветителем Японии». *Альфа и Омега* № 3(44) (2006): 354-368.

Latyshev (2004)   Латышев, Игорь Александрович. *Россия и Япония в тупике территориального спора.* М.: Алгоритм, 2004.

Lensen (1959)   Lensen, George Alexander. *The Russian push toward Japan; Russo-Japanese relations, 1697-1875.* Princeton: Princeton University Press, 1959.

_____ (1961)   _____. "The Attempt on the Life of Nicholas II in Japan." *Russian Review* 20, № 3 (July 1961): 232-253.

_____ (1962)   _____. "Japan and Tsarist Russia – the Changing Relationships, 1875-1917." *Jahrbücher für Geschichte Osteuropas*, 10 (1962): 337-48.

_____ (1964)   _____, ed. *Revelations of a Russian Diplomat: The Memoirs of Dimitrii I. Abrikossow.* Seattle: University of Washington Press, 1964.

_____ (1966)   _____, ed. "White Russians in Wartime Japan: Leaves from the Diary of Dmitri Abrikossow." *Russian Review* 25, № 3 (July 1966): 268-284.

_____ (1970)   _____. *Japanese recognition of the U.S.S.R.: Soviet-Japanese relations, 1921-1930.* Tokyo: Sophia University, and Tallahasee, FL: Diplomatic Press, 1970.

_____ (1973)   _____. *Report from Hokkaido: the Remains of Russian Culture in Northern Japan.* Westport, CT: Greenwood Press, 1973.

_____ (1974)   _____. *The damned inheritance: the Soviet Union and the Manchurian crises, 1924-1935.* Tallahassee, FL: Diplomatic Press, 1974.

Leustean (2010)   Leustean, Lucian N. *Eastern Christianity and the Cold War, 1945-91.* London and New York: Routledge, 2010.

Levine (1996)   Levine, Hillel. *In Search of Sugihara: the Elusive Japanese Diplomat Who Risked His Life to Rescue 10,000 Jews from the Holocaust.* New York: Free Press, 1996.

Limerov (2008)   Лимеров, П. Ф. *Образ св. Стефана Пермского в письменной традиции и в фольклоре народа Коми.* М.: Наука, 2008.

Lukashev (1982)   Лукашев, М. Н. *Десять тысяч путей к победе.* М., 1982.

_____ (2003) _____. *Сотворение САМБО: родиться в царской тюрьме и умереть в сталинской.* М.: «Будо-Спорт», 2003.

Malozemoff (1958) Malozemoff, Andrew. *Russian Far Eastern policy, 1881-1904, with special emphasis on the causes of the Russo-Japanese War.* Berkeley: University of California Press, 1958.

Manchester (2008) Manchester, Laurie. *Holy fathers, secular sons: clergy, intelligentsia, and the modern self in revolutionary Russia.* DeKalb: Northern Illinois University Press, 2008.

Manuel (1979-1989) Мануил (Лемешевский), митр. Куйбышевский, *Русские православные иерархи периода с 1893 по 1965 годы (включительно) / Die russischen orthodoxen Bischöfe von 1893 bis 1965: Bio-Bibliographie.* 6 тт. Erlangen: Lehrstuhl für Geschichte und Theologie des christlichen Ostens an der Theologischen Fakultät der Universität Erlangen-Nürnberg, 1979-1989.

Maruyama (1963) Maruyama Masao. *Thought and behavior in modern Japanese Politics.* London: Oxford University Press, 1963.

Melikhov (1997) Мелихов, Г. В. *Российская эмиграция в Китае (1917-1924 гг.).* М., 1997.

Meyendorff (1981) Meyendorff, John, Prot. *Byzantium and the rise of Russia: a study of Byzantino-Russian relations in the fourteenth century.* Cambridge and New York: Cambridge University Press, 1981.

Michaelson (1999) Michaelson, Aaron Neil. *The Russian Orthodox Missionary Society, 1870 – 1917: A Study of Religious and Educational Enterprise* (Ph. D. thesis). Graduate School of the University of Minnesota, Minneapolis, 1999.

Mikhailova (2008) Mikhailova, Yulia. "Japan's place in Russian and Soviet national identity: from Port Arthur to Khalkhin-gol." *Japan and Russia: Three centuries of mutual images*, eds. Yulia Mikhailova and William N. Steele, 71-90. Folkestone: Global Oriental, 2008.

Mikhailova & Steele (2008) Mikhailova, Yulia and William N. Steele, eds. *Japan and Russia: Three centuries of mutual images.* Folkestone: Global Oriental, 2008.

Minamiki (1985) Minamiki, George. *The Chinese rites controversy: From its beginning to modern times.* Chicago: Loyola University Press, 1985.

Miner (2003) Miner, Steven Merritt. *Stalin's holy war: religion, nationalism, and alliance politics, 1941-1945.* Chapel Hill and London: University of North Carolina Press, 2003.

Mitter (2000)　　　　　　　　Mitter, Rana. *The Manchurian Myth: Nationalism, Resistance, and Collaboration in Modern China.* Berkeley: University of California Press, 2000.

Mizuno (1972)　　　　　　　　水野重郎アントニイ編『盛ハリストス正教会昇天会堂新築成聖記念誌』大船渡：盛ハリストス正教会、1972。

Molodiakov (2004)　　　　　　Молодяков, Василий Элинархович. *Несостоявшаяся ось: Берлин - Москва - Токио.* М.: Вече, 2004.

＿＿＿ (2010)　　　　　　　　＿＿＿. *Россия и Япония. Золотой век (1905-1916).* М.: «Просвещение», 2010.

Morgun (2006)　　　　　　　　Моргун, З. Ф. «Японская газета "Урадзио-Ниппо" во Владивостоке (1917-1922 гг.)». *Известия Восточного института японский спецномер* (1998): 182-199.

Morioka (1976)　　　　　　　　森岡清美『日本の近代社会とキリスト教』東京：評論社、1976。

＿＿＿ (2005)　　　　　　　　＿＿＿『明治キリスト教会形成の社会史』東京：東京大学出版会、2005。

Mousalimas (2004)　　　　　　Mousalimas, S. A. *From Mask to Icon: Transformation in the Arctic.* Brookline, MA: Holy Cross Orthodox Press, 2004.

Mullins (1994)　　　　　　　　Mullins, Mark R. "Ideology and Utopianism in Wartime Japan: An Essay on the Subversiveness of Christian Eschatology." *Japanese Journal of Religious Studies* 21 № 2/3 (1994): 261-280.

＿＿＿ (1998)　　　　　　　　＿＿＿. *Christianity made in Japan. A study of indigenous movements.* Honolulu: University of Hawai'i Press, 1998.

＿＿＿ (2003)　　　　　　　　＿＿＿, ed. *Handbook of Christianity in Japan.* Leiden and Boston: Brill, 2003.

Naganawa (1989)　　　　　　　長縄光男『ニコライ堂の人びと―日本近代史のなかのロシア正教会』東京：現代企画室、1989。

＿＿＿ (1995)　　　　　　　　＿＿＿「日本の府主教セルギイ・チホミーロフ小伝」坂内徳明、栗生沢猛夫、長縄光男、安井亮平編『ロシア　聖とカオス』東京：彩流社、1995、410-429。

＿＿＿ (2001)　　　　　　　　＿＿＿「日本の府主教セルギイ（チホミーロフ）の栄光」長縄光男、沢田和彦編『異郷に生きる―来日ロシア人の足跡』横浜：成分社、2001、189-200。

＿＿＿ (2003)　　　　　　　　＿＿＿「日本の府主教セルギイ（チホミーロフ）の悲哀」中村喜和、長縄光男、長與進編『異郷に生きる II―来日ロシア人の足跡』横浜：成分社、2003、149-159。

_____ (2005)　　　　　　　_____「日本の府主教セルギイ（チホミーロフ）の引退」中村喜和、安井亮平、長縄光男、長與進編『遥かなり、わが故郷—異郷に生きる III』横浜：成分社、2005、171-183。

_____ (2007)　　　　　　　_____『ニコライ堂遺聞』横浜：成分社、2007。

Nakahara (1975)　　　　　　　中原正ペトル編『高崎ハリストス正教会　降誕聖堂新築成聖式記念』高崎：高崎ハリストス正教会、1975。

Nakamura (1996)　　　　　　　中村健之介『宣教師ニコライと明治日本』東京：岩波書店、1996。

_____ (2003)　　　　　　　Nakamura, Kennosuke. "Some aspects of the life and work of St. Nikolai of Japan." In *Saint Nikolai Kasatkin and the Orthodox Mission in Japan: A Collection of Writings by an International Group of Scholars about St. Nikolai, his Disciples, and the Mission*, eds. Michael van Remortel and Peter Chang, 81-106. Point Reyes Station, CA: Divine Ascent Press, Monastery of St. John of Shanghai and San Francisco, 2003.

_____ (2007)　　　　　　　中村健之介「解説『宣教師ニコライの全日記』」ニコライ（カサトキン）・日本の大主教著、中村健之助監修『宣教師ニコライの全日記』1 巻、東京：教文館、2007、15-73。

Nakamura & Nakamura (2003)

　　　　　　　　　　　　　中村健之介・中村悦子『ニコライ堂の女性たち』東京：教文館、2003。

Nakane (1970)　　　　　　　Nakane, Chie. *Japanese Society*. Berkley and Los Angeles: University of California Press, 1970.

New-martyrs database　　　　*Новомученики, исповедники, за Христа пострадавшие в годы гонений на Русскую Православную Церковь в XX в.* База данных Православного Свято-Тихоновского гуманитарного Университета, Москва (http://213.171.53.29/bin/code.exe/frames/m/ind_oem.html/charset/ans).

Nicoll (1897)　　　　　　　Nicoll, Robertson W., ed. *The Expositor's Greek Testament*. 5 vols. New York: G. H. Doran, 1897.

Nishimura (1972)　　　　　　西村康「ニコライ神学校と露都留学生」『ユーラジア』（東京）5 号（1972）52-58。

Nobori & Akamatsu (1981)　　Nobori, Shōmu and Katsumaro Akamatsu. *The Russian Impact on Japan – Literature and Social Thought*, trans., eds., Peter Berton, Paul F. Langer and George O. Totten. Los Angeles: University of Southern California Press, 1981.

Oguma (2002)　　　　　　　Oguma, Eiji. *A genealogy of 'Japanese' self images*, trans. David Askew. Melbourne, Vic.: Trans Pacific Press, 2002.

Oguri (2009)　　　　　　　　　小栗時生「シベリア出兵と日本正教会」生田美智子編『平成 20 年度大阪大学言語社会専攻研究プロジェクト—東北アジアにおける日本とロシア研究』大阪大学大学院言語文化研究科言社専攻生田美智子研究室、2009、115-122。

Obolensky ([1971] 2000)　　　Obolensky, Dimitri. *The Byzantine commonwealth: Eastern Europe, 500-1453*. London: Phoenix Press, 2000 [1971].

Oda (1996)　　　　　　　　　尾田泰彦「大主教ニコライの日本宣教の特色—伝教者制度をめぐって」『キリスト教史』50 号（1996）195-196。

Odawara church (2002)　　　小田原ハリストス正教会編『小田原ハリストス正教会百二十年史』小田原：小田原ハリストス正教会、2002。

Oku (2007)　　　　　　　　　奥武則『露探：日露戦争期のメディアと国民意識』東京：中央公論新社、2007。

Oleksa (1992)　　　　　　　Oleksa, Michael J. *Orthodox Alaska: a theology of mission*. Crestwood, NY: St. Vladimir's Seminary Press, 1992.

Orthodox Encyclopedia (2000-)
　　　　　　　　　　　　　Православная энциклопедия.　　М.:　　ЦНЦ «Православная энциклопедия», с 2000.

Osanai (2005)　　　　　　　小山内道子「ニキータ山下氏に聞く」中村喜和、安井亮平、長縄光男、長與進編『遥かなり、わが故郷—異郷に生きる III』横浜：成分社、2005、3-19。

Ōshita (2004)　　　　　　　大下智一『山下りん—明治を生きたイコン画家』札幌：北海道新聞社、2004。

Ōta (1959)　　　　　　　　太田三郎『翻訳文学』東京：岩波書店、1959。

_____ (2003)　　　　　　太田丈太郎「アレクサンドル・チェレプニンと音楽における日本主義」中村喜和、長縄光男、長與進編『異郷に生きる II—来日ロシア人の足跡』横浜：成分社、2003、73-84。

_____ (2007)　　　　　　太田健一『小西増太郎・トルストイ・野崎武吉郎—交情の軌跡』岡山：吉備人出版、2007。

Paramore (2009)　　　　　Paramore, Kiri. *Ideology and Christianity in Japan*. London and New York: Routledge, 2009.

Patrikeeff (2002)　　　　　Patrikeeff, Felix. *Russian politics in exile: the Northeast Asian balance of power, 1924-1931*. New York: Palgrave in association with St. Antiny's College, Oxford, 2002.

Piankevich (1999)　　　　　Пянкевич, В. Л. *Репатриации и труд военнопленных как источники восстановления экономики СССР после второй мировой войны*. СПб: «Нестор», 1999.

Podalko (2001)　　　　　　　ポダルコ・ピョートル「大正後期・昭和前期の日本の「国際化」と白系ロシア人」長縄光男、沢田和彦編『異郷に生きる―来日ロシア人の足跡』横浜：成分社、2001、15-30。

_____ (2003)　　　　　　　_____「ロシア人はいかに来日したか」中村喜和、長縄光男、長與進編『異郷に生きる II―来日ロシア人の足跡』横浜：成分社、2003、33-46。

Pomazansky (2005)　　　　　　Pomazansky, Michael, Prot. *Orthodox Dogmatic Theology*, trans., ed. Seraphim (Rose), Hieromonk. Platina, CA: St. Herman of Alaska Brotherhood, 2005.

Popov (2004)　　　　　　　　Попов, А. В. «Русская Православная Церковь во времена "русской смуты"». *Антибольшевистская Россия (1917 – 1947) (компакт-диск)*, сост. С. В. Карпенко, (http://www.antibr.ru/studies/ao_rptsgv_k.html).　　　　　М.: Российский государственный гуманитарный университет, Изд-во Ипполитова, 2004.

Pospielovsky (1984)　　　　　Pospielovsky, D. V. *The Russian church under the Soviet regime, 1917-1982.* Crestwood, NY: St. Vladimir's Seminary Press, 1984.

Potapov (2004)　　　　　　　ポタポフ・アレクセイ『明治期日本の文化における東方正教会の位置および影響』東京：日本ハリストス正教会教団・東京大主教々区宗務局、2004。

Pozdniaev (1998)　　　　　　Поздняев, Дионисий, свящ. *Православие в Китае (1900-1997 гг.).* М.: Изд-во Свято-Владимирского братства, 1998.

_____ (1999a)　　　　　　_____. «Духовные школы Маньчжоу-го». *Китайский благовестник* № 1 (1999): 62-69.

_____ (1999b)　　　　　　_____, прот., сост. *История Российской Духовной Миссии в Корее. Сборник статей.* М.: Изд-во Свято-Владимирского Братства, 1999.

_____ (1999c)　　　　　　_____. «К истории Российской Духовной Миссии в Корее (1917-1949)». *История Российской Духовной Миссии в Корее. Сборник статей*, сост. Дионисий Поздняев, прот., 351-362. М.: Изд-во Свято-Владимирского Братства, 1999.

Protopopov (2005)　　　　　　Protopopov, Michael Alex. *The Russian Orthodox presence in Australia: The history of a Church told from recently opened archives and previously unpublished sources* (Ph. D. thesis).　School of Philosophy and Theology, Faculty of Arts and Sciences, Australian Catholic University, Fitzroy, Victoria, 2005.

Quested (1982)　　　　　　　Quested, R. K. I. *"Matey" imperialists?: the tsarist Russians in Manchuria, 1895-1917.* Hong Kong: Centre of Asian Studies, University of Hong Kong, 1982.

Ramet (1988a)　　　　　　　Ramet, Pedro. "Autocephaly and national identity in Church-state relations in Eastern Christiantiy: an introduction." *Eastern Christianity and politics in the twentieth century*, ed. Pedro Ramet, 3-19. Durham and London: Duke University Press, 1988.

＿＿ (1988b)　　　　　　　＿＿, ed. *Eastern Christianity and politics in the twentieth century*. Durham and London: Duke University Press, 1988.

Regel'son (1977)　　　　　　Регельсон, Лев. *Трагедия Русской Церкви: 1917-1945*. Париж: YMCA-Press, 1977.

Remortel & Chang (2003)　　Van Remortel, Michael and Peter Chang, eds. *Saint Nikolai Kasatkin and the Orthodox Mission in Japan: A Collection of Writings by an International Group of Scholars about St. Nikolai, his Disciples, and the Mission*. Point Reyes Station, CA: Divine Ascent Press, Monastery of St. John of Shanghai and San Francisco, 2003.

Rimer (1995)　　　　　　　Rimer, Thomas, ed. *A Hidden Fire: Russian and Japanese Cultural Encounters, 1868 - 1926*. Stanford and Washington: Stanford University Press, 1995.

Robinson (2002)　　　　　　Robinson, Paul. *The White Russian Army in Exile 1920-1941*. Oxford: Clarendon Press, 2002.

Ruisu (2008)　　　　　　　類洲環「輝かしき先輩達9―内村伊蔵を父に、内井照蔵を息子に持つ　内井進」『工学院大学建築系学科同窓会誌 NICHE』31 号（2008）68-73。

Sablina (2006)　　　　　　Саблина, Элеонора Борисовна. *150 лет Православия в Японии. История Японской Православной Церкви и её основатель Святитель Николай*. М.: АИРО-XXI; СПб.: «Дмитрий Буланин», 2006.

Said (1978)　　　　　　　Said, Edward. *Orientalism*. New York: Vintage Books, 1978.

Sandler (1995)　　　　　　Sandler, Stanley, ed. *The Korean War: an encyclopedia*. New York: Garland Pub., 1995.

Sannikov (1990)　　　　　　Санников, Виктор. *Под знаком восходящего солнца в Маньчжурии*. Сидней, 1990.

Sapporo church (1987)　　　札幌正教会百年史委員会編『札幌正教会百年史』札幌：札幌ハリストス正教会、1987。

Sasaki (2004)　　　　　　　佐々木馨『北海道仏教史の研究』札幌：北海道大学図書刊行会、2004。

Sawada (2001)　　　　　　沢田和彦「日本における白系ロシア人の文化的影響」長縄光男、沢田和彦編『異郷に生きる―来日ロシア人の足跡』横浜：成分社、2001、31-46。

_____ (2002)　　　　　_____「白系ロシア人と近代日本文化」日ロ交流協会・第 3 回『日ロ歴史認識問題』シンポジウム、2002・09・19 (http://www.nichiro.org/12_jigyou/sympo_2002_5sawada.html)。

_____ (2005)　　　　　_____「『ルベージュ』誌の在日ロシア人関係記事」中村喜和、安井亮平、長縄光男、長與進編『遥かなり、わが故郷—異郷に生きる III』横浜：成分社、2005、91-102。

Scheiner (1970)　　　　　Scheiner, Irwin. *Christian Converts and Social Protest in Meiji Japan.* Berkeley: University of California Press, 1970.

Schimmelpenninck van der Oye (2001)
　　　　　　　　　　Schimmelpenninck van der Oye, David. *Toward the rising sun: Russian ideologies of empire and the path to war with Japan.* DeKalb, IL: Northern Illinois University Press, 2001.

Schmemann (1963)　　　　Schmemann, Alexander, Prot. *The Historical Road of Eastern Orthodoxy*, trans. Lydia W. Kesich. New York: Holt, Rinehart and Winston, 1963.

Sendai church (2004)　　　教会史編集委員会編『仙台ハリストス正教会史』仙台：仙台ハリストス正教会、2004。

Seraphim (2007a)　　　　セラフィム（辻永）・仙台の主教「セルギイ府主教の死亡広告」『正教時報』1397 号（2007・02・20）16-19。

_____ (2007b)　　　　　_____「「教会報知」から「正教新報」そして「正教時報」へ」『正教時報』1399 号（2007・04・20）12-14；1400 号（2007・05・20）15-17；1401 号（2007・06・20）10-13。

_____ (2007c)　　　　　_____「ＧＡＲＦ所蔵文書とセルギイ府主教の手紙」『正教時報』1403 号（2007・08・20）16-19。

_____ (2007-2008)　　　　_____「セルギイ府主教の晩年　世田谷区太子堂町４５５番地」『正教時報』1407 号（2007・12・20）16-19；1408 号（2008・01・20）14-15；1410 号（2008・03・20）14-17。

_____ (2008-2010)　　　　_____「聖ニコライとセルギイ府主教」『正教時報』1413 号（2008・06・20）14-17；1414 号（2008・07・20）12-15；1415 号（2008・08・20）16-19；1416 号（2008・09・20）14-17；1417 号（2008・10・20）14-17；1418 号（2008・11・20）14-19；1419 号（2008・12・20）16-19；1421 号（2009・02・20）10-13；1422 号（2009・03・20）16-19；1423 号（2009・04・20）12-17；1424 号（2009・05・20）12-17；1425 号（2009・06・20）14-19；1426 号（2009・07・20）16-21；1427 号（2009・08・20）14-17；1428 号（2009・09・20）16-21；1429 号（2009・10・20）14-19；1430 号（2009・11・20）16-21；1431 号（2009・12・20）16-21；1432 号（2010・01・20）10-15；1433 号（2010・02・20）16-21；1434 号（2010・03・20）16-21。

Shepard (2007)   Shepard, Jonathan, ed. *The expansion of orthodox Europe: Byzantium, the Balkans and Russia*. Hampshire, England and Burlington, VT: Ashgate Variorum, 2007.

Shillony (1981)   Shillony, Ben-Ami. *Politics and culture in wartime Japan*. Oxford: Clarendon Press, 1981.

Shimazu (2009)   Shimazu, Naoko. *Japanese society at war: death, memory and the Russo-Japanese war*. Cambridge, UK and New York: Cambridge University Press, 2009.

Shimizu (2001)   清水恵「サハリンから日本への亡命者—シュウエツ家を中心に」長縄光男、沢田和彦編『異郷に生きる—来日ロシア人の足跡』横浜：成分社、2001、77-87。

_____ (2003)   _____「リュボーフィ・セミョーのヴナ・シュウエツさんに聞く」中村喜和、長縄光男、長與進編『異郷に生きる II—来日ロシア人の足跡』横浜：成分社、2003、13-32。

Shin (1989)   Shin, Peter Yong-Shik. *The Ōtsu incident: Japan's hidden history of the attempted assassination of future Emperor Nicholas II of Russia in the town of Ōtsu, Japan, May 11, 1891 and its implications for historical analysis* (Ph. D. thesis). University of Pennsylvania, Philadelphia, PA, 1989.

Shkarovskii (2005)   Шкаровский, Михаил Витальевич. *Русская Православная Церковь при Сталине и Хрущеве (3-е изд., дополненное)*. М.: Изд-во Крутицкого подворья. Общество любителей церковной истории, 2005.

_____ (2007)   _____. *Крест и свастика: Нацистская Германия и Православная Церковь*. М.: Вече, 2007.

_____ (2009)   _____. *История русской церковной эмиграции*. СПб.: Алетейя, 2009.

Shōji (2007)   Shōji Masatoshi John. *The Orthodox Church of Japan, 1912-1954: A time of troubles* (M. Div. thesis). St. Vladimir's Orthodox Theological Seminary, Crestwood, NY, 2007.

Shulatov (2008)   Шулатов, Ярослав Александрович. *На пути к сотрудничеству: российско-японские отношения в 1905-1914 гг.* Хабаровск и М.: Институт востоковедения РАН, 2008.

Simeonova (2007)   Simeonova, Albena. *Japan through Russian eyes (1855 – 1905)*. Sofia: Paradigma, 2007.

Slavinskii (1993)   Славинский, Борис Николаевич. *Советская оккупация Курильских островов, август-сентябрь 1945 года: документальное исследование*. М.: ТОО «Лотос», 1993.

_____ (1995) _____. *Пакт о нейтралитете между СССР и Японией: дипломатическая история, 1941-1945 гг.* М.: ТОО «Новина», 1995.

Sofronov (2005) Софронов, Вячеслав Юрьевич. *Три века сибирского миссионерства, в 3-х тт.* Тобольск: Тобольский государственный педагогический институт им. Д. И. Менделеева, 2005.

Sollogub (1968) Соллогуб, А. А., ред. *Русская Православная Церковь Заграницей. 1918-1968.* Нью-Йорк: Русская Духовная Миссия в Иерусалиме РПЦЗ, 1968.

Stamoolis (1986) Stamoolis, James J. *Eastern Orthodox mission theology today.* Maryknoll, NY: Orbis Books, 1986.

Stark (1970) Stark, Werner. *The Sociology of Religion: A Study of Christendom.* New York: Fordham University Press, 1970.

Steinberg et al. (2005-2007) Steinberg, John W., Bruce W. Menning, David Schimmelpenninck van der Oye, David Wolff and Shinji Yokote, eds. *The Russo-Japanese war in global perspective: World War Zero,* 2 vols., Leiden and Boston: Brill, 2005-2007.

Steiner (1995) Steiner, Evgeny. "Nikolai of Japan." *Monumenta Nipponica* 50, № 4 (Winter 1995): 537-550.

Stephan (1974) Stephan, John J. *The Kuril Islands: Russo-Japanese frontier in the Pacific.* Oxford: Clarendon Press, 1974.

_____ (1978) _____. *The Russian fascists: tragedy and farce in exile, 1925-1945.* New York: Harper & Row, 1978.

_____ (1994) _____. *The Russian Far East: a history.* Stanford, CA: Stanford University Press, 1994.

Sugii (1984) 杉井六郎『明治期キリスト教の研究』東京：同朋舎、1984。

Sukhanova (2008) Суханова, Наталья Анатольевна. *История Японской Православной Церкви в 1912-1970 гг.: Вехи на пути к автономии* (кандидатская диссертация). Институт всеобщей истории РАН, Москва, 2008.

Sutherland (1969) サザランド、ルーシー・スチュアート著、岩間正光シメオン訳『十八世紀政治史上のロンドン』東京：未来社、1969。

Suzuki & Takamura (1998) 鈴木清司、高村功一『重要文化財・日本ハリストス正教会教団復活大聖堂保存修理工事報告書』東京：日本ハリストス正教会教団・文化財建造物保存技術協会、1998。

Takagi (1978-1980)　　　　　高木一雄『明治カトリック教会史』3巻、東京：キリシタン文化研究会、1978-1980。

Tanaka (1993)　　　　　Tanaka, Stephan. *Japan's Orient: rendering pasts into history*. Berkeley, Los Angeles and London: University of California Press, 1993.

Tashiro (2009)　　　　　田代俊一郎『原郷の奄美　ロシア文学者昇曙夢とその時代』福岡：書肆侃侃房、2009。

Thelle (1987)　　　　　Thelle, Notto R. *Buddhism and Christianity in Japan: From Conflict to Dialogue, 1854-1899*. Honolulu: University of Hawaii Press, 1987.

Tokushima church (1980)　　　　　『聖堂建設記念誌』徳島：徳島ハリストス正教会、1980。

Tokyo cathedral (1998)　　　　　東京復活大聖堂修復記念誌刊行委員会編『東京復活大聖堂修復記念誌』東京：東京復活大聖堂教会、1998。

Tomakomai church (1998)　　　　　苫小牧正教会八十年記念委員会編『苫小牧正教会八十年史』苫小牧：苫小牧ハリストス正教会、1998。

Toyama (1981)　　　　　外山操編、上法快男監修『陸海軍将官人事総覧』陸軍篇、東京：芙蓉書房、1981。

Toyohashi church (1979)　　　　　豊橋ハリストス正教会100周年記念事業委員会『豊橋ハリストス正教会100周年記念誌』豊橋：豊橋ハリストス正教会、1979。

Trempelas (1974)　　　　　Trempelas, Panagiotis. *The Autocephaly of the Metropolia in America*. Brookline, MA: Holy Cross School of Theology Press, 1974.

Trukhin (2005)　　　　　Трухин, В. Н. «Николай Японский. Штрихи к психологическому портрету». *Миссионерское обозрение* № 2 (112) (2005): 27-31.

Tsukada (1981)　　　　　塚田理『天皇制下のキリスト教―日本聖公会の戦いと苦難』東京：新教出版社、1981。

Tsukamoto (2005)　　　　　塚本善也「日本ハリストス正教会の台湾伝道」中村喜和、安井亮平、長縄光男、長與進編『遥かなり、わが故郷―異郷に生きる III』横浜：成分社、2005、157-169。

Tsukase (1998)　　　　　塚瀬進『満洲国―「民族協和」の実像』東京：吉川弘文館、1998。

Tsypin (1999)　　　　　Цыпин, Владислав, прот. *Русская Православная Церковь. 1925-1938*. М.: Изд. Сретенского монастыря, 1999.

_____ (2006)　　　　　　_____.　*История Русской Православной Церкви: Синодальный и новейший периоды* (2-е изд., перераб.). М.: Изд. Сретенского монастыря, 2006.

Turbull (1998)　　　　　　Turnbull, Stephen.　*The Kakure Kirishitan of Japan: a study of their development, beliefs and rituals to the present day.* Richmond, Surrey: Japan Library, 1998.

Tyshchuk (1970)　　　　　　Тыщук, А., прот. «Японская Автономная Православная Церковь». *Журнал Московской Патриархии* № 11 (1970): 42-47; № 12 (1970): 43-51.

Ushimaru (1969)　　　　　　牛丸康夫プロクル・長司祭『明治文化とニコライ』東京：教文館、1969。

_____ (1978a)　　　　　　_____『大阪正教会百年史譚』吹田：大阪ハリストス正教会、1978。

_____ (1978b)　　　　　　_____『日本正教会史』東京：日本ハリストス正教会教団・府主教庁、1978。

_____ (1979)　　　　　　_____『パウェル中井木菟麻呂小伝』吹田：大阪ハリストス正教会、1979。

_____ (1985)　　　　　　_____『神のみ旨に生きた激動時代の僕たち』東京：日本ハリストス正教会教団・府主教庁、1985。

Uspenskii (1998)　　　　　　Успенский, Борис Андреевич.　*Царь и патриарх: харизма власти в России: Византийская модель и её русское переосмысление.* М.: Школа «Языки русской культуры», 1998.

Utsumi (1979)　　　　　　内海健寿「東北地方におけるハリストス正教と地域社会—歴史における宗教と経済」『会津短期大学学報』36号（1979・03）42-64。

Vedernikov (1951)　　　　　　Ведерников, А.«Пример церковного законопослушания (памяти Митрополита Японского Сергия)». *Журнал Московской Патриархии* № 7 (1951): 41-53.

Visual Architecture (2006)　　　『建築画報 Visual Architecture―特別号：内井昭蔵と内井建築設計事務所』42巻316号（2006・04）。

Vlasto (1970)　　　　　　Vlasto, A. P. *The entry of the Slavs into Christendom: an introduction to the medieval history of the Slavs.* Cambridge, UK: Cambridge University Press, 1970.

Wada (1981)　　　　　　和田洋一「キリスト教徒はあれでよかったのか」同志社大学人文科学研究所・キリスト教社会問題研究会編／和田洋一研修、杉井六郎、太田雅夫編『戦時下のキリスト教運動―特高資料による』（第一版第三刷）新教出版社、1981、1-19。

_____ (1990)　　　　　　　　和田春樹『北方領土問題を考える』東京：岩
波書店、1990。

_____ (1991)　　　　　　　　_____『開国日露国境交渉』東京：日本放送
出版協会、1991。

_____ (2001)　　　　　　　　和田芳英『ロシア文学者昇曙夢＆芥川龍之介
論考』大阪：和泉書院、2001。

Wakatsuki (1979)　　　　　　若槻泰雄『シベリア捕虜収容所』東京：サイ
マル出版会、1979。

Wells & Wilson (1999)　　　　Wells, David and Sandra Wilson, eds. *The
Russo-Japanese war in cultural perspective, 1904-05.* New York: St. Martin's
Press, 1999.

Widmer (1976)　　　　　　　Widmer, Eric. *The Russian ecclesiastical
mission in Peking during the eighteenth century.* Cambridge, MA: East Asian
Research Center, Harvard University: distributed by Harvard University
Press, 1976.

Williams (2007)　　　　　　　Williams, Brad. *Resolving the Russo-Japanese
territorial dispute: Hokkaido-Sakhalin relations.* London and New York:
Routledge, 2007.

Woodard (1972)　　　　　　　Woodard, William P. *The Allied Occupation of
Japan 1945-1952 and the Japanese religions.* Leiden: Brill, 1972.

Yamamuro (2006)　　　　　　Yamamuro, Shin'ichi. *Manchuria under
Japanese domination*, trans. Joshua A. Fogel. Philadelphia: University of
Pennsylvania Press, 2006.

Young (1998)　　　　　　　　Young, Louise. *Japan's Total Empire:
Manchuria and the Culture of Wartime Imperialism.* Berkeley: University of
California Press, 1998.

Znamenski (1999)　　　　　　Znamenski, Andrei A. *Shamanism and Christianity: native encounters with Russian Orthodox missions in Siberia and Alaska, 1820-
1917.* Westport, CT, and London: Greenwood Press, 1999.